KITCHEN & BATH
BUSINESS AND PROJECT MANAGEMENT

KITCHEN & BATH
BUSINESS AND PROJECT MANAGEMENT

Second Edition

HANK DARLINGTON

ELLEN CHEEVER, CMKBD, ASID

Cover image: (left) © iStockphoto.com/sturti
          (right) © iStockphoto.com/asiseeit
Cover design: Anne Michele Abbott

This book is printed on acid-free paper. ∞

National Kitchen & Bath Association
687 Willow Grove Street
Hackettstown, NJ 07840
Phone: 800-THE-NKBA (800-843-6522)
Fax: 908-852-1695
Website: NKBA.org

Published by John Wiley & Sons, Inc., Hoboken, New Jersey.

Published simultaneously in Canada.

For general information about our other products and services, please contact our Customer Care Department within the United States at (800) 762-2974, outside the United States at (317) 572-3993 or fax (317) 572-4002.

Wiley publishes in a variety of print and electronic formats and by print-on-demand. Some material included with standard print versions of this book may not be included in e-books or in print-on-demand. If this book refers to media such as a CD or DVD that is not included in the version you purchased, you may download this material at http://booksupport.wiley.com. For more information about Wiley products, visit www.wiley.com.

Library of Congress Cataloging-in-Publication Data

Darlington, Hank.
  Kitchen & bath business and project management / Hank Darlington, Ellen Cheever, CMKBD, ASID. – Second Edition.
      pages cm
  Includes index.
  Includes access to companion website.
  ISBN 978-1-118-43912-8 (cloth); 978-1-118-73239-7 (ebk.); 978-111-8-73632-6 (ebk.)
  1. Kitchens–Design and construction. 2. Kitchens–Planning. 3. Bathrooms–Design and construction. 4. Bathrooms–Planning. 5. Interior decoration firms–Management. 6. Contractors' operations–Management. I. Cheever, Ellen. II. Title. III. Title: Kitchen and bath business and project management.
  NK2116.2.D373 2013
  690'.42068–dc23
                                                                    2013016215

Printed in the United States of America

10 9 8 7 6 5 4 3 2 1

Sponsor

The National Kitchen and Bath Association gratefully acknowledges Delta Faucet Company for its generous contribution toward the development of this second edition, which combines the newly revised *Kitchen and Bath Business Management* and *Kitchen and Bath Project Management*.

GOLD SPONSOR

DELTA FAUCET COMPANY

About the National Kitchen & Bath Association

The National Kitchen & Bath Association (NKBA) is the only non-profit trade association dedicated exclusively to the kitchen and bath industry and is the leading source of information and education for professionals in the field. Now 50 years after its inception, the NKBA has a membership of more than 50,000 and is the proud owner of the Kitchen & Bath Industry Show (KBIS).

The NKBA's mission is to enhance member success and excellence, promote professionalism and ethical business practices, and provide leadership and direction for the kitchen and bath industry worldwide. The NKBA has pioneered innovative industry research, developed effective business management tools, and set groundbreaking design standards for safe, functional, and comfortable kitchens and baths.

Recognized as the kitchen and bath industry's leader in learning and professional development, the NKBA offers professionals of all levels of experience essential reference materials, conferences, virtual learning opportunities, marketing assistance, design competitions, consumer referrals, internships, and opportunities to serve in leadership positions.

The NKBA's internationally recognized certification program provides professionals the opportunity to demonstrate knowledge and excellence as Associate Kitchen & Bath Designer (AKBD), Certified Kitchen Designer (CKD), Certified Bath Designer (CBD), Certified Master Kitchen & Bath Designer (CMKBD) and Certified Kitchen & Bath Professional (CKBP).

For students entering the industry, the NKBA offers Accredited and Supported Programs, which provide NKBA-approved curriculum at more than 50 learning institutions throughout the United States and Canada.

For consumers, the NKBA showcases award winning designs and provides information on remodeling, green design, safety, and more at NKBA.org. The NKBA Pro Search tool helps consumers locate kitchen and bath professionals in their area. The NKBA offers membership in 11 different industry segments: dealers, designers, manufacturers and suppliers, multi-branch retailers and home centers, decorative plumbing and hardware, manufacturer's representatives, builders and remodelers, installers, fabricators, cabinet shops, and distributors.

For more information, visit www.NKBA.org.

Table of Contents

INTRODUCTION xv

ACKNOWLEDGEMENTS xxi

CHAPTER 1
GETTING STARTED 1

Do You have What it Takes? 2

Evaluate Yourself 4

Before You Start 8

Why Many Companies Do Not Make It 10

Avoid These Common Mistakes 11

Getting Help from Advisors and Mentors 12

Summary 12

Review Questions 12

CHAPTER 2
PLANNING YOUR BUSINESS 15

What Type of Kitchen and Bath Business are You Going to Operate? 15

Your Business Selection Criteria 17

Deciding on the Right Business 17

Choosing a Name for Your Business 18

Stages of Company Growth 18

Short- and Long-Term Planning 20

How to Create a Strategic Business Plan for a Kitchen/Bath Dealer 21

Researching the Market 33

Preparing Your Business Plan 35

Reviewing Your Plan 40

Summary 40

Review Questions 41

CHAPTER 3
BUSINESS START-UP ISSUES 43

Choosing the Business Legal Structure 43

Other Requirements and Considerations 50

Location, Location, Location 51

Financing the Business 55

A Look at Taxes 60

Selecting Vendor Partners 61

Buying Groups—Sharing Expertise 63

Joining the Business Community 64

Taking Advantage of Outside Help 65

Summary 66

Review Questions 66

CHAPTER 4
ACCOUNTING AND RECORD KEEPING 67

Why You Need to Keep Good Records 69

Establishing Bookkeeping Procedures 70

Choosing an Accounting System 70

What to Keep Track of 71

Accounting Software for Your Business 73

Record-Keeping and Administrative Needs 74

Hiring an Accountant or Bookkeeper 76

Budgeting for Profit and Cash Flow 76

Summary 83

Review Questions 83

CHAPTER 5
FINANCIAL CONTROLS 85

Understanding Financial Statements 85

Chart of Accounts 86

Balance Sheet 95

Cash Flow Analysis 98

Financial Ratio Analysis 103

Gross Margin 105

Ideas on How to Improve Gross Margins 108

Summary 120

Review Questions 120

CHAPTER 6

PROTECTING YOUR BUSINESS.....................................121

Business Legal Structure 122

Professional Advice 122

Contractual Agreements and Personal Guarantees 122

Extension of Credit to Your Customers 123

Copyrighting Your Drawings 123

Developing an Insurance Program 124

Protecting Your Business from Theft 129

Summary 130

Review Questions 130

CHAPTER 7

BASIC TAX MANAGEMENT 131

Small Business Tax Management 131

Special Rules for Small Businesses 132

Tax Responsibilities 134

Specific Substantiation Requirements for Certain Expenses 134

Hints on Preventing an Audit 135

Help from the IRS 135

Other Taxes 136

Summary 137

Review Questions 137

CHAPTER 8

THE BASICS OF HUMAN RESOURCE (PEOPLE) MANAGEMENT......................................139

The Broad Picture of Human Resources 141

Future Human Resource Trends 142

Determining Your Needs 144

Deciding on the Right Compensation System for Your Sales Team 151

Examples of Compensation Plans 155

Resourceful Recruiting 159

Narrowing Down the List: Applications, Résumés, and Testing 162

Art of Interviewing 164

Making the Final Hiring Decision 167

Summary 171

Review Questions 171

CHAPTER 9
HUMAN RESOURCE MANAGEMENT—AFTER
THE DECISION IS MADE 173

The Orientation Period 173

Training and Development 175

Policy and Procedures Manual 177

Creating an Employee-Friendly Work Environment 180

Alternate Working Arrangements 181

Keep Tabs on Company Morale 182

Conduct Regular Meetings 182

Measuring Employee Performance 184

Developing Disciplinary Procedures 188

Defining at-will Employment 189

Terminating an Employee 189

Termination for "Just Cause" 190

Summary 208

Review Questions 208

CHAPTER 10
MARKETING 209

Marketing and Sales are not the Same 210

The Big Picture: The Marketing "Wheel of Fortune" 210

Make the Time 214

Your Marketing Plan and Budget 215

Marketing Budgets 217

Knowing Who Your Customers are 222

Are You Offering the Right Product/Service Package? 224

Knowing Who Your Competitors are 227

Business Image and Branding 230

Establishing Your Brand 235

Finding and Filling a Meaningful Market Position 236

Why It's Important to Have a Great Web Site 237

Develop an Advertising Campaign 238

Getting Your Work Published 240

Social Media Marketing 244

Sales and Selling 247

How to Get Started 247

Your Sales Team Needs a Strong Leader 254

Summary of How to Build a Marketing Plan 256

In Closing . . . 257

Summary 258

Review Questions 258

CHAPTER 11
PROFESSIONAL AND PROFITABLE
PROJECT MANAGEMENT 259

Introduction 259

Project Management Fundamentals: From Information Gathering to
Visiting the Finished Room 260

Summary 265

Review Questions 266

CHAPTER 12
RESPONSIBILITIES OF THE BUSINESS OWNER/MANAGER.....267

The Installation Delivery System 267

Job Site Dynamics: New House versus Old House 268

Job Site Dynamics: Single-Family Dwelling versus Multifamily 269

Installation Service Business Models 269

Key Competencies of Installation Specialists 271

Developing Successful Working Relationships 272

Systematic Approach to Project Management 274

Role of a Manfacturer's Representative 286

Importance of Job Costing 288

Summary 289

Review Questions 289

CHAPTER 13
RESPONSIBILITIES OF DESIGNER OF RECORD.........................291

"Win-Win" Strategy 291

Designer's Role during Project Documentation Process 292

Successful Designers are Detail Oriented 293

Understanding Construction Constraints 293

Summary 311

Review Questions 311

CHAPTER 14
MANAGING CLIENT EXPECTATIONS AND THE JOB SITE 313

Understanding "Remodeling Fever" 313

Managing the Client and the Project 314

Summary 331

Review Questions 331

CHAPTER 15
INDUSTRY STANDARDS FOR MOLDING ORDER
PROCEDURES AND CABINET INSTALLATION 333

Ordering Molding 333

How to Install Kitchen Cabinets 336

Summary 344

Review Questions 344

INDEX 345

Introduction

THE GOAL OF THIS BOOK

It is a career dream of many professionals in the kitchen and bath industry to own their own firm. More experienced business owners are on a continuous quest to learn how to improve their earnings and overall performance. To help you reach these goals, *Kitchen & Bath Business and Project Management* has been written by Hank Darlington, Darlington Consulting, and Ellen Cheever, CMKBD, ASID, Ellen Cheever Associates, in collaboration with respected professionals in the kitchen and bath industry.

This volume offers you a step-by-step management tool to be used to convert the novice business owner's entrepreneurial ideas into a successful business venture. It also provides many ideas for business improvement for the more seasoned business owner and manager.

Learning Objectives of the Book

- Describe good business management practices vital to operating a successful business.
- Identify the three main areas of business management.
- Recognize the importance for Kitchen and Bath businesses owners and managers to build a team of experts.
- Relate how learning to be a good business manager can be easier than becoming a really good Certified Kitchen or Bath Designer.

This book is not intended to take the place of a professional management team: business attorney, accountant, financial planner. Rather, the guidelines and insights within have been gathered and organized with the aim of sharing winning strategies for business management from people recognized as leaders in the field.

ABOUT THE AUTHORS

The coauthors provide a balanced view of proper guidelines to manage a business.

Hank Darlington has over 40 years of experience as a business owner, professional manager, industry consultant, author, and speaker. He founded, owned, and managed a multi-branch kitchen and bath showroom on the West Coast for much of his career. Ellen Cheever is recognized as a leading authority and has over 35 years as a design and marketing consultant in the industry.

Hank Darlington, Darlington Consulting

Hank Darlington has been active in the kitchen and bath industry for the majority of his career. Hank's experience stretches from a large wholesale plumbing distributor organization to an upscale, full-service (one-stop shopping) kitchen and bath showroom with three locations in Northern California.

Hank served as past president of the NKBA Northern California Chapter, served on the NKBA's Board of Directors, and was a founding member of the Decorative Plumbing and Hardware Council. Hank was recognized for his industry contributions when he was inducted into the NKBA Hall of Fame in 2004. Hank was made a Fellow by the Decorative Plumbing and Hardware Association in 2004 for his contributions to that industry.

As the author of four industry textbooks, Hank continues to contribute by presenting seminars for the National Kitchen & Bath Association, writing monthly articles for two national trade publications, and serving as a consultant to manufacturers, distributors, and dealerships.

Ellen Cheever, CMKBD, ASID, Ellen Cheever & Associates

Ellen Cheever is an author and marketing specialist whose practical, yet innovative design solutions and professional writing and teaching helped shape the North American kitchen industry over the past 40 years. When working on residential kitchen projects, she collaborates with noted kitchen specialists throughout the United States, combining her design talents with the product specification expertise and skillful project management of trusted professionals within the client's community. In addition to her residential practice, the firm Ellen Cheever & Associates designs retail showroom spaces, major trade show exhibits, and editorial sets.

A 1992 inductee of the National Kitchen & Bath Hall of Fame, Ellen was recognized as the Designer of Distinction for 2002 by the American Society of Interior Designers, Pennsylvania East Chapter, and won first place honors in the 2004 KWC Kitchen Design Competition.

In addition to these respected professionals, this volume quotes topical articles from major industry trade publications: Kitchen & Bath Design News, Kitchen & Bath Business, Qualified Remodeler, and Remodeling. These sources understand our industry.

As the author of more than fifteen books and technical manuals covering the details of kitchen and bathroom planning standards, Ellen continues to write and speak about emerging design trends, ergonomic planning standards, and winning business strategies within the kitchen design industry.

In addition to Hank and Ellen, the following experienced individuals have made key contributions to the content based on their areas of recognized expertise within the kitchen and bath industry:

- Leonard V. Casey—Strategy Acceleration
- James W. Krengel, CMKBD—Kitchens by Krengel

Leonard V. Casey, MBA, Strategic Acceleration

Educator, corporate executive, entrepreneur, and global leader have all been used to describe Len Casey. After receiving his MBA and teaching at Florida Atlantic University, Len started a twenty-year career with the DuPont Company in 1972. While at DuPont, Len was responsible for such product groups as Teflon/Silverstone, Automotive and Corian. Because of these contributions at DuPont, he was awarded the DuPont Corporate Marketing Excellence award for both the Teflon and Corian businesses.

In the early 1990s, Len and a team of industry leaders purchased a respected upscale cabinet company and, for the next 8 years, he applied his business talent to growing the company into an industry leader. Today, he serves on the boards of several companies, using his experience of over thirty years to advise an array of domestic and international firms and supports a number of non-profit organizations to reach their organizational goals.

James W. Krengel, CMKBD, Kitchens by Krengel

Jim Krengel, CMKBD, began his career in 1966 at Kitchens by Krengel in St. Paul, Minnesota. Today, that design studio is in its third generation of ownership and Jim spends the majority of his time sharing his expertise through professional seminars and via frequent contributions to industry publications.

During Jim's design career, he won numerous design awards, served as the Design Director of Maytag Kitchen Idea Center, and was a consultant to Wilsonart International as well as several other manufacturers. Jim helped form the Minnesota Chapter of the NKBA and was its National President from 1989–1990. The industry recognized his contribution by inducting him into the NKBA Hall of Fame in 2003.

Jim is the author of two design books: *Kitchens: Lifestyle and Design* and *Bathrooms.* He served on the Advisory Board for Kasmar publications, and in collaboration with this respected book publisher, developed the first bathroom and kitchen CDs, each containing over 250 pages of ideas, articles, and portfolios.

ABOUT THE BOOK

This volume is written for business owners, sales managers/directors, and branch managers of kitchen and bath design firms (dealerships) which operate with a showroom, sell cabinets and counters, and provide installation services—either with their own crew or through a network of qualified subcontractors. Where appropriate, comments are made for the independent kitchen designer whose business model does not include representing products or offering installation, but who can still benefit from the business information included.

This volume is particularly valuable to emerging business leaders—great salespeople who now are managing a sales force, for example, as well as individuals with experience in the kitchen industry who may have a career opportunity to manage a branch operation or a second showroom location for their organization. The material is also useful for companies in the midst of a succession plan with new family members who will become owners "learning the ropes" from the current company officers.

We have selected this business model focus because a dealership operating from a showroom is the most typical business model in the kitchen and bath industry, and many people "grow" into business management positions.

It is important to note that this book is a reference book—including material covering all aspects of business management for a new entrepreneur.

It is also valuable to existing companies who are interested in "refreshing" their business practices. Successful firms can benefit by evaluating their current business practices with an eye towards a better organized firm with a renewed focus on profitable projects.

Successful Business Are Led By Balanced Management

Lastly, this entire book is based on the premise that every business is made up of three parts: financial management, human resource management, and marketing management.

The authors understand that there are always two parts of each business for the owner: those things one loves to do, and those things one must do. Most kitchen and bathroom firm owners are fairly strong in the marketing segment (design, sales, advertising, promotions), but are weak in—or, too often, reluctant to invest the time and effort to improve upon—financial management (budgets, financial statements, cash flow) and the human resource (people management) part of the business.

Studying high-profit businesses affirms that balance in all three areas is needed for success.

Business management forms and checklists appear throughout this book. The customizable version of "Forms for Managing People, Profits and Projects" is available online at wiley.com. The forms and checklists can be printed or integrated into your electronic management system.

It is important to start a discussion of business management by recognizing the reason you are considering investing in your own business or have invested in an existing business: you are expecting a reasonable financial return on your investment "ROI". Many individuals in our industry work hard, develop excellent reputations and a strong repeat or referral business but, at the end of the day, have very little return to show on the investment they have made in their business.

Although conservative rate of returns vary with shifts in the economic marketplace—quite simply, you should make a before-tax profit on the money you have invested in your business equal to or greater than conservative returns found in the financial marketplace. Do not be satisfied with a 3% to 5% profit before taxes on your business endeavors—think about the money you've invested in your company and realize that this sum could be invested by your financial planner to reap a specific return for you. Demand of yourself that you spend the time to learn to manage your existing business better, or begin a new business venture managing your operations to enjoy an acceptable rate of return—and an acceptable "ROI."

Make an Appointment with Yourself

To plan properly or to initiate changes in your current business practices, begin by setting aside time to study this material. Consider making an appointment with yourself to work on your weak areas.

A chart detailing the steps that even the simplest new construction/remodeling projects go through follows. Each step involves people management, financial management, and marketing management skills.

Think about your own business and identify areas where you think you could improve. Following this self-evaluation, start the book at the beginning and, much like a novel, read it to the end.

The Kitchen/Bath Project Process

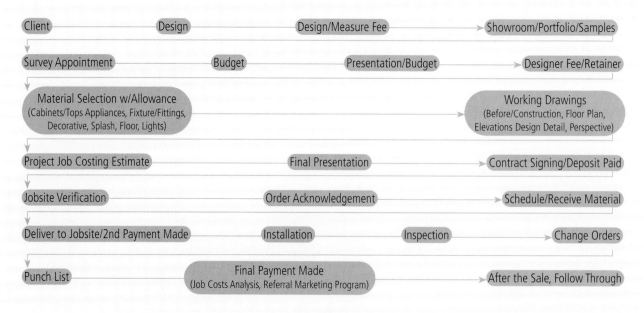

For sales directors/managers or branch managers, consider "The Kitchen/Bath Project Process" detailed above. As you manage a sales team or a branch of your company, look for ways that you can increase the efficiency of the organization in specific areas, or for improvements you might suggest to the business owner. Bring a fresh viewpoint and a new skill set to your management team. Use your experiences to review the process that currently typifies your organization and set time aside with the company's principals or your manager to work on efficiencies of scale.

Common Business Traits of High Profit Firm

- Have solid growth on an annual basis
- Review and use monthly P&L statements as a management tool
- Owners spend time to learn to be better people managers
- Control their product mix and customers to avoid profit erosion
    1. Rely more on cabinets as a percentage of the total sale
    2. Select products that reflect your strategic business plan
    3. Charge design fee retainers
- Sell cabinets installed: view project as a package, not parts
- Have a higher median annual sales volume and a higher average job selling price
- Are paid more quickly
- Complete job cost reviews in a timely manner on all projects
- Achieve superior personnel productivity
    1. Base commissions on gross profit and volume
    2. Use computers to aid design
    3. Offer company benefits with employee contribution
- Achieve higher gross margins
- Effectively manage overhead expenses

Acknowledgements

The NKBA gratefully acknowledges the following peer reviewers of this book:

Mark Goldman, AKBD
David Newton, CMKBD

Getting Started

Millions of people start their own businesses every year. Possibly you've already started yours, or you're giving it serious thought. Whatever the case, many skeptics may try to scare you with the statistics on how many new businesses fail every year, how hard you'll have to work, and how long it will take before you show a profit. But, if everyone listened to the skeptics . . . John Michael Kohler would not have started Kohler Company, Paul Wellborn would not have expanded Wellborn Cabinet, Inc., and the seven Jacuzzi brothers would not have started the now multiproduct Jacuzzi, Inc.

Learning Objective 1: Compare the pros and cons of owning your own business.

Learning Objective 2: Compare your personal leadership traits to the traits and characteristics listed in the chapter.

Learning Objective 3: Review the entrepreneurial innovation assessment and define your personal strengths and weaknesses.

Learning Objective 4: Recognize the characteristics of failed and successful entrepreneurs.

Learning Objective 5: Analyze common mistakes to avoid as an owner/manager of a business.

Pros and Cons of Owning Your Own Business

Pros
- You are your own boss. The sky's the limit.
- You can prove yourself.
- You will have a hand in all aspects of the business.
- You will be able to take pride in promoting and marketing your own business.
- You will be in control.
- You will have creative freedom.

(continued)

- The more the company makes, the more you make.
- You cannot be fired, laid off, or forced to retire.
- You will have the ultimate satisfaction of knowing you started and ran a successful business.

Cons

- There is no guaranteed paycheck.
- It's all on your shoulders.
- You cannot please everyone.
- You will work harder and longer than ever before.
- You will assume the risk of investment.
- There will be constant stress and pressure.
- You will have to adhere to all the laws and regulations.

DO YOU HAVE WHAT IT TAKES?

It All Starts with an Idea

At some point it hits you that, like so many others, you could own and run your own business. You want to step out on your own and take control of your work and financial future. You are confident that you have what it takes to buck the odds and succeed. You also know that owning your own business comes with risks.

Mrs. Fields Cookies

1/4 cup Passion
1/4 cup Perfection
1/4 cup Perseverance
1/4 cup People

Business Success

Debbi Fields Rose, the founder and owner of Mrs. Fields Cookies, had her recipe for success called "the 4 P's." Mrs. Fields defines each "P" this way:

- **Passion.** You have to absolutely and passionately love what you do. In your case, you will have to love designing and selling kitchen and bath (K&B) projects. Never go into business if your first priority is to make money. Money will be the by-product of doing something you love and doing it well.
- **Perfection.** You must constantly strive for perfection because, for your business to succeed and have staying power, you have to do it better than anyone else. Stay focused on constantly improving while stamping out mediocrity.

- **Perseverance.** Stick with it. You'll need guts. Guts to start and guts to believe in yourself. Guts to take on many challenges, guts to face failure, and guts to stick it out.
- **People.** No business can succeed without its greatest asset—people—no matter how good the products and services are. You're not designing and building kitchens and baths, you're helping turn dreams into reality. To achieve this, you will need a team that loves designing, selling, and installing dream projects as much as you do.

Four Keys to a Successful Kitchen/Bath Business

Business Foundation

1. A qualified entrepreneur
2. A researched business opportunity
3. A detailed written plan
4. A sufficient capital fund

Put all four of these together and you have a wonderful chance of success in owning and operating your own business.

Evaluating Yourself

While it is true that starting and running a business is difficult, it's successfully done all the time by many individuals and partners who have built both large and small K&B businesses. You probably know some of these people. If not, you can meet them by actively participating in National Kitchen & Bath Association (NKBA) chapter events or those of other associations. Develop networking opportunities for yourself: Introduce yourself and ask questions to learn what others' keys to success are.

Would You Hire You?

If you've just begun to think about starting your own business or you've been running one for a number of years, you might want to determine if you are the right person for the job.

The position in question is one of being your own boss and running the whole show, which includes bookkeeping, sales and marketing, customer service, supervising employees, vendor relations, and so much more. Most important, your job hinges on your ability to make key decisions (some on short notice) and to utilize your people skills, because most business involves interaction with others. You may not be skilled in all of these key areas. If you're not, you'll have to find others who can assist you by providing strength in areas where you are lacking.

Leadership Traits

Here is a checklist of traits and characteristics you may need to run a business successfully:

❑ Ability to make important decisions
❑ Ability to stay motivated, even when the business has slow times and is not running as smoothly as it might
❑ Knack for organization
❑ Good time management skills
❑ Good communication skills
❑ Stick-to-itiveness, or the drive that keeps you working long hours to get the job done
❑ Good physical health and stamina to survive the long hours and little sleep that may be part of the job
❑ Ability to get along well with many different types of personalities
❑ Ability to harness and manage anger and frustration
❑ Confidence in your skills, knowledge, and abilities to run a K&B business
❑ Ability to find answers to questions you cannot answer easily
❑ Ability to be firm or flexible so you can make adjustments or changes in your plans
❑ Ability to do research and weigh options before jumping into a situation or making a hasty decision
❑ Ability to balance a business and a personal life successfully
❑ Ability to put money aside for difficult times
❑ Ability to network and spread the word about yourself and your business

EVALUATE YOURSELF

Be honest with yourself. Identify how many of the listed skills and talents you possess. How many will you commit to learning? How much of the description just is not you? How many people will you need to hire to fill the void? If you need help with 40 percent or more of the listed items, perhaps you should reconsider starting your own business.

As you analyze yourself, keep in mind that although businesses do fail for a variety of reasons outside of the owner's control, more often actions (or lack of actions) on the owner's part lead to an unsuccessful venture. That's why entrepreneurs need to have a clear picture of both their skills and their shortcomings in order to build on their strengths and shore up their weaknesses.

Complete the next Entrepreneurial Innovation Assessment to help identify your entrepreneurial potential.

Entrepreneurial Innovation Assessment

Read each statement carefully, then mark the answer that most accurately describes your behavior, feelings, and attitude as it actually is—not as you would like it to be or think it should be. Try to mark your first reaction.

	Agree	Disagree
1. My parents encouraged me to take an interest in discovering things for myself.		
2. At least one of my close relatives is an entrepreneur.		
3. Throughout my education I had many part-time jobs.		
4. One or both of my parents had many unconventional or unorthodox ideas.		
5. If I were stranded in an unfamiliar city without friends or money, I would cope well.		
6. I am curious about more things than most people are.		
7. I enjoy a venture in which I must constantly keep trying new approaches and possibilities.		
8. I always seek challenging problems to solve.		
9. I am not very painstaking in my work.		
10. I am able to work for extended periods of time, frequently to the point of exhaustion.		
11. When faced with a problem, I usually investigate a wide variety of options.		
12. While working on a project I learn all I can about it.		
13. Before taking on an important project I learn all I can about it.		
14. When confronted with a difficult problem I try solutions others would not think of.		
15. Once I undertake a new venture I am determined to see it through.		
16. I concentrate harder on projects I'm working on than most people seem to.		
17. I cannot get excited about ideas that may never lead to anything.		
18. When brainstorming with a group of people, I think up more ideas more quickly than others.		
19. I have broader interests and am more widely informed than most people.		
20. When the chips are down, I display more personal strength than most people.		
21. I need social interaction and am very interested in interpersonal relationships.		
22. I find it easy to identify flaws in others' ideas.		
23. I regard myself as a specialist, not a generalist.		
24. When evaluating information, I believe the source is more important than the content.		
25. I am easily frustrated by uncertainty and unpredictability.		
26. I can easily give up immediate gain or comfort to reach long-term goals.		
27. I have great tenacity of purpose.		
28. Things that are obvious to others are not so obvious to me.		

(continued)

Entrepreneurial Innovation Assessment *(Continued)*

	Always	Often	Sometimes	Rarely	Never
29. I get a kick out of breaking rules.					
30. I become upset if I cannot immediately come to a decision.					
31. Ideas run through my head at night to the point I cannot sleep.					
32. I get into trouble because I'm too curious or inquisitive.					
33. I am able to win other people over to my point of view.					
34. I tolerate frustration more than the average person does.					
35. I rely on intuition when trying to solve a problem.					
36. I can stick with difficult problems for extended periods of time.					
37. My problem-solving abilities are stronger than my social abilities.					
38. A logical step-by-step method is best for solving problems.					
39. I can readily allay people's suspicions.					

40. Below is a list of adjectives and descriptive terms. Check 12 words that best describe you.

Energetic ☐	Realistic ☐	Organized ☐	Self-confident ☐
Tactful ☐	Quick ☐	Factual ☐	Fashionable ☐
Dedicated ☐	Cautious ☐	Polished ☐	Persevering ☐
Stern ☐	Alert ☐	Innovative ☐	Good natured ☐
Efficient ☐	Flexible ☐	Inquisitive ☐	Habit bound ☐
Perceptive ☐	Persuasive ☐	Inhibited ☐	Absentminded ☐
Egotistical ☐	Modest ☐	Unemotional ☐	Forward looking ☐
Curious ☐	Original ☐	Clear thinker ☐	Understanding ☐
Informal ☐	Dynamic ☐	Open minded ☐	Self-demanding ☐
Involved ☐	Practical ☐	Courageous ☐	Well liked ☐
Predicable ☐	Formal ☐	Independent ☐	Enthusiastic ☐
Observant ☐	Poised ☐	Thorough ☐	Resourceful ☐
	Helpful ☐	Sociable ☐	

Scoring Instructions

To score the test, circle and add up the values for your answers.

Statement	Agree	Disagree
1.	4	1
2.	3	1
3.	4	1
4.	3	1
5.	4	1
6.	4	1
7.	4	1
8.	3	1
9.	0	4
10.	4	1

Statement	Agree	Disagree
11.	4	1
12.	3	1
13.	4	1
14.	4	1
15.	4	1
16.	4	1
17.	1	4
18.	4	1
19.	4	1
20.	4	1

Statement	Agree	Disagree
21.	1	4
22.	3	1
23.	1	4
24.	1	4
25.	1	4
26.	4	1
27.	4	1
28.	4	1

Statement	Always	Often	Sometimes	Rarely	Never
29.	2	3	5	1	0
30.	0	2	3	5	1
31.	2	4	5	3	0
32.	3	4	5	1	0
33.	3	4	5	1	0
34.	3	4	5	1	0
35.	5	4	3	1	0
36.	4	5	3	1	0
37.	4	5	3	1	0
38.	1	2	5	3	0
39.	3	4	5	1	0

40. These characteristics score 2 points each: energetic, observant, persevering, resourceful, independent, dedicated, original, perceptive, enthusiastic, innovative, curious, involved, and flexible.

   These characteristics score 1 point each: self-confident, forward looking, informal, courageous, thorough, open minded, alert, dynamic, self-demanding, and absentminded.

Interpreting Your Score

125–186   If you scored in this range, you are probably a highly innovative person. Ideas come readily to you. On the whole, you take an innovative approach to solving problems. You also discern possibilities and opportunities in areas where others find little potential. You are original and individualistic, and you have no problem resisting pressures to conform. You have the courage to pit yourself against uncertain circumstances.

77–124   A score in this range indicates that you are moderately innovative. While you lack some of the autonomy, self-sufficiency, and self-confidence of the highly innovative entrepreneur, you compensate with your predilection for method, precision, and exactness. You also have faith in the successful outcome of your current and future entrepreneurial efforts.

27–76   If you scored in this range, you may be more successful operating a franchise or working for someone else than you would be starting and owning your own business. However, remember: Innovative abilities can be developed and cultivated either through on-the-job training or by attending workshops or seminars. If you are determined to own your own business, do not give up.

BEFORE YOU START

Now that you've done the self-evaluation exercises and you still want to pursue owning your own business—or if you are already an owner and "passed" the self-evaluation—you have several more things to consider.

What Are Your Career and Business Goals?

Where are you today? Where do you want to be in three to five years? How do you plan to get there?

What are your goals? Yes, you want to make money, but how much and how fast? Do you see yourself running a small business (fewer than 10 employees) or one with multiple stores and many employees? Is it a business that you hope your spouse, children, or other family members might want to work in and take over someday? Or do you want to work hard for 10 to 20 years and then sell the business and retire? How will you mix personal and business in order to achieve a good balance in your life?

It is important to consider where you want to end up before you even start. Many experts will tell you to start planning your exit strategy the day you start your business.

Separate Home from Business

If your only activity is your business, it's likely your family and social life will suffer. We all know people who are divorced due to problems resulting directly from the pressures of starting and operating a business. Don't let this happen to you.

Think about these words from Lord Chesterfield (1694–1773): "Few people do business well who do nothing else." What this quotation tells us is that you are likely to lose some of the very qualities that will make you a business success if you don't remain well rounded in other aspects of your life. You already know you have to spend a lot of time with your business—but it's imperative that you also set aside time for family, friends, and yourself. Without this relief, you're likely to burn out long before you attain the success you want.

Here are a few suggestions for ensuring a successful balance between your business and home life:

- Plan for the future but live in the present. Don't let the good times pass you by.
- If you do any work at home, designate an area for work only.
- Keep your hobby alive. A hobby can be an excellent source of relaxation.
- Maintain some type of physical activity. Exercise is a wonderful way to reduce tension and clear your mind.
- When socializing, try not to talk about business topics unless asked by others.
- Keep your significant other informed about your business activities, but don't make it the only topic of discussion.
- Although you will be putting in long hours on business, regularly set aside time for activities with family and friends.
- Remember: Problems with family and friends can spell disaster for your business. Be sensitive to their needs as well as your own. Stay involved in activities other than your business to the greatest extent possible.

How Well Do You Understand Business?

You do not need to have an MBA, be a CPA, or read the *Wall Street Journal* from cover to cover to be able to own and operate a successful business.

Business Example from Hank Darlington's Early Career

When I was eight years old, a neighbor playmate, Sally, and I opened up a lemonade stand. A couple of other kids had started one about eight blocks away so we did market research on the best location, then purchased lemons, sugar, cups, and napkins (inventory). We needed a table, chairs, and signage (assets). We established a sell price that was greater than cost, which generated a gross profit. We had a serious human resource issue, which was who would be the boss. (I was older so I won the job.) In the end, we had all the ingredients of a kitchen and bath business and could have generated a profit and loss statement and balance sheet. As I remember, the hot spell lasted about two days, and our interest level was just about as long. Thanks to family and neighbors, I'm sure we put a few coins in our piggy banks. That was my first entrepreneurial experience. I loved it then and love it still!

Beyond operating a lemonade stand when you were a kid, do you have any hands-on business experience? Do you really know all the things involved in running a business? There's a lot to it, including bookkeeping, taxes, payrolls, accounts receivable and payable, marketing, signing contracts, making deals, and operating in accordance with all government laws and regulations.

According to an analysis by Dunn & Bradstreet (www.dnd.com), experience and aptitude count for a lot. Dunn & Bradstreet suggests that poor management is the leading cause of business failure. They estimate that a lack of managerial experience and aptitude accounts for almost 90 percent of business failures.

WHY MANY COMPANIES DO NOT MAKE IT

Since so many small businesses fail in the first six years, it's important to understand why this happens.

- Lack of money
- Lack of business planning
- Inefficient control of costs
- Inferior quality of products and services
- Insufficient inventory control
- Underpricing products and services sold
- Poor customer relations
- Failure to promote and maintain a favorable public image
- Poor relations with suppliers
- Poor management
- Illness of key personnel
- Reluctance to seek professional help
- Failure to minimize taxation through tax planning
- Inadequate insurance
- Loss of key personnel
- Lack of staff training
- Insufficient knowledge of the industry
- Inability to compete
- Failure to anticipate market trends
- Inadequate cash flow
- Growth without adequate capitalization
- Ignoring data on the company's financial position
- Incomplete financial records
- Overextending credit
- Overborrowing
- Overdue receivables
- Excessive demands from creditors

Failure Factors and Characteristics of Entrepreneurs Who Have Failed

Since the failure rate of new businesses exceeds the success rate, it's important to look closely at typical characteristics of businesses that did not make it.

- **Lack of management experience.** Many entrepreneurs do not understand the intricacies of running a business. Too many K&B dealership owners have entered into business with good design and sales experience but little or no management experience. Lack of skills in financial, human resources, and marketing management can lead to failure.
- **Poor financial planners.** A major cause of failure is not having the expertise to write a comprehensive business plan, develop annual budgets, and generate and analyze monthly financial statements. This, plus poor planning in terms of capital requirements, can be the downfall of your business.
- **Poor location choice.** For a K&B dealer, finding the right location is one of the most important decisions. Spend the time and money to be sure the business is in the right area.
- **Ineffective business controls.** Lack of written policies, procedures, systems, and job descriptions, along with poor controls in accounting, job costing, accounts receivable, and inventory control, can kill a business before it even gets started.
- **Being a big spender.** Buying all new equipment and furnishings versus. leasing or buying used is not wise unless the finances allow. Do not overspend on displays and building improvements. Driving expensive cars and taking too much salary can all contribute to a downfall.
- **Lack of commitment and dedication.** In the early years of a new business, the lack of willingness to spend the needed hours or give up non–work-related activities will have a negative impact on the enterprise. At times, family life will be disrupted as the founder works long hours creating a strong foundation for the business.
- **Impulse to overexpand.** When the business gets off to a great start, the first impulse is to expand—locations, products, services, customer base, and so on. Trying to do too much, too quickly can lead to a decline in services rendered, quality of product, and employee performance. The issue of available capital plays an important role in any expansion. A word of advice: Go slowly and be certain before undertaking any expansions.

Success Factors and Characteristics of Entrepreneurs Who Have Succeeded

To succeed, you must define your skills. To help you determine your level of expertise in each category, here is a summary of the skills needed to succeed.

- **Business planning.** The ability to establish and achieve short-term (one- to three-year) and long-term (three- to five-year) planning goals for the business.
- **Finance.** The ability to manage money, create and interpret financial statements, develop and update annual budgets, manage accounts payable and receivable, and successfully seek out funding sources for the business.
- **Accounting.** The ability to accurately record and interpret the income and expenses of the business in a timely manner (preferably monthly). If the business includes installation as one of its services, this would include job costing.
- **Marketing.** The ability to identify target markets (area and clients) and to put together a package of products and services that will be attractive to these clients. Marketing also includes knowing your competition.
- **Sales.** The ability to close sales once clients have been attracted to the business through marketing efforts and the presentation of a solution-slanted functional design plan. This would include learning and teaching sales skills to all salespeople.
- **Advertising, promotion, and public relations.** The ability to create plans, budgets, and campaigns that successfully sell the offerings of your business and attract potential clients to it.
- **Design.** The ability to create space solutions that work.
- **Installation.** The ability to manage a design/build kitchen/bath project with in-house installations or subcontractors.
- **Product knowledge.** The ability to know and sell your products and services better than your competition.
- **Human resource management.** The ability to recruit, hire, train, motivate, manage, and fire people.

AVOID THESE COMMON MISTAKES

Instead of making mistakes and learning the hard way, you can learn from the mistakes of others. Here are some of the pitfalls and common mistakes to be aware of.

- **Being married to your ideas.** Learn to be flexible and be able to adjust and change.
- **Not identifying your target audience.** Are you going to market kitchens and baths to high-end, middle, or low-end buyers? It's unlikely that you'll be able to be all things to all people. Select your niche carefully and thoughtfully.
- **Acting impulsively (i.e., not doing the proper research).** You'll need to learn everything possible about the K&B industry and the marketplace you plan to serve. Make time to learn as much as possible. Have the facts; do not operate on impulse.
- **Not having a business plan.** You will need a business plan that includes a marketing plan, financial projections, and human resource needs.
- **Ignoring the competition.** Study them, "mystery shop" (i.e., visit competitors incognito), research them. Know what their target market is, what main products and services they offer, what price point they offer, what image they project, and so on. In other words, learn everything you can—then use it to your benefit.
- **Underestimating your time frame to profitability.** Having a business plan, knowing your competition, knowing your customers, and offering the right mix of products and services will definitely lead you to profitability in a shorter time frame.
- **Trying to be a one-person show.** Yes, it is your business. No, you cannot do it all by yourself. The most successful businesspeople surround themselves with competent people. Good management is getting the job done through other people.
- **Cutting the wrong corners.** Spending all of your money to build a great showroom but not having money left over to advertise and promote will not get the job done. Be prudent, but be smart.

- **Focusing too much on technology and too little on people.** While technology can do wonders, it will not substitute for good customer, vendor, and employee relations. Do not spend all of your time and money on the latest and greatest computer-assisted design system while you should be training, motivating, and appreciating your employees.
- **Trying to do too much all at once.** Take the whole process one step at a time. Prioritize, set budgets and timelines. Then proceed in an orderly fashion.

GETTING HELP FROM ADVISORS AND MENTORS

Do not try to build a business in a vacuum. Take advantage of the feedback, suggestions, directions, and opinions of others; they can be extremely valuable to help get a business started or to grow an existing business. Certainly seek advice from related trade professionals but also utilize your banker, attorney, accountant, insurance agent, and friends to help in your venture.

SUMMARY

This chapter covered the various pros and cons of owning your own business. You were encouraged to rate your own leadership traits and to evaluate your personal entrepreneurial strengths and weaknesses. Upon completing this chapter, you should have a better understanding of which mistakes to avoid in order to manage a successful business.

REVIEW QUESTIONS

1. List five pros (advantages) to owning your own business. (See "Owning Your Own Business—Pros" pages 1–2)
2. What are the four "P's" that Debbi Fields Rose listed as her recipe for success in operating her company Mrs. Fields Cookies? (See "Business Success" page 2)
3. What are four important building blocks in your business foundation? (See "Four Keys to a Successful Kitchen/Bath Business" page 3)
4. List what you believe are the five most important business leadership traits needed to run a successful business. (See "Leadership Traits" page 4)
5. List five things that will help you ensure a successful balance between your business and your personal life. (See "Separate Home from Business" page 8)
6. List five reasons why your business may not survive. (See "Avoid These Common Mistakes" page 11)
7. List three areas of operating a successful business that you feel are your strongest. (See "Success Factors and Characteristics of Entreprenueurs Who Have Succeeded" page 11)
8. List two areas that are your weakest and explain out how you might improve them. (See "Failure Factors and Characteristics of Entrepreneurs Who Have Failed" page 10)

Resources

American Association of Entrepreneurs
655 15th Street N.W.
Suite 400 / F Street Lobby
Washington, DC 20005
Phone: (202) 659–2979

American Institute for Small Business
7515 Wayzata Blvd., Suite 129
Minneapolis, MN 55426
Phone: (800) 328–2906
http://www.ed2go.com/business/

National Association of Self-Employed
P.O. Box 612067, DFW Airport
Dallas, TX 75261–2067
Phone: (800) 232–6273
www.nase.org

U.S. Small Business Association
403 3rd Street S.W.
Washington, DC 20416
Phone: (202) 205–7701
www.sba.gov

The resources for marketers and entrepreneurs are infinite. Here are a few to get you started:

American Express Small Business Exchange
Phone: (888) 792–0279
www.americanexpress.com/smallbusiness

BizAdvantages
Phone: (800) 223–1026
www.bizadvantages.com

SCORE (Service Corp of Retired Executives)
409 3rd Street, SW, 6th Floor
Washington, DC 20024
Phone: (800) 634–0245
www.score.org

SmartBIZ
www.smartbiz.com

Planning Your Business

Whether you're starting new, have stepped into the family business, bought an existing business, or have been operating a business for some time, you need to evaluate (or perhaps reevaluate) the type of business you want to own.

Learning Objective 1: Compare the three main business models for kitchen and bath businesses.

Learning Objective 2: Explain the stages of company growth.

Learning Objective 3: Explain the components of a detailed business plan.

Learning Objective 4: Explain the difference between a short-term (one-year) and long-term (three- to five-year) business plan.

Learning Objective 5: Explain the advantages of being a niche type of company.

WHAT TYPE OF KITCHEN AND BATH BUSINESS ARE YOU GOING TO OPERATE?

There is no right answer to the question: What's the best business model for a kitchen and bath firm? However, there are several typical business models. Although other models do exist, the next outline is an overview of companies found throughout North America.

Business Model No. 1: A Designer's Studio

An independent kitchen designer operates out of his/her home or a studio location and provides design services for a fee (Figure 2.1). The designer may work closely with area kitchen specialists representing products* or may provide only generic plans. Installation is rarely provided. Often contractors/installers are recommended. The individual is the branded image in the community.

---

* Individual business ethics guidelines and state/province laws determine whether the independent designer can derive income from products purchased by the consumer from referred sources.

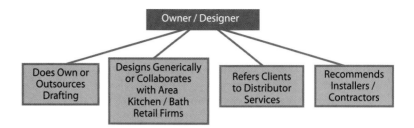

FIGURE 2.1 A designer's studio business model

Business Model No. 2: A Design Practice Firm

A design practice firm (Figure 2.2) offers cabinets and counter surfaces to the consumer. The firm also may provide appliances, fittings, and fixtures. Installation services are offered through in-house staff or subcontractors. The business may be in a destination location, part of a home-based business, or in a retail strip mall environment. The owner is typically the only designer, or the primary designer, for the firm. Both the firm and its owner are known in the community, with the owner as an individual the better-known and recognized entity rather than the firm itself.

Business Model No. 3: A Design Business Firm

A design business firm (Figure 2.3) is a larger organization with a showroom and an attached or remotely located warehouse/shop facility. The business may be a department of a larger business: the kitchen/bath section of a large lumberyard, for example. Such department-style organizations normally use a reference program directing clients to installation specialists rather than maintaining an installation department. Another model is a comprehensive design/build firm where in-house crews or subcontractors provide a turnkey operation.

The owner/manager leads the company and significantly contributes to the sales volume. However, it is the firm that has the branded image, not the individual. Once again, this firm may be in a destination environment, a retail shopping community, or in a trade/retail design center.

This type of firm might have more than one branch location—more than one showroom. The organization also may have a tier of middle management: A sales manager/director may head the team of sales associates and assistants. At each remote location, the organization may have a branch manager who is part of a leadership management team. The sales director/manager and branch manager bring a wealth of knowledge to the organization: Their input about ways to streamline the operation's work procedures, as well as their ability to assist the owner in managing the business, is extremely valuable.

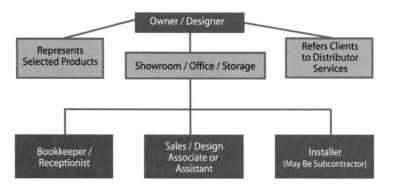

FIGURE 2.2 Design practice firm

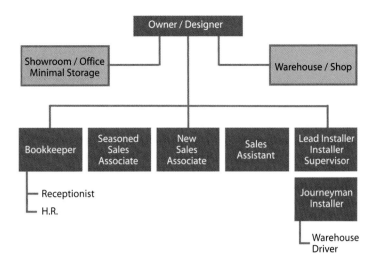

FIGURE 2.3 Design business firm

YOUR BUSINESS SELECTION CRITERIA

Select your ideal business model based on your market research, strategic marketing plan, long-term goals, and exit strategy.

A good business idea is one that will bring you a good profit. Beyond that, a good idea for business should meet some or all of the next criteria:

- Fill a void and/or meet a customer need.
- Offer a faster, better, easier or higher-quality product and service than is currently available.
- Be realistic and within the scope of something that you can do.
- Have a defined target audience.
- Doesn't oversaturate the marketplace.
- Be legal.

What to Do after You Have an Idea

To determine the merits and shortcomings of your business idea, research, crunch numbers, and examine all the practical and not-so-practical aspects of making your idea a reality. Nurture this idea and help it grow into a full-fledged written plan. Then put together the elaborate puzzle that takes your idea from the drawing board and turns it into reality.

DECIDING ON THE RIGHT BUSINESS

A number of significant factors will be part of your decision-making process as you set about finding the right type of K&B business for you. Here are a few of these factors:

- What will you enjoy doing every day that will earn the greatest profit and return on your time and money?
- Will people pay for the products and services that you plan to sell?
- How much financial help will you need and where can you get it?
- What resources (people, vendors, mentors, etc.) can you gather to help run the business?
- How much time and effort can you put into the business without sacrificing other aspects of your life?

Whether you are starting new or taking a fresh look at your existing business, step back and try to design the perfect scenario for yourself.

No, you probably won't end up with the exact same thing, but at least you will have an idea what it is you want to achieve. If after 5 or 10 years you find yourself running a business that is close to what you pictured, then you have done very well indeed. But it all starts with a picture and a plan.

CHOOSING A NAME FOR YOUR BUSINESS

The name of your business is the key to your brand image in your customers' minds. Chosen well, your name will reflect an image that is unique, memorable, appropriate, likable, and capable of advancing a promise for your business.

Following are several questions to ask yourself before committing to a name for a new business or changing the name of an existing business.

- **What kind of name do you want?**
  - **Owner's name:** Darlington Kitchen and Bath Design Studio
  - **Geographical name:** Northern California Kitchen and Bath Center
  - **Alphabetical name:** D & D Kitchens, Baths and Custom Cabinetry
  - **Descriptive name:** Creative Cabinetry
- **What do you want the name to convey?** Words such as "quality," "creative," "premier," "factory direct"?
- **Is the name you want available?**
  - Screen the name for trademark ownership. Check the Patent and Trademark Depository Library (PTDL) at www.uspto.gov.
  - Check if the name is available as a domain name (www.networksolutions.com or www.godaddy.com)
  - Protect the name if it is available. An attorney can do this for a reasonable fee.
- **Is it easy to spell?** Is it phonetically pleasing? Is it a name that works well in normal business conversation?
- **Is it original?** Check several telephone books and the Internet. Aim for an original name that stands apart from the pack.
- **Is it memorable?** Look for a name that reflects a distinct aspect of your company.
- **Can you live and grow with the name?** You are going to have to live with this name for a long time, so the most important questions are: Do you like it? Will it adapt to your future?
- **Are you ready to commit to a name?** Once you have settled on a name and determined that people can spell it, say it, remember it, and relate well to it, you are ready to take these steps to make the name your own:
  - Register the name and trademark in your state/province.
  - Register the domain name.
  - Create a professional logo to serve as the "force" of your name.
  - Look for new ways to advance your name and logo—on vehicle signage, clothing, store signage, letterhead, note cards, advertisements, and so on.

Do all you can to make your name part of your brand.

STAGES OF COMPANY GROWTH

Just as people go through many stages in their lives, companies evolve and change over their years of operation. As you prepare to write a business plan, be sure that you know what stage of growth your business is in—from brand new to well established. Following are the natural evolutionary stages that almost all companies go through. Make sure your plan places you in the right stage.

Stages of Company Growth

1. Idea
2. Planning
3. Funding
4. Start-up
5. Ramp-up
6. Evolution
7. Sustaining

Idea Stage

This stage is when you first start thinking about going into business for yourself and what kind of business it will be.

Planning Stage

This is taking the idea and documenting how the start-up actually will happen. The goal here is to develop a plan that convinces you and others that your idea is a good one and worthy of both the time and money invested.

Funding Stage

This is the stage during which you acquire the money needed to start or change your business. Many K&B businesses are self-funded (i.e., the owner puts up all the money). If you need additional funding, you will become the salesperson and evangelist to banks, partners, family, and any reasonable source. A good job of developing a comprehensive written plan will help immensely in the fundraising stage.

Start-up Stage

This is where you put your plan and funding into action. You select vendors, a location, build the showroom, hire help, and kick off the marketing plan.

Ramp-up Stage

The word is out. Clients are coming in because of referrals, and the business really starts to take off. This is good—but a word of caution is in order: Managing growth can be just as difficult as managing a business downturn. You may need more people or more equipment to become technologically in tune. This stage could last from six months to two years. Growth usually requires additional capital, and you will need to plan for this in advance.

Evolution Stage

When you reach this stage, you will find yourself asking "What will we do next year?" instead of "Will we be around next year?" Your future survival is no longer a major concern. This is where you step back and look at your product and service offerings. Just because things have gone well up to this point does not mean you can become complacent or sit back and rest on your laurels. You must be creative and innovative all over again. Take the next steps that will keep you ahead of your competition and in front of your target audience.

As an example: Maybe you have been marketing and selling K&B design and a selection of higher-end products, but you have not offered installation. You are finding more and more clients looking for turnkey projects, and a few of your competitors are offering this. As a part of your evolution stage, you may want to add installation to your services, and you may want to expand your products to include countertops, appliances, and lighting. After reviewing your projects, you find that 90 percent have been kitchens—you might consider marketing to grow bathroom design and sales.

Over time, you cannot stay at the same level in business. You are either moving ahead or you are falling behind.

Sustaining Stage

This is when you are all grown up. When you reach this stage, you will be an accepted, recognized player in the marketplace and, one hopes, a leader. People will look at you as one of the companies to beat when starting a new business. And they will look at you as one of the companies to emulate when doing their business. Even when you reach this stage, the planning, budgeting, and market research does not stop. It is an ongoing, never-ending process.

SHORT- AND LONG-TERM PLANNING

Nothing happens in the long term without short-term plans and actions that move you toward your desired outcome. These short-term actions cannot help you achieve any particular goal if no goals have been set or no plan has been developed.

You must know where you are going before you can figure out a route to get there:

- Take time to determine your own goals; your company's long-term mission and objectives will guide your daily actions. Without this framework, you and your employees may be busy but the business will not move forward because everyone is pulling in separate directions.
- Make sure everyone knows and understands the goals and objectives of the company. It will make life a lot easier—for you as well as your employees.

For example: You are a Certified Kitchen Designer (CKD). You love designing kitchens enough to win awards. You are okay with the selling process because you know that is what really pays the bills. But now you are involved in the whole business management as well and you have found yourself designing less and hassling with installers more—you are not having fun anymore. This might have been prevented and, in fact, still can be changed by hiring an installation manager, someone you can turn that side of the business over to. Now you can get back to designing and selling—and having fun too.

> ## Start with a Detailed Plan
> - Set goals to identify the actions you must take to get from A (where you are) to B (where your goals are).
> - A plan analysis shows you if your idea is viable or not. It saves you time, money, and heartaches.
> - You and your business associates use the plan as a road map.
> - The plan begins with the company as a start-up, then becomes the evolution plan, followed by the sustaining plan.
> - To make it achievable, be honest, accurate, and reasonable.

Before tackling the step-by-step process of creating a plan outlined by Hank Darlington, we invited industry marketing expert Leonard V. Casey to share his views on the importance of concentrating on the marketing strategy first. Len, an industry veteran with experience leading the DuPont Corian team, running a major cabinet company, and contributing to the strategic planning of a variety of businesses in the K&B industry, suggests the following business focus.

HOW TO CREATE A STRATEGIC BUSINESS PLAN FOR A KITCHEN/BATH DEALER

We all have our own important reasons for going into business—none of these reasons includes paying bills, dealing with banks, understanding suppliers, or writing a business plan. However, over the next few pages, you will find a new and valuable view of a planning process leading to greater enjoyment for your real passion and reasons to have your own business.

A strategic business plan may sound like a lot work and perhaps a little boring. But—if done well—it becomes your best friend the business owner: a place where you can think through your ideas without day-to-day pressures clouding the view. The strategic business plan also helps you gain support from other stakeholders, such as employees, suppliers, and advisors—even customers—by providing a clear view of where the organization is headed.

Having a business plan allows you to evaluate events not as a reaction to short-term opportunities (sometimes turning out to be long-term nightmares) but by measuring opportunities against your strategic yardstick, enabling you to better select the "good" and jettison those things not fitting your plan. This will save time and money and greatly reduce stress.**

A Road Map

A strategic business plan is much like a road map for your business. It allows you to look ahead in such a way as to anticipate needs and the outcome of your actions. If you take full advantage of your strategic business plan, you will have the opportunity of thinking through what you are contemplating, thereby reducing risks and greatly improving chances of success.

In today's business world, there is a great deal of opportunity—far more than perhaps ever before—across a broad spectrum of market segments. A well-engineered, strategic business plan will help you and your employees focus on the most important opportunities for the business, consistent with your values and strengths. It will also give you the conviction to avoid other interesting opportunities that are not a strategic fit.

Strategic business plan: A roadmap to your business

Use the Map
Business plans are often large documents filled with financial data that find a permanent resting place on a shelf, never to be read again once written. But a useful strategic business plan is quite different. It will be read, used, and understood by all stakeholders of the business. It will become a valuable asset. Producing a useful business plan is not easy and involves a great deal of thought, discipline and understanding of your market, but it is worth it.

Difference between a Strategy and a Plan

The name "strategic business plan" implies something more than just the business plan itself. It is made up of two distinct but inseparable parts: first, the strategy and then the plan (Figure 2.4):

1. The strategy of a company is the collection of the important policies designed to allow the business to win (i.e., to meet or exceed its business plan goals and objectives) in the desired marketplace.
2. The plan is the allocation of the company's scarce resources of money, time and people to implement the policies the business is using to win.

The two are inseparable because a business plan not based on a clear strategic direction has no chance of being successful.

**Previous three paragraphs contributed by Leonard V. Casey, MBA.

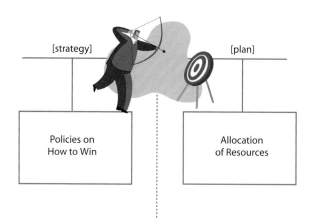

FIGURE 2.4 Strategic Business Plan

Profit Is the Reason for a Business to Exist but Offers No Direction

Many businesses focus a lot of their attention on the notion of the company's profit objective. They sometimes will break down the profit into quarterly, monthly, or even weekly objectives, trying to aim the organization toward the whole idea of earning profit. This, however, may result in a misuse of the concept of profit because it can lead the business in too many directions, wasting resources and, therefore, ultimately producing poor results.

An alert: Sometimes talking about the concept of a misuse of profits leads to confusion because companies *should* earn profit—this is the reward for being successful. However, focusing much of the organization's time on profit itself provides no direction on how to make that profit and does not automatically lead an organization to meaningful solutions.

Look at this concept from another angle.

> Profit is to business as fun is to a vacation. They are both the desired result of specific actions (working, vacationing).

Profit in business has a similar role as fun has to a vacation—it is the goal (the reason you do it). However, both profit and fun offer no direction as to how you are to accomplish the goal. Therefore, they are not useful in shaping your actions. Indeed, in some cases, the quest for profit can even harm the organization because we may think we know where we are headed when we do not.

For example, two friends decide they are going to spend vacation together this winter starting on February 1 to "have fun." They agree to meet, but when they arrive, one is wearing full winter snow gear while the other is clad in a bathing suit and carrying a surfboard. Something was missing in their plan: the lack of strategic intent for what it was they wanted to do (how was fun to occur).

Now, look at this situation with only one improvement—a single element of strategy. The two discuss in advance their desire to have a vacation together and decide they are going to meet in Key West on February 1 (of course, to have fun). If this is the only discussion concerning their vacation, they will accelerate their good experience exponentially. The two probably could have added other items of value, such as booking flights together, saving money on rental cars, and a whole list of things. However, if nothing else did occur, these two will have a good chance of having fun because they have a strategic intent.

It is the same with business profit: Profit is the very reason we are in business. However, profit is nondirectional. Making profit sounds like the right thing to do, and members of the organization may go off in their individual directions—trying to earn profit. But such unfocused efforts may do just the opposite because of the various actions taken. For example, reducing inventory to improve profit may be a good idea. However, if it results in a stock-out, unacceptable delivery delays and—worst of all—a lost customer, the slight savings in inventory could mean disaster for the company.

Profit Is the Result of a Successful Strategy

Organizations need to understand how they will make profit before they begin.

Once you know where you are going, you can measure if you are getting there, and, along the way, you can make improvements to make the profit projections even better. The entire profit opportunity of the company becomes real, measurable, and achievable when you have a clear sense of strategic intent. For example:

- "This year we will increase the total number of kitchens we will complete from 20 to 25 with an increase in the average profit margin from 39 to 42 percent."
- "We will improve our customer referral from 60 to 85 percent during the next two years."

Both of these statements are strategic and directional. Once the organization uses measurable and achievable action elements, the entire profit opportunity of the company becomes real.

Strategy is the things you will do to make profit. Profit is the result.

Break up the process of our strategic business plan into its individual parts (Figure 2.5).

The strategic focus of a company is made up of three important areas: vision, mission, and fundamental strategy. Collectively, these are the most powerful tools a business has. Let's have a look at each individually and how they are interconnected as building blocks with their own hierarchy.

Vision and Mission of Your Company

The vision is the core purpose of why the company exists. It can be called the "soul" of the company. Although the vision says nothing about the day-to-day activities of the organization, it guides everything we do. A company vision functions much like the Constitution of the United States, which does not tell us what we are to do but guides everything we do.

Strategic Focus	Business Plan
Vision	5-year plan
Mission	1-year plan
Strategy	Action plan

FIGURE 2.5 Parts of a business plan

**Vision/Mission:
Much like the Constitution
of the United States**

Without a clear vision, a business will wander from opportunity to opportunity, never reaching its true potential. With a clear and shared vision, every employee will be enabled to focus their energy on the proper variables leading to the success of the business. The vision is only the beginning of the strategic process, but it is the first step. Without it, you can go no further.

Vision Comes from the Top

The vision comes from the top—the founder, the chairperson, the president, and the key people responsible for the business—and must be shared by all. Visions were not always thought of in the formal way we are speaking of today, but visions were always present in all successful businesses. Although a vision may not have been articulated on paper, great businesses have been headed by a leader who was a "visionary." Such a leader had a personal vision that permeated the total atmosphere of the day-to-day life of the organization.

One example: John Hollingsworth, a successful merchant in the mid-1800s, decided to go into the growing business of shipbuilding in Newport News, Virginia. In the first days of his company, standing on the steps of his new office in front of his small staff, he said, "We will make good ships here, at a profit if we can, at a loss if we must, but always good ships."

The importance of John Hollingsworth's words became clearer every day. He set the standard of the way the company existed and why it should exist: "To make good ships." This was his vision. Can you imagine in a bad year a smart purchasing agent who thought he could help profits by purchasing a lower grade of lumber, thereby improving profitability? Hollingsworth's words would go a long way in guiding that purchasing agent and others to look for better solutions and not waste important time on debates about things outside his vision. John Hollingsworth's Newport News shipbuilding company went on to become the most successful shipbuilding company in the world. His vision surely helped.

People often use the words "vision" and "mission" interchangeably, or reverse the order of hierarchy. There is good logic on both sides but, in the end, it is mostly semantics. If the vision of a company is the first building block and the most important abstract view of where the business is going, the mission is the beginning of how we are going to set about the task ahead. Therefore, the mission is the value and belief standards of the organization. The mission statement will help to communicate the organization's belief as an outgrowth of the vision itself.

Consider the next vision and mission statement by a leading faucet and sink manufacturer.

Vision

KWC is known by kitchen and bath consumers, interior designers, architects, and kitchen specialists as a provider of innovative performance-driven water appliances with uncompromising quality, design, and service.

Mission

To reach out to the design professionals in the kitchen and bath industry through a series of design and support programs. KWC will be understood, advocated and the product of choice for the design community.

Strategy

What It Is

The strategy of a business is the written statement of the policies, services, procedures, pricing, and so on that the company will use to be successful reaching its goals in the selected market.

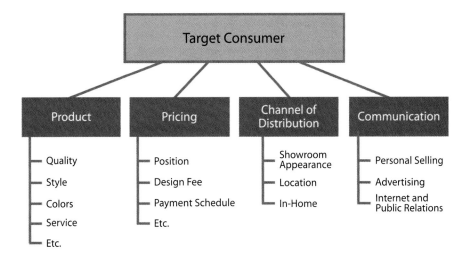

FIGURE 2.6 Market strategy: Target consumer

The Four Key Parts

In its simplest form, a business strategy covers only four major areas (Figures 2.6 and 2.7). Although this may seem oversimplified, all decisions made in business stem from one of these four areas:

1. What products do we offer? Products include physical items, as well as services.
2. At what price will we sell these products?
3. Where will the transaction take place?
4. How do we communicate our message in a manner to stimulate a sale?[1]

On a day-to-day basis, we do not speak of the four decisions of product, pricing, channel of distribution, or communication policies (Figure 2.7). We tend to find ourselves asking questions such as:

• What is the quality and style of the products we are handling?
• Do we provide full installation services? Or offer turnkey construction services?
• What about price?
• Do we charge a design fee? When, if ever, do we give away the plans?
• What is a reasonable payment schedule?
• What about location? How should the showroom look? Where should the showroom be located? Where is the consumer most comfortable?

On a practical basis, these and many other questions are answered day in and day out. And the questions are interrelated: You cannot offer the best in design without some type of advance payment system. Installation cannot be offered if the price does not allow for a profitable installation department. The question, then, is how do we balance the four important variables of price, product, location, and communication in such a way to ensure we are on the correct path forward?

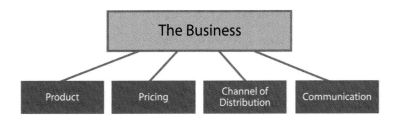

FIGURE 2.7 Market strategy: The business

---

[1]Courtesy of Eugene McCarthy, Author *Principles of Marketing*.

Identify the Target Consumer

Who Is a Target Consumer?

The key element in a business strategy is the proper identification of your target consumer. Without doing so, the balance of your efforts will not work. The more clearly you can identify your target consumer, the easier the answers will become, thereby improving the understanding and execution of your strategy.

Who Is a Target Consumer?

This group should be small enough in size for you to have a clear understanding of their true needs and values yet large enough to be financially interesting.

Target consumers should be a homogeneous group that shares a common sense of quality, values, and needs.

Decisions around these four important variables are interrelated. The answers come from a common denominator: the target consumer you strive to attract. Therefore, the way to ask and answer the questions is to first identify your target consumer and then ask:

- What products does this consumer group need and want?
- What are they willing to pay?
- How does this target consumer learn about products?
- What do they need to know to say yes?
- What service offering does this consumer group want in order to complete the transaction?

When successfully balancing your four major decisions in harmony with your target consumer group, you will have completed your "business strategy."

Comment on the Current Kitchen/Bath Business Environment

As you identify your target consumer, realize that in today's K&B market, it is difficult to serve all types of clients interested in a new kitchen, bath, or other fitted furniture. The old target of trying to offer "good, better, best" selections of products and services (Figure 2.8) is simply too hard to manage in our complex industry today. This outdated business model leads to a few yearly "monuments," or projects that are unprofitable, as well as to time wasted on overdesigned projects for entry-level clients.

Industry leaders suggest that a vertically integrated business model (Figure 2.9) is more successful when it focuses on a limited series of related segments of the market, such as the upper end of the market, the upper middle of the market, or the middle-middle of the market.

When you are successful in segmenting your target consumer, you will find the answers to the questions of product, price, and so on faster and easier to get to. You will clearly know what policies you must follow for a profitable venture. Further, consumers who are similar in nature, values, and needs are your best source of repeat and referral business in the same market segment.

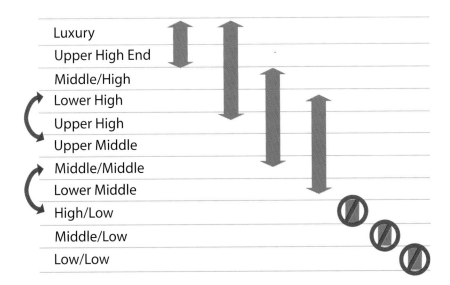

FIGURE 2.8 Outdated good/better/best business model

Engage Your Stakeholders in the Process

When looking to produce your business strategy, it becomes helpful to use your key stakeholders to help you think through the process. Stakeholders should take part in the development and review of the strategy. The end result is a written document describing your target consumer and a policy statement for key business variables of product, price, location, and communications. Once this document has been completed, the business plan becomes a much easier task and alive with insight.

Developing the Business Plan

When armed with a clear strategic focus, the work needed to produce your business plan is easier, less time consuming, and more meaningful, and it receives faster agreement among all stakeholders in the organization. The purpose of your business plan is to drive your business forward to reach the strategic goals you and your organization have set.

The Goal Is Both Financial and Directional

By now, you can see the goal of the strategic business plan is not merely financial—it is directional. A financially successful company is the result of producing a valued offering to a target consumer group. Without providing consistent value over time, the business will fail.

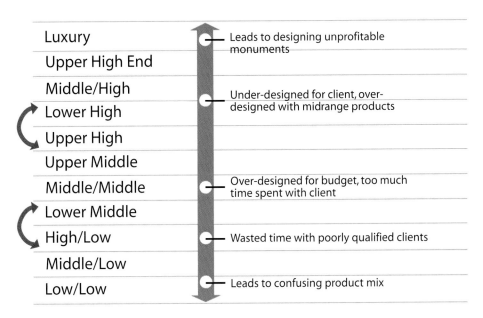

FIGURE 2.9 Vertically integrated business model

The business plan becomes the allocation of your important and limited resources of people, money, and time to perform the necessary work to create the value described in your business strategy, resulting in winning the loyalty of your target consumer. The focus of the plan then becomes describing the tasks or work to be accomplished in a measurable and achievable manner.

Secrets to a Successful Business Plan

- Make the plan measurable and achievable.
- Realize it is not easy to write the plan.
- Make the plan without fear.
- Keep the plan short.

Some important considerations to remember when writing your business plan:

- **The plan must always be measurable and achievable.** Therefore, you must take care to ensure the plan is written in an objective way and is not subjective in nature.

  For example, someone could state this in a business plan:

  > "We will actively promote the value of our organization to the community's opinion leaders throughout the year."

  This statement sounds important and like a good idea. However, it is subjective, impossible to measure, and its implementation often wastes valuable resources of time and money. People within the organization will be trying to do what they *think* you mean by this statement.

  An alternative statement that is measurable and achievable might be:

  > "In order to become known by the community's design leaders (Wilson Design Group, Johnson Interiors, All American Architects), we will host three receptions during May and June for the owners and their staff."

  By making this change, your organization is more empowered to do the intended work. Everyone on your staff now knows who the community leaders are and when the work of courting them will be done. Everyone can add to the list or challenge the validity of the selection. Everyone knows when the effort will take place, and the outcome itself is measurable.

- **Developing the plan is not easy.** Determining the strategic intent driving your target market will take discipline and careful assessment by all stakeholders.
  1. You will need to involve everyone in the process. This will give the plan the best 360-degree view, improving its ideas, performance, and outcome.
  2. You must develop the support staff's agreement and buy-in for the tasks as well as their understanding of the relevance and importance of their work to the whole.
  3. You must establish dates of completion and a clear identification of who is responsible for all actionable plan items.
  4. Everyone must be willing to upgrade the plan.
  5. All stakeholders must understand the plan.

- **Make the plan without fear.** If the plan is used in a negative way to judge people, the organization will not embrace the plan. For example, the people taking on the project of working with the design community leaders (Wilson Design Group, Johnson Interior, All American Architects) are responsible for the events agreed upon but should not be judged on whether the design community leader uses their services. The people responsible for the plan will tend to include only things they know are easy; therefore, you will not get the best from your employees and suppliers. (Make it fun!)
- **Short is better than long.** The shorter your plan is, the easier it will be to read and to communicate and so the better opportunity it has for success. Short plans may also expose a lack of substance. A well-written short plan should offer a complete understanding of the organization: the goals, strategy, and direction of the business.

Your business plan must:

- Translate strategy into action.
- Allow your resources to be apportioned efficiently and properly.
- Provide better communications to associates, customers, and suppliers.
- Provide a timely measurement of success.
- Provide the rationale for financial goals, not just the numbers.
- Establish priorities.
- Be the means of selecting alternative opportunities.
- Be the basis of new plans.

Business Plan Responsibilities

Who is responsible for the business planning process?

- Business owners are the starting place for planning responsibility, accountability, and leadership. Business owners are responsible for the essence of the plan, not just its financial goals. Unless the owners and the top management of the firm are totally familiar with the plan, the organization will never assemble the resources to achieve the financial rewards.
- Management—at all levels of the firm—must be part of the development of the path forward as well as agree to its potential achievability.
- Designers will perform better when they are engaged in the development of the central theme of the organization (its business strategy) and will select customers, develop referrals, and perform closer to the goals if they understand and participate in the development of the plan.
- All support groups, such as accountants, subcontractors, suppliers, and the like, need to be part of the planning process. Each support member sees the opportunity from a unique vantage point. Further, second-guessing from support groups can be detrimental to the potential success.

Formatting the Business Plan

Although the format might not be the most important aspect of a strategic business plan, a consistent format is part of the necessary discipline to deliver the important information to keep the organization on track to achieve success. The next format is highly recommended:

- Five-year view
- One-year view
- One-year action plan
- Review process
- Judging the business plan

Five-Year Business Statement

This is a broad view of where your business is to be five years from now, including a list of the critical events necessary to achieve the five-year business position.

- Keep the broad view to one or two paragraphs, stating both the strategic and the financial consequences of your efforts, plus the key events.
- Keep the five-year view in place for the entire time until it is accomplished (unless it is clearly known to be unsuccessful). This keeps all stakeholders responsible for their efforts and improves the plan's performance.

Follow the five-year view with a one-year view.

One-Year View

The one-year view is also a broad statement of what must happen during the first year of business to be on course for the successful completion of the full five-year plan.

- Write it in terms of its consequences of your actions (always measurable and achievable), followed by the key events to meet the one-year positioning.
- Write it in one or two paragraphs, followed by a list of the three or four most critical events or programs that must happen in order to successfully complete the one-year plan.
- State the most critical events as one-liners, and spell them out in greater detail for those directly involved in their implementation. Provide these details as attachments outside the body of the plan itself. This will provide users with necessary details without overloading the plan itself.

For example, as part of a five-year plan, say:

> "It is mandatory we gain a strong repeat and referral base which will constitute the majority of our future business growth by year 5."

However, you will need to get started; therefore, a one-year plan states what the important elements are:

> "We will implement our 'Customers-R-Forever' program during the second quarter."

For many of the readers of this plan, just knowing that the "Customers-R-Forever" plan will be implemented during the second quarter may be enough information. However, for the plan's "drivers," responsible for implementing the plan, you would have a separate document with a full explanation of what is meant by the "Customers-R-Forever" program, including details of what the plan is, how it will be implemented, how you measure its success, the cost/rewards, and its financial effects.

The program's drivers can refer to the details without going through the entire business plan, while other stakeholders and support members can see the entire plan in context without being distracted by details of important programs.

The five-year and one-year views of the business plan allow stakeholders and support groups an overview of the organization's definition of success. They also allow supporters to see from their own vantage point how they can help. The document is short, clear and concise.

One-Year Action Plan

The Action Plan Spreadsheet provided next should include the most important items to be accomplished throughout the year, who will be responsible, and when these items will be accomplished. The format for this action plan is simple: It should list items, dates, and names of the person responsible. Sometimes the action items may need to be explained in order for others to assist.

Involve the full organization in the business development and its review. Make the central themes of the review teamwork, support, upgrading, and fun. Plans and the plan review often can lead some people to feel uncertain and fearful of being judged wrong. This attitude can—and should—be eliminated. Hold quarterly or monthly reviews. These reviews should be celebrations of the firm's progress. Stakeholders should look forward to the reviews, positive reinforcement of work done, and the opportunity to learn from each other.

Action plan spreadsheet

Action Items	Person Responsible	Start Date	Completion Date	Budget Amount

(continued)

Action plan spreadsheet *(Continued)*

Action Items	Person Responsible	Start Date	Completion Date	Budget Amount

Review Process

Involve the entire organization in the review process. Encourage teamwork and ask for feedback, both positive and negative. The plan review can lead people to feel uncertain but communicate to everyone that open and honest discussion will benefit the company and is valued. Quarterly or monthly reviews are recommended.

Judging the Business Plan

Judge the plan in advance. This may sound difficult; however, it is not only doable, it is necessary. Waiting for five years to consider how successful a five-year business plan is is obviously too late. The best way to judge a plan in advance is to dissect it and prioritize the work and then make sure the work needed to meet the goals of the plan happens in a timely way.

Keys to Success

- **Submit the plan on time.** A plan—no matter how ingenious it may seem—will never reach its full potential if it is late. Therefore, spell out all plans and key elements in a timely manner.
- **Sign off on the plan before implementing.** All plan stakeholders, particularly senior management and writers of the plan, need to sign off on the plan in advance of its implementation. Committing to the plan's resources of time, people, and money make the plan more solid. No one should be willing to sign off on a plan if they do not believe in it. A sign-off is a literal signing of the document at a kickoff meeting.
- **Complete all action items on time.** After the sign-off, the action items are a promise to all stakeholders that you will do what you say and on time. Ensuring this should be an important part of the monthly review.
- **Review plans either quarterly or monthly.** Plan review meetings need to be celebrations of the plan and should be fun. These meetings are the time and place to honor good performance and to offer help where needed.

Judging a plan in advance of its end point will go a long way in helping employees and other stakeholders to stay focused on real issues without second-guessing. The discipline of staying on time for all important plan parts and the sign-off commitment of resources will help the total organization keep focused on what they agreed to do. There is no better way to ensure your plan will have a higher opportunity of success.

Judging a plan in this manner will go a long way in gaining greater understanding by the whole organization in advance of the starting date. The plan will be used as a vehicle for success, not as an indictment for failure. A strategic business plan is much more about events leading to a successful organization than the financial rewards. If the events happen, the financial rewards will occur.

RESEARCHING THE MARKET

Industry leaders follow a systematic approach to the business plan development process.

The key to operating a successful business is to combine your interest and knowledge with the needs of other people in a particular market. After you have determined what type of K&B business you want to be, the next step is making sure there is a market.

Researching the Market

- Analyze how viable your business idea is in your market.
- Determine the size of your market.
- Evaluate your competition.
- Study the upside potential of the industry.
- Identify current and future lifestyle trends for your targeted consumers.

Getting Help

You can ask and pay for outside help in understanding your market, but most likely you will do the majority of market research yourself. Here are a few places you can go to find information:

- Trade publications
- Your local Chamber of Commerce
- The Internet
- Individual company Web sites
- U.S. Small Business Association
- Other K&B business owners
- Your National Kitchen & Bath Association chapter

Knowing What to Look For

Through all of this research, you should be looking for substantial information that supports your ideas and your business plan. In essence, you are conducting a study to see if your plan is feasible based on the current market and economic and competitive climate—and for future prospects.

Examining Your Market Potential

Determine the size of your potential market. Because you will be catering to a specific market by selling a specialized product and service, you will want to know what's happening in new home construction and remodeling.

- **Industry information.** It is important to gauge the overall industry and where it is headed.
- **Competition.** How many competitors are there? Are there already too many players? What companies are capturing the lion's share of the market? What impact have the large multi-branch retailers had, and what is their expected effect in the future? Can you find a niche that others have overlooked? What can you do to differentiate yourself from the competition?
- **Industry trends.** In addition to gathering information on the industry as a whole and on competitors, look at trends (past, present, and future) both in business and in lifestyle. Do-it-yourself (DIY) may be on a decline and do-it-for-me (DIFM) may be on the rise. Statistics show that remodeling accounts for approximately 80% of all K&B products being sold today. We also know that the kitchen and bathroom have become the two most important rooms in the home. Together these trends bode well for K&B businesses.

PREPARING YOUR BUSINESS PLAN

You have evaluated yourself, your idea, and your marketplace, and still believe that starting your own business is a good idea. The next step and one you cannot skip is writing a detailed business plan. Buildings have blueprints, teachers have lesson plans, ball clubs have game plans, and projects have network diagrams. Like so many other endeavors, businesses need a plan of action.

A good business plan will not only keep you on track; like a good outline for a screenplay or novel, it will allow you to put your thoughts and ideas on paper and manipulate them until they are just right. You will then continue expand, change, and tweak them as the business takes shape. When it is complete, the business plan will, like a good mystery novel, answer all the pertinent questions and tie up all the loose ends—which, in your case, will be the details that are essential to running a successful business.

Things to Consider When Writing a Business Plan

- Overall vision of the business
- Goals and objectives
- Overview of the industry
- Company and executive summary
- Market information and analysis
- Comprehensive description of the products and services
- Marketing plan with strategies
- Overview of the competition
- Financial plan, including projected income and expense figures
- Overview of key personnel

The degree of detail and the manner in which the plan is written will vary from business to business and writer to writer. Plans include different information, depending on what is necessary to tell the overall story of how the business will be formed or, if an existing business, how it will proceed over the next three to five years.

The business plan does not have to be written in the order listed. You may start with the areas that you feel the most comfortable or familiar with. The executive summary, which comes near the beginning of a plan, is often actually written near the end of the writing process.

Getting Ready

Writing a business plan for the first time may seem like a daunting task. However, if you set aside some quiet time and take it step by step, you will find it is not as hard as you might think it will be. You'll start with an outline and then move on to a rough draft. As it comes together, you will make revisions and changes. You should share the plan with others for input and feedback. Many find they are overwhelmed at the beginning of the writing process, but as the plan progresses, they begin to enjoy learning about themselves and look forward to carrying out the plan.

- **Where to find guidelines.** Since many business plans have preceded yours, do not feel like you have to reinvent the wheel. Numerous books, articles, and CDs are available on the subject, and you will find a great deal of useful information, including sample business plans, online. One of the best sites for sample business plans is www.bplan.com which offers numerous plans for a wide variety of businesses.

- **Make it clear.** Even though K&B businesses are generally small operations do not be afraid to develop a long and more detailed plan. Remember, the best plan for you does not need to have the most jargon, most pages, or the most buzz words, such as "network," "leverage," or "equity." The best business plan is one that clearly paints a picture of your business and demonstrates how and why it will be successful, will grow, and—most important—be profitable.
- **Make it professional.** Whether you are writing your plan just for yourself or for more formal reasons (to present to a bank or investors to secure financing), make the plan look professional, complete with a cover page and binding. Be sure to proofread and edit the document. Graphs, charts, illustrations, and photos can enhance the plan, but do not add this material just to fill up space; include pertinent information only.
- **Use it.** Far too many businesses fail each year because they either did not have a business plan or had one but left out some key elements. You would never start a long driving trip to an unfamiliar destination without directions; why would you start a business without a detailed business plan?

How to Format the Business Plan

The following are the parts of the business plan document, in order (numbered here for clarity; they would not necessarily be numbered in the document):

1. Title page
2. Table of contents
3. Executive summary
   (a) Business concept
   (b) Financial features
   (c) Financial requirements
   (d) Current business position
   (e) Major achievements
4. Business description and mission
5. Market and industry analysis
6. Competitive analysis
7. Marketing strategy
8. Operations and management
9. Leadership team
10. Financial plan
11. Summary and conclusion
12. Appendix and/or supplementary materials

Step-by-Step Guide

Here we present the information you will need to write a plan.

1. Title Page. This is the reader's first impression of your plan. It should look professional. Show the name of the company; name(s) of the principal(s); business address; telephone, fax, and cell phone numbers; email and Web site addresses; and, finally, the date. If you have a logo or company colors, use them.

2. Table of Contents. A table of contents (TOC) provides an easy way to find key information. The TOC presents an organized overview of what is included within the business plan. It lets readers go back and find each subject without having to look through the entire plan. Keep the TOC simple and straightforward, and try not to exceed one page.

3. Executive Summary. The executive summary is the single most important section of the business plan. Many business owners write this last because they want to be sure that they have covered and included all the most important points of the plan.

It consists of one paragraph (at most) describing each section of your plan. The entire executive summary should be just one to two pages long. Bankers and investors read the executive summary to determine whether to continue reading. Therefore, your summary needs to catch and hold the reader's attention.

Your executive summary should touch on these key elements:

- **Business concept.** Describe the business, its products and services, the market it serves, and the business' competitive advantage.
- **Financial features.** Include financial highlights, such as sales, margins, and profits.
- **Financial requirements.** State how much capital you need for start-up or expansion, how it will be used, and what collateral is available.
- **Current business position.** Furnish relevant information about the company, its legal form of operation, when it was founded, the principal owners, and key personnel.
- **Major achievements.** Point out anything noteworthy, such as awards, major projects, new products or services, unique marketing trials, and the like.

Include your strongest selling points in the executive summary: your location, uniqueness, trend-setting, award-winning, and so on. Be concise. The fewer words, the better.

4. Business Description and Mission. This section of the plan explains your products and services and how they meet the needs of your market. Describe exactly what it is you will be selling and why people will buy it. How will your products and services be different from similar products and services already being offered in the marketplace? If yours is a really revolutionary concept, explain why the market needs this new breakthrough.

Spell out your company's mission. Tell people why the company exists. This simple statement covers, in just a few sentences, the reason for your company's existence. It provides an overall umbrella under which all other goals and actions fall. It says what your company does and who it does it for.

A typical mission statement for a K&B business might be:

> To provide award-winning, functional designs, quality products, service, and installation for kitchens and bathrooms in both new construction and remodeling projects, with the very best one-on-one personalized service from conception to completion

In a perfect world, your mission statement will be short enough that everyone in the company will know it by heart. Consider the next examples.

> Value Cabinets is the low-cost provider of cabinets in Gary.

Or

> Dream Kitchens is the premier kitchen design and installation business in Kokomo.

Notice that these statements are brief and to the point, determining the overall direction of the company. They also set limits. The first statement says "cabinets" and the second, "kitchens and bathrooms," which eliminates room additions, patios, and garages.

The Ritz-Carlton hotel chain uses one of the best, most concise, and to-the-point mission statements. This company builds and operates only five-star properties. Their mission statement, which every employee knows and practices, is "Ladies and gentlemen serving ladies and gentlemen."

Your mission statement does not only explain why you are in business and what you do; it explains to employees, customers, vendors, and everyone else exactly who you are and what you do.

When writing the business description section, do not get sidetracked into talking about all the great things you believe about the company. You may be writing this for a bank or investors; they do not need to hear you sounding like a proud parent bragging about a child. Stick to the facts and focus on what outsiders need to know to entice them to invest in or lend money to your business.

Start by describing your products and services. Explain what your products and services will do for your clients, what benefits you offer, and why clients will want to buy from you. If you offer unique products and services, describe them. (For example, if you provide home offices, entertainment centers, and fireplaces, you might market these as quality custom "furniture" for the home.)

You may want to include a history subsection that describes how the company was started and how it has evolved over the years.

Talk a little bit about where the industry has been and where it is going. Needless to say, you will have to do the necessary research in this area so as not to include incorrect or misleading information.

Tell readers what the legal entity of the business is: sole proprietor, partnership, S corporation, or C corporation. Continue with information on who your main clients are, how big the market is, and how the products and services are distributed and marketed.

5. Market and Industry Analysis. In this section, you present your business in conjunction with the overall industry in which it falls: K&B remodel and new construction. Here you take a step back and look at the big picture, the industry as it currently stands and projected future developments. You will need to do a fair amount of research, with a bit of looking into your crystal ball, before putting this part of the plan together. It will be important to make note of the size and growth of the overall industry.

You can use charts, graphs, or text to explain the various trends culled from your research. In addition to the broader overall industry news, you need to clearly illustrate the market in your area, including growth of remodel and new construction, baby boomers starting to gray and spend money on their homes, and so on. Then tie in your business with the marketing demands and trends.

The end result of this industry analysis should demonstrate why your business will be able to take a nice piece of the pie. This is also important for you, the entrepreneur, to see clearly. If you cannot foresee a potential market share, you will have trouble selling others on what will make your company successful.

6. Competitive Analysis. This is the section where you discuss the competition. This should be a fun exercise. You will need to do some investigative research so that you can adequately describe these businesses. The best way to do this is to visit them. Do it from the point of view of a customer as well as a competitor. You will want to discuss how their businesses operate; their locations, products, services, share of the market; whether they market to the higher-end or mid- to lower-priced market; and if they install and charge design fees. Do they market kitchens and baths only, or have they expanded in other areas of the home? What selection of products do they show and sell?

Next you must describe and make comparisons to your business and explain how you will improve on the products and services offered by the competition. State what makes your business unique. Study what the market wants and show how you can provide solutions in a better way.

You are not trying to denigrate other businesses; you simply are trying to separate what you do from what they do. In your plan, let people know that you're prepared to carve out your own segment of the market and explain how you propose to do it.

7. Marketing Strategy. If no one buys your products or services, you will be out of business quickly. Nothing ends a business faster than no customers. In this section of your business plan, you need to explain how you intend to attract customers. You can have the best products and services, but if you do not spread the word and attract customers, you will not be successful.

Here you need to explain who your target market is. For example: higher-priced older homes that are ripe for remodel and mid- to higher-priced new construction. Since your business will be geared to reach a certain market segment, your marketing effort will have to be geared to that market. You will not be able to be all things to all people, so do not try to market your business to too large an audience.

Gather as much information as possible to support the demographics of your area. Then channel your marketing effort to the group that will be interested in your products and services.

Finally, you will need to explain how you intend to capture a portion of that market. Detail the methods and media you will utilize to market your business. What forms of advertising and promotions will you use? Then assign a budget to your marketing program. A general guideline in the K&B industry is 3 to 5 percent of sales. (This would include any manufacturer co-op monies you can negotiate.) It is very important to justify your marketing plan and to show others—and remind yourself—that you are not throwing money away on a poor marketing strategy. Since you'll be trying to create a specific image for the business, you should describe what that image is and how your marketing plan backs it up. You might also describe, in some detail, any unique or special promotional advertising activities you will use to attract clients.

A good marketing plan takes a fair amount of time and careful consideration to produce. It should be the culmination of researching industry trends and your target market and be a careful evaluation of the proper media and promotional choices for getting your message to your target audience. Whatever you do, be totally realistic in your projected marketing plans.

8. Operations and Management. This section of your plan is designed to describe how the business functions on a continuing basis. It explains who does what and how and where they do it. It tells who is responsible for each aspect of the business. It describes how you work with clients, from meeting and greeting to the finished project (design, selection of products, quotation, writing the order, getting a deposit, installing the products, etc.). Explain the distribution channel for the various products and services: such as cabinets from several manufacturers; countertops from a local fabricator; appliances, lighting, and flooring from local distributors; and some installation (in-house and subcontracted), and so on.

Each company's organizational structure will vary somewhat, so it should be divided into several broad areas:

- Marketing, Design, Sales, and Customer Relations
- Installation and Production
- Administration, Finances, and Human Resources

Expand this section with details and add capital expenditure areas. Possibly include showroom construction and updating costs, new delivery truck, new computer-assisted design system, and others.

When a person finishes reading this section, he or she should have a clear picture of exactly how your business operates.

9. Leadership Team. As mentioned, the K&B industry is composed mainly of smaller firms, so this section of the business plan may be short; nevertheless, it is important. The owner oversees everything and usually sells, orders, and mentors. There may be a need for a bookkeeper/office manager. If the business offers installation, there may be an installation supervisor. List all the key players with short bios and what they bring to the company.

If you have a board of directors or use outside mentors, mention them and what they do because they are important to your success.

10. Financial Plan. Everything else up to this point is presented as the foundation for the financial analysis. If it is a new business, you need to spell out the actual investment required and when and how the business will make enough money to pay it back. If it is an existing business, you will use historic financial data to help build your financial projections for the next three to five years. These pro formas, as they are called, will project sales, margins, expenses, and the bottom line.

This part of the plan also includes a fair amount of looking into a crystal ball. Doing this exercise will help you manage your business more accurately and professionally. It helps you understand cash flow in advance, when to hire or let people go, when money will be available to make capital expenditures, when you will be able to update the showroom, and much more.

This section includes an income statement, balance sheet, and cash flow analysis. If you are starting from scratch or planning to expand and need to borrow money to do it, this is the section that gains either a positive or negative response. Be as realistic as possible because almost everything you do in the business will be guided the bottom line.

Do not be afraid to get help with this section. Ask your accountant and/or banker to help you. In Chapter 5 you will find more detailed information on how to develop an annual budget and how to generate and read profit and loss statements, balance sheets, and cash flow analyses. Review these before tackling this section of your business plan.

11. Summary and Conclusion. Some people do not include this section in their business plans, but it is helpful to summarize the many details in your plan. This final section reiterates what was presented in the Executive Summary but adds additional insight because the reader is now informed on the idea, the market, the competition, and the financial requirements of the business. In this section, you can tie up the plan in a neat package and ensure that readers understand your view of the overall opportunity.

12. Appendix and/or Supplementary Materials. The appendix and supplementary materials consist of material that is referred to throughout the plan. You might include charts, graphs, resumes, and whatever literature is necessary to convince the reader or investors that you have done your homework. Include this information at the end of the plan in order to avoid bogging the text down with too much detail.

Ethics and Your Plan

Be totally honest about everything you present. If you are trying to interest banks or investors in lending you money, it will never happen if they do not trust you or believe the information presented in your plan.

REVIEWING YOUR PLAN

Review your plan carefully when it is complete. Make sure you have included all the key points, that it reads clearly, and that all spelling and grammar is checked and edited. Be sure the plan is printed on quality paper, that it is bound and has a professional appearance.

The completed plan will probably run between 20 and 40 pages. Double space it and allow wide enough margins so the type does not look cramped. Make sure the pages are numbered, and double check that the numbers match those listed in the table of contents.

Remember, the business plan needs to be a realistic portrait of your business, not an abstract design. If the pieces do not fit together or the numbers do not add up, the plan will not work, and neither will the business.

SUMMARY

In this important chapter, several types of business models were presented, and you were encouraged to analyze which one might be best suited for you. Every business goes through various stages of growth. After reading this chapter, you should have a better understanding of where your business is in this evolution. One area that most small business owners overlook and ignore is the all-important business plan. This chapter covered the various parts that make up an effective plan. The chapter outlined how to write a detailed plan that you, your bank, and other interested parties can use to guide and operate the business.

REVIEW QUESTIONS

1. Which of the three business models outlined in the book best describes your business? (See "What Type of Kitchen and Bath Business Are You Going to Operate?" pages 15–17)

2. Why is a clear vision and mission statement important for a business? (See "Vision and Mission of Your Company" pages 23–24)

3. How do you identify who your main target customers will be? (See "Identify the Target Consumer" page 26)

4. What are four parts of a successful business plan? (See "The Four Key Parts" page 25)

5. Why is a one-year action plan important, and how do you build one? (See "One-Year View" page 30)

Business Start-up Issues

If you are just starting a business, you have a lot of important decisions to make. If you've been in business for several years, there are a number of topics that you might revisit. This chapter covers topics such as legal structures for businesses, licenses and permits, taxes, and registering your business name.

Learning Objective 1: Describe the various types of business legal structures.

Learning Objective 2: Discuss the importance of business location and how it can affect ultimate success.

Learning Objective 3: Describe how to package a loan request to your bank.

Learning Objective 4: Explain the various tax laws and the importance of remaining legal and current in how you pay your taxes.

Learning Objective 5: Discuss how to select and maintain strong vendor partners.

CHOOSING THE BUSINESS LEGAL STRUCTURE

Choosing the Business Legal Structure

- Sole proprietorship
- Partnership (limited or general)
- Corporation (S or C)
- Limited liability company

Type of Business: Quick Reference List

Sole Proprietorship

The sole proprietorship is the most common form of business organization. You own and operate the business and have sole responsibility and control. Essentially, you, the owner, are the business. The profits of the business are considered as personal income and, therefore, are taxed at your personal tax rate.

Advantages

- Ease of formation; fewer legal restrictions, usually less expensive than a partnership or corporation.
- Flexibility: quick response to business needs.
- Profits: you have sole ownership of profits.
- Exclusive control and decision making; you are in charge.
- Tax deductions: losses are tax deductible.

Disadvantages

- Unlimited liability: you are responsible for the full amount of business debts, and this liability extends to your personal assets.
- Unstable business life: business could be crippled or terminated by your illness or death.
- Limited investment; investment in the business is limited to the resources that you can raise.

Partnership

A partnership is the association of two or more people as co-owners of a business. It is a legal mechanism that allows for profits and losses to be divided among a group of investors. A limited partnership is a partnership formed by two or more persons with at least one general partner and at least one limited partner. It has some of the attributes of a general partnership and a corporation.

When forming a partnership, you should have a partnership agreement that specifies the legal obligations of each partner. A partnership agreement will:

- Stipulate the initial amount of funding each partner will contribute to the business.
- Determine how management decisions will be made and how authority will be divided.
- Establish methods for settling disputes among partners.
- Set up a procedure for selling the business.
- Specify how each partner's interest will be valued; establish restrictions on selling partner's interest to a third party.
- Specify what would happen to your business if one of the partners dies or becomes physically or mentally incapacitated.
- Specify the rights of the partner's spouse.

Partnerships can be divided into general partnerships and limited partnerships.

General Partnership

In general partnerships, partners participate in the management of the business and are personally responsible for all debts.

Advantages

- Ease of formation.
- More skills and capital available to boost performance and growth.
- Flexibility and decision making with relative freedom from government control and special taxation.
- Tax-deductible losses.

Disadvantages

- Unlimited liability.
- Personal liability of a solvent partner for the actions of unscrupulous partners.
- Unstable life of business; partnership is dissolved if a partner dies or withdraws, unless specifically prescribed for in the written agreement.
- Buying out a partner may be difficult unless specifically prescribed in the written agreement.
- Potential for disagreements between partners could lead to costly dissolution.

Limited Partnership

In limited partnerships, partners are liable only to the extent of their investment and do not share in the management of the business.

Advantages

- A person can invest capital in a partnership business and reap a share of the profits without becoming liable for all debts of the partnership or risking more than the amount of capital contributed.

Disadvantages

- Must have at least one partner who is liable for all debts of the partnership, and other (limited) partners whose liability is limited to their investment in the partnership.
- No voice in the management of the partnership.
- There are other legal and tax considerations involved and legal advice is necessary in choosing this form of organization.
- Formation and operation requires more formality than the formation and operation of a general partnership. Must file with the state.

Corporation

The corporation is the most complex form of business organization. It is made up of three groups of people: shareholders, directors, and officers. A corporation can borrow money, own assets, and perform business functions without directly involving you, the owner, or the other corporate owners.

Advantages

- The stockholder's liability is limited to a fixed amount, usually the amount invested.
- Business looks more credible than a sole proprietorship to potential suppliers, employees, and bankers.

(continued)

- Ownership is readily transferable.
- Separate legal existence.
- Relative ease of securing capital in large amounts and from many investors.

Disadvantages
- Activity is limited by the corporation's charter and various laws.
- Extensive government regulation and burdensome federal, state, and local reports.
- Considerable expense in forming corporation.
- Greater administrative expenses on an annual basis.

The legal structure you choose depends on a number of things involving your type of business, individual situation, goals for the business, and other personal and financial factors. Before deciding what is best for you, discuss your situation with your accountant and attorney. Make sure you are prepared to describe your business plans in some detail. This consultation will be money and time well spent. Making the right choice can help you avoid a mistake that can be costly in terms of possible future liability.

There are three basic options to consider, and each has its own unique advantages and disadvantages.

Sole Proprietorship

A sole proprietorship is the most popular legal structure for a small business. According to the Small Business Administration (SBA), almost 75% of the 23 million small businesses in the United States are sole proprietorships. As the name implies, ownership is totally with one person. It is the easiest structure to establish because no legal formalities are necessary. The only business requirement may be a license from your local jurisdiction.

Advantages of a Sole Proprietorship

- Easy and quick and usually the least expensive to establish.
- You have total ownership and control of the business.
- All profits of the business belong to you, the owner.
- No additional federal taxation on business profits—meaning no double taxation.
- No periodic business reporting to the Internal Revenue Service (IRS) or other government agency is required.
- Income tax filing is simply part of your annual personal tax return. (You would use a Schedule C or Canada Revenue Agency Form T4002.)

Disadvantages of a Sole Proprietorship

- The owner is personally liable for all business debts.
- It is generally more difficult to borrow money or obtain outside investment than with other types of legal structures.
- If the owner is incapacitated for any reason, the business is likely to fail.
- All management responsibility is with the owner, which can be a heavy burden.
- You must pay self-employment tax on the business's net income.

Note: If you are a designer doing business from home (i.e., a "home-based business"), you are most likely a sole proprietor. However, just because you conduct business from your home does not exempt you from possible legal or other liabilities.

Partnership

A partnership is just what the name implies: Business ownership is divided between two or more partners. The general partnership is the most common and is formed to conduct a business with two or more partners fully involved in the operation of the business. All the partners share both the profits and the liabilities. A limited partnership, as the name implies, provides for limited liability of partners. This liability can be no greater than the partner's investment in the partnership. In a limited partnership, there must be at least one general partner who remains liable for all the debts of the partnership.

Advantages of a Partnership

- There is synergy as a result of pooling partners, different areas of expertise.
- The partnership does not pay federal income taxes.
- An informational tax return (IRS Form 1065 or Canada Revenue Agency Form T4002) must be filed that shows the pass-through of income/loss to each partner.
- Liability may be spread among partners.
- Investment can come from the partners in the form of a loan, which creates interest income for the partners and a business deduction for the partnership.

Disadvantages of a Partnership

- Formation and subsequent changes in structure are complex.
- Problems with partners stem from misunderstandings, different goals, and other issues and can adversely affect or destroy the partnership.
- Limited partners are liable for debt if they are active managers in the business. General partners have unlimited liability, and such partners also be liable for commitments of the partners. Limited partners are not liable for the debts of the limited partnership unless they are active managers in the business.

Corporation

There are two types of corporations: the C corporation (regular corporation) and the S corporation (or S corp.). Both forms are complex legal entities. Their detailed structure may vary from state/province to state/province. Incorporating a business in a given state/province allows you to conduct business only in that location. It is essential for you to obtain legal advice if you are thinking about forming a corporation. Because each state/province has its own set of corporation laws, contact the appropriate office in your state/province. Usually the Office of the Secretary of State can provide additional material and procedures.

Most people immediately think of incorporating in order to minimize their personal liability. The liability of stockholders (owners) in a corporation is limited under certain and complex conditions. Today, with the U.S. Tax Reform Act of 1986 and other legislation, there are few good tax reasons to incorporate a business in the U.S. (with the exception of dividing corporate profits). The reason for incorporation is, in fact, limited liability.

However, there is no such thing as total insulation from liability resulting from doing business as a corporation.

Record keeping and tax matters for a corporation are complex and time-consuming tasks usually requiring the services of an accountant. Keep this in mind when considering operational costs for your business.

Avoid do-it-yourself incorporation guides. The process is complex and not a task you should take on by yourself. Legal fees for setting up a corporation can run from $350 to $1,500, assuming it is relatively straightforward.

Regular Corporation

A corporation is a taxable entity and as such pays taxes. This results in the "double taxation" you may have heard about. The corporation pays corporate taxes on its profits, and then you, the owner (shareholder), pay personal taxes on the dividends the corporation pays you. This is one of the biggest disadvantages of a corporation.

However, incorporating your business usually makes it easier to establish credit with suppliers and to borrow from banks. If you expect to use outside investors for business capital, a corporation is necessary.

Advantages of a Regular Corporation

- Shareholders (the owners) enjoy personal limited liability.
- It is generally easier to obtain business capital.
- Profits may be divided among owners and the corporation in order to reduce taxes by taking advantage of lower tax rates.
- The corporation does not dissolve on the death of a stockholder (owner) or if the ownership changes; the corporation has perpetual existence unless it is legally dissolved.
- There are favorable tax treatments for employee fringe benefits, including medical, disability, and life insurance plans.
- Seventy percent of any dividends received by a corporation from stock investments are deductible as long as they weren't purchased with borrowed money.
- Shares in a corporation are easily transferable (unless limited by a shareholders' agreement).

Disadvantages of a Regular Corporation

- More expensive and complex to set up than other legal structures.
- Completing tax returns usually requires the help of an accountant.
- Double taxation on corporate profits and dividends paid to owners.
- Recurring annual corporate fees.
- Tax rates are higher than individual rates for profits greater than approximately $75,000.
- There is a 28% accumulated earnings tax on profits in excess of $250,000.
- Business losses are not personally tax deductible.

S Corporation

The S corporation offers the limited liability advantages of a corporation but does not pay federal taxes. All of the earnings of an S corporation are passed through to the shareholders (owners). Losses also can be passed through if the shareholder has basis (economic investment). The S corporation is a popular form of incorporation in the start-up years of a business, but there are some subtle disadvantages that need to be considered as you grow. To qualify as an S-corporation, a corporation must file IRS Form 2553 in a timely fashion; some states require a separate election. Again, because of the complexities involved, consult your attorney and/or accountant.

Advantages of an S Corporation

- Owners enjoy personal limited liability as in a regular corporation.
- Owners have no federal income tax liability and, in most cases, no state income tax.
- Profits are passed to owners with no double taxation.
- Losses are passed through to the owners if they have basis.
- Wholly owned subsidiaries are permitted.

Disadvantages of an S Corporation

- More expensive and complex to set up than other legal structures.
- Maximum of 75 shareholders (usually not an issue in our industry).
- Only one class of common stock is permitted, and no preferred stock is permitted.

Limited Liability Company

A limited liability company (LLC) blends the tax advantages of a partnership and the limited liability advantages of a corporation. Owners of an LLC are called "members." An LLC also has some limitations. You can get information from your state/province and consult with your attorney and accountant to see if an LLC is the way to incorporate your business.

Advantages of an LLC

- Owners have limited personal liability, as with a corporation and unlike a partnership.
- Owners pay no federal taxes, like a partnership.
- There is no limit on the number of stockholders, unlike an S corporation.
- More than one class of stock is permitted, unlike an S corporation.
- Business losses may be deducted on your personal tax return, like an S corporation.
- The IRS and most states allow for single-member LLCs for sole proprietors who want limited liability but do not want to incorporate.

Disadvantages of an LLC

- Earnings are generally subject to self-employment tax.
- State law may limit the life of an LLC.
- Lack of uniformity in LLC statutes. Businesses that operate in more than one state may not receive consistent treatment.
- Some states do not tax partnerships but do tax LLCs.
- Conversion of an existing business to LLC status could result in tax recognition on appreciated assets.

Choosing Your Legal Structure

It is impossible to give specific advice on this important decision in this volume because every situation is unique. Assess the advantages and disadvantages described here based on your particular situation. It is important to discuss your plans with advisors, including both an attorney and an accountant, before making your final decision.

When discussing your plans with advisors, keep the following points in mind:

- The LLC is worth looking into.
- Saving on taxes is one of the most important considerations for selecting a business structure. Keep in mind that there are generally few tax advantages with a corporation if your total taxable business income is more than $75,000.
- Do not select the corporation structure based on possible tax advantages of profit-sharing plans because the 401(k), SEP (Simplified Employee Pension Plan), and Simple IRA (Savings Incentive Match Plan for Employees) plans available to sole proprietorships are equally beneficial.
- If you consider a partnership, be certain to have a complete partnership agreement drawn up by your attorney.
- Consider an S corporation if you expect business losses for the first year or two. These losses can be passed through to the owners as tax relief, but they provide no current benefit in a regular corporation if a shareholder has basis.

OTHER REQUIREMENTS AND CONSIDERATIONS

There are a number of items to address when starting and operating a business, regardless of the legal structure and type. Review the following items so that you stay compliant in all areas and do not overlook important acts or issues.

Business Licenses and Permits

Depending on your type of business and your location, various licenses and permits may be required. Check with your state/province, city, and county/municipality governments for information on these items. Be diligent because fines could be levied for any omissions.

Business Name

Once you have selected the business name, if you are a sole proprietorship or partnership, be sure to register for a "fictitious name" with your state/province. (It is "fictitious" because the name most likely will not be your own full legal name.) Filing with the state/province costs from $10 to $100. Be sure no one else has selected the same name or one very close to it. If you develop a logo for the business, you can apply for a trademark for this. If you think you will ever do business in more than one state/province, register the business name in each state/province.

Tax Payments

You will be required to make periodic estimated federal and sometimes state/province tax payments regardless of your business legal structure so you must obtain a tax identification (ID) number from the tax authority. The requirements vary so discuss this with your accountant. Late tax payments will accrue costly penalties.

Collection of Sales Tax

Most kitchen and bath (K&B) businesses sell products to end user customers (the public), which means it's likely you will collect sales tax for the state/province and/or local government. Check with your state/province and local tax departments on the requirements because every state/province is different. You probably will have to apply for a sales tax ID number that will identify you to the local and state/province government as a seller of goods. The process is easy and usually there is no cost involved. There may also be monthly reporting requirements.

Operating in More than One State/Province

Assume that your business grows and you want to operate with stores or offices in more than one state/province. The good news is, this is possible. The bad news is that you may need to perform some filings and registrations to qualify in each state/province where you do business. In addition, you will have to file tax returns in each of these states/provinces. Once again, get professional help in this area.

LOCATION, LOCATION, LOCATION

Business Location Choices

- Home-based location
- Studio/boutique location
- Destination location
- Shared location
- Retail shopping location
- Trade/retail "mart" location

When starting a new business, be sure to select the best location. If you are already in business, step back and look at your current site.

Not all locations are created equal. And not all businesses need a great location. But for a kitchen and bath business that wants to attract homeowners, interior designers, contractors, and architects, location is important, visibility, access, and exposure are all essential to consider.

The first thing to ask is: Have you targeted the right community? Consider:

- Is the population base large enough to support your business?
- Does the demographic profile closely match that of the market you wish to serve?
- Does the community have a stable economic base that will promote a healthy environment in which your business can operate?
- What are the community's attitudes or outlook?

The answers to these questions require that you know the demographic profile of your potential clients. Look for:

- **Purchasing power.** What is the percentage of disposable income in the community? This would include the income levels of the homeowners.
- **Residences.** Are the homes owned or rented? What is the current and projected value of homes in this marketplace?
- **Means of transportation.** Do your prospective clients own vehicles or use public transportation?
- **Age range.** What is the age range of your target audience? Generally, you will be looking for homeowners in the 35+ age bracket. Are they aging baby boomers, young professionals, or retirees?
- **Family status.** Are the residents mostly married, or are there more who are single?
- **Leisure activities.** What type of hobbies and recreational activities do people in the community participate in?

Other considerations for your location:

- **Traffic and accessibility.** Is your location easy to get to? Will a lot of drive-by traffic help the business? (Usually, yes.)
- **Competition.** How many competitors are in this marketplace? Where are they located?
- **Related building product businesses.** Being close to tile/granite, lighting, appliance, flooring, and window and door businesses is usually a big plus. Clients like one-stop shopping whenever possible.
- **Visibility.** Is the location easily seen from the street or highway?
- **Signage.** Good signage is invaluable. Check local restrictions and regulations.
- **Facilities.** Do the area and building project the image you want and need? How is the parking, lighting, and landscaping?
- **Landlord.** Is the landlord responsive and easy to work with or just the opposite?
- **Rent.** Cost is important. Can you afford it? Conversely, if it is a great location, can you not afford it? Plan to provide references to the landlord.
- **Miscellaneous.** This category includes storage of merchandise, shipping and receiving areas, regulations regarding garbage, pickup and deliveries, snow removal, and the like. Utilities, office and support space, windows for displays, ceiling height, public restrooms, good security and neighbors, and additional fees if in a mall-type location are all things to consider.

The ideal location would be in an area that meets many of these needs and offers growth opportunity, terrific demographics for your products and services, little direct competition and is in an area where you feel safe and can attract the high level of experienced personnel you will need to help make the business a success.

Home-Based Design Business: No Showroom

- Appointments with clients in their homes or at distributor/supplier's showroom
- No storage/warehouse facilities

Design/Build Destination Showroom

- Appointments in showroom
- Separate storage and/or shop facility on-site
  or distance away

Retail Shopping Area Showroom

- Appointments in showroom
- Retail shopping location, storage area attached,
  no warehouse/shop facility on site

Trade/Retail "Mart" Location Showroom

- Appointments in showroom
- Trade design center location open to the public; storage/warehouse off-site

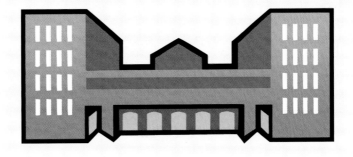

TABLE 3.1 Location Checklist

Answer each question on a scale of 1 to 3, with 1 being "Good," 2 being "Fair," and 3 being "Poor."			
Questions	**Good**	**Fair**	**Poor**
1. Is the facility large enough for your business?			
2. Does it meet your layout requirements?			
3. Does the building need any repairs?			
4. Are leasehold improvements completed?			
5. How accessible is the facility to your target audience?			
6. How convenient is it for employees in terms of commuting, parking, comfort, and safety?			
7. How consistent is the facility with the image you want to project?			
8. How safe is the neighborhood?			
9. How likely will neighboring businesses help attract clients?			
10. How close are competitors located to the facility?			
11. Can suppliers conveniently make deliveries?			
12. Does the facility allow room to expand?			
13. Rate the visibility and signage.			
14. Are there windows to show off your displays?			
15. Is there plenty of convenient parking?			
16. Is the outside and inside lighting sufficient?			
17. Will the public restrooms meet your needs?			
18. How is the car and foot traffic?			
19. Are the lease and rent terms favorable?			
20. Is the location zoned for your type of business?			
21. Can you live with all regulations and restrictions?			
22. Are other building product businesses near the facility?			

Table 3.1 is a Location Checklist to help you in this important decision. Add other items that would be important to you.

Your numerical ratings combined with your good judgment when weighing the relative importance of each item will assist you in comparing potential sites.

Tax Ramifications of Claiming an Office in Your Home

Some designers choose to operate from a home office. This might be the ideal business location for an independent designer.

Too often, people automatically assume working out of their home provides specific tax advantages. When certain conditions are met, the IRS/Canada Revenue Agency allows you to deduct the costs associated with using a portion of your home for business.

Conditions

In most cases, you must use your home office exclusively for business activities. In other words, you cannot use the area for both business and personal purposes. The area could be a room or another identifiable space.

The area generally must be either your principal place of business or a place where you meet with clients or customers. However, a separate structure (such as a garage) that you use in connection with your business also may qualify.

If You're an Employee

If you are an employee who works out of your home, you may qualify for a home office deduction if all the above requirements are met and you are using the office for your employer's convenience.

What's Deductible?

Deductible expenses include a portion (based on the percentage of space in the home used for business) of real estate taxes, mortgage interest or rent, utilities, depreciation, insurance, and maintenance costs.

What If I Sell My Home?

Consult a tax professional regarding the ramifications of selling your home if you claim a portion of it as a home office.

FINANCING THE BUSINESS

Whether you are considering a brand-new business or you have been in business for some time, the money hunt is never ending. Cash is king during good times and bad, during expansion and cutbacks. Because it is so important, spend time thinking about how to keep your business well financed.

Having the money available to finance your dream or to continue to grow it can happen only if you have a solid financial foundation in place. If you are thinking about securing funds from a lender or an investor, you should know exactly how much money you need to get started or to grow and stay open. Knowing this will put you well ahead of most other small business entrepreneurs. The big question is: Where will you find the money to start or grow your business?

A number of sources provide funding. These include:

- Banks, venture capitalists.
- Personal loans and individual investors.
- Your own savings. (However, if you are using your own savings, do not take away from living expenses or savings earmarked for college tuitions or retirement.)

If you have the money to invest, use it cautiously and stick to your business plan.

A Word of Experience from Hank Darlington

Even if you are going to self-fund the business, through savings, selling assets, credit cards, or some other plan, a financial foundation is no less important. It is the basis for creating a solid kitchen and bath business.

Questions to Consider for Your Loan Proposal

- Who are you?
- What is your management ability?
- What are you going to do with the money?
- When and how do you plan to pay it back?
- What is your ratio of business debt to net worth?
- What is your debt paying record?
- What are the company's past earnings?
- What is the value and condition of your collateral?
- Does the amount requested make suitable allowances for unexpected business developments?

Packaging Your Loan Proposal

By Melvin Pfeif

Mark Twain once said that a banker is a fellow who lends his umbrella when the sun is shining and wants it back the minute it rains.

While there may be some truth to that, it is important to remember that bankers *want* to make loans. Making loans is how banks earn a profit. But keep in mind that the banker wants to make loans to businesses that are solvent, profitable, and growing. Your job is to convince the banker that you fit (or soon will fit) that description. Many different outlines are available for preparing a loan proposal. The Small Business Administration; SCORE, a nonprofit association dedicated to helping small businesses get off the ground; your bank; and others have developed guidelines for clearly and effectively communicating your financial needs and anticipated sources of prepayment. Which outline is the right format for your business is a matter of preference.

Regardless of your choice, always begin your proposal with a cover letter. Clearly and quickly explain who you are, your background, the nature of your business, the amount and purpose of your loan request, your requested terms of repayment, how the funds will benefit your business, and how you will repay the loan. Keep it simple and direct. You have the rest of the package to fully explain the details of your proposal.

Then follow your chosen outline to provide more depth and discuss the specifics in detail. Don't assume the reader is familiar with your industry and your individual business. Include industry information and anything else that will make the reader comfortable with how your business works and what the industry trends are.

The loan officer must feel satisfied with the answers to these questions:

Who are you?	Your character comes first, then your ability to manage your business.
What are you going to do with the money?	The answer to this will determine the type of loan, short or long term. Money to be used for the purchase of seasonal inventory will require faster repayment than money used to buy fixed assets.
When and how do you plan to pay the loan back?	Your banker's judgment of your business' ability to repay the loan will be a deciding factor in the answer to this question.
Does the amount requested make suitable allowance for unexpected developments?	The banker determines the answer to this question on the basis of your financial statement, which provides for the unexpected developments and considers the collateral pledged.
What is the outlook for business in general and your business in particular?	When assembling this information, pay close attention to the preparation of income and cash flow projections to support your ability to repay the loan. These projections are critically important for a new venture or a business that has not yet established a track record of profitability to clearly substantiate repayment.
What is your management ability?	If you are starting a business or purchasing an existing one, you will generally be expected to demonstrate previous management experience in your field. Without this prior background, the potential risk of business failure usually precludes conventional bank financing or an SBA loan.
What is the ratio of business debt to net worth?	The lender will look closely at your tangible dollar investment in the firm. Don't expect a bank or the SBA to finance a venture you are unwilling to risk your own funds in. For start-ups or buyouts, you should plan to invest at least $1 of your own funds for every $2 of loan. The more debt a firm takes on, the more risk to the business owner and the lender.
What is your debt-paying record to suppliers, banks, home mortgage holders, and other creditors?	Check your credit rating. Your banker will. Contact business and personal credit reporting services and ask for a copy of your file. You may have to pay a fee for this information, but it may be money well spent. Errors and inaccuracies in these reports can occur. It is easier to correct any mistakes before you apply for a loan rather than try to provide explanations to your lender after the problem arises.
What are the company's past earnings?	If these earnings don't support your ability to repay the loan, you have your work cut out to convince the lender. Remember to emphasize what the loan will do for the firm. Point out the benefits of the loan and what will happen to the company as a result. And remember to support your projected figures with clear, logical explanations.
What is the value and condition of your collateral?	Every loan must have at least two identifiable sources of repayment: cash flow generated from profitable operations of the business and collateral pledged to secure the loan. Keep in mind that lenders typically will view business assets, such as inventory, accounts receivable, and equipment, as worth much less than you might think. If you can't sell the inventory, imagine how difficult it will be for the lender to find a buyer at a reasonable price.

Finally, take another look at the proposal to make sure you have included everything necessary. If your proposal is fairly complex, it may consist of a substantial amount of material. But remember that excessive content sometimes can be a red flag in itself. The lender will want to read everything that is pertinent to the proposal but may become impatient if superfluous material is presented just to make an impressively thick package.

Investors, regardless of who they are, are looking for:

- A good idea.
- A solid, comprehensive business plan.
- Someone with the experience, drive, determination, and skills to make that plan happen.

Borrowers, on the other hand, are looking for:

- Someone who understands their idea or shares the same vision.
- Someone who will let them maintain control of the business.
- An individual or institution with the funding to help make their plan happen.

Warning

Obtaining financing is often tied to control issues:

- If you obtain a loan, arrange to pay back the money with interest but with no other strings attached.
- Realize that if you take on an investor, whether it is a friend, relative, or stranger, you may have to give up some degree of control over your business and some percentage of the profits.

Therefore, whenever taking on investors, determine specifically what they want for their investment. Are they seeking profits, control, or some of each? Try to reach an agreement that makes you feel comfortable—and put it in writing!

Funding Sources

Banks

A bank will not want any ownership or control of the business—it will leave the day-to-day business decisions to you. A bank will want to secure its loan with collateral on your part. In simple terms, it will want to know that it will get its money back one way or another. A bank will want to see a complete and detailed business plan and to know specifically what the money will be used for (i.e., expanding your displays, new furniture, equipment, inventories, etc.). It will want to know exactly how much money you want, no rough estimates.

Your background, character, and capability to run a business and to repay a loan are other key factors that a bank will consider. Your past financial statements, credit history, and references are also important information to back up your loan application.

Several programs featuring loans for small businesses are also available through the SBA. Check with local banks or look at the SBA's loan programs on its Web site (www.sba.gov).

You can also join a credit union and apply for a smaller, shorter-term loan.

Venture Capital Firms

Most venture capitalists are more interested in helping mature businesses with growth and expansion, although some will work with start-up businesses.

Once again, you will have to show them a sound business plan and prove your worthiness. They will expect to earn a reasonable rate of interest on their investment and may want to exert some control. Remember, this is not a loan—these firms are making an investment.

Individual Investors

Finding backing for your business gets interesting with individual investors. These investors can range from family, to friends, to neighbors. Regardless of who the individual investor might be, present your proposal and plan in a professional manner. Pitch your idea to these investors exactly the same way you would to a bank.

Should you elect to take this route, put the entire agreement in writing. If it is a loan with interest, document this. If it is an investment in future profitability or part ownership, spell out the details and cover the control issue.

Stockholders

In order to secure financing, and if your business is a corporation, you may need to sell a piece of the business to investors. They would become shareholders and would most likely expect to receive some share of the profits on a regular basis, usually yearly. If the business is sold, the number or percentage of shares investors hold determines how much of the selling price they receive. Once again, be sure to cover the control issue. Put all details in writing to eliminate any misunderstandings.

Financing Your Business

Six C's of Credit

1. Capital
2. Collateral
3. Character
4. Capability
5. Coverage
6. Circumstances

Six C's of Credit

Bankers use what they refer to as the six C's of credit. The higher you rate in these categories, the greater the likelihood of getting your loan approved. And the better the rate will be!

1. **Capital.** The amount of money already invested in your business or available for future investment
2. **Collateral.** The assets you own that could be used to secure your loan
3. **Character.** Your personal experience, reputation, and credit history
4. **Capability.** Your ability to repay the loan based on past, current, and future income flows
5. **Coverage.** The insurance or safety precautions needed to protect the lender's investment
6. **Circumstances.** The current financial situations of both your business and the economy as a whole

If deficiencies exist in any area of your business, do not try to hide them. Be open and honest. Show what you are doing to correct the problem and emphasize other favorable factors. Bankers want to lend money and handle your banking needs, but it is up to you to demonstrate that you are a good risk. If the first bank you visit turns you down, learn from your mistakes, correct them, and visit another bank.

When You Have the Money

Now that you've obtained a loan from a bank or investor, the money is yours to do with whatever you choose, right? Wrong. You requested this money for a specific purpose, and that is exactly where that money needs to be spent. The bank and/or investors will want to stay informed about what is happening. Do what you say you are going to do at all levels. You may need to revisit this source again in the future, and you will want a favorable response. Look at these sources of funding as partners in the business even though legally they are not.

A LOOK AT TAXES

Although you most likely will not welcome the tax man with open arms, you do need to know how to prepare for tax payments once you become a business owner. There will be federal, state/province, county, and city taxes to be paid. Other than the IRS/Canada Revenue Agency, the rates and regulations will vary by area. You, your bookkeeper (if it's someone other than yourself), and your accountant all need to be informed and involved. Here are just a few tips to help you remain legal and minimize your tax obligations.

Keep Good Records

One of the most basic principles of paying taxes is sound preparation, which entails good record keeping. Studies show that more people run into problems with their various tax returns because of their record-keeping system than for any other reason.

Your record-keeping system provides a clear picture of all income and expenses. Keep information on all sales transactions, receipts, and canceled checks for all purchases and expenses made for the business. Make sure all paperwork is dated and filed according to categories such as rent, utilities, auto expenses, advertising, accounts payable by vendor, and so on. Your system should be easy to follow, to update, and to access.

What You Need to Pay and When

The legal entity of your business dictates when, at what rate, and how much you have to pay in taxes. Whether you operate on a calendar or fiscal year also has some bearing.

Your bookkeeper, accountant, or both will help with taxes, but the final responsibility is yours. The IRS/Canada Revenue Agency, states/provinces, and other agencies are unforgiving when it comes to not paying taxes. Do not delegate and do not forget. Be sure to pay your taxes in a timely and correct manner.

There are lots of opportunities and temptations where taxes are concerned. Do not jeopardize your business or personal life by taking shortcuts—play it straight.

Obtain Good Professional Help

The tax laws and regulations are long and varied so it is in your best interest to obtain the best professional help you can find. A good tax professional can advise you how to legally minimize both business and personal taxes. Avail yourself of this expertise. Here are a few tips to use when looking for the right tax professional. Choose someone:

- Whom you trust implicitly.
- Who will take the time to review your situation and provide you with advice and guidance on an ongoing basis.
- Who has all the necessary credentials in the field.
- Who is familiar with your type of business on a broad level.
- Who likes working with small business owners.
- Who knows the federal, state/province, and local regulations and requirements.

A good tax professional can quite literally mean the difference between success and failure in business. Take your time and choose someone you believe can help you make the right tax decisions and devise the best tax plan for your business.

SELECTING VENDOR PARTNERS

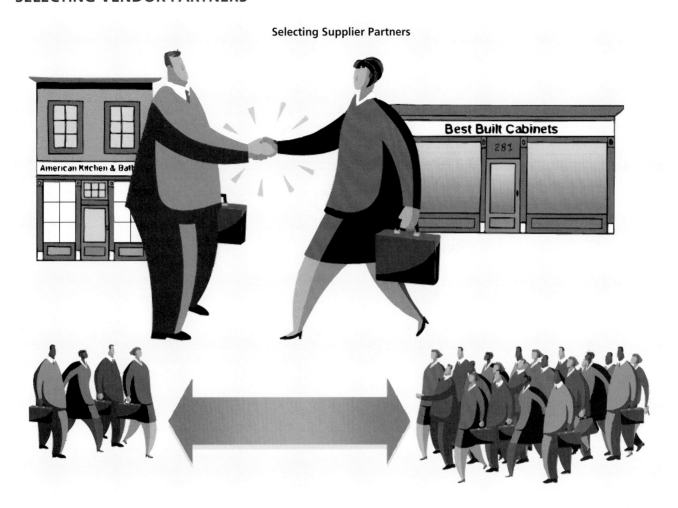

Selecting Supplier Partners

One of the most important marketing decisions you make is selecting the products you want to sell. Because yours is a kitchen and bath business, cabinets will be one of those products. Your market research should have told you what other products you might add to your product package. Many kitchen and bath businesses are showing and selling countertops (natural and synthetic); some show and sell appliances, tile, plumbing, lighting, flooring, doors, and windows. What is or will be your product offering?

Once you have made this important decision, you must decide who your vendor partners will be. Make your decision almost as if you are entering into a marriage, because the attributes that make for a strong personal marriage are similar in a business marriage. Good communication, openness, honesty, commitment, loyalty, and respect all apply to both.

Part of the decision process will be selecting your niche—luxury, high end, middle range, or entry level (most competitive).

Some try to combine two or three of these niches; however, it is very difficult to be all things to all people. It is easier, less costly, and more productive to be a specialist in just one area, with the possibility of overlapping into another.

Once you have selected your niche, start looking for vendors that supply this price and quality range of products. There is such a wide range of wood species, styles, colors, and finishes and variety of custom offerings from manufacturers that you may have to select three or four cabinet partners. Some businesses elect to work with just one or two cabinet suppliers; others work with seven to ten. One or two lines may not give you all the offerings you need, but

TABLE 3.2 Vendor Selection Checklist

Rate each area on a scale of 1 to 5, with 1 being the lowest value to your business and 5 being the highest value to your business. Or come up with your own rating. Feel free to add any other items that would be important to you at the bottom of the list to prioritize the results. Assign weight to each item based on its importance to your business.

Review Product Line by:	Weight	×	Rating	=	Total
Breadth and Depth					
Quality					
Price point					
Overall service					
Style of product					
Brand recognition					
Purchase cost (multiplier)					
Sales and profit potential					
Exclusivity					
Market share					
Company history and growth					
Company financial status					
Product warranty program					
Local representative					
Terms of purchase					
Cash terms					
Days due					
Delivery					
Lead times					
Freight					
Co-op programs					
Training					
Volume rebate program					
Special event dollars					
Web Site, literature, and brochures					
Order placement procedures					
Vendor advertising and promotions					
Do they sell to multi-brand retailers?					
Do they sell through buying groups?					
Display programs					
Return goods policy					
Customer testimonials					
Quality of reps					
Total score					

seven to ten may dilute the amount of business you can give to each. Remember, you want to be an important partner to every vendor you work with.

There is a long list of items to use to rate the various vendors. Not each line item will be of equal importance to you. This varies by business so you should assign your own weighting for each item. To rate importance, you might use the numbers 1 to 5, with 5 having the most value to your business and 1 the least. When comparing like vendors, use the guide to rate each. Do not fall into the trap of "I like the rep." The rep who calls on you is important, but is only one of the items rated on the Vendor Selection Checklist (Table 3.2). There are many other factors to consider. When feasible, visit vendors, take the tour, meet their people, and check their financial statements. They will insist on seeing yours, so it is only fair, and good business too, to review theirs.

Countertops, appliances, plumbing, and the many other products you might decide to show and sell will most likely be supplied by local vendors or distributors. Choose the very best partner wisely, as you will want the marriage to grow and last.

BUYING GROUPS—SHARING EXPERTISE

Buying groups have been around in most industries for decades, but the K&B industry is still a relative newcomer to the buying group concept. Two of the major buying groups participating in our industry are Bath and Kitchen Buying Group (BKBG) and SEN Design Group.

Buying Groups Offer You

- Sharing expertise/networking
- Receiving industry specific financial information
- Participating in shared expense marketing programs
- Receiving rebate financial rewards

Advantages of Participating in a Buying Group

- Monetary benefits—rebates, cash, and other discounts generally not available to individuals.
- A direct and greater voice to the top management of vendor/supplier partners.
- Access to kitchen/bath industry–focused marketing programs.
- The opportunity to network with fellow professionals at buying group meetings once or twice a year.
- The opportunity to attend kitchen/bath industry–focused educational conferences.
- Assistance with business management issues by individuals completely focused on the kitchen/bath industry.
- The opportunity to participate in a consumer magazine program.

Although the financial benefits are normally the main reason for joining a buying group, members often cite other advantages that become more important as they participate. These include:

- The opportunity to share financial information with businesses following a similar model. Some consider receiving focused advice on how to improve financial performance from one meeting to the next a major benefit. To gain this benefit, participants must be willing to share accurate—and, often, confidential—financial information.

- Networking opportunities with others in the same business.
- Learning how to expand your business, or being introduced to business practices or marketing programs in a more focused environment rather than in association meetings or other activities that have a more diverse business membership. As one individual said, "It becomes an ongoing school for finding best practices in the industry and sharing them."
- The opportunity for national exposure through consumer publications often published by the buying group. These "'advertorial' formats have proven successful for participating dealers. The consumers value the information and the examples of great kitchen design and often consider these books on a par with other special interest issues.

Why Dealers Have Not Joined Buying Groups

- They do not understand the membership fee structure or the rebate program.
- They do not want to pay annual dues, and do not like the idea of submitting a letter of credit.
- They believe they can buy just as competitively on their own.
- They are not interested in carrying the product lines represented by the buying group.
- The buying group does not represent enough of their vendor partners.

A buying group may not be in the best interest of dealerships whose business models are quite different from the majority of the buying group's membership. For example, a boutique business with an annual sales volume of less than $1 million and that focuses on the high end might not benefit from a buying group catering to larger retail organizations.

Selecting Vendors Is a Group Responsibility

Dealers typically are hesitant about joining buying groups because of concerns about the supplier partner elements of the group.

> To be successful, a buying group must do a volume of business with specific vendors. This means all members must participate and purchase all or some of their product mix from the participating manufacturers. In all groups, the members actually choose the manufacturers to represent. Additionally, while members are encouraged to buy from this select group (and receive greater rebates when they do), members certainly can still choose to buy other products from nonmember vendors, assuming they make their minimum purchase requirements for the buying group.

> *Kitchen & Bath Design News*

Buying group membership requirements vary but typically include:

- A one-time membership fee and some type of annual fee. (The annual fee may be used for other buying group services or may be waived based on the minimum purchasing level met by the dealer.)
- A minimum yearly annual sales volume from the participating manufacturers.
- The firm may be required to have a showroom and not belong to a competing buying group.
- There may be a minimum annual sales volume requirement.
- Participating members must attend at least one of the buying group's two yearly conferences.

JOINING THE BUSINESS COMMUNITY

By virtue of being located in a community, you are part of it. You will have to follow local ordinances and pay local taxes. There will be various business and civic organizations to join for both learning and networking opportunities, such as the local Chamber of Commerce. These organizations offer seminars and learning opportunities for small business owners. By being a member, you can network with other small business entrepreneurs.

By becoming involved, you will develop relationships that can help you and your image, leading to good public relations. Support from leaders in the community can help your business draw attention to itself. Sponsoring an event to help a charitable organization will enhance your public image.

By contributing to your community, you will draw positive attention from the media. They, in turn, will reflect to the public a positive image of you and your business.

You will be busy running your business so initially you may not be able to afford the time to become a leader of an organization, but being an active member and supporter can only create positive results.

TAKING ADVANTAGE OF OUTSIDE HELP

It is difficult to build a business in a vacuum. Feedback, suggestions, opinions, and guidance from others can be valuable in helping you run your business. The sources and resources are innumerable. Some help you may have to pay for (attorney, accountant, consultants, etc.); other help may be free for the asking (banker, Chamber of Commerce, SBA, etc.).

Consider Your Banker a Key Business Associate

Your bank is more than a place where you keep a checking account. It provides many important services that will be required for your business operations. Choose carefully.

- Is the bank in a convenient location?
- Does the banker understand your business?
- Is the bank small enough so you can deal with senior management?
- Will your banker be willing to act as a mentor and be willing to coach you?
- Does the bank have an SBA loan department?
- In the United States, is the bank a member of Federal Deposit Insurance Corporation (FDIC) and the Federal Reserve Bank? In Canada, is the bank a member of the Canada Deposit Insurance Corporation (CDIC)?
- Does the bank provide the services you will need now and in the future?
- Is the bank's capitalization/asset ratio greater than 6%? (This is a good measure of the bank's health.)
- What are the fees for various transactions?
- Are the fees competitive?
- What are the fees and interest rates associated with their credit cards? Are they competitive?
- What balances are required on interest-bearing checking accounts?

National Kitchen & Bath Association

One great resource is the National Kitchen & Bath Association (NKBA). Local and national activities provide invaluable networking opportunities. As you meet and become acquainted with other owners at NKBA events, you will be able to pick up the phone or fire off an email to discuss almost any issue that may surface. Do not try to reinvent the wheel, just improve on it. There is no better way than by sharing experience with others who have been there and done that.

Advisory Board

Establish an advisory board for your business. Include your accountant, attorney, and banker, and add a friend or relative who may have small business management experience. If you work with an advertising or public relations firm, ask them to be a member. Bring the group together quarterly or as necessary. Have an agenda and start brainstorming. It may cost you a few dinners and gifts during the holidays, but the results will be more valuable than you could imagine. Help is out there—go find it.

SUMMARY

In this chapter we explained that there's more to operating a successful K&B business than simply being a good designer. Knowing how to select the proper legal structure for the business may protect you, your family, and your employees. The phrase "location, location, location" is every bit as important for your business as it is for your home. Having a solid financial foundation for the business and a strong working relationship with a bank is another important key to success, as is staying legal and current with local, state, and federal taxes, both personally and professionally. Selecting the right vendor and business advisory partners is another big responsibility of the owner and management team.

REVIEW QUESTIONS

1. What are the advantages of an S or C corporation for the legal structure of your business? (See "Corporation" pages 47–49)
2. After completing the business Location Checklist, are you satisfied with your current location? Explain your answer. (See "Location, Location, Location" pages 51–52).
3. What are the six C's of credit for financing your business? (See "The Six C's of Credit" page 59)
4. What are some of the tips you should follow in selecting the right tax professional? (See "Obtain Good Professional Help" page 60)
5. Explain the benefits of using the Vendor Selection Checklist to analyze your current list of key vendors. (See "Vendor Selection Checklist" page 62)
6. List four advantages of belonging to a buying group. (See "Advantages of Participating in a Buying Group" pages 63–64)

Accounting and Record Keeping

After the excitement and anticipation of a great business success comes a more mundane yet vital task. Business accounting is your way to keep score on how well the business is doing. If the main purpose of operating a business is to make a profit, then proper business accounting is required in order to know how well you are doing and if you really are generating profits.

Learning Objective 1: Describe the three main components of businesses.

Learning Objective 2: Explain good record-keeping and financial tracking records.

Learning Objective3: Explain the benefits of having both an in-house and an outside "expert" to help you manage these areas of your business.

Learning Objective 4: State why developing timely budgets is your road map for financial success.

Learning Objective 5: Construct a sample budget and a format that you can use in your business.

You Must Be Balanced

Design Talents   Business Skills

People Skills

Remember, there are two parts to your business: the things you love to do (designing, selling, and creating kitchen and bath projects) and the things you must do (accounting, managing people, and solving problems). Accounting falls into the latter group. Bookkeeping is not glamorous and it's not the reason you went into business, but it is the backbone of a successful business. Without accurate books and business records and without the skills to generate and analyze these records, you will be unable to get a clear picture of just how well, or how poorly, your business is doing.

Most kitchen and bath business owners fall short in this all-important area. But the difference between just eking out a living versus having a successful business is often the owner's involvement in and understanding of the financial area of the business.

What can you do to become a good financial manager? Be a balanced business owner.

Balanced

Every business consists of three parts:

1. Marketing management
2. Human resource management
3. Financial management

All three areas need to be equally strong for a business to be truly successful. Most K&B business owners are fairly strong in the marketing segments (design, sales, advertising, promotion) but are weak and often reluctant to improve on the human resource (people management) and financial areas (budgets, financial statements, cash flow) of the business.

Owners who do not work to become stronger in the human resource and financial management sides of their businesses will most likely not be in business five or ten years from now. The stronger and better-managed competitors, may they be large or small, will outperform them and squeeze them out of the marketplace.

WHY YOU NEED TO KEEP GOOD RECORDS

It is elementary that good bookkeeping and record keeping are essential to operating a small business. When you own a business, you must understand why these daily chores are important so that you will be motivated to keep up with them. Here are a few reasons why good record keeping is important.

Keeping Good Records Helps You...

- Monitor and track performance of your business.
- Pay the right amount in taxes.
- Pay yourself and others.
- Manage the business.
- Sell the business.
- Borrow money.

Monitor and Track Performance of Your Business

Close monitoring tells you whether you are making or losing money. Monitoring allows you to gauge which products and services are selling and which are not and which are profitable and which are not. Monitoring will give you a clear understanding of expenses in order to manage them accordingly.

All business decisions should be based on where you stand financially. Before you change out a display, take on new products, expand your services, hire more people, buy a new truck, or do anything that requires a financial outlay, you need to know how your decision will impact your business financially. Good bookkeeping and record keeping provides you with this essential information.

Pay Your Taxes

It is much easier to calculate tax return figures and pay taxes when you are working from a set of accurate financial records. If you are a corporation, you will have to pay quarterly taxes in a timely manner. In addition, the many rules and regulations governing sales taxes and payroll taxes will be much easier to comply with if you know where to look for the correct numbers.

Pay Yourself and Others

The rule should be to pay yourself first. But how much? You cannot pay yourself or distribute profits to other partners or investors if you do not know what the profits are.

Manage the Business

Good accounting and the ability to interpret the numbers will tell you when it is appropriate to expand or necessary to cut back. They allow you to truly manage the business to maximize profitability and the return on your investment.

Sell the Business

You will need up-to-date and accurate accounting records if you ever decide to sell the business. You'll need them in order to arrive at a fair selling price, and prospective buyers will need to review them to know how the business is doing before they can make an educated decision on whether to move forward with the purchase.

Borrow Money

To pursue investors, you will need to show accurate financial statements. Good, solid bookkeeping is the only way to produce the information everyone will need.

ESTABLISHING BOOKKEEPING PROCEDURES

The newness and size of your business will dictate whether you'll have to keep the books or whether you can afford to hire a bookkeeper to handle these responsibilities. The size and volume of the operation will determine whether you can have someone on staff full or part time to perform the bookkeeping duties.

Basic bookkeeping starts on a day-to-day and sale-by-sale level. The variety of software packages available make much of the work quite simple. Whether you're using a software program or doing the bookkeeping manually, you'll need to keep a journal of sales and cash receipts. Doing this will allow you to track your sales totals, know which products and services were sold on credit, and keep track of payments for each sale.

Your cash disbursements journal (or expense journal) will provide you with information on how much you are spending and to whom you are paying the money.

Do not defer all financial and accounting questions and decisions to the bookkeeping department or an outside accountant. Doing this can lead to trouble. Bookkeepers provide you with accurate books; an accountant will help you prepare financial statements and make recommendations. But it's up to you to make final and informed decisions. Therefore, get in the habit of meeting with your accountant and/or bookkeeper on a regular basis to review your financial situation.

You may want to seriously consider taking a basic accounting class or two online or at your local community college to gain a basic understanding of accounting and financial management.

CHOOSING AN ACCOUNTING SYSTEM

There are two basic types of accounting methods: the cash method and the accrual method.

Cash Method

In the cash method, you record income only when you receive it from your customers. Likewise, when you write a check or pay cash out, you record that as well. This system is simple because you are keeping track of cash coming in and going out. However, most businesses, including kitchen and bath businesses, are not cash-only. It is common today to extend credit to customers or, in the case of kitchen and bath businesses, to take deposits for products and services to be rendered at a future date. A cash accounting system does not account for these types of transactions. Therefore, if you use this method, you won't have the whole picture of what you have actually earned or spent.

Accrual Method

Much more common today, especially with kitchen and bath businesses, is the accrual method of accounting. Here, each transaction is recorded when it occurs, regardless of whether you have received the cash or spent the cash at that time. This method generally will provide you with a more accurate picture of your profits and losses, especially where deposits are received, product is purchased, work is performed, and invoices are paid at varying intervals. To get the best picture of where you stand in your kitchen and bath business, you will benefit by using the accrual method. If you maintain inventory, you do not have a choice: The Internal Revenue Service (IRS) says you must use the accrual system.

Selecting a Single- or Double-Entry System

Another choice you may have is whether to use a single-entry or a double-entry accounting system. Most software programs come with the double-entry system already built in. In these programs, you make one entry and the programs make the second: Both a debit and a credit entry are made for each transaction. Another reason the double-entry system is preferred is that it provides a check-and-balance system (credits must equal debits), allowing you to find errors more easily.

Establishing Your Fiscal Year

An accounting "period" is a set amount of time where the financial reports of the business can be compared with those from another set amount of time. The accounting period can be months, quarters, or years. One year in a company's financial life is called a fiscal year. A fiscal year can follow a yearly calendar (January 1 to December 31) or any other 12-month period you select (e.g., March 1 to February 28). S corporations typically have to be on a calendar year.

There Are No Shortcuts

Be leery of accountants, bookkeepers, or any online offers that offer dramatic shortcuts to handling the tasks of record keeping. While technology can speed up your accounting methods, anything that appears to be fast or takes shortcuts is probably missing some vital steps that may haunt you later.

WHAT TO KEEP TRACK OF

What to Keep Track Of

- Accounts receivable
- Accounts payable
- General ledger
- Balance sheet
- Operating income statement
- Job costing

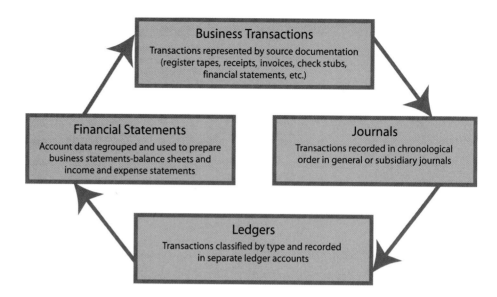

FIGURE 4.1 You must keep accurate business records

Choosing the right system is one thing, but after you make that decision, you need to know what to keep tabs on. Otherwise your accounting system will not do you any good. Figure 4.1 illustrates the important things you will want to track.

Accounts Receivable

You'll need to keep track of all accounts receivable—that is, the money owed to you by customers. For each customer, you will keep an individual list of account receivables. This will allow you to see how much you are owed by each customer and in total. It will also show you whether this money is due or overdue.

Accounts Payable

The money that you owe and need to pay to others is your accounts payable. You may owe money to suppliers and vendors or others from whom you have purchased merchandise, equipment, or services. By keeping a separate ledger account for each supplier or vendor, you will be able to see exactly whom you owe money and how much you owe at any given time. In this way, you will be able to plan your payments and take advantage of any cash discounts offered.

General Ledger

This is where you start to organize your financial statement. The general ledger summarizes data from other journals, including cash disbursements, or your expense journal and your sales and cash receipts journal. This is where you will find the balance between debits and credits when you finish posting your entries.

Balance Sheet

The balance sheet is one of the key financial statements to prepare based on your bookkeeping and accounting procedures. It will present you with an overview of your business at the present time. A balance sheet includes all of your assets and liabilities. The balance sheet is the next step after posting to the general ledger, adjusting entries, and completing the trial balance.

As the name implies, the balance sheet must balance, meaning your assets will equal your liabilities plus your capital. The balance sheet shows you who owns the majority of your business, you and your investors or banks, vendors, and other creditors. See Chapter 5 for more details.

Operating or Income Statement

The operating or income statement is the one that will require the most attention from you, as well as any banks or investors you might be working with. This financial statement, also known as the profit and loss (P&L) statement, shows your net income or loss and gives you an overall perspective on where the business stands.

The P&L statement is simply a final, rounded-off (to the next full dollar) summation of what you have earned and what you have spent. The main items shown on the P&L statement are sales, cost of goods sold, gross profit, expenses, and net income or loss. This report gives you the all-important "bottom line." (This is the final line of the report showing a profit or a loss.)

You will find more detail and examples on this important financial statement in Chapter 5.

Job Costing

Job costing is one record-keeping activity often overlooked by business owners who also design, sell, and supervise installations (see Chapter 11). It is important that your estimating forms flow into your accounting records so that as invoices are received, they can be matched up with the estimated costs for that aspect of the project. It's not unusual for a high-volume seller to actually generate fewer profits than another member on the team who does not generate as much cash but does a better job estimating and managing the project, resulting in more profit.

ACCOUNTING SOFTWARE FOR YOUR BUSINESS

Modern technology requires the right software for the right task, whether for design, project management, inventory, graphics, communications, or financial management. An accounting software package should be easy to learn and should include features appropriate to your particular business. Talk with your accountant and well-established K&B business owners before deciding which financial software package would be best for you. Keep in mind that the software will have to be compatible with your computer system.

There are a number of programs and online services available, ranging in cost from under $100 to several thousand dollars. Following are a few of the more popular programs that should cover most of your small business accounting needs. Due to the popularity of software packages for small businesses, most accounting professionals now offer assistance with these programs as part of their services.

Accounting Software

Accounting is the language of business, and good accounting software can save time and money and help business owners and managers do a better job of managing their business.

There is no substitute for an accounting pro who knows the ins and outs of tax law, but today's desktop software packages can help you with everything from routine bookkeeping to payroll, taxes, and planning. Each package also produces files that can be handed off to an accountant as needed.

Today, business managers have more accounting software options than ever before, including subscription Web-based options that don't require their users to install or update software. Many businesses, however, including those that need to track inventories or client databases and those that prefer not to entrust their data to the cloud, may be happier with a desktop tool.

Here are three excellent general-purpose small business accounting packages that are popular in the kitchen and bath industry: Account Edge Pro (both the product and the company were previously known as MYOB), Intuit QuickBooks Premiere, and Sage 50 Complete (the successor to Peachtree Complete). All three packages offer a solid array of tools for tracking income and expenses, invoicing, and managing payroll and operating reports.

These full-featured programs are not inexpensive. Account Edge Pro at $299.00 is the least expensive. Prices climb if you opt to use common time-saving add-ons such as payroll services or if you add licenses for multiple user accounts.

All three are solid on the basics, but they have distinct differences in style and focus. The more you know about your accounting requirements, the more closely you'll want to look at the software you're thinking of buying.

Sage 50 Complete appeals to most to people who understand the fine points of accounting and can use the product's many customization features (especially businesses that manage inventory).

QuickBooks works hard to appeal to newbies who need only the basics and might be intimidated by the level of detail and technical language in the other two packages. It has a number of third-party add-ons that meet specific needs and greatly expand its capabilities

Account Edge Pro balances accessibility with strong features at an affordable price. It's especially suitable for businesses that need to provide simultaneous access to multiple users.

Be sure to carefully review your computer system's requirements for any software package as well as upgrades you may have to purchase in order not to invest money in software that your computer system is too outdated to run.

RECORD-KEEPING AND ADMINISTRATIVE NEEDS

Besides all the financial records of sales, expenditures, profits, and losses, you'll also need to maintain other records. These include the names and addresses of your suppliers, accurate client records, and up-to-date employee data. If you keep any inventory and other such records in your computer, it is in your best interest to also keep hard copies of key information as a backup.

Your personnel files should include these items:

- Tax information for each employee, including Social Security number
- Personal contact information, including emergency numbers in case of injury or illness
- Employment history including resume, initial job application
- Employment record with your company, including pay rate, dates of pay changes, accrued sick days and vacation days

For clients and customers, you will need to maintain these files:

- Up-to-date contact information
- Copy of credit application with signed personal guarantee, if appropriate
- All correspondence
- Records of all transactions

Additional files to keep on hand:

- Permits, licenses, and registrations
- Property lease agreements
- Equipment leasing contracts or receipts for purchases
- Important correspondence with landlord, regulatory agencies, and government officials
- Supplier contact information and terms of purchase, including any specially negotiated deals
- Contact listings for local and industry governing bodies, including the National Kitchen & Bath Association, the local Chamber of Commerce, zoning committee, and the like
- Legal papers, including claims you've made and claims against your company
- Lease/property/equipment insurance (i.e., the insurance needed to operate, etc.)

Even though much business is transacted through email, it is important to take the time to run hard copies of all key documents and store them safely in your files. Businesses that rely solely on their computers are taking enormous risks. Have backup data available at all times.

One of the biggest—yet least discussed—causes of business failure is poor record keeping. And this does not mean just financial records. Businesses also close because they let licenses and registrations lapse. Companies find themselves in financial trouble because they neglected legal matters. It is vital to have a solid record-keeping and filing system in place from the beginning.

How Long Should You Retain Your Records?

The following list includes suggestions for the minimal amount of time that various types of corporate records should be retained:

Record Type	Retain
Corporate Records	
Bylaws, charter, minute books	Indefinitely
Capital stock and bond records	Indefinitely
Checks (taxes, property and settlement contracts)	Indefinitely
Contracts and agreements (current)	Indefinitely
Copyrights and trademark registrations	Indefinitely
Deeds, mortgages and bills of sale	Indefinitely
Labor contracts	Indefinitely
Minute books of directors/stockholders (including bylaws and charter)	Indefinitely
Mortgages, notes and leases (expired)	8 years
Patents	Indefinitely
Property appraisals	Indefinitely
Proxies	Indefinitely
Retirement and pension records	Indefinitely
Stock and bond certificates (canceled)	7 years
Tax returns and working papers, revenue agent reports	Indefinitely
Correspondence	
General	3 years
Legal and tax	Indefinitely
Routine (customers, vendors)	1 year
Personnel	
Contracts (expired)	7 years
Disability and sick benefit reports	6 years
Employment applications	3 years
Personnel files (terminated)	6 years
Withholding tax statements	6 years

Accounting	Retain
Auditors records	Indefinitely
Bank reconciliations	1 year
Bank statements and deposit slips	3 years
Cash books	Indefinitely
Chart of accountants	Indefinitely
Cancelled checks	8 years
Depreciation schedules	Indefinitely
Dividend checks (cancelled)	6 years
Expense reports	7 years
Financial statements (end of year)	Indefinitely
Fixed assets detail	Indefinitely
General ledgers and journals	Indefinitely
Inventory of products, materials, and supplies	7 years
Payroll	
Time cards	3 years
Individuals' earnings records	8 years
Records and summaries	7 years
Petty cash vouchers	3 years
Physical inventory tags	3 years
Subsidiary ledgers (accounts receivable, accounts payable, A/R and A/P)	7 years
Trial balances (monthly)	7 years
Vouchers for payments to vendors, employees, etc.	7 years
Insurance	
Accident reports	7 years
Claims (after settlement)	Indefinitely
Policies (all types—expired)	4 years
Safety reports	8 years
Purchasing/Sales	
Purchase orders	7 years
Requisitions	7 years
Sales contracts	7 years
Sales invoices	7 years

HIRING AN ACCOUNTANT OR BOOKKEEPER

Because a number of owners have difficulty dealing with the financial aspect of their businesses, they need professional advice and assistance in this all-important area. They may be award-winning designers, outstanding salespeople, and great marketers, but when asked to analyze a P&L statement, their eyes glaze over. Even the best and most powerful accounting software is useless if you cannot input or understand the data. Most of the time, hiring an accountant or bookkeeper is a smart business decision.

Although accountants and bookkeepers cannot guarantee your success, they can be an important adjunct to your business. Their basic services include keeping track of how much your business owes, how much it's owed, creating financial statements (such as balance sheets, income statements, cash flow statements), and reconciling bank statements. They might also handle:

- **Taxes.** A good accountant/bookkeeper can save your business and possibly you thousands of dollars through proper tax planning.
- **Payroll.** Often this is outsourced, however.
- **Financial statement preparation** (compilation, review or audit). This may be required if you have bank loans or outside investors.
- **IRS audits.** Accountants and bookkeepers can be invaluable if the IRS audits your business.
- **Business and financial planning.** An accountant can help with business succession and estate planning or help to prepare and value the business for sale.

So, where do you find a good accountant or bookkeeper? Referrals are the best source. Network with others in your local industry. Consult other small business owners as well as your friends, banker, and attorney.

After you have a few names, set up appointments and interviews to determine:

- **Their experience.** You want someone who deals with small businesses, especially in your field.
- **If timely service is delivered.** Numbers are constantly coming in from your business, so make sure they will get reports to you at least monthly. (No later than the tenth of the month.)
- **Who will service your account?** Will it be the person you are meeting with or an associate you have not met?
- **What service you can expect beyond reporting?** Will they handle your taxes, payroll, and the like?
- **If you will be able to get business consulting as well.** A good accountant or book-keeper should become a valuable member of your team.
- **How much will it cost?** You should know fairly accurately how much time the accountant will put in each month and what you should expect to pay.
- **How well will you relate to this person?** Is his or her personality one that you can work with? Do you have other interests in common, and can you possibly become friends as well as business associates?

Accountants are professionals, and their fees are not inexpensive. Here are a few ways to keep your accounting costs down.

- Keep excellent records. Organize your receipts. Maintain a legible and current ledger. If possible, automate your records.
- Handle the small tasks in-house.
- Use a bookkeeper for the daily and monthly accounting. Use the accountant for taxes, audits, and year-end reporting.

BUDGETING FOR PROFIT AND CASH FLOW

You cannot open the doors to your business each day without having some idea of what to expect. And you cannot close its doors at the end of the day not knowing what happened. The Boy Scouts have a great motto: "Be prepared." A business should follow the same motto. It should plan ahead and prepare for its future, and it should control its performance to reach financial goals.

Business owners/managers have these broad options:

- They can wait for results to be reported to them on a look-back basis.
- They can look ahead and plan what profit and cash flow should be and then compare actual results against the plan.

The latter option is the essence of budgeting.

What Is a Budget?

Be careful how you use the term "budgeting." Budgeting does not refer to putting a financial straitjacket on a business. Rather, business budgeting refers to setting specific goals and developing the detailed plans necessary to achieve those goals.

Business budgeting is built on realistic forecasts for the coming period. It requires that owners/managers have a thorough understanding of the profit blueprint of the business and the financial effects of profit-making activities. A business budget is an integrated plan of action, not simply a few trend lines on a financial chart.

Difference between Budgeting and P&L Statements

Financial statements (see Chapter 5) are prepared after the fact—after sales, expenses, and profits are recorded. Budgeted financial statements, however, are prepared *before* the fact and are based on future transactions expected to take place based on the profit strategy and financial goals of the business.

Budgeted financial statements are not reported outside the business; they are strictly for internal management use. The only exception to this would be if you need a bank loan. The bank would most likely want to see some projected numbers, also known as pro formas.

Accounting software has made doing an annual budget much easier. Using the computer beats the old do-it-by-hand method.

How to Develop a Business Budget

If yours is a new business, your budget will be all "crystal balling." You will not have the historical numbers of a more mature business. A business that has been operating for several years offers the budget preparer (owner/manager) the advantage of real numbers documented for management and tax purposes. Therefore, you can build your budget on historical data using statistical growth formulas.

The first time you sit down to do an annual budget, it may seem daunting, and to some degree it is. It takes quiet and time. If you operate on a calendar fiscal year, January 1 through December 31, you should start the process two months before the end of your fiscal year, meaning you would start work on your budget on November 1.

Start by having the financial statements from the past two or three years in front of you. Then do some "futuristic" market survey information collecting. Ask your sales staff what they believe next year will bring. Ask your suppliers the same question. Check what other small business owners in your market predict for the future. Call other K&B business owners and ask for their input. Contact your local Chamber of Commerce to ask what it believes the business climate will be in your area for the next 12-month period. In other words, ask anyone and everyone for their opinions.

The Revenue Stream: A Sales Plan

A sales plan is simply a compilation of the amount of product and/or services that the company anticipates selling over a defined period of time.

Experienced sales managers in the K&B industry offer these general rules for the generation of a sales plan:

- Agree that a defined period of time is one year.
- Because of the cyclical nature of K&B sales, it is easier to forecast sales on a calendar-year basis.
- Base sales forecasting on incoming orders (orders signed and sold for the period) rather than the accounting definition of invoiced sales.
- Forecast yearly sales by month and by quarter. Geographic areas vary; a typical quarterly breakdown for K&B sales is:

  First Quarter: 20%

  Second Quarter: 25%

  Third Quarter: 30%

  Fourth Quarter: 25%

- Chart sales monthly, by salesperson. Industry experience suggests salespeople should be capable of generating between $500,000 to $750,000 in sales per year. This consists of cabinets, countertops, delivered and installed.

  After identifying the average time from lead to contract to deposit and final payment, you'll be able to estimate the number of months it will take a new salesperson to reach peak performance during your sales forecasting annual period. In a number of well-run businesses, salespeople achieve sales of $750,000 to $1 million per year.

- If you are not significantly increasing or decreasing your sales force, once you have a "feel" for what the next year may bring, apply it to your historic data. If your sales have been growing at 10% a year and the forecasts are for more of the same, use a 10% increase in sales as your number for the next year.

Study Your Expenses

The third step in developing a budget is to zero in on the expenses your firm incurs during normal operations and in executing every project you sell.

Do this by looking at every line item on your income statement and reviewing expenses. Will they go up or down? Will rent increase? Will health and medical expenses continue to climb? Will you have to hire another salesperson or installer because sales are projected to grow? After you've made your best, most informed guess on each of these items, add it all up to see what the bottom line says. Will it meet or exceed your expectations?

For start-up businesses or those in an evolutionary stage, look at every line item and review expenses. For businesses on a fast-track growth pattern, decisions about the marketing plan may dramatically affect the expenses. For example, if you are predicting a large increase in sales, you may need to hire more people to handle that increase: doing this will dramatically increase your cost of doing business.

Compensation and Operating Expense Reporting

Your operating expense reporting is dramatically influenced by how you pay yourself and what you pay your sales/design staff. Study the information in Chapter 8 to better understand the importance of paying yourself a salary commensurate with the work you are performing as a member of your company's leadership and sales team. The chapter also provides an in-depth discussion about the pros and cons of various salary/commission compensation packages for your sales/design staff.

TABLE 4.1 Acme Kitchens, Inc. Income Statement—6-Month Period 01/01/13 to 06/30/13

Net Sales	$ 555,819	100.00%	$555,819
Cost of Sales			
Product Repairs/Warranty	432	.08	432
Repair Contract Labor	112	.02	112
Repair Product	1,264	.23	1,264
Installation Costs	2,662	.48	2,662
Supplier Purchases	360,230	64.01	360,230
Purchases—Warranty and Repair	54	.01	54
Purchase Discounts	[660]	[.12]	[660]
Freight Out	3,510	.63	3,510
Total Cost of Sales	367,604	66.13	367,604
Gross Profit	188,215	33.86	188,215
Operating Expenses	180,164		110,550*
Net Income before Other Items	8,051		77,665
Interest Income	98		98
Interest Expense	5,550		5,550
Rental Income	2,850		2,850
Income (Net Loss)	5,449		75,063
*Does not include owner wages and fringe benefits.			

Table 4.1 presents hypothetical numbers generated by Acme Kitchen.

Keep Up the Markup

Just what are average overhead factors in our industry (Figure 4.2)?

- Overhead is at least 25 to 35 percent of the total project costs for most firms that offer installation.
- The sales function accounts for 6 to 8 percent.

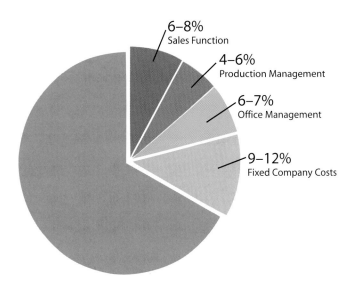

6–8%
Sales Function

4–6%
Production Management

6–7%
Office Management

9–12%
Fixed Company Costs

FIGURE 4.2 Keep Up the Markup (Overhead 25%–35% of Costs)

Source: Walter Stoeppelwerth, *Remodeling Magazine* (July 2004).

- Production management accounts for 4 to 6 percent.
- Office management accounts for 6 to 7 percent.
- Fixed company costs account for 9 to 12 percent.

Once you've completed your sales forecast, margin analysis, and expenses review, run the numbers. If your before-tax profits are below expectations, you can:

- Raise sales forecasts.
- Raise margin goals.
- Lower expenses.

The balance of this chapter explains how to initiate one of these three profit-producing business initiatives.

Budget: Your Road Map

The budget should be on a spreadsheet that shows all 12 months and a total. The budget spreadsheet should be set up exactly like your income statement, balance sheet, and cash flow statement. (Yes, you will prepare a projected balance sheet and cash flow analysis from the information you gather.)

As the actual numbers of the new year are reported, you will match them to your budgeted numbers. Some will be high and some will be low. If at the end of the first quarter you are way off with some budgeted numbers, you should adjust them at that time.

The advantage of doing an annual budget is that it helps to eliminate surprises. It helps you to plan when you'll have to hire more people. It tells you when you'll be able to afford to update part of your showroom or buy a new truck. And, more important, it sets sales, expense, and profit goals that help you maximize your investment in money and hard work.

Budgeting has advantages and ramifications that go beyond the financial dimension and have more to do with business management in general. Here are some additional benefits of budgeting:

- Budgeting forces owners/managers to forecast better.
- Budgeting motivates managers and employees by providing useful yardsticks for measuring performance.
- Budgeting can assist in communication among the owner, supervisors, and employees.
- Budgeting is an essential part of the all-important business plan (see Chapter 3).

Table 4.2 is a Sample Budget Spreadsheet to guide you in your annual budget preparation. If your current chart of accounts is detailed enough and works well for you, use your own format.

TABLE 4.2 Sample Budget Spreadsheet

Income	Description	Jan	Feb	Mar	Apr	May	Total
Sales							
	Cabinets						
	Countertops						
	Plumbing						
	Lighting						
	Appliances						
	Instillation						
	Freight Income						
Cost of Goods Sold							
	Sales						
	Cabinets						
	Countertops						
	Plumbing						
	Lighting						
	Appliances						
	Installation						
	Freight and delivery						
Gross Profit							
	Sales						
	Cabinets						
	Countertops						
	Plumbing						
	Lighting						
	Appliances						
	Installation						
Expenses							
Operating Expenses							
	Personnel						
	Officers						
	Payroll—Exempt						
	Payroll—Nonexempt						
	Commissions						
	Bonuses/Incentives						
	Overtime						
	Payroll Taxes						
	Insurance—Health/Medical						
	Insurance—Workers' Comp						

(continued)

TABLE 4.3 *(Continued)*

Expenses *(Continued)*	Description	Jan	Feb	Mar	Apr	May...	Total
Facilities and Equipment							
	Depreciation						
	Car/Truck Rental						
	Fuel						
	Office Equipment Rental						
	Building Rent						
	Vehicle Maintenance						
	Building Maintenance						
	Insurance—Fire and General						
	Insurance—Vehicle						
	Utilities						
	Property Taxes						
Other Operating Expense							
	Advertising—Publications						
	Advertising—Newspaper						
	Advertising—Radio and TV						
	Advertising—Direct Mail						
	Advertising—Yellow Pages						
	Advertising—Other						
	Promotions						
	Conventions and Meetings						
	Travel and Entertainment						
	Dues and Subscriptions						
	Legal Fees						
	Accounting Fees						
	Supplies						
	Postage						
	Phone (Less Yellow Pages)						
	IRA—Pension Contributions						
	Provision for Bad Debt						
	Bank—Service Charges						
	Donations						
	Licenses—Auto and Business						
	Computer Expenses						

TABLE 4.3 *(Continued)*

Expenses *(Continued)*	Description	Jan	Feb	Mar	Apr	May	Total
	Employee Training						
	Showroom Expenses						
	Cleaning Services						
	Alarm Expenses						
Total Expenses							
Total Net Operating Income							
Other Income/Expenses							
Other Income	Discounts and Purchases						
	Interest Income						
	Refunds and Adjustments						
Total Other Income							
Other Expenses	Interest on Line of Credit						
	Interest Expense						
	State Income Tax						
Total Other Income							
Net Other Income							
Net Income/Loss before Taxes							
Net Income							

SUMMARY

In this chapter we explained the three main components of good business management: financial, human resources, and marketing. The financial management segment may not be a business owner's favorite part of the business, but to be successful, the owner must acquire at least a basic knowledge of financial management. The importance of finding outside professional help in this area was explained. Developing and keeping budgets was also reviewed.

REVIEW QUESTIONS

1. What are the three main components of virtually every business? (See in chapter introductory text page 68)
2. How does keeping good business records benefit you? (See "Why You Need to Keep Good Records" page 69)
3. What is an operating income statement (P&L statement)? (See "Operating or Income Statement" page 73)
4. Why is it important to have an accountant or bookkeeper working with you? (See "Hiring an Accountant or Bookkeeper" page 76)
5. Why is it important to do business budgeting on a yearly basis? (See "Budgeting for Profit and Cash Flow" pages 76–77)

Financial Controls

Communication is a wonderful thing when it works. Communication takes on a new importance when it's about money. Money is a necessity of life, and many people treat threats to their money as threats to their person. Accounting procedures and statements provide a standardized way for people to communicate about financial and business situations.

The purpose of the highly structured world of accounting is to provide the business owner/manager and others with the information needed to manage a business or evaluate investments. Accounting is how businesses keep score, and just like keeping score in sports, there are numerous rules and procedures to accurately reflect the results of actions on the field.

Learning Objective 1: Explain the three main types of financial statements and how to use them.

Learning Objective 2: Discuss charts of accounts and how they organize the financial activities of the business.

Learning Objective 3: Discuss the importance and use of the income statement.

Learning Objective 4: Define a balance sheet and explain why it is an excellent financial management tool.

Learning Objective 5: Describe cash flow analysis.

Learning Objective 6: Explain gross profit margin.

UNDERSTANDING FINANCIAL STATEMENTS

Even if you have, or plan to have, an accountant or bookkeeper manage your financial records, you still need to understand basic financial terms so that you can make reasonable financial decisions.

Using financial statements effectively, along with a valid sales/profit/expense forecast, gives you a preview of good times and bad times so that you can take proactive measures.

Basic Financial Statements

This chapter introduces you to financial statements and explains their basic purpose. There are three basic financial statements:

1. Income statement, also known as the profit and loss (P&L) or operating statement
2. Balance sheet
3. Statement of cash flows

The income statement shows you the sales revenue, expense, and net income (or loss) of your company during a specific accounting period, which is usually a fiscal month, quarter, or year. The balance sheet shows you how much you own and how much you owe at a particular point in time. This is usually calculated at the end of a fiscal quarter and on the last day of the fiscal year. The statement of cash flows shows exactly how much cash you actually received and how much cash you spent on a periodic basis. You must watch your cash flow statement carefully because it tells you how much money you have or will have in the bank, so that you can pay your bills. Most likely, your accountant will advise you to operate your business on the accrual method of accounting, mainly because you receive deposits from clients and not all your products and services are delivered at the same time.

CHART OF ACCOUNTS

One of the procedures accountants use to make record keeping easier and more understandable is summarizing transactions so that similar transactions are grouped together. They do this by using a chart of accounts. This chart lists all the possible categories of transactions and organizes them in such a way as to produce financial statements.

- Group accounts that summarize the assets and liabilities of the company to form the balance sheet.
- Group accounts that summarize the sales and expenses of the company to form the income statement.
- If you are using the accrual method of accounting, you will also need a financial statement that details cash flow activity, which is likely to be different from the activity shown on the income statement. Cash-basis companies might not need as elaborate an analysis to generate a good understanding of their cash flows, but they should still be aware that lags between billing and collection could adversely affect their cash position.

Those statements, taken together, describe the total financial condition and results of operations for the company. The statement of cash flow uses information from both income and balance sheet statements.

It is critically important to set up these accounts for tax purposes and for the financial management information (reports) you need to make effective monetary decisions. Remember, you may not get to report any taxes on income if you don't manage your business well enough to have a positive net income at the end of the year.

Follow Industry Leaders

You don't have to reinvent the wheel when creating your chart of accounts. Talk to other successful kitchen and bath business owners to determine if they would share theirs with you—not their financial numbers, just their chart of accounts by name and number. This is an easy way to get started. The software package you decide on may even include it.

Table 5.1 is a sample chart of accounts that the typical kitchen and bath business might use. You are not limited to the number (quantity) of accounts that you choose to use. Our recommendation is to use as many as possible. The more you break down the expense portion of the income statement, the easier it is to monitor and control expenditures. Breaking out sales by product also allows you to track progress and profitability.

TABLE 5.1 Sample Chart of Accounts

BALANCE SHEET

Assets	Account No.	Description
Current Assets	100	Cash
	110	Savings Account
	120	Accounts Receivable
	130	Inventory
	140	Prepaid Expenses
	150	Other Current Assets
Total Current Assets		

	Account No.	Description
Long-term Assets	200	Land
	210	Buildings
	220	Equipment and Machinery
	230	Vehicles
	240	Furniture
	250	Other Equipment/Computers
	260	Other Long-term Assets
Total Long-term Assets		

Liabilities and Owner's Equity

	Account No.	Description
Current Liabilities	400	Notes Payable (less than 1 year)
	410	Accounts Payable
	420	Client Deposits
	430	Taxes Payable
	440	Accrued Expenses
	450	Other Current Liabilities
Total Current Liabilities		

	Account No.	Description
Long-term Liabilities	500	Notes Payable (more than 1 year)
	510	Mortgage Payable
	520	Installment Debt Payable
	530	Other Long-term Liabilities
Total Long-term Liabilities		

	Account No.	Description
Owner's Equity	600	Paid-in Capital
	610	Retained Earnings
Total Owner's Equity		

Total Liabilities and Owner's Equity		

(continued)

TABLE 5.1 *(Continued)*

PROFIT AND LOSS STATEMENT

Income

	Account No.	Description
Sales	700	Sales
	700.10	Cabinets
	700.20	Countertops
	700.30	Plumbing
	700.40	Lighting
	700.50	Appliances
	700.60	Installation
	700.70	Freight Income
Cost of Goods Sold	800	Cost of Goods Sold
	800.10	Cabinets
	800.20	Countertops
	800.30	Plumbing
	800.40	Lighting
	800.50	Appliances
	800.60	Installation
	800.70	Freight and Delivery
Gross Profit	900	Gross Profit
	900.10	Cabinets
	900.20	Countertops
	900.30	Plumbing
	900.40	Lighting
	900.50	Appliances
	900.60	Installation

Expenses

	Account No.	Description
Operating Expenses	1000	Operating Expenses
	1010	Personnel
	1010.10	Officers
	1010.20	Payroll—Exempt
	1010.30	Payroll—Nonexempt
	1010.40	Commissions
	1010.50	Bonuses/Incentives
	1010.60	Overtime
	1010.70	Payroll Taxes
	1010.80	Insurance—Health/Medical
	1010.90	Insurance—Workers' Compensation

PROFIT AND LOSS STATEMENT

Expenses *(continued)*	Account No.	Description
Facilities and Equipment	1100	Facilities and Equipment
	1100.10	Depreciation
	1100.20	Car/Truck Rental
	1100.30	Fuel
	1100.40	Office Equipment Rental
	1100.50	Building Rent
	1100.60	Vehicle Maintenance
	1100.70	Building Maintenance
	1100.80	Insurance—Fire and General
	1100.90	Insurance—Vehicle
	1100.100	Utilities
	1100.110	Property Taxes
Other Operating Expenses	1200	Other Operating Expenses
	1200.10	Advertising—Internet
	1200.20	Advertising—Publications
	1200.30	Advertising—Radio and Television
	1200.40	Advertising—Direct Mail
	1200.50	Advertising—Yellow Pages
	1200.60	Advertising—Other
	1200.70	Promotions
	1200.80	Conventions and Meetings
	1200.90	Travel and Entertainment
	1200.100	Dues and Subscriptions
	1200.110	Legal Fees
	1200.120	Accounting Fees
	1200.130	Supplies
	1200.140	Postage
	1200.150	Telephone (less Yellow Pages)
	1200.160	IRA—Pension Contributions
	1200.170	Provision for Bad Debt
	1200.180	Bank—Service Charges
	1200.190	Donations
	1200.200	Licenses—Auto and Business
	1200.210	Computer Expenses

(continued)

TABLE 5.1 *(Continued)*

PROFIT AND LOSS STATEMENT

Expenses *(continued)*	Account No.	Description
	1200.220	Employee Training
	1200.230	Showroom Expenses
	1200.240	Cleaning Services
	1200.250	Alarm Expenses

Total Expenses		

Total Net Operating Income		

Other Income/Expenses

Other Income	1300	Discounts and Purchases
	1400	Interest Income
	1500	Refunds and Adjustments
Total Other Income		

Other Expenses	1600	Interest on Line of Credit
	1700	Interest Expense
	1800	State Income Tax
Total Other Expenses		

Net Other Income		
Net Income/Loss before Taxes		

Net Income		

Income Statement

Your income (P&L or operating) statement shows whether your business is profitable. The statement totals the amount of revenue and then subtracts the expenses associated with making that revenue. The result is the pretax profit. After taxes are paid, you will have your net income.

Income statements show you how much you sold and how much it cost you to create these sales during a particular period. Unfortunately, many K&B businesses have their income statements prepared at year end or once a year for tax purposes. This is the only time the owner knows for sure how the business is doing. It is recommended that very K&B business should generate monthly income statements. This way, if something is out of kilter and the business

Impact of Monthly P&L Statement Review

Ramifications of Yearly P&L Statement Review

is not performing well, you can respond, act, change, and correct whatever it is that is not working. Those who wait until year end to learn that the business has been operating at a loss will have a much tougher time turning things around. It is much easier to plug a hole in a rowboat when you first see the leak than when the boat is sinking.

Once you and your accountant/bookkeeper have created your chart of accounts and you input the numbers into the software daily, it is easy and no more costly to run the income statement report monthly than it is to do so once a year.

The key is that you, the owner/manager, have to discipline yourself to spend the time it takes to analyze the monthly income statement in a timely manner. You should get the statement by the tenth of the following month, and you should review it within two or three days. This is your report card. It is the management tool that says either you are doing a great job and earning a nice return on your investment or you're doing a poor job and need to make some serious adjustments.

Once you learn how to read and analyze your financial statements, you will look forward to getting them and you will benefit from spotting those areas that still need a little attention and work. If you are going to invest all the money to start the business and you are going to commit the bulk of your waking hours to it, shouldn't you try to run the best business possible?

If you cannot find a half hour or so each month to review how you are doing, the next book you read should be on time management. If you had invested $250,000 in the stock market, you would likely check the Dow Jones on a daily basis. Doesn't your business deserve the same attention?

Sales Revenues

Sales revenues are the first numbers on an operating statement. They show what your sales are for a given period (monthly, quarterly, yearly). If you sell multiple products and services, break them out by category (i.e., cabinets, countertops, appliances, installation, etc.) so you will be able to track each category and make sound business decisions.

Expenses

Expenses fall into two categories: cost of sales expenses and operating or fixed expenses.

Cost of Sales Expenses

Cost of sales expenses, also referred to as cost of goods sold (COGS) are those directly related to your products and installation (if you install). These costs generally include the cost of the products—namely, what you paid your suppliers. If you install, COGS are the cost of your labor and any outside subcontractors. You monitor these costs with timely job-costing reviews. Unmonitored, you may be suffering from gross profit margin erosion and not know what the cause is.

Categorized COGS will be exactly like sales to enable you to determine profitability by product category. Subtract COGS from the total sales to get your gross profit or gross margin. These are profit dollars you made on the sale.

Operating and Fixed Expenses

The next part of the income statement is your operating and fixed expenses. These are the expenses associated with running your business. They include payroll (including your salary), rent, utilities, insurance, and so on. Operating expenses also include a few items that are not necessarily fixed in terms of dollar amount but are still are shown in this section as regular monthly expenses; these might include, for example, commissions or advertising expenses, which will vary from month to month. As mentioned earlier, the more chart of accounts (i.e., listing of expense items) that you show here, the easier it is for you to track and compare where the dollars are going.

The next and most important section of the income statement is the bottom line, or net income. This is the number that tells you whether making that monetary investment and working 60 to 80 hours a week has been worth it.

To summarize:

Net Sales	**1,550,000**	**100.0%**
– Cost of Goods Sold	990,000	64.0%
= Gross Profit	560,000	36.0%
– Expenses	490,000	32.0%
= Operating Profits	70,000	4.0%
– Taxes	21,000	1.4%
= Net Income (Profit)	**49,000**	**3.7%**

If the business is showing a net profit, the government will want its share. Do not fight it. In fact, be happy you have to pay taxes—it means you made money. Your accountant will work with you through good tax planning to help you minimize your taxes, both for the business and personally.

Table 5.2 is a detailed sample of an income statement. It reflects the chart of accounts discussed previously and shows all of the parts that make up what might be a typical P&L statement for a kitchen and bath business. Compare this to what you currently generate. If it makes sense to make some changes, meet with your accountant and make them.

TABLE 5.2 Sample Income Statement

PROFIT AND LOSS STATEMENT

Income	Account No.	Description	Amount
Sales	700	Sales	
	700.10	Cabinets	
	700.20	Countertops	
	700.30	Plumbing	
	700.40	Lighting	
	700.50	Appliances	
	700.60	Installation	
	700.70	Fright Income	
Cost of Goods Sold	800	Cost of Goods Sold	
	800.10	Cabinets	
	800.20	Countertops	
	800.30	Plumbing	
	800.40	Lighting	
	800.50	Appliances	
	800.60	Installation	
	800.70	Freight and Delivery	
Gross Profit	900	Gross Profit	
	900.10	Cabinets	
	900.20	Countertops	
	900.30	Plumbing	
	900.40	Lighting	
	900.50	Appliances	
	900.60	Installation	

Expenses

Operating Expenses			
Operating Expenses	1000	Operating Expenses	
	1010	Personnel	
	1010.10	Officers	
	1010.20	Payroll—Exempt	
	1010.30	Payroll—Nonexempt	
	1010.40	Commissions	
	1010.50	Bonuses/Incentives	
	1010.60	Overtime	
	1010.70	Payroll Taxes	
	1010.80	Insurance—Health/Medical	
	1010.90	Insurance—Workers' Comp	

(continued)

TABLE 5.2 *(Continued)*

PROFIT AND LOSS STATEMENT

Expenses *(continued)*	Account No.	Description	Amount
Facilities and Equipment	1100	Facilities and Equipment	
	1100.10	Depreciation	
	1100.20	Car/Truck Rental	
	1100.30	Fuel	
	1100.40	Office Equipment Rental	
	1100.50	Building Rent	
	1100.60	Vehicle Maintenance	
	1100.70	Building Maintenance	
	1100.80	Insurance—Fire and General	
	1100.90	Insurance—Vehicle	
	1100.100	Utilities	
	1100.110	Property Taxes	
Other Operating Expense	1200	Other Operating Expense	
	1200.10	Advertising—Internet	
	1200.20	Advertising—Publications	
	1200.30	Advertising—Radio and Television	
	1200.40	Advertising—Direct Mail	
	1200.50	Advertising—Yellow Pages	
	1200.60	Advertising—Other	
	1200.70	Promotions	
	1200.80	Conventions and Meetings	
	1200.90	Travel and Entertainment	
	1200.100	Dues and Subscriptions	
	1200.110	Legal Fees	
	1200.120	Accounting Fees	
	1200.130	Supplies	
	1200.140	Postage	
	1200.150	Telephone (less Yellow Pages)	
	1200.160	IRA—Pension Contributions	
	1200.170	Provision for Bad Debt	
	1200.180	Bank—Service Charges	
	1200.190	Donations	
	1200.200	Licenses—Auto and Business	
	1200.210	Computer Expenses	
	1200.220	Employee Training	
	1200.230	Showroom Expenses	
	1200.240	Cleaning Services	
	1200.250	Alarm Expenses	

Total Expenses			

Total Net Operating Income			

PROFIT AND LOSS STATEMENT

Other Income/Expenses	Account No.	Description	Amount
Other Income	1300	Discounts and Purchases	
	1400	Interest Income	
	1500	Refunds and Adjustments	
Total Other Income			

Other Expenses	1600	Interest on Line of Credit	
	1700	Interest Expense	
	1800	State Income Tax	
Total Other Expenses			

Net Other Income
Net Income/Loss before Taxes

Net Income

BALANCE SHEET

An income statement reflects the flow of money in and out of your business during a specific period of time. Alternatively, the balance sheet (Table 5.3) shows the amount of assets and liabilities at a particular point in time. The balance sheet is based on a fundamental equation of accounting: assets = liabilities + owner equity.

Assets

Assets are those items of value that the company owns, such as cash in the checking account, accounts receivable (money clients owe you), inventory, furniture, equipment, and property. Base the value of an asset on its initial purchase price minus any applicable depreciation (the account-tracked decrease in value that occurs as an asset ages).

Liquid and Fixed Assets

The definition of assets is broken out even further: some assets are referred to as liquid assets and others as fixed assets. Liquid assets include cash and anything you own that you can quickly convert into cash in less than 12 months (inventory, vehicles, furniture, etc.). Fixed assets are those that are more difficult to convert quickly (buildings, machinery, etc.).

Assets have three values:

- Initial purchase cost;
- Book value (purchase cost minus depreciation); and,
- Market value (what someone would pay for the asset today, disregarding any depreciated value.)

Liabilities

On the other side of the ledger of the balance sheet are the liabilities. These are the amounts of money that you owe. Typical liabilities might include accounts payable (reflecting the monies you owe to suppliers), loans (banks, credit unions, etc.), credit cards, taxes, and any people or institutions to whom you owe money.

TABLE 5.3 Sample Balance Sheet

BALANCE SHEET

	Account No.	Description	Amount
Current Assets	100	Cash	
	110	Savings Account	
	120	Accounts Receivable	
	130	Inventory	
	140	Prepaid Expenses	
	150	Other Current Assets	
Total Current Assets			

	Account No.	Description	Amount
Long-term Assets	200	Land	
	210	Buildings	
	220	Equipment and Machinery	
	230	Vehicles	
	240	Furniture	
	250	Other Equipment/Computers	
	260	Other Long-term Assets	
Total Long-term Assets			

Liabilities and Owner's Equity

	Account No.	Description	Amount
Current Liabilities	400	Notes Payable (less than 1 Year)	
	410	Accounts Payable	
	420	Client Deposits	
	430	Taxes Payable	
	440	Accrued Expenses	
	450	Other Current Liabilities	
Total Current Liabilities			

	Account No.	Description	Amount
Long-term Liabilities	500	Notes Payable (more than 1 year)	
	510	Mortgage Payable	
	520	Installment Debt Payable	
	530	Other Long-term Liabilities	
Total Long-term Liabilities			

	Account No.	Description	Amount
Owner's Equity	600	Paid-in Capital	
	610	Retained Earnings	
Total Owner's Equity			

Total Liabilities and Owner's Equity			

Year	$ Earnings/Loss
1	<10,000>
2	20,000
3	50,000
4	90,000
5	130,000
	$280,000

FIGURE 5.1 Retained Earnings. The retained earnings for this five-year period would be $280,000.

Liabilities are broken out as:

- Short term (or current) liabilities, which are monies that will be paid back within a 12-month period.
- Long-term liabilities, which are monies that are not due within the next 12 months (i.e., those that will be paid back in 13 months or longer).

The next part of the balance sheet is owner equity. This is the part that makes a balance sheet balance. When you subtract liabilities from assets, the result is owner equity. You are taking what you owe away from what you own. Owner equity is derived by adding the initial investment of your company stock and the accumulated retained earnings of the business together. Retained earnings are the accumulation of each year's profit or loss from year 1 to the current year (Figure 5.1).

As your company grows, the numbers on your assets, liabilities, and equity lines will usually grow larger too. This happens because you will be purchasing new equipment, computers, software, and inventory (if you carry any). Accounts receivable will also be growing. Companies just starting out typically will have small numbers on their assets, liabilities, and equity lines. Your focus as an owner should be on generating positive net income. Doing this creates positive and growing retained earnings, thereby increasing the owner equity.

Figure 5.2 is a simplified example of a balance sheet.

Paying Taxes Is a Good Thing to Do

All too often, small business owners manage their businesses and finances so that they show a very small or negative income and, as a result, pay little or no taxes.

Assets	
Cash	$25,000
Accounts Receivable	$100,000
Inventory	$25,000
Fixed Assets	$175,000
Total Assets	**$325,000**
Liabilities	
Short Term	$65,000
Long Term	$100,000
Total Liabilities	**$165,000**
Owner Equity	
Capital Stock	$10,000
Retained Earnings	$150,000
Total Owner Equity	**$160,000**

Assets ($325,000) = Liabilities ($165,000) + Owner Equity ($160,000)

FIGURE 5.2 Simplified Example of a Balance Sheet

Since small, privately owned companies do not face the same scrutiny that larger investor-owned businesses face, there is minimal pressure to show a positive net income. If you take this approach with your business, be prepared to answer some pretty tough questions if you ever need to present negative income financial statements to outside investors, such as bankers, venture capitalists—or worse, the Internal Revenue Service.

Moreover, if you decide you want to sell your business, it will not command a good selling price. Many buyers include a multiplier of three to seven times earnings as part of the formula to value a business they are considering. EBIDA (earnings before interest, depreciation, and amortization—a formula banks and business brokers use to value a business—reflects that $5 \times$ Nothing = Nothing. Again, get your professional accountant's advice in this area.

CASH FLOW ANALYSIS

A cash flow analysis is a very important financial statement because it tells you whether you have or will have enough cash to pay your bills. The key challenge is keeping more cash coming in than is going out.

A cash flow analysis, or statement of cash flow, looks a lot like an income statement. The major difference is that your income statement focuses on earnings from operations, whereas the cash flow analysis also reflects investments, borrowings, repayments of loan principals, and other balance sheet changes. Cash flow from operations might also be significantly different from reported earnings, especially if you are using the accrual method of accounting. Remember also that your income statement might be based on accrual accounting methods, whereas your cash flow statement is based on *actual* cash in and out flows.

The reason you need both an income statement and a cash flow statement is that you might have a good month of sales followed by a bad month of sales. The bad month may be so bad, in fact, that you may have to get a loan to cover your expenses.

By watching your cash flow analysis, you can see in advance when you will start to run out of cash during that month. However, because an income statement is based on an accrual basis of accounting records when obligations are made, and not when the cash is either spent or received, the good months and bad months often even themselves out. You would not know by looking at your income statement that August (the bad month) almost put you out of business due to lack of available cash. However, your monthly cash flow analysis would alert you to potential problems before they become real ones. Therefore, it is imperative that you use all three financial statements to get an accurate picture of your company's financial condition.

Cash flow is your lifeblood—without it, your business will not survive. One more reason, then, to create a budget is to ensure you will have adequate cash flow. Without consistent, sufficient cash flow to buy inventory, pay bills, handle payroll, pay yourself, and do marketing, you will go out of business. Preserving and defending your cash flow is critical.

Aside from creating a budget, there are three more ways to control your cash flow.

1. **Live by this rule:** Without cash, your business will not survive.
2. **Create cash flow projections.** You need to know what will come in and when. Realistic cash flow projections are essential. The question to ask is: What do you expect your cash balance to be in six months?
3. **Keep the pipeline open.** A client or customer you acquire today may sign a contract and give you a deposit, but it may be several months before you finish the work and collect the final payment. You have to keep acquiring new clients and work to keep the cash flow spigot open.

A cash flow crunch is usually the result of poor planning. All businesses have cycles, so plan for them. Most kitchen and bath dealers experience cyclical sales: slower winter sales and stronger spring, summer, and fall sales. Using sales and promotions during the slower period may help to balance out your cash flow.

Managing cash flow can be difficult in both good and bad times. Knowing in advance—through good forecasting—will help you stay on top of this critical piece of your financial plan. Tables 5.4 and 5.5 provide useful templates to help you manage cash flow.

Managing the Cash Flow

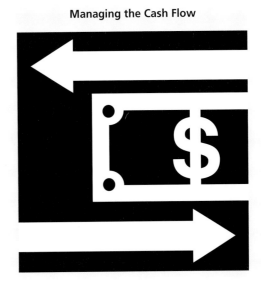

TABLE 5.4 Cash Flow Template

	JAN	FEB	MAR	APR	MAY	JUNE	JULY	AUG	SEPT	OCT	NOV	DEC
1. Cash on hand at beginning of month (equals line 15 from prior month)												
CASH IN												
2. Cash sales												
3. Payments on open accounts (accounts receivable)												
4. Deposits on new sales												
5. Other cash in												
6. TOTAL CASH IN (add lines 1–5)												
CASH OUT												
7. Purchases for cash (inventory)												
8. Payment on invoices (accounts payable)												
9. Variable expenses												
10. Fixed expenses (operating expenses)												
11. Other cash out												
12. TOTAL CASH OUT (add lines 7–11)												
13. Capital expenditures (fixed asset purchases)												
14. Loans (+ /–)												
15. NET CASH Month-end (Line 6–Line 12) +/– Line 13 +/– Line 14 Total carries to first line of next month												

Fixed expenses are recurring items that can't easily be changed, such as rent, debt, and payroll. Variable expenses include advertising, supplies, promotion, consulting, and other expenses that can easily be increased or decreased from month to month. Capital expenditures are purchases of equipment, furniture, etc.

TABLE 5.5 Weekly Cash Flow Report

Week Ending:	Total Cash Received: $

Customer Deposits Received: $	
Customer Name:	Payment Amount:
Customer Name:	Payment Amount:
Customer Name:	Payment Amount:
Customer Name:	Payment Amount:
Customer Name:	Payment Amount:
Customer Name:	Payment Amount:

Customer Payments Received: $	
Customer Name:	Payment Amount:
Customer Name:	Payment Amount:
Customer Name:	Payment Amount:
Customer Name:	Payment Amount:
Customer Name:	Payment Amount:
Customer Name:	Payment Amount:

Total Booked Sales:	
Sales Tax Liability:	
Total Available Cash	$
Checking Account Balance	$
Money Market Account	$
Special 2% Account	$
Line of Credit Available	$

Cash Flow Forecast

Once you have completed your sales and operating statement forecast, you can move onto the all-important cash flow forecast.

The cash flow forecast is important to you, as the owner or manager of a kitchen and bathroom firm. It is the one statement you can use most effectively to guide your business through the maze of hidden costs. Without such a plan, you may have to pay interest and penalties if you cannot pay your bills and taxes on time. Or, if you estimate a job based on a discounted price for materials you may be unable to take advantage of that discount because you do not have the funds available. Too often, people confuse cash flow with profits, but they are not the same thing. You can operate your business unprofitably for a long time before you realize you are in trouble because there is a steady cash flow through the business. You can also operate a business with a profit from the first day, but you may be out of business at the end of the first 30 days if you do not have sufficient cash flowing into the business. Insufficient capital or cash flow is the single most devastating cause of small-business failures.

The statement of cash flow really amounts to a calendar or schedule whereby you plot the payments that must be made within a specific time frame, and at the same time, try to anticipate which funds will be available to meet those obligations. Then you make arrangements to offset any expected shortfalls. By doing this ahead of time to avoid any penalty assessments or interest charges, you will avoid hidden charges which systematically eat away at your profit margins.

Don't Spend the Cash Too Fast

One of the dangers of cash flow management in the kitchen and bath industry is the temptation to spend deposit and second-payment monies received from work in progress on expenses for marketing initiatives rather than on the actual products purchased for the project.

It is not unusual in our industry to be cash rich and profit poor. Whether required or not, many successful kitchen and bath design firms follow a rigorous policy of paying large deposits on the products ordered for each project in tandem with client payments received. Some states require such a payment policy by law.

When planning major expansions or marketing initiatives, you must budget the expenses over a period of time so the cash needed to pay for these activities comes from profits generated by jobs already under way.

Don't Use the Cash Flow Statement
to Your Disadvantage

Your cash flow statement should show salaries for owners from the start of the business. Not including these salaries is unrealistic and is generally done only to show early profitability. This will not impress bankers, lenders, and investors. They want the facts as they really are, so produce your cash flow statements listing your salary and showing both profitable and unprofitable periods. Some businesses do not become profitable for quite some time, and astute lenders and investors already know how and where to find that information. Prepare two statements: one reflecting your cash position that shows where it really stands before any bank loans or investments, and a second version that shows the impact of the loan(s) and your ability to repay them within the limits of your projected revenues and cash flows.

Managing cash flow includes responsibilities with respect to the management of a firm's current assets:

- **Make deposits in a timely and routine manner.** If deposits are not in the bank, you will not be able to take advantage of early payment discounts. Furthermore, you may be subjecting your business to unnecessary fines and penalties.
- **Invoice in a timely manner.** If you employ a charge system for your clients, you need to ensure that they are billed as quickly as possible. At this point, they are using your money, and good cash management dictates that you convert your receivables to cash as quickly possible.
- **Work your aged receivables.** The faster you can turn your receivables into cash, the more quickly you can pay your own bills and avoid fines and penalties. You will also increase your ability to pay your bills early and thus take advantage of early payment discounts. Perhaps most important of all, you will increase the chances of collecting your money without hassle. If your customers are aware of how serious you are about collecting your money, no doubt you will be paid first.
- **Keep inventory levels low but profitable.** You must have inventory on hand to sell when customers are ready to buy; otherwise they will shop elsewhere. The problem is that, too often, a business will buy a large amount of inventory in order to get the best possible price and terms.

In order to manage the business effectively, you need as much flexibility as possible when it comes to your current assets. While inventory is a current asset, it is the least flexible in terms of liquidity. Be sure you maintain enough on hand to meet your requirements but not so much that you tie up the firm's ability to meet its short-term obligations.

What Happens to Cash Flow When You Hire an Untrained or Inexperienced Designer?

If you are the owner of the company and also its primary designer/salesperson, you might need to add an additional design specialist to your team. Adding such a person can wreak havoc with your cash flow during the training period. Your sales will dip as you spend more time in your management and training mode. The new designer may make some costly mistakes if you do not supervise him or her closely.

A new and inexperienced designer may require almost a full year of your attention before he or she can generate a reasonable sales volume. This expansive period is caused by the length of time consumers take to make decisions regarding new kitchens or baths, the ordering time for such projects, and the installation time. Assume a three-month getting-to-know-one-another period, followed by a three-month period of carefully supervised project planning and presentation, concluding with a six-month trial period where you continue to keep a watchful eye on the designs produced and the estimates prepared by this new individual. Carefully review client satisfaction with a new designer during this preliminary training period. Make sure you adjust your cash flow projections so that you can manage a decrease in revenue as well as budget for the nonproductive start-up period required by a new employee.

Accounts Receivable Aging Report

The accounts receivable aging report (Table 5.6) is another invaluable tool. It tells you who still owes you money and how far past due they might be with their payments.

You may or may not offer open credit accounts to your customers. For most homeowners, it is not a requirement, but homebuilders and remodel contractors may require it. Regardless, in the course of operating a kitchen and bath business, you may expect to take multiple deposits for products and services as the job progresses, but experience has shown that this does not always happen. A client may fall behind in payments for any number of reasons. Your job is to stay on top of the money owed to you (accounts receivable) and be sure that you are paid in full in a timely manner. Since cash is king and you cannot operate your business without it, you have to manage it from all directions. If you keep your collections in order, your need for extra cash will diminish or be eliminated all together.

TABLE 5.6 Sample Accounts Receivable Aging Report

Customer Name	0–30 Days	31–60 Days	61–90 Days	90+ Days

FINANCIAL RATIO ANALYSIS

All the numbers in a financial ratio analysis can seem overwhelming when you are trying to see the big picture and make general conclusions about the financial performance and condition of the business.

One useful way to interpret financial reports is to complete ratios: that is, divide a particular number in the financial report by another number.

Financial statement ratios are also useful because they enable you to compare a business's current performance with its past performance or with the performance of another business, regardless of whether sales revenues or net income was bigger or smaller for the other years or the other business. Using ratios cancels out size differences.

You will not find many ratios in financial reports. Publicly owned businesses are required to report just one ratio (earnings per share [EPS]), and privately owned businesses generally do not report any ratios. So why bring it up? Ratios are terrific indicators on how the business is performing. When buying a house, you or your real estate agent may do comparatives (or comps) on other homes in the same neighborhood. These comps might be on selling price or, more likely, on cost per square foot (total cost divided by square footage). Certainly there are other variables (condition and age of the home, quality of the kitchen and bath, etc.), but at least the square footage ratio gives you a guide.

In the kitchen and bath industry, there are several sources for guidelines, benchmarks, and comparative figures.

- **National Kitchen & Bath Association.** NKBA currently offers a number of surveys and research findings (NKBA.org).
- **Trade magazine reports.** Several industry publications regularly report on specific and general financial ratios or business systems.
- **Cabinet company dealer counsel shared reports.** Some manufacturers assist their dealers with business management by creating a platform where similar business models can exchange financial ratio information.
- **Buying groups.** Similar to cabinet company networking, these groups offer a platform for firms to share information.

Estimates put the number of kitchen and bath dealers in the United States and Canada between 7,000 and 8,000. Some 2,000 are members of the NKBA.

Following is a sample income statement (Table 5.7) and balance sheet (Table 5.8) for a typical kitchen and bath business. These will serve as the example for the rest of this chapter. Notice that there is no statement of cash flow here, because no ratios are calculated from data in this financial statement.

TABLE 5.7 Income Statement for Year

Sales Revenue	$1,550,000
Cost of Goods Sold	$990,000
Gross Margin	$560,000
Operating Expenses	$490,000
Operating Profit	$70,000
Earnings before Tax	$70,000
Net Income	$49,000

TABLE 5.8 Balance Sheet at End of Year

Assets

Cash	$75,000
Accounts Receivable	$89,000
Inventory	$25,000
Current Assets	$189,000
Fixed Assets	$93,000
Accumulative Depreciation	$38,000
Total Assets	$320,000

Liabilities

Accounts Payable	$40,000
Short-term Notes Payable	0
Current Liabilities	$85,000
Long-term Notes Payable	$20,000

Owner Equity

Capital Stock	$10,000
Retained Earning	$165,000
Total Liabilities + Retained Earnings	$320,000

Gross Profit Margin Ratio

Making bottom-line profit begins with making sales and earning sufficient gross margin from those sales. "Sufficient" means that your gross margin must cover the expenses of making sales, operating the business, as well as paying interest and income tax expenses, so that there is still an adequate amount left over for profit. Calculate the gross profit margin as follows:

Gross Margin ÷ Sales Revenue = Gross Margin Ratio

Gross Margin $560,000

Sales Revenue $1,550,000 = 36.13% Gross Profit Ratio

In the kitchen and bath industry, the gross profit margin ranges from as low as 30 percent to as high as 45 percent. For a firm operating in a showroom environment and offering installation services, the NKBA Dealer Profit Report average of 36.13 percent is marginal. Most industry experts believe a (very achievable) goal for all kitchen and bath businesses should be 40 percent and higher. You have invested too much money, too much work, and offer too many features and benefits not to achieve a higher gross profit margin.

Profit Ratio

Businesses are motivated by profit so the profit ratio is critical. The "bottom line" is not called the bottom line without good reason. The profit ratio indicates how much net income was earned on each $100 of sales revenue.

Net Income ÷ Sales Revenue = Profit Ratio

Net Income $49,000

Sales Revenue $1,550,000 = 3.16% Profit Ratio

This means that for every $100 in sales, the average kitchen and bath business earned $3.16. Comparatively speaking, that is poor. An average profit ratio for small business owners would be in the 5 percent to 10 percent range.

If the gross profit margin for kitchen and bath dealers had been the 40 percent we encouraged earlier, the profit ratio would have improved to 7 percent, or $7.00 earned for every $100 in sales. This would have been much more respectable.

Current Ratio

A test of the short-term solvency of a business is its capability to pay the liabilities that come due in the near future (up to one year). The current ratio is a rough indicator of whether cash on hand plus cash to be collected from accounts receivable and from selling inventory will be enough to pay off the liabilities that will come due in the next period.

As you can imagine, lenders (banks, credit unions, etc.) are particularly keen on punching in the numbers to calculate the current ratio. Here is how they do it:

Current Assets ÷ Current Liabilities = Current Ratio

Current Assets $189,000

Current Liabilities $85,000 = 2.22% Current Ratio

A business is are expected to maintain a 2 to 1 current ratio, which means its current assets should be twice its current liabilities. In fact, some lenders may legally require a business to stay above a minimum current ratio.

Our example shows K&B businesses at a very healthy 2.22 to 1 current ratio, mainly because the current liabilities are relatively low.

Quick Ratio

The quick ratio compares cash and accounts receivable to current liabilities and assesses the ability of your business to meet its current financial obligations in the event that sales decline and inventories cannot readily be converted to cash. The quick ratio is also called the acid test because it measures only ready assets. Here is how it works:

Cash + Accounts Receivable ÷ Current Liabilities

Cash $75,000 + Accounts Receivable $89,000

Current Liabilities $85,000 = 1.93

An acid test (quick) ratio of 1 to 1 is considered acceptable, given the fact that an adequate means of collecting accounts receivables exists.

Using actual K&B industry numbers in this example shows a very respectable 1.93 to 1 acid test. The bankers would be pleased.

GROSS MARGIN

As you can see, using these ratios is not difficult, if you have the financial statement information and formulas for the ratios in front of you. It is logical that everyone who has invested money, sweat, love, and tears into a business wants to know what the business performance is compared to local competitors and peers in the industry. Putting these ratios to work tells you where you stand, where you are doing well, and, more important, where you need to improve.

At the very top of the income (P&L) statement shown earlier is "sales revenue". The next line is "cost of goods sold," followed by "gross margin" (often referred to as gross profit). A lot of people get confused with exactly what gross margin is because the income statement also has a line item called net profit (the very last line of the operating statement). That's why people refer to net profit as the bottom line—that's exactly what it is, the bottom line of the operating statement.

Net profit is what the business made (or lost) after all expenses, interest, and taxes have been paid.

Gross margin (or gross profit) is the profit on goods and services sold, less the cost of those goods and services, but before operating expenses. Here is a simplified example: You have sold a kitchen full of cabinets for $10,000. Your cost, including delivery of the cabinets to the job site, from your supplier is $6,000. By subtracting the cost of goods sold ($6,000) from the sale price of $10,000, you have a gross margin (profit) of $4,000. After this, you need to subtract the expenses related to operating the business (payroll, rent, utilities, advertising, supplies, etc.), which will give you the operating profit. From this, subtract any interest paid on loans and taxes, and you finally reach the bottom line or net profit.

For example:

Cabinet sale	$ 10,000
Cost of cabinets and delivery	$ 6,000
Gross margin on this sale	$ 4,000

If a business is going to operate profitably, the total gross margin dollars have to be larger than the total operating expense dollars. The NKBA Dealer Profit Report shows the participating businesses averaged a 36 percent gross profit margin and their operating expenses averaged 32 percent. The difference of 4 percent is what the profit was before taxes. The gross profit margin should be higher (40 percent or more), and the expenses should be lower (30 percent or less). Many kitchen and bath businesses currently operate at the better numbers. The challenge to you is to set goals of 40 percent gross profit margin and 30 percent on operating expenses.

Difference between Profit and Markup

It is surprising how many business owners and salespeople do not know the difference between profit and markup and do not know how to calculate it. Here are some examples that will clarify it.

You want to make a 40 percent margin on a cabinet sale. The cost of cabinets and delivery to you is $6,000:

Wrong calculation:

$1.4 \times \$6,000$ cost = $8,400 selling price or

$2,400 gross margin or

28.6% gross profit margin

Correct calculation:

100% minus 40% = 60%

$6,000 cost

.60 = $10,000 selling price or

$4,000 gross margin or

40.0% gross profit margin

When calculating, you do not multiply the cost of goods sold times the margin you want to make. Start with 100 percent, subtract the margin you want to make, and then divide this number into your cost of goods sold.

Profit and Markup Are Not the Same

Increase Markup Multiplier to Increase Margin

1.50 multiplier	=	33.0% margin
1.60 multiplier	=	37.5% margin
1.65 multiplier	=	39.0% margin
1.72 multiplier	=	42.0% margin
2.00 multiplier	=	50.0% margin

Gross Profit Margin Adjustment

The Power of Percentage Points

After establishing your sales goals, understand the power of percentage points. To make more money on the sale, raise your margins.

Once you have established your sales forecast, you will move on to gross profit. Will your margin increase, decrease, or stay the same? Plug in this number.

Gross Profit Margins

What a 3 percent Improvement in gross profit margin would mean to profit before taxes.

	Actual	w/Improvement
Sales	$1,550,000	$1,550,000
Cost of goods sold	990,000	943,950
Gross margin dollars	560,000	606,050
Gross margin percent	36.1%	39.1%
Operating expenses	490,000	490,000
Operating profit	70,000	116,050

This is only a $46,050 increase in operating profit before taxes and represents a 65.8 percent improvement in operating profit. Yes, all of this on a 3 percent improvement in gross profit margin. Make margin improvement a major focus of your business. Many well-run kitchen and bath businesses enjoy gross profit margins of 40 percent. This should be your goal. Margin is more important than sales volume. Be sure to really study your gross profit margins.

Do You Charge the Same Markup on All Parts of the Project?

There is no one right answer in our industry: Some industry experts will stress that once you have identified your desired profit margin within the budget, every single item receives that same markup. Others suggest that different areas of the business should operate as individual profit centers and may carry lower margins. In the kitchen industry, the norm is for cabinets installed to carry the desired margin of the firm. Appliance sales—and sometimes countertop sales—may carry a lower margin because of competitor pressures. Large projects where you are subcontracting out major renovation costs may be another area where lower margins are appropriate.

To determine the best business decision for your organization, study your competitive market, look at your business model, estimate the third stage of the budgeting process, and then decide what is right for you.

IDEAS ON HOW TO IMPROVE GROSS MARGINS

Two of the most important functions you will carry out as a kitchen and bath business owner are generating profitable sales and controlling expenses.

When these two things are done well, the business will be profitable and worth all of your hard work.

The Great Cash Hunt

Strategy No. 1: Increase Your Margin

A list of ideas that will help you grow your margin follows. Not all of them will feel good to you, but try out those that you feel make sense for your business. Every point you bump your margin up will be money in your pocket.

- Know which products and services are the most profitable to your business, and work hard to sell them. Make sure your salespeople know what those products are.
- Always start by trying to sell the higher-priced products. It is much easier to come down than it is to go up.
- If you sell from a manufacturer's suggested list price and give a discount off list, reduce the discount.
- If you work from a manufacturer's cost on products and add a markup (multiplier) to it, increase the markup multiplier.
- Mix up the discount or multiplier. Do not use the same number across the board. Make more on accessories, add-ons, and the less shopped items.
- Know the features and benefits of your salespeople, company, and products. Then be sure to articulate them to your clients. When you add value, price becomes less important.
- Sell a diversity of products. Make yourself the one-stop shopping headquarters for kitchens, baths, libraries, entertainment centers, fireplace mantels, home offices, and so on.
- Market yourself as a design-build firm. Price the complete project, including all products and installation. Make it difficult for the clients to "shop you" (get alternative estimates based on the exact same specifications). Sell kitchens, not cabinets.

- Sell add-ons and always at better margins. Be sure to have one "wow" kitchen and bath display that shows every "bell and whistle" possible. Then be sure your clients are aware of the features—and make a higher margin on the extras and add-ons.
- Make a profit on freight. If freight to you averages 12 percent from the manufacturer, charge your clients 14 percent or 15 percent.
- Encourage (insist on) job site delivery from your manufacturers. There will be less handling and less breakage.
- Negotiate better deals with your vendors. You don't know if you don't ask. You can make as much money on how you buy as how you sell.
- Be a valued partner with your suppliers. The more important you are, the easier it will be to negotiate better deals.
- Study the advantages of being a member of a buying group.
- Price change orders at higher margins.
- Ask for referral fees from suppliers and subcontractors. If you are referring a lot of business to them, it should be worth something to you.
- Do not ever give out product names or numbers. Do not make it easy for the client to shop you.
- If you must warehouse products because a job is not progressing on schedule, charge a warehousing fee (unless, of course, it is you who held up the schedule).
- Know and shop your competitors. Know what products and services they offer and at what price point.
- Add a contingency percentage (1 percent, 2 percent, or 3 percent) to every quote to cover all the things that can and do go wrong on jobs.
- Tie your salespeople's compensation to sales and margin performance (i.e., the higher the sales and margin, the higher the compensation). Motivate them to increase margins.
- Teach salespeople how to sell in order to maximize the gross profit margin. Teach the basics, then practice, practice, practice!

Sales volume is very important, but a profitable sales volume driven by a good gross margin is most important.

Strategy No. 2: Pay Yourself First

Go for the Low-Hanging Fruit First

(Easy Profit Improvements)

Two Percent Is Heaven Sent[1]

The most important cash that we can earn is the cash that flows through to *you*, the business owner. After all, if there is no money for you at the end of the day, then you are going to be very unhappy. It is doubtful that you will be hiring any new staff, enlarging your showroom, or buying a new car. If you are not enjoying personal cash, then why put up with the headaches of being a business owner? If you are not generating personal cash, it is a good bet that your growth rate will be as flat as your wallet. Remember, profits are good, and cash is paramount.

Often it is difficult to understand the true profitability of a small, closely held business. Bottom-line net profit often ranges from 2 percent to 5 percent. If we generate additional profit, we try to spend monies on goods and services that will improve our business.

Let's assume that your firm is generating 2 percent or more net profit. At the end of the year, are you going to look at your bottom line and wonder where the cash went? It happens to business owners all the time! The answer to that quandary is to take your cash up front.

Open an interest-bearing account at the financial institution of your choice. Then every day take 2 percent of every dollar that your firm receives and put it into that account. Make sure that only you, the business owner, can access the funds that accrue. In our firm, we call it the special account, and it appears as an entry on our balance sheet. At the end of the year, you will no longer be wondering where your 2 percent profit went. It will be right there, earning interest!

Let's assume that your business had $800,000 in sales this year:

$$.02 \times \$800,000 = \$16,000$$

If your business grows by 5 percent each year for five years:

$$.02 \times \$800,000 = \$16,000$$
$$.02 \times \$840,000 = \$16,800$$
$$.02 \times \$882,000 = \$17,640$$
$$.02 \times \$926,100 = \$18,522$$
$$.02 \times \$972,405 = \$19,448$$

The total 2 percent saved up front in five years is $88,410 plus interest!

You already know that you are going to generate 2 percent or more net profit this year. Taking the 2 percent up front ensures you that cash will be there for you when you need it. Use it for your retirement, to pay college tuition, or buy your own building. Best of all, when you have a tough day—and we all have plenty of those in our business—it is gratifying to check out your 2 percent account and find that it is bigger than it was the day before.

Strategy No. 3: Once the Project Is Sold, Minimize Profit Drain by Closely Watching Cost Discrepancy

The Great Cash Hunt

There is no question that your time is more valuable on the sales floor or creating a great design. Let your office personnel handle all of the other non–income-producing tasks. You do not need to open the mail, review purchase orders, or log invoices for payment. You should, however, make sure that every check being sent out has your signature on it. With every check ready to be signed, insist that the gross profit made on the items being paid for be noted along with the check. If you thought that you should be grossing 40 percent on your stainless sinks and the note attached to the check shows 33 percent, then you've got a problem. If the margin is not what you think it should be, give it back to your office manager with instructions to find out why. A sharp office manager will already have determined where the problem lies.

In our business, we use "blue slips" (we print these forms on blue paper to make them stand out) for cost discrepancy reports. Our sales and design staff hate to see them coming! Figure 5.3 is an example of one of our blue slips.

COST DISCREPANCY REPORT

Job Name _____   Date _____

Item in Question_____

Item Cost on Purchase Order $ _____

Item Cost on Vendor Invoice $ _____

Difference between Anticipated Cost and Amount Invoiced $_____

Explanation/Action to Be Taken _____

Signature _____

FIGURE 5.3 Sample cost discrepancy report form

Strategy No. 4: Do Not Allow Salespeople to Alter Your Targeted Margins

Don't Cut Markup Factor to Lower Selling Price

1.72%
1.60%

20 Things to Do before Cutting the Price

Price is the most common objection kitchen and bath salespeople hear. Too often, salespeople try to overcome price objections simply by lowering the price—and their profit margins along with it. Here are 20 things to do before cutting the price.

1. Hold the conviction that your price is right. Fear of price is the weakest point in selling. If you aren't sure your price is fair, how can you convince your customers that it is? Confidence will win their respect.
2. Know your product.
3. Discuss the products that you offer. Someone can always offer an inferior product at a lower price.
4. Get all the facts. Check the local competition. What do they sell? How much do they charge?
5. Look for a catch in a competitive price. It is nearly always there. This is especially true with Internet pricing.
6. Find out if customers are bluffing. Do they really have a better offer elsewhere?
7. Sell your product and your service. Convince customers that differences in product quality justify your price.

8. Be flexible. Adjust the model quoted, the materials used, and so on, and then recalculate your price on the reduced package.
9. Feature your exclusive brands and the services that you provide that no local competitor can offer.
10. Cite some examples of dissatisfied people who bought on price alone—there are many.
11. Sell the qualities of your dealership. Emphasize all your good points: service, stock, reputation. Salesmanship can win over price alone.
12. Demonstrate the difference between price and value. Avoid arguments. Talk customer benefits.
13. Be sure to figure your own costs carefully to make sure you are on firm ground when price discussion becomes necessary.
14. Offer a concession. Make your customers feel that you are working for them and are always trying to find ways to give them better merchandise at a fair price.
15. If your service record is better than your competitor's, advise the prospective buyer to check on your reputation for service, deliveries, and general character. Make it the policy of your dealership to stand behind the products you sell. If something goes wrong with the product, tell customers that you will take responsibility personally.
16. Offer more. Offering accessories that your competitor does not, sometimes gives you an opportunity to enhance the deal for the prospective buyer.
17. A frank discussion of good business sense will show prospects that your price is fair and that they'll get better service from a firm that operates on a sound financial basis.
18. Show a different model. Then you and your competitor aren't competing on the same item.
19. Think of the future. Consider the ethics and future results of cutting a price today. Are you willing to offer that price to other prospects? Consider the problems of cutting prices too often.
20. Remember that in any price concession, every penny comes right out of your profits.

If They Tell You They Are "Shopping"

If prospects immediately tell you that they've already been looking around at other kitchen and bath dealerships, you might want to ask them these three questions: What have you seen? What have you seen that you've really liked? Why didn't you buy it? This will allow you to see their true objections.

Strategy No. 5: Look for Little Ways to Conduct Your Business More Efficiently

Loose Change: A penny saved is a penny earned.

Bottom-Line Boosters: 16 Ways to Cut Costs and Improve Your Profits

1. **Be a penny pincher on postage and overnight delivery.** The United States Postal Service (USPS) continues to raise prices. Here are some money savings ideas.
   - Sorting by zip code, zip+ 4, and printing bar codes on envelopes can net savings of almost 20 percent. Ask your local postmaster for details. The USPS will convert your mailing list (it must be on a computer disk) to zip+4 at no charge. Call the USPS Address Information Center at 800–238–3150 for information.
   - If your volume is not big enough for postal discounts, fine out if there is a postage "presort" company in your area. These firms collect mail from small businesses, do the presorting and bar coding, and everyone shares in the savings.
   - Get tough on private postage. Remind employees that stamps and the postage meter are not for their personal use.
   - Use postcards. They're quick, inexpensive, and convenient.
   - Use Priority Mail envelopes and boxes to take advantage of flat-rate mailing charges regardless of weight and delivery address.
   - Buy lighter envelopes.
   - Purge your mailing lists: Eliminate waste in your marketing efforts. Consider marketing alternatives.
   - Return damaged meter tapes to the USPS for refunds of up to 90 percent.
2. **When using FedEx and UPS, select the most cost-effective delivery schedule to take advantage of discounted shipping rates.**
3. **Reduce payroll frequency.** If you pay weekly, switch to every other week. Approximately 30 percent of small businesses still pay weekly, thus incurring higher costs.
4. **Reduce telephone costs.**
   - Directory assistance calls are no longer free. Make sure your employees use the Internet or telephone book.
   - Some long-distance carriers have a service available when calling from a hotel in order to avoid multiple access charges. Contact your long-distance operator to see if this service is available to you for your next hotel meeting.
   - Shorten long-distance calls if your land line charges extra for them; have a checklist prepared.
   - Review your cell phone plan to make sure it is the best one for your calling patterns.
   - Cut unauthorized employee calls by stating your policy and enforcing it. You can also purchase a device that hooks to your phone system and blocks expensive calls to 900, 976, 411, and other numbers.
   - Encourage more incoming faxes from customers and vendors. Get rid of your fax cover sheet to quicken each outgoing call
   - Use email whenever possible in lieu of telephone calls or faxes.
5. **Stop wasting money on office supplies, equipment, and printing.**
   - Do not photocopy items you should be printing. Copies cost 5 to 15 cents each. Printing can cost as little as 3 cents.
   - Select business forms of equal size. When printing them, have multiple forms combined in a gang run instead of printing them separately. This can save you up to 40 percent.
   - Review your office equipment service contracts. You may want to cancel contracts for fax machines, laser printers, and personal computers, because generally you will have fewer problems with these pieces of equipment. Be sure you do not have any ghost contracts for equipment you no longer use. Insist on single-year contracts.
6. **Review all advertising expenses.** Check the performance on all advertising by tracking results.
7. **Manage your inventory.** Inventory is cash sitting on the shelf. The cost of carrying excess, outdated, or slow-moving inventory can be costly.
8. **Tighten up on legal and accounting costs.** If you're using an accounting or law firm, especially a large one, put the business out to bid. You may be pleasantly surprised.

9. **Do not incur bank fees on things you can get for free.** Shop around for the best bank for your business.

10. **Refinance debts.** If interest rates are low, it may be a good time to consolidate your debts.

11. **Pay down your debt.** Interest on loans is expensive; pay them off.

12. **Review your insurance coverage.** Consider raising deductibles. Possibly self-insure in some areas. Increase the waiting period for disability coverage. Put your insurance package out to bid. Conditions change rapidly—both yours and the insurance company's. Rates may have decreased. Do not just automatically renew your contract annually.

13. **Check your company job classification under workers' compensation.** Be sure you are not paying for higher-risk coverage on job descriptions that have changed.

14. **Be tough on collections (accounts receivable).** The sale is not final until you have collected the money.
    - Invoice quickly.
    - Be sure your invoice contains all pertinent data and details.
    - Eliminate questions and delays.
    - Use the phone for collections—it is much more effective than letters.
    - Bring in a collection agency quickly if your own efforts fail.

15. **Recycle.** Options vary widely, but you may be able to turn trash into cash by collecting and recycling cardboard, newspaper, metal, aluminum, and other materials. This could also cut your trash hauling costs.

16. **Set up a suggestion box.** Nobody is closer to what is happening than your employees. Ask for cost-saving ideas. Tie an incentive to it. Get their input.

Strategy No. 6: For Every Cent or Dollar Saved, Your Profits Increase

This strategy—of ways to make fundamental changes in your business to make it more profitable—includes proven ideas developed some years ago by this author along with Ellen Cheever, CMKBD, ASID and Ken Rohl, CEO of Rohl. As board members of the NKBA, at the time, we got together to discuss ways a business could become more profitable during difficult times. Interest rates then were soaring to near 20 percent. Clients were delaying renovation or new construction projects because of these astronomical rates.

The following content includes the recommendations that came out of that meeting.

Operations

Elimination or reduction of profit centers, product lines, and other operations having marginal profits may result in cost savings in overhead, energy, marketing, and interest payments. The sale or discontinuance of low-margin product lines or second showroom or facilities may free cash for debt reduction and for expansion of more profitable operations.

Cost reduction and control are critical to maintaining profitability in economically difficult times. However, do not indiscriminately cut costs. Cut fat, not muscle. Arm yourself with knowledge of your operations. Identify the activities and costs of providing services or fabricated products. Determine the causes of certain expenses and what the effects of reducing or not reducing those costs will be.

- Close or sell marginal or unprofitable branches, production facilities, and subsidiaries. Establish a P&L status for each stand-alone business.
- Review production and distribution of products with an eye toward reducing warehousing and transportation costs while maintaining or improving customer service.
- Consolidate job functions to reduce staffing, warehousing, administration, and office support expenses.
- Share with another company the costs of certain operations, space, and other overhead costs or product purchases.
- Curtail capital expenditures and expansion plans until a thorough financial analysis provides reasonable expectations.
- Sign all checks for expenses personally.

Administration

Many expenses are fixed. However, there are many variable expenses that can be reduced for meaningful savings. Do not overlook anything, however small.

- Allocate administrative charges to branches, production shops, and subsidiaries. Treat each distinct part of your business as a separate profit center. Eliminate unprofitable areas.
- Review all dues and subscriptions.
- Review telephone, fax, and other communication costs.
- Compare rates and proposals of long-distance communication and equipment providers. Eliminate personal telephone calls charged to the company.
- Reduce premium overnight shipment of products and documents.
- Sell or scrap excess office/warehouse furniture and equipment.
- Good housekeeping alone can improve employee morale and customer perceptions.
- Defer additional computer hardware and software upgrades unless they will achieve worthwhile payback.
- Review insurance costs. Get competitive proposals and an assessment of current coverage and insurance costs.
- Minimize professional (legal and accounting) costs.
- Review borrowing and credit card interest costs.
- Tightly control all approvals for capital expenditures.
- Reduce and eliminate excess reports and other questionable paperwork.
- Renegotiate present and future leases.

Design

You cannot tolerate marginal design efforts or results. It is important to personalize the plan for the client to receive the best design solution. This is far more important than specifying gadgets or creating one-of-a-kind installation ideas that are time consuming and difficult to execute. You also need to think of ways to employ design to increase your profits.

- Do not lower your prices on the jobs you generally do. Rather, increase your expertise in other types of projects offering higher-margin opportunities.
- Consider using an outside design/drawing service rather than adding a draftsperson or as a substitute for one full-time draftsperson.
- Keep solutions simple, based on products/craftspeople you are familiar with. Doing this makes estimating your ideas accurately easier.
- Use products in your designs that are not easy for the client to shop.
- Increase the perceived value of your presentation by presenting better-looking plans to the client.
- Keep the showroom creative and neat.
- Ask every client about potential cabinetry needs in other areas of the home.
- Devote your best design efforts to key accounts or repeat/referral clients.
- Talk about the increased real estate value your design will add to the client's home.
- Do not design monuments. Jobs that require a great deal of design time or installation supervision rob you of the precious time needed to design more projects and increase profit levels.
- Attend a design seminar/workshop to stay current on what's new.
- Read consumer magazines and trade journals to keep your designs fresh.

Installation

Most kitchen dealerships experience some slippage between the anticipated gross profit margin on the job and the actual amount of money made after the installation is completed. It is critical to be accurate in your estimates so that you protect every possible profit dollar coming to your company. To do this, you need to take the guesswork out of the estimating process and shorten the cycle time it takes from tear-out to job completion.

- Avoid time and material or hourly wages. Work on unit price sheets or fixed bids.
- Hold a one-hour production meeting each week, during which problem solving and tightening the cycle time is your primary focus.
- Cost out each job 30 days after it is completed.
- Schedule a pre-installation meeting on all jobs.
- Double-check job site dimensions and orders to eliminate errors.
- Visit the job site often, start the punch list early. Get the touch-up work done while the crew is still on the job.
- Improve your relationship with workers so that they focus on making money as well.
- Keep your trucks properly stocked with miscellaneous equipment so that trips to the lumberyard or warehouse are minimized.
- Insist that hourly employees track their activities by project for proper cost accounting.
- Review profitability comparisons between subcontracting installations versus maintaining an in-house crew.
- Have installers/subcontractors attend manufacturer-sponsored training programs to ensure that they are handling, installing, and protecting all materials properly.
- Prepare clear and simple project documents that meet NKBA Graphics and Presentation Standards.
- Stay in touch with the client. If there is a problem, fix it immediately.

Warehousing and Distribution

Making your warehousing and distribution functions more efficient may benefit your bottom line.

- Determine the most active products within the warehouse and make them the most readily accessible.
- Evaluate warehouse housekeeping and safety.
- Be familiar with your state's Occupational Safety and Health Administration (OSHA) and workers' compensation law.
- Review your on-time delivery performance.
- Review vendor on-time delivery performance.
- Check vehicle maintenance programs.
- Review security and other physical controls over inventory and equipment.
- Frequently check the most critical inventory items and adjust your records accordingly.
- Keep accurate inventory records to reduce excess inventory.

Purchasing

How effective is your purchasing function? Companies can make more money in the way they buy than in the way they sell.

- Press suppliers for the best terms.
- Consider joining a buying group.
- Consider buy versus make items.
- Evaluate lease versus buy items.
- Reduce rush procurement. Take time to shop the market and seek competitive bids.
- Have product delivered to job sites by suppliers to reduce your inventory.
- Evaluate all product lines. Consolidate products and/or vendors.
- Consolidate purchases for maximum discounts, freight terms, and so on. (Doing this saves on paperwork and telephone calls.)

Payables

Be sure that your people are open and honest with your suppliers. Pay on the longest terms possible without penalties, loss of credit, or premium prices. Make certain that your disbursement function is well managed. Unless you are taking advantage of a worthwhile discount, paying bills early costs you money (i.e., if you normally pay in 30 days, 2 percent/10 terms will save you 36 percent over 360 days).

- Pay bills when due, not before.
- Limit expense authorizations to the owner.
- Negotiate the longest possible terms with vendors without affecting agreed-on pricing.
- If a vendor requires cash in advance, discuss a discount to compensate for your loss of normal trade terms.
- Review expenditures to determine if certain payments, such as insurance premiums, can be made annually rather than quarterly. But do not be trapped into an unnecessary prepayment situation.
- Consider a short-term (30 days or less) loan to pay a vendor that offers a cash discount—you will save money.

Take the Discount

Borrow to Discount

Vendor accounts payable	$50,000
2% cash terms available	$1,000
Net payable to vendors	$49,000
Cost to borrow for 30 days	$245 (6% × $49,000 ÷12)
Net saved for 30 day loan	$755
($1,000 − $245 = $755)	

- Taking every cash discount is easier said than done; but is a first step to boosting your cash. If your business purchased $500,000 worth of materials, with an average prompt-pay discount of 3 percent, that's a total of $15,000 of found cash. Think of all you could do with an extra $15,000!

Moving Cash Faster

Look at order-processing and cash-collection cycles. For every day that you shorten the cycle, you improve customer service and speed up the flow of cash and profitability. Be conscientious in paying suppliers and subcontractors. Do not expect them to be your bank. Lines of credit with lending institutions are easier to arrange when you do not need the funds. If you do not know how to develop a credit line, ask your banker.

- Determine how long it takes between the receipt of an order and the shipment or performance of the job. Discuss ways to streamline the process. Find out why orders are backlogged.
- Once the job is complete or the service is performed, determine how long it takes to get the bill out. Invoice daily.
- When the customer makes a payment, see how long it takes to get the payment deposited. Deposit daily.
- Make certain that high-volume invoices receive priority.
- Sweep excess funds into interest-bearing accounts.
- Review alternatives to bank balances that are not earning interest.

Managing Cash Flow

Your company's ability to manage and control its investments in receivables and inventories while simultaneously achieving the longest reasonable terms on payables can materially offset the future of your business. Your readiest source of additional financing may be the dollars you can free from your own working capital pipeline. The investments here are substantial.

- Tap your own capital and make it works double-time. The older the receivable, the less likely you are to collect it. Fewer than 20 percent of receivables over nine months old are ever collected.
- You need timely information on your receivables and a quick follow-up process on delinquent accounts.
- Your credit policies should be tight enough to minimize bad debt losses yet flexible enough to optimize sales and to be competitive.
- Your company's gross margins may determine how conservative or liberal you need to make your credit policies.
- Banks do not count receivables over 60 days as assets against borrowed funds.

Credit and Collections

Good management of accounts receivable is critical to the success and survival of your business.

- Have a top-notch person responsible for credit and collections.
- Good communications with accounts receivable is the best way to speed up payment. Establish standard collection procedures, including collection letters and a schedule of actions and correspondence. Call customers for delinquent payments. Calls demand answers; letters can be ignored. Set up a tickler file to follow up on payment promises made by customers. Settle customer billing disputes promptly.
- Perform credit investigations of new construction or design/build customers, and obtain relevant financial information and references. Update credit information on existing new construction or multihousing customers on an annual basis. Review current credit applications for completeness. Include a personal guarantee where warranted. Insist that this be signed if the customer is incorporated.
- Stay close to your key customers. Keep an ear to the ground for early signs of trouble. Closely monitor accounts receivable balances of key customers. Contact customers immediately when their average collection period increases.
- Renegotiate long-overdue accounts to get immediate cash flow.
- Consider partial but immediate payments with a realistic schedule for future payments. Obtain a signed payment agreement note that is secured by real property.
- Link sales commissions to final payment. Involve designers/salespeople in collection efforts.
- Offer cash discounts to encourage earlier payments. Rebill customers for discounts taken but not earned. Charge interest on past-due accounts.

- Develop and stick to your own deposit/collection schedule. (Many kitchen/bathroom dealers use a 50 percent deposit, 40 percent on delivery, and 10 percent on completion schedule.)
- Use your deposit/collection schedule on all change orders.
- If necessary, hand-carry payments on change orders.
- Make certain your invoices are clear and understandable.
- Get credit card equipment to reduce processing charges for credit card sales. Negotiate with your bank for two-day turnaround on your payables at no more than a 1.5 percent service charge.
- Utilize all legal means to collect your money—including Small Claims Court, mechanics liens, and collection attorneys. You worked hard to deliver your products and services, and you deserve to be paid for them.

SUMMARY

In this chapter we presented an in-depth look at the three main financial statements—operating, balance sheet, and cash flow—that you should generate on a monthly basis to help you manage the business. We discussed how a detailed chart of accounts allows you to break out and summarize every single business transaction. Examples of each of the important financial statements were provided. This chapter also includes several suggestions that a business owner might use to reduce expenses.

REVIEW QUESTIONS

1. What are the three main financial statements that you should generate and review on a regular basis? (See "Basic Financial Statements" page 86)
2. What is the function of a chart of accounts? (See "Chart of Accounts" page 86)
3. What are the main segments of the income statement? (See "Income Statement" pages 90–91)
4. What does the balance sheet tell you about the business? See under "Balance Sheet" page 95)
5. How does a cash flow statement help you manage the business? (See "Cash Flow Analysis" pages 98–99)
6. What is an accounts receivable aging report? (See "Accounts Receivable Aging Report" page 102)
7. What is the difference between gross profit margin and net profit? See "Gross Margin" pages 105–106)

Protecting Your Business

Learning Objective 1: Identify various ways that you can protect your business.

Learning Objective 2: Compare the types of insurance available to help you protect your business.

Learning Objective 3: Explain why business owners should develop an errors and omissions policy to cover their kitchen and bath designs.

Learning Objective 4: Analyze the insurance needs of your business using the Business Insurance Planning Worksheet.

Learning Objective 5: Discuss ways that you can protect your business from internal and external theft.

Just what does "protecting your business" really mean? Protection includes those steps we take to ensure continuity of business operations in the event of unforeseen problems. It also includes protecting your personal assets from business creditors in the event of a business problem.

Part of owning and operating a business includes being fully aware of the potential liabilities that may result from any number of situations, such as selling a product that somehow injures someone. Would a refrigerator falling on someone be an example? Probably not, but other events may occur.

- Your showroom could be damaged or a company-owned vehicle could be involved in an accident.
- Your installation specialist may hook up a gas stove incorrectly, resulting in an explosion and injury to someone. Or you could be sued by a customer or employee for a number of reasons.
- Designers who "sell" plans are in jeopardy of being sued for a design error that costs the client money or causes harm in some way because of a planning, construction, or code violation.

The list is endless, and the key word is "awareness." Once you are aware of the potential problems, you can take steps to limit your liability and business disruption in the event of unforeseen circumstances. Keep in mind that as a practical matter, you can only limit your liability, not reduce it to zero. You must take steps to keep your potential liability at acceptable limits. That is, you must determine how much you can afford to lose without becoming "insurance poor" (i.e., buying too much insurance).

The following recommendations will help to Protect Your Business:
- Choose the most suitable business legal structure.
- Obtain professional advice when required.
- Fully understand contracts and personal guarantees.
- Use credit bureaus to help scrutinize clients for open accounts.
- Develop an insurance program.
- Build in systems and procedures to help protect you from theft.

BUSINESS LEGAL STRUCTURE

Chapter 3 covers the various business legal structures. They range from the sole proprietorship to various forms of corporations. Take time to understand the advantages and disadvantages of each business legal structure. The legal structure you choose relates directly to your potential personal liability and therefore to your insurance program. Always consider your personal exposure when selecting a legal structure.

PROFESSIONAL ADVICE

Protection starts with appropriate financial and legal advice on all tax, contractual, and human resource matters relating to your business.

Do not take chances, especially in the legal world. "After the fact" is too late. With legal, financial, and human resource matters, do not be penny wise and pound foolish. Business legal problems can sneak up on you, and you must be ready. You do that by having your attorney review contracts and other business documents before signing them. Do not be pressured by time constraints.

Likewise, you should have a human resource attorney review all of your various employee related forms: everything from the job application form, to your employee handbook, to termination paperwork.

Your accounting professional should help you make sure that all taxes are paid on time and that any other forms and payments due the various governmental agencies are handled properly.

CONTRACTUAL AGREEMENTS AND PERSONAL GUARANTEES

Many of your larger suppliers, and some smaller ones too, will ask you to complete a detailed credit application in order to do business on terms rather than cash. They will also want to see current financial information and will ask you to sign a personal guarantee. With a signed personal guarantee, you are liable for the guaranteed amount of money owed regardless of your business's legal structure. Because personal guarantees are usually executed when business is going well, one tends not to think of the potential downside.

As recommended before, consult with your business advisors. Do not ever sign a personal guarantee on the spot.

Review the guarantee considering the worst-case scenario. For example, assume your business has gotten off to a great start. You started out in a small retail space and now you want to move to a larger space in an even better location. The owner of the property insists that, along with the standard commercial space lease contract, you sign a personal guarantee. You sign, you move, and two years later disaster strikes. You file for bankruptcy and close your business down. But, you still have three more years to go on the lease. Since you signed the personal guarantee, you will be personally responsible for the final three years of the lease—and the fine print in the personal guarantee may state that you must also pay for improvements made while you were a tenant if the landlord wants to restore the location to its original condition.

With personal guarantees—and indeed with anything you are considering signing—recall the advice of H. Jackson Brown Jr. In his *Life's Little Instruction Book*, "Read carefully anything that requires your signature—because the big print giveth and the small print taketh away."

Be careful and cautious when it comes to signing a personal guarantee. And require a personal guarantee to you on any open accounts that you choose to work with—if the business is a corporation. If it is a sole proprietorship or partnership, the individual's signature on the credit application will suffice as this states that he or she will be responsible for all payments.

EXTENSION OF CREDIT TO YOUR CUSTOMERS

Your suppliers will be demanding, and they will insist on signed commitments from you. You need to treat your customers the same way. If you offer an open account to any client, and many kitchen and bath businesses do, have a legally approved credit application and personal guarantee approval system in place. Insist that the application be completely filled out and signed. Ask for credit references, and check them out. Use credit bureaus to help you. They are not expensive and are reliable. If the client is a corporation, you might consider using Dunn & Bradstreet's services for checking past payment history and related information. You can find the company on the Internet at www.dnb.com or call 866-314-6335 (United States) or 800-463-6362 (Canada).

Virtually every state/province has mechanics lien/builder's lien laws that are in place to protect homeowners, contractors, and suppliers. The regulations vary by state/province, so learn how these regulations work in your state/province and use them. They are a great tool to help ensure that you are paid.

COPYRIGHTING YOUR DRAWINGS

It is the industry standard that the copyright ownership of drawings belongs to the firm, not the designer. Your plans should include a copyright notice. Plans should have a disclaimer detailing what purpose your drawings are intended for. Your final plans should be dated and signed by the consumers so there is little opportunity for preliminary plans to be mistaken for final ones. The NKBA recommends that all of this information appear in a drawing title block (see samples in Figures 6.1 and 6.2).

Sample Copyright Statement for Drawings

Copyright © 2013

Design plans are provided for the fair use by the client or his agent in completing the project as listed within this contract. Design plans remain the property of ABC Design Studio and cannot be used or reused without permission.

FIGURE 6.1 Example of Drawing Title Block

Sample Intended Use of Plans Disclaimer

These design plans are not provided for architectural or engineering use. It is the respective trades' responsibility to verify that all information listed is in accordance with equipment use, applicable codes, and actual job site dimensions.

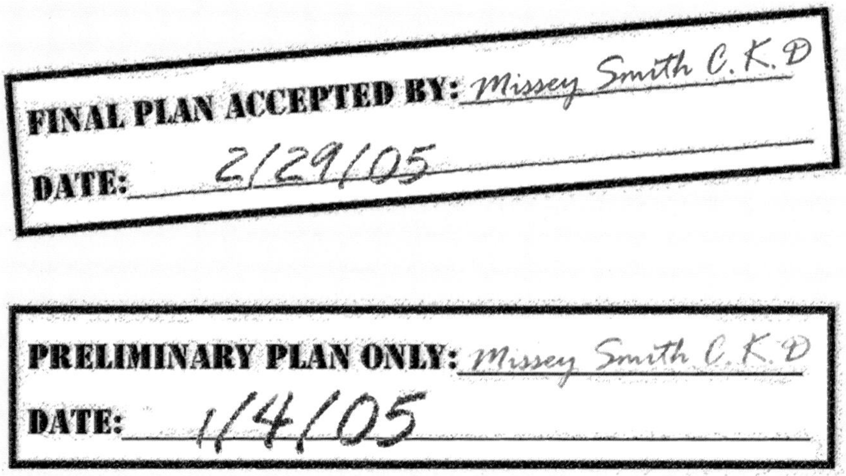

FINAL PLAN ACCEPTED BY: *Missey Smith C.K.D*

DATE: *2/29/05*

PRELIMINARY PLAN ONLY: *Missey Smith C.K.D*

DATE: *1/4/05*

FIGURE 6.2 Documentation can protect your business should conflicts arise.

DEVELOPING AN INSURANCE PROGRAM

The importance of insurance cannot be overemphasized; neither can the danger of paying for insurance you do not need. Solicit the advice of an independent business insurance agent. Do not forget to shop. Talk to three or four agents, and compare recommendations and prices. Some agents may suggest coverage that you just do not need. This, after all, is how they make their living. To learn more about this important piece of your business puzzle, visit the Independent Insurance Agents of America web site at www.iiaa.org.

In some cases, you can obtain insurance coverage at favorable group rates through various professional associations or your local Chamber of Commerce.

Whatever your final insurance program, revisit it at least every six months. Your business can change rapidly, especially in the first several years of operation, and your insurance needs will change with it. Keep in touch with your insurance agent, using him or her as a mentor in this important aspect of your business. Do not be afraid to make changes when necessary.

Business Interruption Insurance

Business interruption insurance protects against loss of revenue because of property damage. For instance, this insurance would be used if you could not operate your business during the time repairs were being made because of a fire or in the event of the loss of a key supplier. The coverage can pay for salaries, taxes, and lost profits.

Burglary, Robbery, and Theft Insurance

Comprehensive policies protect against loss from burglary, robbery, and theft, including those crimes committed by your own employees. Be certain that you understand what is excluded from this coverage.

Disability Insurance

Cover yourself by disability insurance whether you decide to purchase key person insurance or not. This insurance, along with business interruption insurance, ensures that your business will continue to operate in the unfortunate event that you are unable to work. Pay particular attention to exactly how "disability" is defined in the policy, the delay time until payments start, when coverage terminates, and adjustments for inflation.

Errors and Omissions Insurance

Regardless of what kind of business you own, customers can claim that something you did on their behalf was done incorrectly, and this error cost them money or caused them harm in some way.

In the litigious world we live in, many business owners protect themselves with errors and omissions (E&O) insurance. This type of insurance may be appropriate for anyone who gives advice, makes educated recommendations, designs solutions, or represents the needs of others, such as teachers, consultants, software developers, ad copywriters, Web page designers, placement services, telecommunication carriers, or inspectors. It is essential if you sell plans as part of your product offering.

Although formalizing a contract with your clients and listing the proper disclaimers on your plans can help limit your liability, the big expenses in an E&O claim is the legal defense needed to prove liability or innocence. E&O policies are designed to cover many of these defense costs and ultimately the final judgment, if the business owner does not win the case.

Fire Insurance

Fire insurance, like all insurance, is complicated, and you should understand what is and is not covered. For example, a typical fire insurance policy covers the loss of contents but does not cover your losses from being out of business for several months while the rebuilding takes place. Do not forget to check whether the contents are insured for their replacement value or for actual value at the time of loss.

Consider a co-insurance clause that reduces the policy cost considerably. This means that the insurance carrier will require you to carry insurance equal to some percentage of the value of the property, usually around 85%. With this type of clause, it is very important that you review coverage frequently so that you always meet the minimum percentage required. If this minimum is not met, a loss will not be paid no matter what its value.

Health Insurance

Most employees need, want, and expect to receive health insurance as one of their benefits. For employers, it has become a major issue due to spiraling costs. A number of economically attractive packages are offered to small businesses (small groups are usually defined as 25 or fewer employees). Most of the kitchen and bath businesses in the United States and Canada fall into this category.

Two questions small business owners face when considering health insurance are: What kind of benefits should I buy?, and How much can I afford to pay? Regarding the first, buy the benefits that will protect you, your employees, and your families in case of emergency. Regarding the second, it depends on your age and the age of your employees, gender, and whether families will be covered.

Be sure to explore the wide range of options available in health care coverage today, including:

- **Fee for service.** Fee for service provides eligible employees with services of a doctor or hospital with partial or total reimbursement, depending on the insurance company.
- **Health maintenance organization (HMO).** An HMO provides a range of benefits to employees at a fixed price with a minimal contribution or sometimes no contribution from the employee, as long as the employees use doctors or hospitals specified in the plan. Many HMOs have their own managed care facilities.
- **Preferred provider organization (PPO).** PPOs are considered managed fee-for-service plans because some restrictions are put in place to control the frequency and cost of health care. Under a PPO, arrangements are made among the providers, hospitals, and doctors to offer services at an alternative, usually lower, price. Most of the time there is a copay amount for each visit.
- **Health savings account (HSA).** An HSA combines a high-deductible health insurance plan (HDHP) with a tax-free savings account that works like an individual retirement account, except the money is intended to be used for qualified health care costs. The primary advantage of this plan is lower premiums plus protection from big medical bills. HSAs also encourage employees to make more intelligent medical decisions because they are actually spending their own money.
- **Flexible benefit plan.** A flexible benefit plan allows employees to choose from different fringe benefits. It is sometimes referred to as a cafeteria plan. Check with your insurance agent for more details on the wide variety of health care plans that are available.

Key Person Insurance

Key person insurance is particularly important for small mom-and-pop businesses, where the loss of the owner/manager or lead design/sales person, from illness, accident, or death could render the business inoperable or severely limit its operations. This insurance, although expensive, can provide protection for this situation.

Liability Insurance

Liability insurance is probably the most important element of your insurance program. It provides protection from potential losses resulting from injury or damage to others or their property. Think about some of the big cash awards you have read about that have resulted from lawsuits concerning liability of one kind or another, and you will understand the importance of this insurance. If your agent recommends a comprehensive general policy, make certain that it does not include items you do not need. Pay only for insurance you really need. Do not confuse business liability coverage with your personal liability coverage. They are both recommended. Your personal coverage will not cover a business-generated liability. Check to be certain that you have both types of coverage.

Compare the costs of different levels of coverage. In some cases, a $2 million policy costs only slightly more than a $1 million policy. Economies of scale are true with most forms of insurance coverage. That is, after a certain value, additional insurance becomes very economical.

Life Insurance

Life insurance is one of the lowest-cost benefits you can offer your employees. For a small additional fee, health insurance providers allow you to purchase life insurance plans either from them or from another company.

Owner's Disability Insurance

The disability insurance discussed earlier is for the business. If something happened to you, the owner, the money would go to the business because you are not there to run it. Personal disability insurance covers you in the event you are disabled and unable to work. Normally the amount paid out is slightly less than your current salary. Cost for this coverage varies considerably, depending on your profession, salary level, how quickly the benefits start, and when they end. Benefits paid are tax free only if you, not the company, pay the premium.

Workers' Compensation Insurance

If you have employees, most states/provinces will require you to cover them under workers' compensation. The cost of this insurance varies widely and depends on the type of work performed and your accident history. It is important that you classify your employees properly to secure the lowest insurance rates.

Guidelines for Developing Your Insurance Coverage Package

It is possible to purchase insurance for just about any peril you can imagine, if you can afford to pay the premiums. When considering your insurance coverage, use these guidelines:

- Before speaking with an insurance representative, prepare a clear written statement of what your expectations are.
- Do not withhold important information from your insurance representative about your business and its exposure to loss.
- Get at least three competitive bids using brokers, direct agents, and independent agents. Note the interest that each agent takes in loss prevention and suggestions for specialty coverage.
- Avoid duplication and overlap in policies; do not pay for insurance you do not need.
- Note that complete insurance packages for small businesses do exist in some areas. Ask for a BOP (business opportunity plan).
- Ask whether the insurance firm is licensed to transact business in your state. If so, make sure it has a solvency fund should a catastrophe put the insurance company in danger of going under.
- Reassess insurance coverage on an annual basis. As your firm grows, so do your needs and potential liabilities. Being underinsured is one of the major problems growing businesses face. Get competitive bids on your total package every two or three years.
- Keep copies of your insurance policies and complete records of premiums paid, itemized losses, and loss recoveries. This information can help you get better coverage at lower costs in the future.

Table 6.1 is a business insurance planning worksheet that lists every type of insurance to help you put together the insurance program that is right for your business.

TABLE 6.1 Business Insurance Planning Worksheet

Type of Insurance	Required	Yearly Cost	Cost per Payment
General liability insurance			
Product liability insurance			
Errors and omissions liability insurance			
Malpractice liability insurance			
General liability insurance			
Automotive liability insurance			
Fire and theft insurance			
Business interruption insurance			
Overhead expense insurance			
Personal disability insurance			
Key employee insurance			
Shareholders' or partners' insurance			
Credit extension insurance			
Term life insurance			
Health insurance			
Group insurance			
Workers' compensation insurance			
Survivor—income life insurance			
Care, custody and control insurance			
Consequential losses insurance			
Boiler and machinery insurance			
Profit insurance			
Money and securities insurance			
Glass insurance			
Electrician equipment insurance			
Power interruption insurance			
Rain insurance			
Temperature damage insurance			
Transportation insurance			
Fidelity bonds			
Surety bonds			
Title insurance			
Water damage insurance			
Natural disaster insurance			
TOTAL ANNUAL COSTS			

PROTECTING YOUR BUSINESS FROM THEFT

Theft is not a pleasant subject to talk about, but it is a necessary one. Every business is subject to theft, ranging from a handful of paper clips to hundreds of thousands of dollars. The thief can be someone unknown to you breaking into your business and stealing product, cash, computers—anything of value. Or it could be a longtime, trusted employee.

Employee Theft

Employee theft is one of the most emotionally devastating things that can occur in a business. It can cast a shadow of doubt over everyone working for the company until the person who is responsible for the theft is caught. You should be alert to these problems:

- Missing office supplies and equipment
- Missing inventory
- Cash missing from the cash box
- Accounting books that do not balance
- Checks written to people and/or companies that you do not recognize
- Purchases made for products and services that are never delivered
- Employees who do not charge friends or relatives for products
- Overtime exaggerated
- Excessive vacation and sick days

Protect Yourself

To help limit your losses from employee theft, thoroughly check the background of all prospective hires. Get to know your employees so that you can detect signs of financial or personal problems. If they trust and respect you, they may ask for help before taking their problems out on the business.

Here is a list of things you can do to limit both internal and external theft:

- Install a security system. It should include alarms on all doors and windows and sound and motion sensors. The system should be tied into a central "reporting" station. Put signage on windows and doors to show people you are protected. Be prudent when sharing the access code.
- Have outside lights that automatically come on at dusk and go off at dawn. Keep the property well lighted.
- Balance the cash box every night.
- Have someone you know come into the business and purchase something for cash. Then track the cash and paperwork all the way through your system and into the bank. Let everyone know you have done this and that you will continue to do it on a random basis.
- Conduct a surprise check of products loaded on a truck ready for delivery. Make sure there is not more product leaving the building than the paperwork calls for.
- Be alert to employees leaving the premise with boxes, bundles, and bags that they did not come in with.
- If employees park their cars right next to storage areas, be alert to unscheduled trips to their cars during working hours.
- You, the owner, should open every bank statement. Review every check written to be sure you know to whom it was written and what it was for.
- Require two-signature checks—you being one of the signers.
- Check all time cards on hourly employees.
- Review each pay register verify that employees are being paid the correct amount.
- Review your financial statements monthly. Be on the lookout for unusual expenditures or changes in cash flow.

- Let employees know that theft is a major concern of yours, and even though you trust them, you will continually be checking on everything to make sure that theft does not happen.
- Lock cash and all valuable documents in a fire safe every night.

Theft, especially employee theft, is a delicate and sensitive subject. By being wise, alert, prudent, and smart, you can avoid some of the opportunities for theft.

Protecting your business is no easy task. This guide should help you in getting started. As in several other areas of the business, take advantage of all the professional help you can.

SUMMARY

In this chapter we discussed the importance of protecting your business and included a number of different things that you might consider doing to protect your business. We talked about how to choose the most suitable business legal structure, why using outside professional help can be beneficial, and why having a comprehensive insurance plan can help protect your business.

REVIEW QUESTIONS

1. List three types of health insurance plans. (See "Health Insurance" page 126)
2. Why is it important to have an errors and omissions (E&O) policy? (See "Errors and Omissions Insurance" page 125)
3. What is the difference between business and personal liability insurance? (See "Liability Insurance" page 126)
4. List five things that you might do to protect yourself from internal theft. (See "Protect Yourself" pages 129–130)

Basic Tax Management

This is a great time to be a small business owner. Not only is small business the major force in the American economy, but it is also the benefactor of new tax laws that make it easier to write off expenses *and* minimize the taxes you owe. Your business needs to use every tax-saving opportunity to survive and thrive at this time. Tax laws seem to always be changing and evolving. It is important for you not only to be up to date on current laws but to make a commitment to stay current in the future.

Learning Objective 1: Recognize the importance of selecting the best business structure for your business and the importance of good record keeping.

Learning Objective 2: Identify resources that you can use to help maximize your income tax savings.

Learning Objective 3: Discuss the special rules on taxes that apply to small businesses.

Learning Objective 4: Describe the importance of claiming deductions and what doing so can mean to the bottom line of your business.

Learning Objective 5: List common business expense deductions and how they must be substantiated.

SMALL BUSINESS TAX MANAGEMENT

According to the National Federation of Independent Business (NFIB), 88% of small businesses use paid preparers to file their income tax returns. The percentage rises to 95 percent for businesses with 20 or more employees. So why should you pay close attention to this chapter? The answer is simple: *You*, not your accountant or other financial advisor—and not software—run the business. You can't rely on someone else to make decisions critical to your activities. You personally need to be informed about tax-saving opportunities that continually arise so you can strategically plan to take advantage of them. Being knowledgeable about tax matters also saves you money; the more you know, the better you are able to ask your accountant key tax and financial questions that can advance your business while you meet your tax responsibilities.

This chapter focuses primarily on federal income taxes. State requirements vary a great deal. It is your responsibility—along with that of your outside advisors—to be knowledgeable in that area also. Following sales and government regulations, federal taxes are a big concern in running a small business. Most businesses are required to pay and report many other taxes, including state income taxes, employment taxes, sales and use taxes, and excise taxes. We include some information about these taxes in order to alert you to your possible obligations so that you can then obtain further assistance if necessary.

It is important to continually stay alert for future changes!

The purpose of this chapter is to make you acutely aware of how your actions in business can affect your bottom line from a tax perspective. The way you organize your business, the accounting method you select (see Chapter 4), and the types of payments you make all have an impact on when you report income and the extent to which you can take deductions. This chapter is *not* designed to make you an expert. We strongly suggest that you consult with a tax advisor before making important decisions that will affect your ability to minimize your taxes.

In Chapter 3, we covered the different forms of business organization that you can choose. We discussed pros and cons and the tax ramifications of each form. In Chapter 4, we emphasized the importance of good record keeping. You must learn how to keep the necessary records to back up your write-offs in the event your return is questioned by the Internal Revenue Service (IRS).

The Small Business Administration (SBA) has teamed up with the IRS to provide small business owners with help on tax issues. A special DVD called *A Virtual Small Business Tax Workshop* is available free of charge at www.irs.gov, and IRS tax experts now participate in SBA Business Information Centers where tax forms and publications are also available. Please take advantage of all of the help you can.

As a small business owner, you work hard and try to grow your business—and you hope to make a profit. What you can keep for yourself from that profit depends in part on the income tax that you pay. Income tax applies to your *net* income, not your gross income or gross receipts. You are not taxed on all of the income you bring in by way of sales, fees, commissions, or other payments. Instead, you are essentially taxed on what you keep after paying off the expenses of providing products and services or making the sales that are the crux of your business. Deductions for these expenses operate to fix the amount of income that will be subject to tax. So deductions, in effect, help to determine the tax you pay and the profits you keep. The number of tax credits has been expanded in recent years and can offset your tax to reduce the amount you ultimately pay.

SPECIAL RULES FOR SMALL BUSINESSES

Sometimes it pays to be small. The tax laws contain a number of special rules exclusively for small businesses. You may wonder just what a small business is. The SBA usually defines a small business by the number of employees. Size standards range from 500 to 1,500 employees, depending on the industry or the SBA program.

Reporting Income

While taxes are figured on your bottom line (your income less certain expenses), you still must report your income on your tax return. Generally all of the income your business receives is taxable unless there is a specific tax rule that allows you to exclude the income permanently or defer it to a future time.

When you report income depends on your method of accounting and the fiscal year you have chosen. How and where you report income depends on the nature of the income and your type of business organization. Over the next several years, declining tax rates for owners of pass-through entities (e.g., sole proprietorships, partnerships, and limited liability companies) and S corporations will require greater sensitivity to the timing of business income as these rates decline.

Claiming Deductions

You pay tax only on your profits, not on what you take in (gross receipts). In order to arrive at your profits, you are allowed to subtract certain expenses from your income. These expenses are called deductions.

The IRS dictates what you can and cannot deduct. Within this framework, the nature and amount of the deductions you have often vary with the size of your business, the industry you are in, where you are based in the country, and other factors. The most common deductions for business include these:

- Car and truck expenses
- Utilities
- Supplies
- Legal and professional services
- Insurance
- Depreciation
- Taxes
- Meals and entertainment
- Advertising
- Repairs
- Travel
- Rent for business property and equipment
- Home office (in some cases)

What is the legal authority for claiming deductions?

Deductions are a legal way for you to reduce the amount of your business income subject to tax. There is no constitutional right to tax deductions. Instead, deductions are a matter of legislative grace; if Congress chooses to allow a particular deduction, so be it! Therefore, deductions are carefully spelled out in the IRS Code.

In many instances, the language of the IRS Code is rather general. It may describe a category of deductions without getting into specifics. For example, it contains a general deduction for all "ordinary and necessary" business expenses without explaining what constitutes these expenses. "Ordinary" means common and accepted in business, and "necessary" means appropriate and helpful in developing and maintaining a business.

What Is a Tax Deduction Worth to You?

The answer depends on your tax bracket. The tax bracket is dependent on the way you organize your business. If you are self-employed and in the top tax bracket of 35% in 2012, then each dollar of deduction will save you 35 cents. Had you not claimed this deduction, you would have had to pay 35 cents of tax on that dollar of income that could have been offset by the deduction. Deductions are even more valuable if your business is in a state that imposes income tax. This book does not discuss the impact of state income tax and special rules for state income taxes. However, you should explore the tax rules in your state and ascertain their impact on your business income.

When Do You Claim Deductions?

Like the timing of income, the timing of deductions (when to claim them) is determined by your tax year and method of accounting. Your form of business organization affects your choice of tax year and your accounting method.

Even when expenses are deductible, there may be limits on the timing of those deductions. Most common expenses are currently deductible in full. However, some expenses must be capitalized or amortized, or you must choose between current deductibility and capitalization. "Capitalization" generally means that expenses can be written off as amortized expenses or depreciated over a period of time.

Credits versus Deductions

Not all write-offs of business expenses are treated as deductions. Some can be claimed as tax credits. A tax credit is worth more than a deduction since it reduces your taxes dollar for dollar. Like deductions, tax credits are available only to the extent that Congress allows them.

TAX RESPONSIBILITIES

As a small business owner, your tax obligations are broad. Not only do you have to pay taxes and file income tax returns, but you must manage payroll tax taxes if you have any employees. You may also have to collect and report on state and local sales taxes.

It is very helpful to keep an eye on the tax calendar so you will not miss out on any payment or filing deadlines, which can result in interest and penalties. You might want to view and print out or order (at no cost) from the IRS Publication 1518, Small Business Tax Calendar (www.irs.gov/pub/irs-pdf/p1518.pdf). You can obtain most federal tax forms online at www.irs.gov. Nonscannable forms, which cannot be downloaded from the IRS, can be ordered by calling toll free at (800) 829–4933.

Two other important factors in when and how you do your federal income taxes are what accounting period or tax year that you select and the accounting method that you choose. Both of these topics are discussed in Chapter 4.

Tax law does not require you to maintain books and records in any particular way. It does, however, require you to keep an accurate and complete set of books for your business. We covered this important part of operating your business in Chapter 4.

SPECIFIC SUBSTANTIATION REQUIREMENTS FOR CERTAIN EXPENSES

The law requires businesses to keep and maintain books and records and to provide special substantiation for certain deductions. A negligence penalty can be imposed for 20% of an underpayment resulting from failure to keep adequate books and records and to substantiate items properly. Next we discuss some areas that most kitchen and bath businesses should be concerned about.

- **Travel and entertainment.** You need only two types of records to claim deductions for your travel and entertainment deductions:
  - Written substantiation in a diary, log book, itemized expense report, or other notation system containing certain specific information.
  - Any documentation evidence (receipts, canceled checks, or bills) to prove the amount of the expense. Smart phones and other mobile devices may be used for written substantiation in lieu of a log book.
- **Gifts.** You must show the cost of the gift, the date it was given, and a description of the gift. You also need to show the business reason for the gift or the business benefit gained or expected to be gained by providing it. Include the name of the person receiving the gift, his or her occupation or other identifying information, and his or her business relationship to you.
- **Car expense.** You must show the number of miles driven for business purposes (starting and ending odometer readings), the destination, the purpose of the trip, and the name of the party visited (if relevant). Simply jot down the odometer reading on January 1 to start a good record-keeping habit. Keep a log book in the car, and keep track not only of business mileage but also of expenses for gas, oil, parking, tolls, and similar items.
- **Cell phones.** In the past, record keeping for phone usage (business and personal) was required for cell phones. However, as of January 1, 2010, cell phones are no longer treated as listed property, so no special records are required.

HINTS ON PREVENTING AN AUDIT

- Be sure that every employee is properly classified (employee versus independent contractor and exempt versus nonexempt).
- Report all of your business income. (Don't put cash in your pocket.)
- Keep accurate records.
- Formalize agreements between corporations and shareholders. (Have signed contracts on leases and notes on loans.)
- Be careful when claiming deductions and credits. Make sure you meet eligibility requirements before taking write-offs.
- Supply all necessary information when completing business returns.
- Review the IRS appropriate audit guide. There are several, based on various industries, are available from the IRS.
- Ask the IRS for an opinion if you're not sure of something.
- File on time.
- Get good advice.

HELP FROM THE IRS

The IRS has offices in most cities in the United States. It also has a Web site exclusively for small businesses and self-employed individuals at www.irs.gov/Businesses/Small-Businesses-&-Self-Employed/.

The IRS also provides a number of publications that can give you important information on income and deductions. These publications are available directly from the IRS by calling (800) 828–3676 or by visiting your local IRS office, the post office, or a library. Following is a list of IRS publications that may be of interest to you:

Publication Number	Title
15	Circular E, Employer's Tax Guide
15-A	Employer's Supplemental Tax Guide
15-B	Employer's Guide to Fringe Benefits
334	Tax Guide for Small Business
463	Travel, Entertainment, Gift and Car Expense
509	Tax Calendars
521	Moving Expenses
526	Charitable Contributions
535	Business Expenses
536	Net Operating Losses
537	Installment Sales
538	Accounting Periods and Methods
541	Partnerships
542	Corporations
544	Sales and Other Dispositions of Assets
547	Casualties, Disasters and Thefts (Business and Non-Business)
550	Investment Income and Expenses
551	Basis of Assets
552	Record Keeping for Individuals
560	Retirement Plans for Small Business

(continued)

Publication Number	Title
583	Starting a Business and Keeping Records
587	Business Use of Your Home
590	Individual Retirement Arrangements (IRA's)
908	Bankruptcy Tax Guide
946	How to Depreciate Property
963	Federal-State Reference Guide
969	Health Savings Accounts and Other Tax Favored Health Plans
1518	IRS Calendar for Small Businesses and Self-Employed
1779	Employee Independent Contractor Brochure
1932	How to Make Correct Federal Tax Deposits
3066	Have You Had Your Checkup This Year for Retirement Plans?
3402	Tax Issues for Limited Liability Companies
3780	Tax Information for Small Construction Businesses
3998	Choosing a Retirement Solution for Your Business
4222	401(K) Plans for Small Businesses
4263-E	Small Business Tax Workshops
4333	SEP Retirement Plans for Small Businesses
4334	SIMPLE IRA Plans for Small Businesses
4591	Small Business Federal Tax Responsibilities
4806	Profit Sharing Plans for Small Businesses

The IRS provides a number of free resource tools on CD-ROM. These include the "Small Business Resource Guide," the "Virtual Small Business Workshop" (mentioned earlier), and "Introduction to Federal Taxes."

Another valuable source of assistance are the instructions for particular tax returns. For example, the instructions in Form 1120S, U.S. Income Tax Return for an S Corporation, provide guidance on claiming various tax deductions.

You may want to attend a free IRS seminar offered to new business owners. Topics covered in these seminars include record keeping, tax filing requirements, employment taxes, and federal tax deposit rules. To find a seminar in your area, call the IRS Taxpayer Education Coordinator (listed in your local phone book and available through the IRS general number, 1-800-829-1040).

If you are having problems with the IRS that are causing you financial difficulty or significant cost, including the cost of professional representation, contact the National Taxpayer Advocate Service at http://www.irs.gov/uac/Contact-Your-Advocate! for free and confidential help.

OTHER TAXES

Federal income tax may be your primary concern and your greatest tax liability, but as a business owner, you may have other tax obligations as well. You may owe state income and franchise taxes, employment taxes, sales and use taxes, and excise taxes. Due to space limitations and differences by state, we do not cover each of these in this book. You can obtain more information on various "other" taxes by obtaining these IRS publications: No. 15 Circular E, Employer's Tax Guide; No.15-A Employer's Supplemental Tax Guide; No. 15-B Employer's Guide to Fringe Benefits; and No. 510 Excise Taxes.

SUMMARY

In this chapter we explained that, as the business owner, *you* have an important responsibility to be involved in the tax management of your business. You must keep accurate records and pay taxes in a timely manner. By staying current with federal, state, and local laws, you can put more dollars on the bottom line of your business.

REVIEW QUESTIONS

1. Explain why *you*, the owner/manager of your business, must be knowledgeable in the area of taxes and not delegate the responsibility entirely to an outside professional.(See "Small Business Tax Management" pages 131–132)

2. Which IRS tool can help you become a good tax manager? (See "Tax Responsibilities" page 134)

3. Identify three expense deductions that kitchen and bath dealers can use to reduce their tax consequences—and what record keeping is necessary for each. (See "Specific Substantiation Requirements for Certain Expenses" page 134)

4. List several hints that you can use to help prevent a federal IRS audit. (See "Hints on Preventing an Audit" page 135)

The Basics of Human Resource (People) Management

Earlier we mentioned that every business is comprised of three major management areas: financial management, marketing management, and human resource (people) management. Owners and managers of today's kitchen and bath businesses must be equally strong in all three areas.

Being a good people manager is a learned art and skill.

Learning Objective 1: Relate the difficulty an owner/manager may have in finding a good balance in managing all aspects of their business.

Learning Objective 2: Discuss the different areas of human resources that owners/managers are responsible for.

Learning Objective 3: Identify human resource trends of the future.

Learning Objective 4: Explain the rules and regulations that apply to human resource management.

Learning Objective 5: Explain the purpose of a comprehensive job description for every employee.

Learning Objective 6: State the difference between an employee and an independent contractor.

Learning Objective 7: List various compensation plans and the pros and cons of each.

Learning Objective 8: Describe recruiting and interviewing practices.

Large companies have separate departments, helped by professional human resource managers, who are dedicated to handling this part of running a successful business. Because of their small size (generally 20 or fewer employees), most kitchen and bath companies do not have the luxury of hiring specialists to manage different segments of the business. So the owner ends up doing everything. Those owners who recognize they must become well-rounded professional managers will be the survivors in this increasingly competitive market (Figure 8.1a, b).

Employees represent the intellectual capital that can make or break a firm's ability to remain competitive. People are your most important asset. But if they are not well managed, they can also be a liability.

As business becomes more complex, so does the human resource function, which encompasses everything from addressing staffing needs more strategically to launching effective training initiatives, interpreting federal and state/provincial codes, and implementing policies and benefits that safeguard workers while protecting company interests. The stakes are high. The legal and economic consequences of a major human resources misstep can be enormous.

For many kitchen and bath business owners, human resource management is an intimidating prospect. This and the next chapter cover this important subject: This chapter covers the basics, and Chapter 9 is directed to the owner/manager of the business or the head of human resources, if the business has one.

(a) To be a successful owner of a kitchen and bath design business in the evolving stage, you must balance:

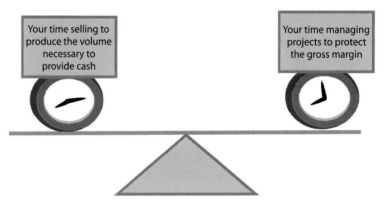

(b) To be a successful owner of a kitchen and bath design business in the evolving stage, you must balance:

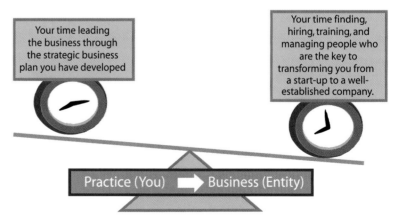

FIGURE 8.1 A Key to Success

THE BROAD PICTURE OF HUMAN RESOURCES

Most people in business agree that being sensitive to and doing your best to meet the "people needs" of your employees is in your best interest as an employer. However, debate exists concerning just how much responsibility a company must assume with respect to those needs and how much time and money a company must devote to the needs and priorities of employees as opposed to those of its business operations and customers (Figure 8.2).

That is where you come in. As the owner, and probably the human resource manager, your job is to focus on the practices and policies in your company that directly affect the welfare and morale of your most important asset: employees. It is up to you to help your company to strike the optimum balance between the strategic needs of your business and the basic needs of your employees. Most kitchen and bath business owners would agree that the task is not only harder than ever before, it is more important than ever before.

For one thing, the market for employees with the skills and knowledge that growing technology-driven businesses require is extremely competitive today. Consequently, your ability to attract good employees relates more closely than ever to the "human" side of the day-to-day working experience (i.e., the general atmosphere that prevails in the workplace) and the extent to which your company practices help people balance the pressures of work and home.

Whether called human resources management or personnel administration, this important facet of business is generally described as the decisions, activities, and processes that must meet the basic needs and support the work performance of employees.

Human Resource Managers

Are responsible for:

- Staffing
- Basic workplace policies
- Compensation and benefits
- Regulatory issues

The most common areas that fall under human resource management include these:

- **Staffing.** Strategically determining, recruiting and hiring the people to help operate your business
- **workplace policies.** Orienting your staff on policies and procedures such as schedules, safety, and security

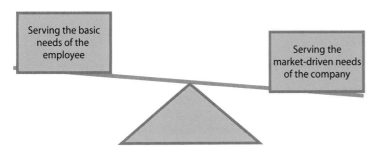

The best human resource managers find a balance between:

Serving the basic needs of the employee

Serving the market-driven needs of the company

FIGURE 8.2 Human resource management

- **Compensation and benefits.** The salary and company services that ensure your staff stays with you and grows in knowledge and experience to help your company grow and expand
- **Regulatory issues.** What your company must do to stay in compliance with the ever-increasing number of federal, state/provincial, and local regulations.

Human Resource Management Is All about People

- Finding and recruiting them
- Training and developing them
- Creating a safe/healthy/productive place for them to work
- Communicating with them
- Motivating them
- Compensating them

Every company, regardless of size, location, or purpose, must deal with human resource issues in one way or another. The only exception would be a work-at-home, self-employed designer.

You Are the Human Resource Manager

Most small business owners function as the human resource manager. You will be/are responsible for personally overseeing and conducting all human resource functions at your company: hiring/firing employees, researching compensation and benefit packages, writing paychecks and keeping appropriate records, training and developing employees, and communicating with employees.

You need to become a good human resources manager if you hope to thrive and survive in the business world. However, when and how will this happen when you are still the number one salesperson and marketing person in the business? These are tough questions to answer, but they need answering nevertheless. Reading these chapters is a good start. The next step is putting various methods, policies, procedures, and forms to work for you; buying some books and CDs on the subject, taking advantage of online learning, and attending seminars or community college classes is always recommended.

Outsourcing May Be the Answer

Outsourcing is a growing trend in human resource management that can help the owners of small businesses. Engage outsiders to help administer operational functions, such as the payroll and the benefits package. They can give advice on almost every human resource issue that may arise. Several outsourcing companies specialize in small business human resource needs. Speak with your accounting and legal advisors or other business owners for a reference. You can also do an online search for companies in your area.

FUTURE HUMAN RESOURCE TRENDS

There have been more changes in human resource management in the past 15 years than in the 100 years before that, and the changes in the next 10 years may be even more dramatic.

Managing the Human Side of Change

One of the challenges that you will surely face in the decade ahead will be managing change, and the number one contribution you can make in this human resource area is to become a catalyst for change in your organization. You may be a one-person management team, but it will be up to you to envision the kinds of changes that will take place and to adapt to those changes in a timely manner.

Adapting to the Changing Nature of Jobs

The most significant change in the organizational structure of most companies has less to do with the fundamental structure of companies and more to do with the fundamental nature of jobs and the working arrangements of the people who hold these jobs.

Today's workplace is not necessarily an office or showroom where employees perform their jobs. Today is the age of the telecommuting and the virtual office. More and more employees are performing some or all of their work from home.

Today is also the age of flextime, with many companies providing some or all of their employees with an opportunity to modify the normal nine-to-five schedule in ways that suit their lifestyles. When you have a showroom that needs to be covered and only one or two salespeople on staff, building in flextime can be difficult, but being aware of the trend and trying to work with your employees is important.

Some working parents want to spend more time with their children expanding the number of part-time positions filled by qualified professionals. However, part-time positions can be difficult to coordinate with your customers' demands.

A trend that is favorable to our industry is that people are working longer, past the normal retirement age of 65. Do not overlook this growing source of employees.

Workforce Diversity

The demographics of the American workforce has changed dramatically in just the past 50 years. White males dominated the workforce in the past. Today, the workforce consists of females and males of all ethnic backgrounds.

These changes in demographics have forced human resource managers and business owners to alter the structure and administration of their benefit packages. There is no longer a one-size-fits-all benefits package. The trend today and for the future is cafeteria-style offerings, where employees receive an allowance and have the opportunity to select which benefits best meet their needs.

The biggest challenge that diversity poses is how to manage this mixture of genders, cultural backgrounds, ages, and lifestyles at a time when companies are moving away from the old-style way of management and replacing it with a more open, empowered, and team-oriented approach to decision making.

The challenge to companies in general and human resource professionals in particular is not to simply adapt to diversity but to capitalize on it. Many kitchen and bath businesses are discovering that they are competing in a much different marketplace than they were 20 years ago. Customers and workforces are better educated and more diverse. Use this to your competitive advantage.

Using Technology to Help Manage Human Resources

Computers streamline almost all aspects of the human resource function. There is some excellent human resource software available to help you manage your human resource department, even if you are the whole department.

Rules and Regulations

A workforce that is free of hazards, sexual harassment, and discrimination is no longer considered a benefit in today's environment; it is something that employees have every right to expect. It is also something that federal, state/provincial, and local government agencies are using their authority to ensure.

Many rules and regulations have been introduced in the past 25 years, and this trend will surely continue.

If you do not have a human resource background, your challenge will be to familiarize yourself with all the various government-mandated regulations and programs with which your company must comply.

The government-mandated regulations that most companies need to remain aware of today involve almost every aspect of the human resource function, including safety and health, equal employment opportunity, sexual harassment, pension reform, and work environmental issues. Someone in your company must make sure that everyone is following the rules and regulations; probably that someone is you.

Becoming Family Friendly

Is your company family friendly? It should be if you want to attract and retain top performers. Being family friendly means that your company's scheduling and general operating policies take into reasonable account the personal needs of the employees—in particular, their desire to balance job responsibilities with family responsibilities.

It has become increasingly apparent in the past 10 years that family-oriented policies do more than simply enhance a company's recruiting initiatives. They also produce a number of bottom-line benefits, such as reduced absenteeism, fewer disability claims, and fewer workplace accidents. Chief among the practices and policies typically found in companies actively pursuing work and family initiatives are flexible scheduling (flextime), telecommuting, individual arrangements, employee assistance programs, and benefit programs that enable employees to select those benefits that are relevant to their particular needs.

DETERMINING YOUR NEEDS

Hiring is a multistep process. The first and most important step is to form a clear understanding of your staffing needs. You must identify not only what position to fill but when to fill it and what the costs will be.

Too often, owners/managers of kitchen and bath businesses operate using spontaneous decisions regarding who, what, and when to hire. They do not have well-thought-out strategies, written job descriptions, or documented compensation plans to guide them in the process. You should not simply be filling jobs. You should constantly be seeking to bring to your company the skills, experience, and attributes that it needs to meet whatever challenge it may face.

Document the Job

Once you've determined need and affordability, establish the following:

- A written job description for the position that outlines, in detail, all aspects of the job.
- Minimum and maximum compensation to be paid, including fringe benefits.
- Type of compensation program you will be using (straight salary, straight commission or salary plus commission).
- Performance goals for sales, gross profit, number of jobs, and so on. This should be done for a 12-month period.

- Qualifications and experience required to perform the job (i.e., AKBD, CKBP, CKD/CBD, computer skills, selling experience, etc.).

Document the Hiring Plan

Once you've documented the job, develop your plan for hiring:

- Identify where and how to find new people—local or regional ads, university referrals, local workforce development offices (often the same office as unemployment), word of mouth, and so on.
- Set a timeline for advertising, interviewing, checking references, hiring, and training.
- Determine if part-time, backup, or a subcontractor will fill the need.

Building Competency Models

Competency modeling is determining what particular mix of skills, attributes, and attitudes will produce superior performance at your business. This strategy applies not only to hiring decisions but also to training and development strategies.

For example, the core of your business is designing and selling kitchen and bath projects. Many owners put design skills ahead of the skill of selling. Certainly, producing winning designs is important, but selling the products and services is even more important. Everything starts with the sale. This is what pays the bills. Great designs are important to helping consummate the sale, but selling skills are even more important.

Therefore, the competency model for a design/sales position should take into account the skills, attributes, and attitudes of both the design and selling side of the position.

You may not always be able to fill every position with people who meet the total competency model, but you should be able to identify any skill deficits (i.e., gaps between the requirements of the job and the qualifications of the candidate). Then you can work to close these gaps through training and coaching.

Developing an Employee's Skill Inventory

Once you gain a general sense of the competencies that will produce superior performance, you are nearly ready to take the next step in a strategically driven hiring process, which is developing an employee skill inventory.

A skill inventory is exactly what the name implies: a portfolio of the human capital in your company—a catalog of the individual skills, attributes, credentials, and areas of knowledge that currently exist. The focus should be on any skills and attributes that have led to successes and accomplishments (i.e., the better-performing employees) in the past.

Segments of the Employee's Skills Inventory

The key to developing a practical, user-friendly employee skills inventory lies in how you organize various categories of information.

A typical list of employee skills inventory should include some of these fields:

- **Skills/knowledge areas.** Business-related functions or activities in which the employee has a special knowledge or a proven record of proficiency.
- **Special preferences.** Statements that the employees have made about their own career aspirations or other jobs in the company they would like to pursue.
- **Educational background.** Schools, degrees, credentials, and subjects that the employee has been exposed to.
- **Job history at your company.** Details about work history and performance.
- **Previous job history.** Experience, skills, and performance at previous jobs.

- **Training courses and seminars.** List of programs with topics covered that identifies knowledge/skill set the employee has previously developed.
- **Test results.** If applicable.
- **Licenses, credentials, and affiliations.** These should be work related and limited to the tasks and responsibilities of the job. NKBA certifications are meaningful, and if you offer installation, a contractor's license will also be important.

Developing a Job Description

The job description (Table 8.1) has long been the tool of hiring for well- managed businesses. Unfortunately, most kitchen and bath businesses do not have detailed written descriptions for each position in the company. This is unfortunate because job descriptions are important in the hiring process and to the employee when hired as well as during job performance evaluations.

Job Description

- Spells out *in detail* what the job entails
- Is the basis for key hiring criteria
- Ensures the candidate has a clear understating of what to expect if hired
- Becomes a reference tool during evaluation process
- Acts as a benchmark for performance after you hire the candidate
- Establishes a minimum–maximum compensation range

Executed correctly, a well-thought-out job description:

- Describes in detail what the job entails, ensuring that the boss and all involved in the hiring process will be on the same page
- Serves as a basis for hiring criteria
- Ensures that candidates have a clear understanding of what to expect if hired
- Serves as a reference tool during the evaluation process
- Serves as a benchmark for performance after you hire the candidate
- Establishes a compensation range

Think of a job description as a snapshot of the job. It should communicate clearly and concisely the responsibilities and tasks that the job entails and indicate the key qualifications for the job, the basic requirements, and, if possible, the attributes that equate to superior performance.

A well-written job description should include:

- Title of the position
- Department (if applicable)
- Direct report (to whom the person reports)
- Responsibilities
- Necessary skills
- Experience necessary

TABLE 8.1 Sample Job Description

Position/Title: _____
(i.e., Designer/Salesperson)

Department: _____
(i.e., Sales)

Reports to: _____
(i.e., owner)

Overall Responsibility: _____
(i.e., design/sell kitchen and bath projects)

Key Areas of Responsibility

- Meet and greet clients visiting the showroom.

- Articulate personal features and benefits and those of the company and the products and services offered.

- Qualify clients: Who are they? Why are they there? What is their time frame? Have they been shopping? What is their budget? Do they need design services? What products (styles finishes, wood species, etc.) are they interested in? Do they have a contractor? Are they looking for a turnkey job? How do they plan to use this space and what about it is important to them. And any other information that allows the salesperson to proceed.

- Help the client in product selection.

- Complete designs that meet and exceed client needs.

- Develop a complete list of all products.

- Quote prices on products and services.

- Follow up all project quotes until clients accept or reject.

- Manage the project through completion.

- Work with the installation team to coordinate the project.

- Communicate with clients, vendors, subcontractors, and others involved with the project in a timely manner.

(continued)

TABLE 8.1 *(Continued)*

Key Areas of Responsibility *(Continued)*

- Maintain complete, detailed files on each client and project.

- Use CAD system for designs.

- Participate in ongoing training programs to maintain a high level of skills in design, sales, product knowledge, computer, company policies and procedures, and industry trends.

- Achieve mutually agreed-on sales and profit goals.

- Be active in industry associations (NKBA, ASID, etc.).

- Be professional in dress, language, and all personal aspects.

- Be a good team member and assist others when needed.

Skills and Attributes

- Strong product knowledge.

- Strong design skills.

- Strong sales skills.

- Strong people skills.

- Detail-oriented.

- Good organization skills.

- Good time-management skills.

- Good team player.

- Good knowledge of installation.

Experience/Ability Requirements

- Minimum 3 years design and sales of kitchens and baths.

- High school graduate.

- NKBA certification a plus.

- Minimum 3 years CAD experience.

Alternatives to Full-time Employees

Kitchen and bath dealers frequently use independent contractors to provide services for their businesses. It is important, however, to be aware of proper payroll deductions because the U.S. Internal Revenue Service (IRS) and Revenue Canada keep a close watch on how small businesses classify independent contractors and employees.

Pros and Cons of Independents

Independent contractors are essentially self-employed individuals who provide services using their expertise and their equipment to accomplish the job. They may or may not work on your premises. An independent contractor is neither a consultant nor a vendor. A consultant generally advises management, while an independent contractor performs specific tasks. A vendor typically provides goods and services and operates at a separate established location, while an independent contractor works in your showroom environment.

Dealers use independent contractors as a way to control hours and expenses and to manage the ebb and flow of day-to-day business. Since many independent contractors have worked for a variety of businesses, they bring a depth of experience and knowledge. They are more likely than employees to provide you with unbiased opinions and input.

On the downside, it can be tougher to earn loyalty from independent contractors. Maintaining focus can also be a problem, as can confidentiality.

The best use of independent contractors is for filling in gaps rather than handling everyday functions. They can also manage pilot programs or test markets.

Meeting Tax Laws

The IRS has been keeping particularly close tabs on small businesses to make sure they appropriately classify independent contractors and employees. In the event of an IRS audit, your firm could be liable for back employment taxes if the IRS determines that one of your independent contractors does not meet its definition of an independent contractor. Discuss your job description with your legal and accounting advisors to determine if it meets the IRS definition of an independent contractor.

Both the IRS and individual states often use the "20 Common Law Factor" test in determining whether to reclassify the tax treatment of a worker. For a detailed discussion of these factors, consult your business attorney and your certified public accountant.

Employee versus Independent Contractor

1. Is the individual providing services required to comply with instruction on when, where, and how the work is done?
2. Is the individual provided with training to enable him or her to perform the job in a particular manner?
3. Are the services performed by the individual a part of the contractor's business operations?
4. Must services be rendered personally?
5. Does the contractor hire, supervise, or pay assistants to help the individual performing under the contract?
6. Is the relationship between parties a continuing one?
7. Who sets the hours of work?
8. Is the individual required to devote full time to the party for whom the services are performed?

(continued)

9. Does the individual perform work on another's business premises?
10. Who directs the sequence in which the work must be done?
11. Are regular oral or written reports required?
12. What is the method of payment: hourly, weekly, commission, or by the job?
13. Are business or travel expenses reimbursed?
14. Who furnishes the tools and materials necessary for the provision of services?
15. Does the individual have significant investment in the tools or facilities used to perform his or her services?
16. Can the individual providing services realize profit or loss?
17. Can the individual providing services work for a number of firms at the same time?
18. Does the individual make his or her services available to the general public?
19. Can the individual be dismissed for reasons other than nonperformance of contract specifications?
20. Can the individual providing services terminate his or her relationship at any time without incurring a liability for failure to complete a job?

Following are some helpful points offered by D. S. Berenson, the managing partner of Johanson, Berenson LLP, a Washington, DC–based national law firm specializing in the home improvement industry. His comments are reprinted from *Remodeling* magazine's February 2004 issue and should be considered for informational purposes only and not construed as legal advice.

Have a detailed written agreement with your installer. A word of warning: State audits are usually triggered by a disgruntled individual, often filing for workers' comp. On occasion, it may be faster and less expensive to pay a small claim rather than assert that the worker was an independent contractor and face a full examination.

If an examination takes place, the IRS and some State tax agencies may request that an employer or worker complete a "Form SS-8." This is a heavily biased form designed to support reclassification, and completing it almost always subjects the business to a reclassification examination. Disgruntled workers often provide the most damaging statements on these forms (which are hard to refute because the identity of the worker is not disclosed). Any business should first consult legal counsel before completing an SS-8.

Is the New Position Exempt or Nonexempt?

An exempt employee normally is an executive, manager, or professional. Other types of exempt employees are those who are "learned" or "artistic" professionals. All others are nonexempt employees who are subject to the wage and hour laws of your state. Merely placing an employee on salary or straight commission does not exempt that person from wage and hour laws. Salaried workers who are nonexempt employees earn overtime the same as hourly wage earners. Only qualified exempt employees do not earn overtime or any other right enumerated in the Industrial Welfare Commission orders.

Many kitchen and bath dealers, as well as other small business owners, do not comply with the federal and state/provincial laws that apply to this subject.

The line between exempt and nonexempt employees can be a difficult one to draw. Many owners and managers have difficulty distinguishing between the two. Seek guidance from your financial or legal consultants to learn what federal and state/provincial laws affect your business. The laws vary, and, in some instances, the state laws supersede federal laws.

Before meeting with your counselor, have written and detailed job descriptions for all employees. If you know exactly what responsibilities are to be performed, you will have an excellent starting point to help you classify your employees correctly.

The kinds of job responsibilities performed will help define an exempt employee. The Fair Labor Standards Act (FLSA) of 1938 (and amended many times since then) regulates methods of wage payments and hours of work for your employees. The FLSA also details laws concerning child labor, minimum wage, and overtime pay.

Human Resource Forecasting

Do you normally wait until someone quits or you terminate them to start looking for a replacement? Do you wait until everyone is overloaded, complaining, or about to quit because the workload is bigger than the current staff can handle? These situations put pressure on how to fill the slot. In such cases, too often the slot is filled with the available candidate come along. Pressure makes it difficult to hire properly.

Chapter 2 explored the importance of a business plan, and Chapter 4 discussed the annual budget. Both of these are important business management tools to help forecast the business's staffing needs. These tools will tell you when you should be starting the next hiring process. Don't wait until everyone's plate is so full that service levels and morale suffer. Anticipate, when possible, when the next salesperson should be brought on board. Track sales, expenses, and profits—and know what's happening day to day—so you know when to start your search.

When you build in time to search for, interview, hire, and train staff, you will have a much smoother transition.

With sophisticated computer software, it is easier to track workload than ever before. Sales numbers are important, but numbers of projects (in process and forthcoming), numbers of work orders, invoices, purchase orders, and the like are guides as well. Use this information to help forecast for future human resource needs.

Important Questions to Ask before Hiring

- Is the business profitable? (Don't add expenses if it's not.)
- Are projections for continued growth positive? (Do some market research.)
- Can the business support an additional person?
- How will adding an additional design/sales person affect the current staff? (Will it take business away from them?)
- Does continued good customer service dictate hiring the additional person?

DECIDING ON THE RIGHT COMPENSATION SYSTEM FOR YOUR SALES TEAM

The compensation package for employees is one of the main engines that drives your business. If your company is like most companies, it's an expensive engine to maintain and probably your number one expense.

People costs are between 50 percent and 60 percent of total operating expenses for small businesses in America. According to the NKBA's most recent Dealer Profit Report, total payroll expenses were 56.4 percent of the total operating expense (right in line with national small business averages). What's yours? Be sure to include all related people costs (salary, taxes, benefits, perks, commissions, bonuses, etc.), including the owner's.

Payroll is more than simply an expense. How much you pay your employees and the factors that you use to establish pay scales and award bonuses and other incentives can profoundly affect the quality of your workforce. Equally important, it can affect your ability to attract and retain productive, reliable employees.

At industry business management workshops, usually one of the liveliest topics is compensation. "What pay structure do you use—salary, straight commission, or a combination?" is frequently asked/ If commission, "Is it on sales, gross profit, or both?" "How much should I pay a sales/design person?" (Productivity has a lot to do with this.)

There are no right answers to these questions, because there are too many variables. But there are some guidelines and parameters. Some basics are presented next.

Basics of Employee Compensation

The language of employee compensation (unless you specialize in human resources and, more specifically, employee compensation) can be confusing. Here a list of common terms.

- **Compensation.** This is the general term for anything that employees receive in exchange for their work, including base pay, commissions, bonuses, and other incentives.
- **Base wage and salary.** The salary or wage that employees receive before deductions are subtracted and before other incentives are included.
- **Incentives.** These are special rewards for productivity, such as commissions, bonuses, profit sharing, and so on, that you offer employees in addition to base wage or salary.
- **Benefits.** Benefits are any other compensation that you offer to employees in addition to base wage or salary. Examples include health insurance, stock options, 401(k) retirement plans, vacation, and sick days.
- **Exempt workers.** These are employees who receive salaries (those paid on a flat weekly, biweekly, or monthly as opposed to an hourly basis) and who are ineligible, in most cases, for overtime pay.
- **Nonexempt workers.** These are full-time and part-time workers to whom you pay an hourly wage. The provisions of the Fair Labor Standards Act (FLSA) and comparable state/provincial laws, particularly with respect to minimum hourly wage and overtime pay, cover nonexempt employees. Be sure to check your state/province on the criteria that constitutes and clarifies the difference between exempt and nonexempt employees. They vary from state to state/province to province.
- **Commission.** A commission is a percentage of a price or gross margin earned on the sale of products and/or services. It can be the total wage or can be combined with salary or hourly wages.

Setting the Foundation for an Effective Compensation System

To establish a foundation for an effective compensation plan, first think system and then think strategy, with a constant eye toward the needs and goals of your business. An effective compensation system is a well-thought-out set of practices that helps to ensure that:

- Your employees receive a fair and equitable wage (from both the owner and employee's perspective) for the work they perform.
- Your payroll costs are in line with the overall financial health of your business.
- Your employees understand your basic philosophy of compensation, which has strong support of managers and employees alike.
- The pay scale for the various jobs in the company reflects the relative importance of the job and the skills that performing these jobs require.

- Pay scales are competitive with others in your region in order to retain and attract employees. (You don't want to lose key people to competitors.)
- Your compensation policies (and levels) are in line with state/province and federal laws involving minimum wage and job classification.
- Your compensation policies keep pace with the changing nature of today's labor market—particularly in recruiting and retaining the knowledge workers who are in strong demand.

Establishing a Compensation Philosophy

Do you just try to meet the minimum compensation it will take to bring a new employee on board and then react to wage increases based on employees' demands? Or do you have a well-thought-out strategy that becomes the basis for your wage and salary decisions? To develop an acceptable compensation strategy, some questions you may want to ask yourself are:

- Will you make your pay scales simply competitive with the going rate in your area, or will you try to pay just a little more?
- Will you try to determine how much each position in the company is worth to the business? Or will you set up salaries on an individual basis, based on the qualities and potential of the person filling the position?
- To what extent are the monetary rewards you offer your employees going to take the form of salary, commissions, performance incentives, or benefits?
- Will you base the salaries on how well people perform or on other factors, such as how long they stay with you or the credentials (certifications) they bring to the job?
- Are you going to award incentives based on individual performance, tie them to company results, or use a combination thereof?

There are no right or wrong answers to these questions. Every situation is different. What's important is that your compensation philosophy takes into account your company's mission and strategic goals. If your goal is to be the biggest and best kitchen and bath business in your area, you probably will have to pay just a little more in order to attract and retain the best people. If your goal is to increase productivity and performance, you may want to build in incentives to reward employees for their individual and/or collective efforts.

Common Compensation Plans

In the kitchen and bath industry, there are almost as many compensation plans as there are businesses. Here is a brief look at the pros and cons of four of the most popular plans.

Regular (Straight) Salary Plan

This straight salary plan pays the employee a set amount of salary (exempt employees) or hourly (nonexempt employees) on a regular (weekly, biweekly, monthly) basis.

Employee
- Pros
  - Security
  - Guaranteed same dollars each month
  - Easy to budget
  - Earns the same regardless of productivity or performance
- Cons
  - Does not provide incentive

Management
- Pros
  - Easy to plan and budget
  - Easy to administer
  - Total control

- Cons
  - Does not provide incentive
  - Employee earns the same regardless of production

Commission-only Plan

The commission-only plan usually applies only to salespeople. It pays a certain percentage on monthly (the most often time period used) sales, gross margin, or a combination of both.

Employee
- Pros
  - Big incentive to sell more or at higher margins
  - No limit on how much employee can earn
- Cons
  - Can have variance in income.
  - Difficult to budget for household expenses

Management
- Pros
  - Only pay for productivity
  - May attract very productive salespeople
- Cons
  - Harder to administer
  - Cannot plan/budget as well
  - Less incentive to be a "team player" (more individualistic)
  - Employee can be too aggressive
  - Lose control of employee
  - If on sales, no incentive to achieve margins

Combination Salary/Commission Plan

In the combination salary/commission plan, compensation is made up of a percentage of salary (guaranteed) and commission (driven by productivity). Management sets both with a goal that the total will offer both security and incentive. There are pros and cons for each party:

Employee
- Pros
  - Partial guarantee
  - Partial incentive
  - More security than straight commission
- Cons
  - Guaranteed portion only accounts for part of total comp.
  - Productivity incentive may negatively impacted

Management
- Pros
  - Partial incentive
  - Employee has to be productive
- Cons
  - Harder to administrate
  - Incentive to produce may not be enough
  - Can only plan or budget for part of it

Guaranteed Draw against Commission

A guaranteed draw against commission plan is a straight commission plan (can be on sales, margin, or both), but instead of waiting for sales/margin results, the employee gets a guaranteed amount in advance that is then subtracted from the commissions when results are in.

Employee
- Pros
  - No waiting for commissions
  - Incentive to sell more, increase margins, or both
  - No limit on how much they can make
  - Can plan and budget
- Cons
  - Can fall behind and owe company

Management
- Pros
  - Same minimum pay every month (+/– commissions)
  - Easy to plan and budget
  - Incentive for employee
  - Pay only for productivity
  - May attract big sellers
- Cons
  - May be hard to collect from an employee who falls behind
  - Harder to administrate
  - Harder to plan/budget
  - Employee can be aggressive
  - Can lose some control
  - If commission on sales or margin only, could lose incentive

EXAMPLES OF COMPENSATION PLANS

How much do you want/have to pay a design/salesperson to produce x amount of sales and/or gross margin? For purposes of our examples, let's assume a yearly compensation of $60,000 per year. One way is simply a straight salary plan, regardless of sales or gross margin:

$5,000 per month = $60,000 per year

However, it is important to note that in the kitchen and bath business, sales professionals are rarely paid a straight salary. Salaries are typically an entry-level compensation plan when a designer is starting. A modest salary often is paid during the training period. Afterward, individuals typically move to a split salary and commission and then on to either a draw against commission or straight commission.

You can make any one of the previously described commission or combination commission/salary plans work. Simply plug in the numbers or percentages to make that happen. Each of the three examples that follow uses the same set of underlying assumptions:

Monthly sales	$80,000	Yearly sales	$960,000
Monthly GP %	40%	Yearly GP %	40%
Monthly GP $	$32,000	Yearly GP $	$384,000
Monthly compensation	$5,000	Yearly compensation	$60,000
(Less benefits)		(Less benefits)	

Here is how you do it:

Example 1. Straight commission-on-sales plan

Monthly sales	$80,000	Yearly sales	$960,000
Commission %	6.25%	Yearly commission %	6.25%
Monthly Commission	$5,000	Yearly compensation	$60,000

Example 2. Straight commission on gross margin ($)

Monthly GP ($)	$32,000	Yearly GP	$384,000
Commission %	15.625%	Yearly commission %	15.625%
Monthly commission	$5,000	Yearly compensation	$60,000

Example 3. Combination salary/commission-on-sales plan (you determine the salary portion)

Monthly base pay	$2,500	Yearly base pay	30,000
Monthly sales	$80,000	Yearly sales	960,000
Monthly commission %	3.125%	Yearly commission %	3.125%
Monthly commission $	$2,500	Yearly commission $	$30,000
Total monthly compensation	$5,000	Yearly compensation	$60,000

Example 4. Combination salary/ commission-on-gross-margin plan (you determine the salary portion)

Monthly base pay	$2,500	Yearly base pay	$30,000
Monthly GP %	40%	Yearly GP %	40%
Monthly GP	$32,000	Yearly GP	$384,000
Monthly commission %	7.8125%	Yearly commission %	7.8125%
Monthly commission $	$2,504	Yearly commission $	$30,048
Total monthly compensation	$5,004	Yearly compensation	$60,048

You decide how much you want to pay, what plan will work best for you, and how much productivity (sales and gross profit (GP) margin) you expect to achieve for the dollars paid, and then plug in the numbers.

Examples 3 and 4 offer some guaranteed compensation ($2,500 per month) and build in an incentive that encourages more sales and gross margin. You can even increase that incentive to benefit the company by building in a sliding-scale commission based on monthly gross margin. When the margin goes up, so does the commission percentage. When the GP dollars go down, so does the commission percentage.

Here is an example of a sliding scale commission plan that is driven by both sales and gross margin productivity. You decide what the monthly base pay should be in order to achieve your goals. (Again, make the numbers work for you):

Monthly commission percentage	Monthly gross margin percentage (commission % × monthly GP $)
44% and over	10%
42–43.99%	9%
40–41.99%	8%
38–39.99%	7%
36–37.99%	6%
34–35.99%	5%
32–33.99%	4%
Less than 32%	0%

For example, if monthly sales were $100,000 and the gross margin percentage was 40 percent, the gross margin dollars would be $40,000. You would pay a commission of $3,200 (8% × $40,000).

Running the Numbers

Straight salary is easy to budget, but here are some examples of how you might approach commission structures.

Assumption: You want/expect the salesperson to achieve $50,000 sales per month at 40 percent gross profit. You can either pay 10 percent commission on total sales or 25 percent commission on gross profit dollars.

- Commission only: Per month

  10 percent commission on $50,000 = $5,000

  Total compensation, with no benefits $5,000

  Or

  40 percent gross profit on $50,000 Sales = $20,000

  25 percent commission on $20,000 = $5,000

  Total compensation, with no benefits $5,000

- Combination plan: Per month

  Base salary of $1,500

  7 percent commission on $50,000 = $3,500

  Total compensation, with no benefits $5,000

  Or

  Base salary of $2,500

  40 percent gross profit on $50,000 Sales = $20,000

  12.5 percent commission on $20,000 = $2,500

  Total compensation, with no benefits $5,000

Or you can pay commission on a sliding scale based on performance rather than on a fixed rate. Here is an example of such a sliding scale might be, paying commission on gross profit:

Monthly Average Gross Profit Margin Percent	Monthly Gross Profit Commission Rate
44% +	14%
42%–44%	13%
40%–42%	12%
38%–40%	11%
36%–38%	10%
34%–36%	9%
42%–34%	8%
30%–32%	7%
25%–30%	5%
Below 25%	0%

Set goals and communicate those goals to your employees at the start. If your employees exceed the goal, consider a special bonus.

Employment Contracts

Regardless of what payment method is used, make up a contract with each salesperson that addresses each of these six points:

1. How is the salesperson to be paid?
   a. Salary + commission
   b. Commission on sales
   c. Commission against draw
   d. Commission on gross profit
   e. Earned commission
2. What is the commission paid on?
   a. Sales volume
   b. Profit margin of each project
3. What is the basis for the payment calculations?
   a. Sales amount without taxes
   b. Gross profit, including overhead calculations, or only job-related costs
   c. Any design fees shared between the salesperson and customer
   d. Commission rate(s) for all products and services (i.e., will the rate be the same for cabinets, appliances, countertops, plumbing, installation, etc.?)
4. What is the payment schedule/timing of payments? For a salary or draw, is it:
   a. Calendar basis (weekly, biweekly, etc.)
   b. When the draw stops
   c. What relationship, if any, exists between the draw payments and commission payments?

Straight Commission Program Based on Gross Profit–An Example

Straight commission salespeople are the most productive and profitable when paid on a percentage of the gross profit earned on the job. Our sample company bases its straight commissions on these following formulas:

- Commission rates: a minimum of 30 percent and a maximum of 40 percent of the gross profit generated on a job.
- Minimum gross profit required: 30 percent. Maximum acceptable gross profit: 50 percent. Gross profit under 30 percent receives no commission.
- Company overhead, gifts or other charges may be included in the gross profit calculations as a cost to the job.
- 60 percent of the estimated gross commission is paid to the salesperson in the next pay period providing they provide the following to the company's satisfaction:
   a. A signed contract
   b. The required deposit
   c. The plans and elevations required
   d. A job cost estimate sheet
   e. Other appropriate materials identified by the company
- The 40 percent balance of the commission is paid in the next pay period after:
   a. The job is completed.
   b. All costs are entered.
   c. All costs are reconciled.
   d. The actual gross profit can be determined. The job is fully paid.

5. When the company terminates salespeople, what happens to:
   a. Their draw?
   b. Commissions earned?
   c. Future commissions?
   d. Their overdraw?
   e. Jobs in progress?
   f. Jobs almost sold?
   g. Jobs that still must be completed?
   h. Jobs that run over cost?
   i. Leads generated while employed?
6. If salespeople leave the company, what happens to:
   a. Their draw?
   b. Commissions earned?
   c. Future commissions?
   d. Their overdraw?
   e. Jobs in progress?
   f. Jobs almost sold?
   g. Jobs that still must be completed?
   h. Jobs that run over cost?
   i. Leads generated while employed?

RESOURCEFUL RECRUITING

The recruiting stage of the hiring process is a lot like fishing. Success depends not only how well you do it but where and what "bait" you use.

There are numerous ways to go fishing for qualified candidates. Some strategies require more time, effort, and cost than others. The key to effective recruiting is to make sure that whatever options you select are logically and strategically aligned with your priorities.

The number one question is: Where can I find good people? There is no easy answer. If you are operating a highly successful business, where the environment is professional and fun and the people are happy, motivated, and well compensated, you'll have prospects knocking on your door. Good news travels, and word will get out that your business is a good company to work for.

Another option is to develop your own highly qualified employees. Hire bright, well-educated, motivated, hardworking people who will be a good fit to your company. The long-term benefits usually outweigh the short-term effects.

For example, hire for Job A (a less responsible job requiring less experience), then train and move employees to Job B. Receptionists can meet and greet clients, answer phones, do paperwork, chores, and so on. They learn your system and procedures, attend all staff meetings for product knowledge and selling skills, and, in the course of a year or two, are often ready to move into the sales department. It is a good practice to promote from within. It builds morale, motivates, and allows you, the boss, to build your own team.

Recruiting Is More than a Numbers Game

When preparing to hire a new person, it is a common misconception that you should interview as many prospects as possible. But, quality is more important than quantity, and you want to attract only the highest-quality candidates. When you advertise or visit local colleges during a job fair, you'll be making a statement about your company. It is important that the statement is positive. To recruit the best talent, establish a positive, professional image and reputation for your company. This carries through to the interview stage as well.

Getting Started

Recruiting—finding qualified candidates—is probably the most challenging part of hiring. Consider using these sources:

- Classified advertisements (trade journals and/newspapers)
- Vendor reps
- The NKBA job posting Web site www.kitchenandbathcareers.com
- The Internet
- Personnel agencies (that specialize in the K&B industry)
- Industry meetings and events
- Job fairs/open houses
- Colleges with interior design or kitchen/bath design curricula
- Family and friends

Remember, prospects will often seek you out if they've heard that you pay well and that yours is a great place to work.

Make Recruitment an Ongoing Process

Companies known for their ability to attract and hire good employees are always recruiting, even if they don't have any current openings. If recruiting is part of your responsibility as the owner, always be on the lookout for people who can contribute to your organization's success, even if they are working somewhere else at the time and you have no immediate personnel needs. At the very least, keep an active file of names and résumé of individuals who have the experience and qualities you may need.

Create a Strategy

You need a plan. What sources do you plan to use? When will you start? When do you hope to have all the résumé in to start reviewing? How long will the interviewing process take? When do you want to have someone on board? If you set time frames and deadlines for each of these, you'll have a better chance of achieving your goals. Allow for flexibility.

Keeps Tabs on Your Progress

Monitor your efforts on a regular basis; not just the quantity of inquiries but also the quality. Depending on internal needs and the response, you may have to increase or decrease your efforts.

Recruiting from Within

As mentioned previously, there are several advantages to recruiting from within. It helps keep morale and motivation levels high, and you won't need to worry about employees fitting into your culture since they already know the territory.

There are, however, two possible drawbacks to promoting from within. First, you may have a limited range of candidates, and there may be someone more qualified on the outside. Second, promoting one person may upset another.

Classified Advertisements

Whether you're placing an ad in a trade magazine or on the Internet, on sites such as LinkedIn, Monster, and CareerBuilder, you can be reasonably sure that people looking for jobs in the kitchen and bath field will be reading it.

How to Write a Classified Ad

Keep the following considerations in mind when writing a job ad:

- The goal of a classified advertisement is not only to generate responses from qualified candidates but also to screen out candidates who are unqualified. You're better off getting 10 responses from people who deserve an interview than getting 100 responses from people who are unqualified.
- Think "sell." You are advertising a product: your company.
- Every aspect of your advertisement must seek to foster a favorable impression of the position and the organization.
- If you've done a good job writing a detailed job description, a good part of the ad is already written. Think of the ad as a synopsis of the existing job description.

The next list describes elements to keep in mind as you compose the ad.

- **Headline.** Usually the job title
- **Job information.** One or two lines about the general duties and responsibilities of the job
- **Company information.** Description of what your company does
- **Qualifications and hiring criteria.** Level of education and experience required
- **How to respond.** Let applicants know the preferred way to get in touch with you: email, phone, mail, or fax

Bear in mind the following key components:

- Convey some sense of your organizational cultural values with a few phrases ("family-oriented," "team-driven," "client focused," etc.).
- Use active voice and action words throughout the ad ("successful," "fast growing," "well respected," etc.).
- Create a buzz, a sense of enthusiasm, arousing applicants' interest.
- If there's something special about the job or company, spell it out (award winning, live in California, the playground of America, etc.)

Figure 8.4 is an advertisement for a designer/sales position. The sample is for a print ad, but the example would work equally well for an online classified ad.

CLASSIFIED ADVERTISING

KITCHEN-BATH DESIGN SALES PROFESSIONAL

A successful, growing and award-winning kitchen and bath business seeks an experienced, well-organized person to work in its newly remodeled showroom. This opportunity offers living in beautiful Northern California and working in a family, team-oriented business. The successful candidate will work with clients in designing and selling high-end, quality kitchen and bath products. The business offers one-stop shopping and turnkey projects to a growing list of clients. The company offers above-average compensation. A minimum of five years experience, strong sales record and NKBA certification is highly desired. Respond via email.

FIGURE 8.4 An example of a classified (print) ad.

NARROWING DOWN THE LIST: APPLICATIONS, RÉSUMÉS, AND TESTING

Most would agree that the job interview is the most important element of the hiring process. However, another important key is effective screening. If you do not do careful screening, two things may happen—both bad. First, you may inadvertently "weed out" candidates who deserve a second look. Second, you could waste valuable time on candidates who are clearly unqualified.

Job Applications

In the past, this was the primary method of screening. However, thanks to the résumé, applications do not figure as prominently in the hiring process. There are probably two reasons for this. The résumé contains all or most of the information and, Equal Employment Opportunity (EEO) legislation now prohibits the interviewer from asking many of the questions that were standard in the past. Items relating to age, marital status—even birthplace—are illegal to ask.

A comprehensive legal application form does provide a uniform means of reviewing the information and it may force the candidates to furnish facts that they might otherwise omit.

Office supply stores offer basic preprinted applications but you may elect to create your own. If you do your own, think about how much information you really need. As a general rule, less is more. If you prepare your own, have it reviewed by a human resource attorney.

Here are questions to avoid:

- Race
- Religion
- Gender or sexual orientation
- Age
- Ancestry or national origin (although you can ask if a candidate is eligible to work in the United States)
- Military service
- Height/weight
- Political preference
- Handicaps/disabilities
- Whether the candidate owns or rents a house
- High school/college graduation dates (allows you to determine age)
- Maiden names
- Pictures before they are hired

Final rule: If you do not need specific information, do not ask for it. A well-designed application form should provide you with the following four types of information:

- Vital statistics—name, address, etc.
- Educational background
- Detailed work history
- Background information

Always have the applicants sign the form and affirm the accuracy of the information they furnish. This does not guarantee that all of the information is true, but it gives you some protection if, after you hire an applicant, they do not work out and you discover that they made misrepresentations on the application.

Screening System

There are no set rules for screening, other than common sense. Here is a system that works well:

- Scan for the basics such as core qualifications for the position you are seeking to fill.
- Screen for criteria. Using the written job description as your guide, focus on the more specific hiring criteria. Start with a high standard of evaluation, with only those applications

meeting most or all of your criteria placed in a follow-up file. This eliminates those who do not meet the criteria.

- Set up a separate file for the finalists. At this point, you'll want to establish a separate file for each of the candidates who pass the initial screening process. Attach a flow sheet to the front of each file to keep up to date with each candidate. The flow sheet lists the steps in the screening process with spaces for the date and initials of the person completing the step.
- Extend an invitation. Depending on how many finalists you have, take it to the next step. If you have several finalists, you can make telephone calls to help expand or clarify information. If you haven't received a completed copy of your application form, invite the candidate to come in to complete it.

Analyzing Résumés

Analyzing résumé can be a difficult process. Most candidates have learned how to write a résumé that makes them look like theperfect candidate; those who can't often hire someone to do it for them.

Résumé come in two different forms:

1. **Chronological.** All the work related information appears in a chronological sequence.
2. **Functional.** The information appears in various categories (skills, achievements, qualifications, etc.).

Both serve the purpose and one should not be favored over the other. Some candidates may use a combination of the two.

Here are some points to remember:

- Many résumé are professionally prepared and designed to create a winning, but not necessarily accurate, impression.
- Résumé screening is tedious—you may have to sift through the stack several times.
- Do not delegate the screening.

Reading between the Lines

Because people get help in creating their résumé, it's more difficult than ever to get an accurate reading. Here are some characteristics worth looking for:

- **Lots of detail.** The more details a candidate furnishes, the more reliable (as a rule) the information often is. However, résumé over two pages are generally not recommended.
- **A history of stability and achievement.** Watch out for people who have traveled job to job, regardless of the reasons they give. Work history should show steady progression to greater responsibility. Don't go by job titles alone. Look at what the candidate did.
- **A strong, well-written cover letter.** Assuming the candidate wrote it, it is generally a good indication of the person's communication skills.

Red Flags

Sometimes what is *not* in a résumé or careless mistakes can reveal quite a bit about a candidate. Here are some of the things to look for:

- Sloppy overall appearance
- Unexplained chronological gaps
- Static career pattern
- Typos and misspellings
- Vaguely worded job descriptions
- Job hopping
- Overemphasis on hobbies or outside interests

Testing

Pre-employment testing is probably the most controversial of all the screening options in use today. Most people agree with the basic rationale that test results often can alert you to attributes and potential problems that you will not pick up from résumé and that might not surface during interviews. There is, however, no conclusive proof that testing results equate to better hires.

Tests are simply tools. Each type measures a specific aspect or quality of an applicant's skills, knowledge, experience, or—more controversially—personality (or psychological makeup).

Literally hundreds of tests are available. In our industry, it is easy to test design skills, done by hand or using a CAD system. It is more difficult to test selling skills. Some personality tests will help determine if the candidate would be a good fit for your corporate culture.

An excellent, proven, inexpensive test is the DISC Personality Test. It can be taken online and results are almost immediate. DISC stands for four personality traits: dominance, influence, steadiness, and conscientiousness. For approximately $70 you can learn a lot about your top candidates. You can find the tests at www.thediscpersonalitytest.com or by calling 888-585-9414.

Hiring the right person the first time is important (and cost effective), so try some testing. Why not use all the tools you can to help you make the right hiring decisions?

ART OF INTERVIEWING

Conducting an interview is an art—a learned skill—and it may seem easier than it is. Too many kitchen and bath owners/managers take interviewing for granted. They do not invest the time, effort, and concentration that effective job interviewing requires. Unfortunately, too many interviewers wing it. They do not thoroughly prepare in advance. It is a proven that well-prepared, organized interviews equate to better, more productive, longer-lasting employees. Here are some tips.

- **Look out for "professional" interviewees.** They are more schooled and practiced at putting on a good performance. This can be a positive thing but can also mean that they know how to give the answers you want to hear. Do your best to distinguish one from the other.
- **Who is conducting the interview anyway?** Many applicants approach interviews with the attitude that they are checking out the company and the position rather than the other way around. It's important that both parties have their questions answered but if you find the candidate is asking all of the questions, you have lost control of the interview.
- **Sour grapes, legal issues.** Now that more candidates are well versed in antidiscrimination legislation, those who do not get the job are more likely than ever to claim, justifiably or not, that your company's interviewing practices are discriminatory. It's important to conduct every interview within legal guidelines. Basics of Interviewing

Job interviews enable you to perform the next four tasks that are essential to making a sound hiring decision:

1. Elicit firsthand information about candidates' backgrounds and work experience that augments or clarifies what you have already learned from their resume, application form, or previous interview.
2. Get a general sense of candidates' overall intelligence, aptitudes, enthusiasm, and attitude, with particular attention to how these attributes match up to the requirements of the job.
3. Gain insight, to the extent possible, into candidates' basic personality traits.
4. Estimate candidates' ability to adapt to your company's work environment.

Five Deadly Sins of Job Interviewing

Here are five common interviewing mistakes:

1. **Not taking enough time.** You fail to give the interviewing process the time and effort it deserves. With all the hats that kitchen and bath owners have to wear, it's easy to understand how they can neglect to take the time needed to do a good job. Considering the cost of making poor decisions and the effect on the company and other employees, can you afford *not* to take the time to do a good job?
2. **Getting bored with the repetition of the interview.** The most successful interviews have a plan. You need structure so you won't miss or overlook anything and so you can make comparisons.
3. **Talking too much.** Let candidates do most of the talking. If you're talking more than 20 percent of the time, you're talking too much. If you do most of the talking, the only thing you'll learn is that candidates are good listeners.
4. **Placing too much emphasis on one particular aspect of a candidate's overall presentation** (credentials, interests, etc.).
5. **Looking for subconscious meanings in what candidates say.** Being able to read people is a valuable skill for anyone who conducts interviews. However, you are not a psychologist or psychiatrist, so don't try to seek out the subconscious meaning behind everything candidates say or do.

Setting the Stage

Being well prepared for an interview is one of the keys for success. Here are a few things you can do to prepare yourself for the interview process:

- Familiarize yourself with the written job description, especially the hiring criteria.
- Review everything the candidate has submitted to date: job application, résumé, cover letter, and so on. Make notes on anything (positive and negative) that jumps out at you.
- Set up a general structure for the interview.
- Write down the questions you intend to ask, and keep the list in front of you.
- Set up a timetable, allow yourself plenty of time.
- Conduct the interview in a room that's quiet, private, and reasonably comfortable. Clear your desk, close the door, put calls on hold, and avoid interruptions.

Introduction (Warming Up)

Your first priority is to put the candidate at ease. If you are seated when candidates come in, stand, shake their hand, smile, and let them know you are pleased to see them. Start with some small talk (keep it to a minimum), giving candidates an overview of what you are expecting to get out of the interview. Let them know approximately how long the interview will take (45–60 minutes), unless you determine early on that this is not the right candidate. If that's the case, end the meeting sooner in a polite way.

Art of Asking Questions

- Have a focus, know what information or insights you are looking for.
- Make every question count.
- Pay attention. *Do not* think ahead; listen to what candidates have to say.
- Do not hesitate to probe.
- Give candidates of time to answer.
- Hold your judgments.
- Take notes.

The Art of Questions and Answers

The following are guidelines for the question-and-answer process:

- **Have a focus.** Before you start to ask questions, you'll want to have a reasonably specific idea of what information or insights you're expecting to gain from the interview. Review the hiring criteria you developed in your job description.
- **Make every question count.** Every question should have a specific purpose.
- **Pay attention.** Be a good listener; ask, then listen (remember the 80 percent listening guideline). Fight the tendency to think ahead.
- **Do not hesitate to probe.** If you ask a specific question and receive a general answer, come back and ask another question that will give you the specific information you're seeking. For example, when a candidate for a sales job says she was the number one salesperson, ask for a specific sales number.
- **Give the candidate time to respond.** A bit of silence while the candidate thinks about the answer to your question is fine. If the silence lasts 10 seconds or more, you may want to consider restating the question.
- **Hold your judgments**. Try to keep your attention on the answers you're getting instead of making interpretations or judgments. Be careful not to prejudice yourself in the beginning of the interview so that you may fail to accurately process information that comes later.
- **Take notes.** If you're interviewing more than two candidates, you may have a difficult time keeping the facts straight unless you take notes. Try to be unobtrusive in the note taking so candidates do not feel they have to slow down and wait for you. Use a separate sheet of paper rather than the résumé to make your notes.

General Interview Questions

1. Tell me a little about yourself.
2. What do you know about our company, and why do you want to work here?
3. What interests you about this job, and what skills and strengths can you bring to it?
4. Can you tell me a little about your current job?
5. I see that you have been unemployed for the past _____ months. Why did you leave your last job, and what have you been doing since then?
6. What would you describe as your greatest strength as an employee? Your greatest weakness?

7. Who was your best boss ever, and why? Who was the worst, and, what could you have done to make that relationship better?
8. How do you think your best boss would describe you? Your worst boss?
9. What was/is your greatest achievement at your prior/current job? What was/is your greatest failure?
10. What things do you think your prior/current/last company could do to become more successful?
11. Describe a typical day at work in your prior/current job.
12. What sort of work environment do you prefer? What brings out your best performance?
13. Where do you see yourself and your career in three years? Five years?
14. Tell me about an important decision you made at work and how you arrived at it.
15. How do you handle conflict? Give me an example of how you handled a workplace conflict in the past.

Closing on the Right Note

If you've managed time well during the interview process, you should have enough time left for the candidate to ask you questions. These questions can be important because they will give you an idea of candidates' interests and how much preparation they did for the interview. Questions about the job itself versus questions about salary, perks, and the like can be more revealing.

Finally, in ending the interview, you can:

- Offer candidates a broad summary of the interview.
- Let candidates know what comes next.
- End the interview on a formal note.

As soon as possible after each candidate's departure, take time to collect your thoughts and summarize your views of the interview and your notes. This will help you when going back to review the finalists.

MAKING THE FINAL HIRING DECISION

The decision-making process in the final stages of hiring is no different from the process of making any complex decision—whether you're buying a new computer system for the business, changing your cabinet supplier, or changing the showroom location. Look at your options, weigh the pros and cons of each, and make your choice.

Some base their decisions on intuition, or a gut feeling, while others are highly systematic. Some people rely entirely on their own judgment, while others seek input from others. You can never be certain the decision you make is going to yield the desired result. But you can be certain that you manage the decision-making process in a disciplined, intelligent way. To do this, you should perform four tasks:

1. Early in the hiring process, identify your needs and prepare a job description that pinpoints the combination of skills, attributes, and credentials that a particular job requires.
2. Gather enough information about each candidate through interviewing, testing, and observation so you have a reasonably good idea of each person's capabilities, personalities, strengths, and weaknesses.
3. Remain objective (no easy task) in evaluating candidates. Don't allow personal biases to steer you away from your hiring criteria.
4. Sell candidates you favor on the job and make them enthusiastic about the position.

Much of the hiring process involves guesswork, but by doing the things listed above, it will be educated guesswork.

What to Look For

The resources available to make a hiring decision regarding a given individual are limited. Only a handful of information is available. Here are a few sources you might be able to use.

Past Experience

The best indicator of a candidate's future performance is past performance.

Interview Impressions

The impressions you pick up during an interview usually carry a great deal of weight in the hiring decision. The problem with interview impressions is that they are just that—impressions.

Test Results

Arguments for and against testing exist. Some candidates are great testers, while others freeze. If you do decide to use test results in your decision-making process, make sure of these two things: the validity of the tests (whether they do indeed predict the quality of future job performance) and their legality (whether their use complies with all state and federal laws and does not result in discrimination).

References and Other Third-Party Observations

Reference data are useful and necessary components of the hiring process. But in today's litigious environment, most former employers are reluctant to say anything negative about an employee for fear of a lawsuit. Use reference information as a secondary source—to verify impressions and other information.

Firsthand Observation

Watching candidates actually perform some of the tasks they would be doing if hired is clearly the most reliable way to judge their competence. That is why many companies have instituted combination training and probationary periods. Ask a sales/design candidate to do a simple kitchen or bath design, both by hand and on the computer. How fast is he or she? How accurate?

Another trend in hiring today is the practice of starting out a new employee as temporary, with the understanding that if he or she works out, the job will become full time.

Rating Scale

Rating scales can be tricky. Instead of simply looking at the candidate as a whole, you look at each of the criteria you set down and rate the candidate based on how he or she measures up in that particular area.

By weighing each performance category, you show which is more important to the success of the job:

- Using a weighted scale to compare one candidate to another requires both subjective and objective opinions from you.
- Constructing a weighted scale by category may be difficult, but breaking out different parts of the job should help in the selection process.

Table 8.2 is a sample of a weighted evaluation scale. Make this scale work for you by adding or deleting any categories and by changing any of the assigned weights. What may be the most important categories for one many not be for the other.

To explain the concept of a "weighted scale": Individual business needs will establish priorities. Therefore, by having two employee rating systems, you are able to evaluate each point on its own merit. Then rank the importance of the skill, talent, or ability according to your needs.

TABLE 8.2 Weighted Evaluation Scale

Candidate's Name:			
Position:			
Performance Category	**Weighted Importance** **1 (Low)–5 (High)** ×	**Candidate Rating** **1 (Low)–5 (High)** =	**Total Score**
Design Skills (hand)	3	5	15
Design Skills (CAD)	4	3	12
Selling Skills	5	1	5
Design skills (hand)			
Design skills (CAD)			
Selling skills			
Time management skills			
Organizational skills			
Communication skills			
Previous employment			
Reliability; work ethics			
Team player			
Past work history			
Professionalism			
Product knowledge			
Follow-through			
Motivation			
Enthusiasm			
Fit with the company "culture"			
TOTAL			
(Note: Column 2 is the weight of importance you assign to each category; column 3 is how you rate the candidate.)			

Factoring in the Intangibles

The difficult part of any evaluation procedure is attaching numerical ratings to the intangibles—those attributes you can measure only through observation. Several of the intangible factors commonly included in the criteria for most jobs, along with some suggestions on how to tell whether candidates measure up, are listed next.

- **Industriousness and motivation**

  Definition: Candidates' work ethic—how hard they are willing to work and how important it is to them that they perform to the best of their ability.

  Possible ways of measuring: Verify accomplishments in their last jobs.

- **Intelligence**

  Definition: Mental alertness, thinking ability, capability to process abstract information.

  Possible ways of measuring: Testing. Evidence of good decision-making ability in previous jobs.

- **Temperament and ability to cope with stress**

  Definition: General demeanor—whether the candidate is calm and levelheaded, hyperactive, or hotheaded.

  Possible ways of measuring: Personality testing. Examine stress levels in previous jobs.

- **Creativity and resourcefulness**

  Definition: The ability to think outside the box—to come up with innovative solutions to problems.

  Possible ways of measuring: Examples of previous work (portfolio of designs). Previous accomplishments or awards.

- **Orientation to teamwork**

  Definition: Whether the candidate can work harmoniously with others and share responsibility for achieving the same goal.

  Possible ways of measuring: Previous work experience (did they work on their own, or in groups), leisure preferences (are they solitary or group oriented?).

Making the Offer

You have made your final choice about whom you want to hire. Now you must make the offer and convince the candidate to come to work for you. Without the proper execution of the offer, you might lose the candidate:

- **Don't delay.** Once you've made up your mind, make the offer as soon as possible.
- **Put everything on the table.** Give the candidate all of the details about pay, benefits, hours, and any extras. You should have a standard job offer letter that you can customize. Always put the job offer in writing.
- **Set a reasonable acceptance deadline.** The candidate may need time to make his or her decision—but allow no more than a week.
- **Employment contracts (yes or no).** There is no need for long, formal legal documents. Use a one-page letter that specifies the job title, duties, responsibilities, conditions of employment, and severance arrangements. This eliminates questions, surprises, and misunderstandings.
- **"Selling" the candidate.** If this is someone you really want to have work for you and he or she is are showing some reluctance, you'll have to find out (via questions and answers) what is causing the reluctance. Here are some factors that may have bearing on how excited the candidate feels about your offer:
  - Nature of the job and its responsibilities
  - Advancement opportunities
  - Salary (commission) structure and frequency of reviews

- Benefits package—how does it compare to the candidate's previous job?
- Culture and company working style
- Policies toward work/family balance issues, such as flexible scheduling, telecommuting, child care, and so on
- Commuting considerations—how long will it take them to get to work?
- Reporting relationships; personality of the immediate supervisor
- Self-development opportunities (company training, NKBA courses, certification, etc.)
- Relocation of the candidate and family
- Perceived strength, solvency, and market competitiveness of the company

How far you are willing to go to accommodate a reluctant candidate generally depends on two factors:

1. How much you want the candidate
2. Company policies and precedents

There are three questions to ask yourself:

1. Are there any other equally qualified candidates available?
2. How long would it take to pursue them?
3. Has the position been particularly hard to fill?

If your initial attempts to woo a reluctant candidate fail, the best thing to do may be to cut your losses and move on. Sometimes you just have to walk away. The goal should be to leave the candidate with a feeling of fair treatment.

SUMMARY

In this chapter we have explained the importance of good human resource management. We identified the rules and regulations that must be followed and pointed out human resource trends of the future. The importance of having written job descriptions and hiring plans was discussed in detail. We introduced the subject of compensation and compared various options for sales consultants. Finally, we discussed the importance of recruiting methods and provided many recommendations for successful hiring.

REVIEW QUESTIONS

1. What are the owner/manager responsibilities in human resource management? (See "The Broad Picture of Human Resources" page 141)
2. What are the pros and cons of a combined salary and commission compensation program for sales consultants? (See "Common Compensation Plans" page 153)
3. List 5 resources you can use for recruiting new employees. (See "Getting Started" page 160)

Human Resource Management—After the Decision Is Made

People are your most important asset—your real key to success. The human resource topic is the subject of many books. In this volume, we are concentrating on the basics and the areas of human resources that are the most important to kitchen and bath business owners and managers.

Learning Objective 1: Describe the things you must do in the area of human resource management to build the best team.

Learning Objective 2: Describe in detail why having a written training program is important.

Learning Objective 3: Explain why a company policy and procedures manual is a valuable tool for business owners, managers, and employees.

Learning Objective 4: Describe various disciplinary procedures.

Here are five areas of human resource that, if done well, will almost guarantee the success of your business.

1. Hire the best.
2. Train the best.
3. Communicate the best.
4. Motivate the best.
5. Compensate the best.

THE ORIENTATION PERIOD

Almost every new hire will be a bit apprehensive and unsure of what to expect and what to do in those first few days on the job. Everyone needs a period of acclimation to a new company and teammates. This is commonly known as the orientation period. Large companies tend to have formal programs, but small businesses have less formal ways of welcoming new employees.

Regardless of its form, the basic goal of every orientation process is that, after a reasonable amount of time, your new "partners" will know their responsibilities, be productive, and feel like they're part of the team.

Some Things Not to Do

- Leave the employee alone to learn the ropes simply by observing and asking questions.
- Let the new person just follow a more experienced person around.
- Show the new employee nothing more than a short video on your orientation program.

Some Things to Do

- **Ease anxieties.** The main purpose of an orientation plan is to accelerate the process of making employees feel at home. Here are seven suggestions to help make that happen:
  1. Let all the other employees know that a new person will be starting. Tell them who, what, when, and why.
  2. You, the owner, should meet the new employee and take the person to his or her workstation.
  3. You, the owner, should take the new hire around the building and introduce all other employees.
  4. You, the owner, should give the new hire a tour of the facility, pointing out restrooms, lunchroom, and so on.
  5. Provide the new person with a company roster that includes names, phone numbers, and job titles.
  6. Take the newcomer to lunch on the first day—perhaps with one or two other teammates.
  7. Give a clear sense of tasks and expectations, including:
     - A written copy of their job description.
     - Review of the job description in detail.
     - Explanation of expectations.
     - Explanation of your performance evaluation system and the standards you will use to measure them.
     - Explanation of your compensation review policy.
- **Review the company mission statement and goals.** Review, in detail, exactly what the company does.
- **Give the new hire the company policy and procedures manual or employee handbook.** Advise him or her to review it in detail. Answer any questions and clear up any misunderstandings. Have the new employee sign a form acknowledging he or she received, read, and understood the content of the policy manual and/or employee handbook.

A word of caution: Do not provide too much information too quickly. Think of the orientation as a process, not an event. Set priorities. Stay in close touch. Be proactive.

Mentoring: The Secret to Success

What employees see happening around them affects them as much as what they hear and see during a formal orientation program. The best way to make sure that this works in your favor is through the use of mentors. Other employees acting as mentors can show the new person the ropes and be available to answer questions and provide whatever support the individual might need.

In small kitchen and bath businesses, the mentor may very well be the owner. In this case, you, the owner, have to make the time and effort to help the new employee get started in a positive way. First impressions are important.

TRAINING AND DEVELOPMENT

You are off to a good start. You have hired the best candidate. You have done a great job with the orientation program, and the new employee is settling in nicely. Now the real work begins: training. Training starts with the employee's first day of work—and never really ends. Training is one of the five components of good human resource (HR) management. (Hiring, motivating, communicating, and compensation are the other four.)

Unfortunately, most kitchen and bath owners do not have formal training and development programs. Most of the training is on-the-job training with the owner or coworkers helping when they can. Sometimes you are lucky and you're able to hire well-trained, productive people; sometimes not. In either case, almost every employee can improve. It's your job to help them do that. It is good for employees (the more productive they are, the more they can earn), and it's good for you (the more productive they become, the more you will earn)—a win-win situation for all.

Larger, more sophisticated companies do something called "needs assessment." They actually develop a method to evaluate their needs in terms of training. Because you are a small business with 10 or fewer employees, you will know who needs training and in what areas, and how much they need. Your challenge is making it happen.

Training can be fun, inexpensive, and rewarding. It becomes part of the employee's job description, and it becomes one of your main management focuses.

Areas to Concentrate On
- Product knowledge
- Sales skills
- Design skills
- Communication skills
- Time management and organizational skills
- Compensation
- Computer/technology skills

You cannot do everything all at once. Identify priorities (which may vary by employee). Establish time frames and budgets. Look at training and development as a long-term, ongoing process.

An important part of building your training program is to know what your company's long-term goals and objectives are. Your training program should be designed to meet these goals and objectives. For instance, if you want to grow sales from $1 million to $2 million over the next three years, you'll need sales/design people. Your annual and three-year budgets, coupled with cash-flow projections, will tell you when to add people.

In our industry, there are several methods of training.

- **In-house training.** You or someone else acts as the coach and mentor, spending as much time as necessary to "grow" each employee. Hold weekly staff meetings on the same day, at the same time, every week, with mandatory attendance. Use a percentage of these meetings for product knowledge training (either by you or a manufacturer's representative). Some would be for sales training (again, by you or an outside professional). Some would be for internal policies and procedures. Others might be state-of-the-company communication. And still others might be open topic brainstorming.
- **Manufacturer rep or factory product training.** This can take place at your place of business or at the factory.
- **NKBA and other organizations, schools, and seminars can provide training both in person and online.**
- **Books, audio and visual CDs on a variety of topics.** Maintain a resource library and offer an incentive to encourage use. (Or make it a mandatory part of the job.)

- **CAD system training.** Again, this training can take place in-house, off-site, or online.
- **The Internet.** More and more good training programs are becoming available online.
- **Community colleges.** Use of this resource depends on the courses offered and training needed.

For employees other than sales/design (installers, bookkeeping, general office, warehouse, etc.) different programs are available. Training should be an ongoing process for all of your employees.

Because your goal is to help employees increase their productivity and enjoy their work more, it can be beneficial if you can tie in some rewards and incentives.

Training does not just apply to employees. It's just as important for you—the boss—to continually work to improve yourself. The better you are, the better the employees will be.

Be proactive. Do not wait for someone else to do it for you.

NKBA Professional Development

When you enroll in the National Kitchen & Bath Association's professional development, you take the first steps toward becoming one of the finest professionals in the kitchen and bath industry. Whether you simply want to improve your professional development one course at a time, or you want to work toward NKBA certification, you will gain knowledge that will enhance the level of service you provide to your clients.

What Is NKBA Professional Development?

In order to meet the increasing need for qualified professionals in the kitchen and bath industry, the NKBA has developed eight learning paths which offer an individualized approach to professional development.

They are:

- Design & Inspiration
- Talent Management
- Communication
- Adapt & Innovate (Change Management)
- Focus on the Customer
- Business Management
- Leadership
- Sales & Marketing

Each learning path contains a variety of courses, webinars, and other learning experiences to enhance professional skills and/or prepare for the NKBA multi-level certification. Learn more at NKBA.org.

For students entering the industry, the NKBA offers accredited and supported programs throughout North America where an NKBA-approved curriculum is offered at two- and four-year learning institutions.

Who Attends NKBA Professional Development Courses?

All levels of professionals in the kitchen and bath industry, as well as individuals in the construction, remodeling, design, and other related fields attend professional development courses. Kitchen and bath professionals attend courses to enhance their careers by staying up to date on the latest trends and techniques, to obtain continuing education units to support NKBA certifications, or to gain experience in a new aspect of the industry.

The NKBA offers certification for both design and non–design K & B industry professionals. The NKBA developed its certification programs as a way for kitchen and bath professionals to enhance their careers and market themselves as experts in their field. NKBA certification is based on in-depth testing and extensive industry experience. The primary body of knowledge for NKBA certification is the nine-volume *Professional Resource Library* and the NKBA Kitchen & Bathroom Planning Guidelines. Types of certification offered are:

- **Associate Kitchen and Bath Designer (AKBD).** An AKBD is a certified professional, knowledgeable in product selection, space planning, materials, and finishes. Applicants must document a minimum of two years' experience. At least one year must be specifically within the kitchen/bath industry. The second year of experience may be in a related industry. The candidate for this certification must meet specific educational requirements and pass a comprehensive academic exam.
- **Certified Kitchen and Bath Professional (CKBP).** The CKBP is a non-design-oriented certification. The focus of this certification is in the areas of residential construction, general business knowledge, materials and product knowledge, and project management. This certification path is for the dealer, distributor, fabricator, installer, remodeler, manufacturer, sales representative, or any other segment of the industry to validate knowledge, experience, dedication, and professionalism in the K&B industry. The candidate for this certification must meet specific education and experience requirements and pass a comprehensive academic exam.
- **Certified Kitchen Designer (CKD) and Certified Bath Designer (CBD).** CKDs and CBDs specialize in the design, planning, and execution of residential kitchens and bathrooms. They have advanced knowledge of technical and personal communication skills required to succeed as a design specialist. The candidate for this certification must meet specific education and experience requirements and pass a comprehensive academic and design exam.
- **Certified Master Kitchen and Bath Designer (CMKBD).** This master level is synonymous with advanced achievement and experience. The CMKBD is awarded to designers who have 10 years of full-time experience since their first certification. An advanced level of certification recognizes industry professionals for their achievements and dedication to continuing their education.

POLICY AND PROCEDURES MANUAL

A policy and procedures manual that incorporates an employee handbook is an invaluable tool for you and your employees for the following reasons:

1. It spells out everything about how your business is run.
2. It puts everyone on the same level.
3. It ensures that everyone works according to the same rules.
4. It allows the boss and supervisors to manage in a fair and consistent manner.

The manual covers everything from unlocking the doors in the morning to turning off the alarm to making the coffee—how the coffee is to be served to clients—and every detail about your business. A manual is a great deal of work to put together, but start with one section at a time and build from there.

The policy and procedures manual informs all employees exactly how the business operates. It enforces a consistency that most small businesses do not enjoy. And, most important, it adds value—sometimes substantial value to the business, should you decide to sell it. Why? Because it is the systematic, time-saving how-to manual for the new owner.

Excellent software is available to help you in the process of writing a manual. If you want to be successful owner/manager in our industry, make writing a formal, detailed policy and procedures manual a high priority.

Outline for a Policy and Procedures Manual

ABC Kitchen and Bath Company Main Street Anywhere, USA, or Canada

Table of Contents

1. All about ABC Kitchen and Bath Company
   A. Where do I work?
   B. What are the house rules?
   C. Company Mission Statement
   D. Organization Chart
      (1) Job Descriptions
         a. Sales/Design Consultant
         b. Sales/Design Assistant
         c. Office Manager
         d. Office Support
         e. Installation Supervisor
         f. Installer
      (2) Job Performance Evaluations
         a. How They Work
         b. Employer's Responsibility
         c. Timing
2. Products and Services
   A. Products We Sell
   B. Services We Offer
      (1) Company Brochures
   C. Working with Clients
      (1) Kitchen and Bath Retainers
   D. Showroom Etiquette
3. Design, Estimating, and Sales Presentations
   A. Company Pricing Worksheet
   B. Requesting Supplier Quotations
   C. Setting Margins
   D. Figuring Freight Costs
   E. Learning and Practicing Selling Skills
   F. Protocol for Presenting Projects
4. Project Paper Flow
   A. Sales Agreements
   B. Deposits
   C. Creating a Job File
   D. Invoices
   E. Purchase Orders
   F. Change Orders
   G. Order and Purchase Order Editing
   H. Margin-Buster Report
   I. Delivery Information
      (1) Job Site Directions
      (2) Final Plans for Delivery

5. Equipment Use and Etiquette
   A. Using the Telephone
   B. Understanding the Alarm System
   C. Using the Copy Machine
   D. Computer Usage
   E. Processing Credit Card Transactions
   F. Using the Fax Machine
   G. Email Protocol
6. Installation Services
   A. Installation Estimate Procedure
   B. Installation Payment Schedules
   C. Referral Programs
   D. Installer Performance Agreement
7. Office Follow-up Services
   A. Shipping and Receiving Documents
   B. Product Expediting
   C. Billings and Collections
   D. Job Costing
   E. Product and Service Warranties
   F. Service Calls
   G. Customer Service Surveys
      (1) 60-Day Follow-up
      (2) One-Year Anniversary Follow-up
   H. Customer Thank-Yous
      (1) Notes
      (2) Gifts
   I. Referral Cards/Gifts
8. Being a Staff Member
   A. Commission Procedure
   B. Retirement Plan
   C. Professional Growth Plan
   D. Employee Handbook
9. Personal
   A. AIDS
   B. Americans with Disabilities Act
   C. Attendance and Punctuality
   D. Compensation Practices and Pay Schedule
   E. Discipline and Offense Descriptions
   F. Dress
   G. Drug and Alcohol Abuse
   H. Employee Assistance Programs
   I. Employee Discipline
   J. Employee Relatives
   K. Equal Employment Opportunity
   L. Ethics and Personal Conduct
   M. Family and Medical Leave Act
   N. Grievance Procedures
   O. Holidays

(continued)

P. Housekeeping
Q. Jury Duty
R. Leaves of Absence
S. Management Rights
T. Manual Development Guide
U. Maternity Leave
V. Military Leave
W. Orientation
X. Overtime Availability
Y. Peer Review
AA. APerformance Reviews
BB. Personnel Records Access
CC. Probationary Period for New Employees
DD. Reporting Improper Behavior
EE. Safety and Health
FF. Safety Rules
GG. Sexual Harassment
HH. Sick Leave
II. Smoking
JJ. Telephone Usage
KK. Termination of Employment
LL. Time Cards
MM. Transfer and Relocation
NN. Vacation
OO. Wage Garnishment

CREATING AN EMPLOYEE-FRIENDLY WORK ENVIRONMENT

According to a survey by Robert Half International, Inc., the world's largest specialized staffing firm, nearly two-thirds of Americans say that they would be willing to reduce both their work hours and compensation in exchange for more family or personal time. It's important for every K&B business owner to recognize this fact and try to promote quality-of-life HR policies as both a recruitment and employee retention tool. For many K&B businesses, being both customer and employee "friendly" has been a major key to success. The following six areas must be considered to ensure employee job satisfaction.

1. Pay and benefits
2. Opportunities
3. Job security
4. Pride in work and company
5. Openness and fairness
6. Camaraderie and friendliness

Basics of an Employee-Friendly Workplace

Employee Well-Being as a Core Value

If you treat your employees as cherished assets, you are well on your way to creating that friendly workplace. Employee-friendly businesses routinely take the welfare of their employees into consideration when making bottom-line decisions.

Make a Reasonable Commitment to Job Security

In the event of a market downturn, the owner and top management should take the first and biggest cuts. Then an across-the-board 5% decrease in salary is often better than letting someone go.

Create a "People-Friendly" Facility

State/provincial and federal laws dictate that a workplace must be safe. Having a comfortable break room, clean restrooms, and convenient parking are also important.

Be Sensitive to Work/Family Balance Issues

Being sensitive to work/family balance issues is more important than ever before. It can be difficult for people today—especially parents with young children—to juggle family responsibilities with work responsibilities. Small businesses owners have the flexibility to support their employees whenever there is a medical emergency or—on a more pleasant note—some special event at their children's school. It is not just the permission given; it is the manager/owner's attitude that goes with it.

Empower Your Employees

The more you empower your employees to make decisions and do things their way (as long as you get the results you are looking for), the happier they will be. You'll find that they will work harder and do a better job when they're accountable for their own decisions and actions as opposed to simply following orders.

Open Communication

Secrecy breeds suspicion. The old notion of not sharing financial information or allowing employees to be involved in important decisions is disappearing (or at least decreasing). Keep your staff informed, during both good times and bad.

Create a Sense of Ownership

Create a sense of ownership with your employees. You may not choose to share any part of actual ownership, but you can create a profit-sharing program that allows all employees to share in the fruits of their labors.

ALTERNATE WORKING ARRANGEMENTS

Alternative work arrangements are those that deviate from the traditional Monday to Friday, 9:00 a.m. to 5:00 p.m. workweek. Many K&B businesses are open on Saturdays and some evenings. Some 84 percent of American companies offer some form of flexible work arrangement, and the number is growing.

The idea here is that you give employees some measure of control over their work schedules, making it easier for them to manage personal or nonbusiness responsibilities. The hope is that happier employees will be more productive and loyal. These situations should be handled on a case-by-case basis so that they don't favor certain employees over others.

Options for Alternate Work Arrangements

- Flex time. One employee may choose to work 8:00 to 3:00 to be home when the children get home from school; another employee may opt for 10:00 to 5:30 to avoid commuting delays.
- Compressed workweek. Instead of working five 8-hour days, an employee could work four 10-hour days or six 6.5-hour days. Check your state/provincial wage and hour laws on workdays longer than 8 hours. You do not want to pay overtime.

- **Job sharing.** In this arrangement, that two part-time employees share the same full-time job. This could save you money on the benefits package, but the skills of a design/sales person and the continuity of client service would make sharing this position difficult. However, there may be positions (receptionist, warehouse) where this might work.
- **Telecommuting.** Telecommuting refers to any work arrangement in which employees—on a regular, predetermined basis—spend all or a portion of their workweek working from home or another company location. In the case of a showroom design/sales person, this can be difficult. However, this could work if you have three or more salespeople.
- **Permanent part-time arrangement.** In a permanent part-time arrangement, the hours usually are in the 20- to 30-hour-per-week range. If possible, the employee could pick the days and times. In smaller kitchen and bath businesses, where a bookkeeper would be a great addition, but there is not a full week's work, a part-time arrangement could work very well. You might also save on benefits normally provided to a full-time employee.

KEEP TABS ON COMPANY MORALE

You can usually tell, simply by the general atmosphere in the workplace and by the manner in which employees interact with one another, whether morale is high or suffering. Good, open communication (up or down) and careful observation are the tools for judging employee morale.

CONDUCT REGULAR MEETINGS

Holding productive meetings will support your communication efforts. Professionally conducted meetings set goals, clarify responsibilities, and create future leaders for your company. Meetings should not become gripe sessions fostering negativity. They should not bore the attendees or distract them from the real work that needs to be done.

"Calling a Meeting," an article by Linda Case, CAR (Remodelers Advantage Inc., Fullton, Maryland) in the May 2004 issue of *Remodeling* magazine offered excellent guidelines for a well-run meeting.

According to Case, "Planned and conducted properly, meetings are not a waste of time and money. Well-run meetings help your team achieve goals and be accountable for results in their day-to-day roles." Here are some important points:

- Schedule weekly meetings—if the manager or owner is on vacation, have the meeting run by a key team member.
- Have an agenda, collect information via email from the entire team before the meeting. Prioritize the issues, in case there is too much on the agenda, and circulate the agenda before the meeting.

Sales Meetings
- Many companies have a sales meeting once a week; others find it more useful to meet monthly.
- Sales meetings might be reserved just for the sales staff or might include the entire organization. Whether weekly or monthly, the sales meeting is often scheduled late in the day so as not to take away from time in the field or on the phone
- Sales meetings should be a forum for reporting goal achievement, assistance, encouragement, problem solving, training, and general communication.

- Sales meetings are also an excellent time to have supplier partners or other specialists address the group.
- Make meetings fun, educational, and productive.
  - Avoid individual problems.
  - Stick to the agenda.
  - Focus on group concerns and opportunities.
  - Avoid overemphasizing the negative.
  - Avoid "product information" overload.
  - Stress the best methods for getting clients to buy.

Salespeople need and want encouragement, challenge, training, incentives, respect, answers, positive environment, and rewards. Focus your sales meetings on providing these motivations.

If your sales meetings are floundering, make them productive using these tools:

- Have a clear purpose.
- Review guidelines for behavior at the meeting.
- Develop a written agenda.
- Stay within a defined time period.
- Consider hiring a facilitator.
- Prepare and disseminate minutes.
- Present a weekly or monthly flash report of sales performance.

Successful Meetings

- Run the meeting like clockwork. Start on time and end on time.
- Do not allow anyone not in attendance to interrupt the meeting unless it's an actual emergency.
- Hold it regularly. If the manager or owner is on vacation, a key team member should run the meeting.
- Follow an agenda based on feedback from the entire team before the meeting, which is prioritized and circulated before the meeting.
- Have a flash report—a concise one-page report with key data for each attendee: leads taken in, sales made, jobs closed, and client evaluation scores received.
- Take minutes. Email them to all attendees after the meeting. Clearly note who is responsible for which tasks or projects identified or assigned during that meeting. At the start of the next meeting, follow-up on these items.

State-of-the-Company Address

Employees like to be part of the big picture. One California kitchen/bath dealer makes a state-of-the-company presentation to employees at least once a year, usually at year-end, but more often if the situation dictates. All company employees are expected to attend and the owner makes a 45- to 60-minute presentation. General financial information is shared (i.e., sales up, margins down, expenses holding).

If you choose to do likewise, keep in mind that successful presentations require planning and rehearsal. Communication is effective only if your message is clearly understood. Plan ahead. Prepare the points you want to make and the visual aids and handouts you will use.

State of the Company
Preparing the Address

- Prepare an outline of the points you want to make in the order in which you plan to present them.
- Determine how much time you will need, keep the presentation as concise as possible.
- Practice your presentation several times until it comes naturally.
- Allow for questions and answers. Good communication is a two-way street.
- Prepare your responses to possible questions so that as you interact with your employees you are able to go with the flow.

MEASURING EMPLOYEE PERFORMANCE

Few management practices are more basic or more widespread than performance evaluations (appraisals)—except in small mom-and-pop businesses like the majority of kitchen and bath dealers. Few kitchen and bath businesses have formal performance evaluation programs or even do performance reviews with their employees. This is unfortunate because evaluations are extremely helpful for the owner, the company as a whole, and the employee in particular.

Performance evaluations are a vital management function, and it is up to you to implement a structured, meaningful, and well-administered and delivered appraisal system. Performance evaluations are report cards on how employees are doing. Everyone needs to know and deserves to know exactly where they stand. Do evaluations at least once a year, although twice a year is recommended.

Overview of the Process

Creating and implementing a structured performance evaluation process takes time and work. A formal evaluation forces you to establish goals and to identify the behaviors necessary to achieve them. The very nature of an appraisal system puts both the employee and the supervisor into situations that many find uncomfortable. Some supervisors find it difficult to be both candid and constructive when conducting an appraisal session that involves negative issues.

So why go through the trouble to create and implement this process? Simply put, the benefits of an effectively structured and administered performance evaluation process far outweigh the time and effort the process requires. Here is a list of things that a well-designed, well-implemented performance evaluation system can do for your company.

Benefits of a Performance Evaluation System
- Enhances the impact of the coaching that should be taking place between employees and their supervisors.
- Motivates employees to improve their job performance.
- Provides an objective—and legally defensible—basis for key HR decisions, including merit pay increases, promotions, or terminations.

- Establishes a reasonably uniform set of performance standards that are in accord with company values.
- Confirms that employees possess the skills and attributes needed to successfully fill a particular job.
- Verifies that existing reward mechanisms are logically tied to outstanding performance.
- Irons out difficulties in the employee/supervisor relationship.
- Gives employees who are underperforming the guidance that can lead to better performance.
- Keeps employees focused on business goals and objectives.
- Validates hiring strategies and practices.
- Reinforces company values.
- Assesses training and staff development needs.
- Motivates employees to update their skills and knowledge so that they can make a more meaningful contribution to your company's success.
- Provides a forum for open communication.

Conducting the Performance Evaluation
Before the Interview

- Make sure the employee understands the purpose of the evaluation.
- Both parties review the job description.
- Both parties review previous documentation.
- Both parties prepare comments that are concise with backup examples.
- Make sure the employee knows the format of the review process.
- Set a date and time for the review

Preparing for the Evaluation

The following additional information supports steps recommended to prepare for the evaluation meeting.

- **Make sure that the employee understands the purpose of the evaluation process.** It can include setting goals, providing constructive feedback, and analyzing strengths and weaknesses, for example.
- **Review the job description.** Both you and the employee should review the job description so that when you meet, you both of you know what the specific job expectations are. Focus on the job as it was described and performed, not on the employee's personality or personal issues. He or she must also evaluate the past 12 months, not just the most recent month or two. This is also a good time to revise and update the job description to reflect current duties and responsibilities.
- **Review previous documentation.** During the course of the year, you should accumulate the necessary information to prepare the evaluation. This information should include the prior year's appraisal, sales and margin goals (for salespeople), and all notes and information, both positive and negative, that will help you evaluate the employee's past 12 months' performance.
- **Be concise but precise.** Use bullet points, not paragraphs. Give examples to back up comments. Be as specific as possible. Do not draw generalized conclusions.
- **Involve the employee in the evaluation.** Ask the employee to do a self-evaluation using the same basic form you'll be using. This helps keep the lines of communication open and gives you valuable insight as to how the employee perceives him- or herself.

Many times employees are tougher on themselves than you are. For more employee involvement, ask the employee to be prepared to answer questions like these:
- What do you feel your major accomplishments have been during the year?
- What could you have done better?
- What can I do to help you do a better job?
- Is there anything you would like to see changed in your job?

- **Set goals and objectives.** Once the current year's performance is evaluated, establish the goals and objectives for the following year. All the goals and objectives must be achievable. They should be easy to understand and measure. After deciding the goals, you and the employee must agree on three things:

  1. Steps the employee must take to achieve the goals.
  2. The method to measure achievement of the goals.
  3. Benchmarks throughout the year to monitor progress toward achieving the goals.

- **Set the date and time for the review.** Give yourself and the employee at least two weeks to prepare, especially if you use the employee self-appraisal system.

- **Rehearse what you are going to say.** Because reviews can be emotional, especially for employee, it's a good idea for you to have a written agenda. You should know in advance what you're going to say during each part of the review. By doing so, you will be sure you're successful in delivering the message you intend regardless of the employee's response.

Conducting the Performance Evaluation

During the Interview

- Make sure the room is comfortable and well lit and that the setting is private with no interruptions.
- Plan a relaxing greeting.
- Present an overall summary.
- Start with strengths.
- Identify areas to improve.
- Ask for feedback.
- If necessary, discuss salary.
- Close on a positive note.

Conducting the Performance Evaluation

Now that you and the employee are well prepared, it is time to have your meeting.

- **Be sure the meeting room is comfortable and well lit.** Alert everyone that you do not want to be disturbed. No interruptions.
- **Greeting.** Start with a warm greeting and perhaps some brief small talk to help the employee relax and to create an atmosphere conducive to the review.
- **Overall summary.** Explain where the employee's overall performance ranks, starting with the more general comments and leading into specifics.
- **Strengths.** Unless the employee's performance is totally unsatisfactory, you will be able to identify some strong points. Compliment him or her on both major and minor strengths as they relate to the job. You want to start on a positive note. You can be either specific or general in covering the strengths.
- **Weaknesses.** Unless you have the perfect employee with truly exceptional performance, you will have identified some areas that need improvement. In reviewing weaknesses, be

as specific as possible. Instead of saying "You are always late," mention the exact dates and how late. If there is a long list of weak points, do not go through all of them. Prioritize them and cover just two to four. One of your goals should be to maintain the employee's self-esteem throughout. A browbeating will not accomplish your goal.

- **Feedback.** When—and hopefully if—you both agree on the areas that need improvement, you need to establish a system/method that will cause improvement to take place. Both you and the employee should contribute to the plan for improvement. (Employees who are part of helping build a plan are more apt to want to see it succeed.) Both of you must reach agreement on the steps to be taken and the time frame. (Create a mini-contract.) You want honest feedback, so give employees the opportunity to air their thoughts. Listen politely. Do not interrupt. Good feedback is helpful to all parties concerned.

- **Salary.** Most companies tie a salary review to the performance review. But this may not be the best strategy. Why? If employees know that salary is covered at the end of the review, it is what they are going to be thinking about, and they may miss all the important things you have been talking about. Conduct the compensation review at a different time, one to two months after the performance review. This also acts as a motivator for employees to follow through on improving weak areas.

- **Closing.** Unless the reviews are very bad, end on a positive note. Thank them for the effort they put into preparing for the review and for being good, open-minded listeners. Tell them that you appreciate them as employees and are glad they work for you.

Performance Evaluation Legal Issues

The most frequent job-related legal problems are often a direct result of unrealistic employment reviews. Managers too often avoid conflict by failing to appraise a poor employee's performance accurately and truthfully. Later, if the employee is fired, it is easier for him or her to claim discrimination and offer performance reviews as evidence of adequacy to carry out the job requirements.

- **The first step.** Make sure to give each employee an honest and realistic review. All reviews should be issued in writing—including all "agreements" or "disagreements" that come out of the review. The reviewed employee should receive a copy of the review and should sign a copy acknowledging that this is what took place. If an employee refuses to sign a negative review, ask a witness to verify that you asked for a signature and the employee refused.

- **Develop consistent review criteria.** Have a written performance evaluation procedure. Be sure all employees are familiar with it and that your attorney has reviewed it and the evaluation forms. Reviews must be much more specific than general.

- **Other steps you can take to avoid legal issues over reviews.**
  - Establish grievance procedures.
  - If possible, have more than one person provide input on each employee's overall performance rating during the preappraisal period.
  - Give employees feedback throughout the year to avoid performance review surprises.
  - Work closely with employees who have received poor performance ratings to help them improve.

In Summary

- **Evaluate all year long.** Have frequent conversations about how the employee is doing, even if they're informal. Employees feel better when they know that their manager is interested in their work.
- **Handle more important issues immediately.** Don't wait for the formal evaluation.
- **Do not make the evaluation a surprise.** If you evaluate performance on a regular basis, you have the opportunity to make your employees aware of their mistakes before they evolve into big problems.

- **Document, document, document.** Keep notes about performance issues, both good and bad. Do not rely on your memory only to write the review. Such documentation can also help you legally, especially if you foresee a termination.
- **Get the employee involved.** Ask employees for feedback throughout the year. At review time, have them do a self-appraisal and get them involved in establishing strategies to improve.
- **Evaluate performance, not the person.** Measure behavior or output against prearranged, agreed-on standards.
- **Maintain the employee's self-esteem.** Agreeing upon methods for improvement can give the employee renewed confidence to meet goals.
- **End on an upbeat note.** Despite the review, end with a positive statement.

DEVELOPING DISCIPLINARY PROCEDURES

Not many years ago, if employees were not performing up to standard or had done something wrong, you could fire them without worrying about a possible lawsuit. Not today. All termination decisions must be reviewed carefully to ensure that they are not improper or could be argued as being improper before a jury or government agency. Unfortunately, in employment litigation, what the jury believes is what matters, irrespective of the actual facts surrounding the discharge. Some employers elect to adopt a formal disciplinary process, one that reasonably and systematically warns employees when performance falls short of expectations. Consistency in following the process is a key. The owner/manager, all supervisors, and the employees need to know what the process is—and that it is followed carefully.

The specifics of the process can vary, but most disciplinary procedures are structured along the same lines.

- **Initial notification.** The first step in a typical progressive disciplinary process is informing employees that their job performance or workplace conduct is not measuring up to the company's expectations and standards. This initial communication typically is delivered verbally in a one-on-one meeting between the employee and his or her manager. A written record signed by the employee is put in the employee's file.
- **Second warning.** This applies if the performance or conduct problems raised in the initial phase worsen or fail to improve. The recommended practice is for you to have another one-on-one meeting with the employee and accompany that oral warning with a memo that spells out job performance areas that need improvement. It's important at this stage in the process that the employee be made aware of how his or her behavior is affecting the business. You should try to work with the employee to come up with a plan of action that gives the employee the opportunity to improve. You should also advise the employee that failure to improve/ change could lead to a termination. This requires another signed form for your files.
- **Last-chance warning.** This phase of discipline usually takes the form of a written notice. The notice informs the employee that if the job performance or workplace conduct problems continue, the employee will be subject to disciplinary action or termination. Should the employee be terminated this may protect you from legal repercussions. This requires another form, a signature, and filing.
- **Termination.** This is the last step in the process—the step taken when all other corrective or disciplinary actions have failed to solve the problem.

These progressive disciplinary steps are meant to serve as general guidelines. However you decide to structure your disciplinary plan, the process should meet these criteria:

- Have clearly defined expectations and consequences.
- Have early intervention.
- Ensure the discipline is appropriate for the offense.
- Be consistent—always.
- Have rigorous documentation.

DEFINING AT-WILL EMPLOYMENT

For a long time, employers in the United States have operated under a doctrine generally known as at-will employment. This simply means that in the absence of any contractual agreement that guarantees employees certain job protections, you have the right as an employer in the private sector to fire any of your employees at any time and for any (or no) reason. In other words, you may terminate an employee without cause and with or without notice. At the same time, your employees have the right to leave at any time, for any (or no) reason, even without giving notice.

There is more to this subject than can be covered adequately here. Learn more about at-will employment before deciding if it is appropriate for your business. If it is, make firing at will an item in your policy and procedures manual. However, seek legal or professional advice before implementing.

TERMINATING AN EMPLOYEE

Even when you have ample cause for doing so, terminating an employee is always a cause for stress and heartache—not only for the employee who is losing his or her job but also for the manager who has to make the decision and perform the action. It is also hard on coworkers who may have established close relationships with the employee.

As the owner or manager of your company, you can do a great deal to help ensure that your company's approach to firing meets two critical criteria:

1. Maintaining the dignity and rights of the terminated employee.
2. Protecting the company from retaliatory action by a disgruntled former employee.

Who Should Do It and Where

You, the owner, or the immediate supervisor should deliver the termination notice. Since you or a supervisor have been doing the performance evaluations and warnings, you should be most familiar with the facts. Deliver the message in person and in a private location. Depending on the circumstances, it might be advisable to have a third person present. However, coworkers should not be involved.

Preparation

Regardless of why an employee may be leaving your company, it is essential that the termination meeting be as conclusive as possible, which means you need to have everything ready before the meeting takes place. Here are some things to consider when you prepare your list of to-dos:

- **Final payment.** Ideally, the dismissed employee (regardless of the reason) should walk out of the termination meeting with a check that covers everything he or she is entitled to, including severance. Depending on your company's policy—and on the circumstances that led to the employee's departure—the amount of the check probably will include money from some or all of these areas:
  - Salary obligation (prorated through the day of dismissal)
  - Severance pay (if applicable)
  - Any outstanding expense reimbursements due the employee
  - Money due for accrued vacation, sick days, or personal day benefits
- **Security issues.** Go into the meeting with a prepared list of all items related to company security, including keys, access cards, and company credit cards. It's also advisable to change locks and alarm codes after a dismissal.
- **Company-owned property.** If the employee is still in possession of any company-owned property, that property should be turned over immediately. If the property is off-site

(computer, uniforms, etc.), arrangements for pickup should be made immediately. (You may want to hold part of the final check if there is a lot of money involved.)

- **Extended benefit information.** If your company is subject to COBRA (Consolidated Omnibus Budget Reconciliation Act) regulations—and most are—you are obligated to extend the employee's medical coverage—with no changes—for 18 months. Who pays for it—the company or the employee—is your call, but you are under no legal obligation to pay. Just be sure the employee leaves with all the information needed to keep the coverage going. Make sure, also, to resolve all questions regarding an employee's 401k or pension plan during the meeting, including up-to-date information on what options, if any, the employee has with regard to these benefits.

- **Notification of outplacement or other support mechanisms.** If your company has set up outplacement arrangements (or any other services designed to help terminated employees find another job), make sure that you have all of that information available.

- **Delivering the news.** There is no perfect script for letting employees know that they are being discharged, but come right to the point. Be direct, be firm, and do not allow yourself to get into an argument. The decision has been made. End of conversation.

- **Spelling out reasons—or Not.** If you have a legally approved terminate-at-will clause, you do not want to give any reasons for the termination. If you have done a good job with performance evaluations, termination will not come as a surprise to the employee. If you do decide it's appropriate to give reasons, no more than a few short, factual sentences will do. There is no need for drawn-out explanations. Tact and sensitivity are important, but so is honesty. Be very careful about what you say and how you say it. You don't want legal problems to result because of mistakes you made during the termination meeting. You should have a termination form. It should be completely filled out—including final payments. You must ask the employee to sign it. If he or she refuses, ask a third person to witness that you asked the employee to sign but he or she refused. Then have the witness sign the form attesting to the facts.

- **Posttermination protocol.** Or what happens immediately following the termination meeting. The departure should be as clean as possible—albeit with due respect to the feelings and the dignity of the fired person. Harsh and humiliating as it may seem, you or the manager should accompany the dismissed employee back to the workstation, give the employee the opportunity to collect personal belongings, and escort him or her out of the building. If the company has confidentiality agreements, employees should be reminded—in writing—of their legal obligations. Advise terminated employees that they are no longer authorized to access the company's computer system and any online accounts.

TERMINATION FOR "JUST CAUSE"

There really is no "best" time to conduct a termination meeting. Experience shows that late in the day (5:00 p.m.) and early in the week (Monday, Tuesday, Wednesday) are best. Late in the day spares dismissed employees the embarrassment of having to clear out their work areas in the presence of others. Early in the week gives employees a chance to get started on a job search during the work week.

Certain employee infractions and misdeeds are so blatant that you can generally terminate the employee without going through the normal disciplinary channels. Your employee handbook or policy and procedures manual should include offenses that lead to immediate dismissal. Here are some you might consider including in your manual:

- Stealing from the company or from other employees
- Possession or use of drugs or alcohol on the job
- Distribution or selling of illegal drugs
- Blatant negligence that results in the damage to or loss of machinery or equipment
- Falsifying company records
- Violation of confidentiality agreements
- Misappropriation of company assets

- Making threatening remarks to other employees or managers
- Engaging in activities that represent a clear case of conflict of interest
- Lying about credentials

Are You a Candidate for a Top 10 CEO Award?

Having a great company is possible if you become a great leader. Running a small business can be as challenging as leading a large corporation. You can learn from the leadership strengths of major corporation chief executive officers (CEOs).

- In today's world, a CEO must focus on a number of elements to be effective, but there are three critical areas on which he or she must concentrate.
    1. A CEO must establish the *highest ethical standards* for the organization and implement them through written and verbal communication as well as through personal example.
    2. A CEO must establish a *strategic vision* that creates a competitive advantage for the organization and significantly enhances profitability.
    3. A CEO must *motivate* employees by empowering them and must clearly communicate the company's goals.
- Although a company's leaders need to be knowledgeable, intelligent, approachable, hardworking, and effective communicators, *honesty* may be the most important attribute of truly good leaders. Leaders must be honest in all they do in order to secure and maintain employee, consumer, investor, and partner trust. In return, they need honest people surrounding them in order to lead their organizations effectively.
- Attributes of a good CEO, president, or chairman are honesty, integrity, consistency and a strong sense of *fair play*. Additionally, a good CEO needs to be a good communicator and delegator.
- Good CEOs are goal setters, coaches, and cheerleaders for their people. They keep everybody's eye on the ball, *focused* on the ultimate goal of the company, whether it's manufacturing, marketing, sales, or systems. A leader must have wisdom, authority, courage, and *benevolence* in order to achieve long-term success. It is not always easy to decide right from wrong. Always err on the side of being fair. Treat people as if they are important, and they will help make you successful.

Six Top Attributes of the "Ideal" CEO
1. Honesty
2. Integrity
3. Effective communication
4. Long-term vision
5. Leadership by example
6. Fairness, firmness, and consistency

The following forms are provided as samples only. You are encouraged to consult with a human resource specialist and other legal advisors as to their appropriate use. The NKBA accepts or provides no warranties for the use of these materials.

- Job description form (Table 9.1)
- Employment application (Table 9.2)
- Weighted evaluation scale (Table 9.3)
- Rate schedule for sales commission plan (Table 9.4)
- Health insurance payroll deduction authorization (Table 9.5)
- Employment status form (Table 9.6)
- Employee performance evaluation (Table 9.7)
- Employee self-evaluation (Table 9.8)
- Time sheet (Table 9.9)
- Leave request (Table 9.10)
- Employee conference summary (Table 9.11)
- Termination notice (Table 9.12)

TABLE 9.1 Job Description Form

Job Title:	Location:
Supervisor:	Date Needed:
Estimated Starting Pay: $	Budgeted: [ ] Yes [ ] No

REASON FOR HIRE

[ ] New Position	
[ ] Replacement For:	Date Vacated:

TYPE OF EMPLOYMENT (Check one in each column)

[ ] Regular, Full Time	[ ] Exempt	[ ] Commission	[ ] Class A Truck Driver
[ ] Regular, Part Time	[ ] Non-Exempt	[ ] Non-Commission	[ ] Class B Truck Driver
[ ] Temp, Full Time			[ ] Forklift Driver
[ ] Temp, Part Time			[ ] Other [ ] N/A

WORK EXPERIENCE/SKILLS	PHYSICAL REQUIREMENTS	EDUCATIONAL QUALIFICATIONS
Required:	Required:	Required:
Desired:	Desired:	Desired:

PRIMARY RESPONSIBILITY OF POSITION (Essential Job Functions)

ADDITIONAL COMMENTS

APPROVALS

Submitted by:	Title:	Date:
Approved by:	Title: General Manager	Date:
Approved by:	Title: President	Date:
Received by:	Human Resources	Date:

THIS SECTION TO BE COMPLETED BY HUMAN RESOURCES

Sources Contacted:	
Date Filled:	Name of Candidate Selected:
Source:	
Hired By:	Position:
Starting Date:	Rate:

TABLE 9.2 Employment Application

An Equal Opportunity Employer Please Print in Ink		FOR COMPANY USE ONLY		
		To Start (Date):	Emp. #	
		Pay Rate:		
Date:		$ per	Commission	Yes or No
Position applying for:		Location:		
		Position:	Job #	
		Supervisor:		
Location applying to:		Hired By:		
		Hire Source:		
		Pay Rate:		

Check	[ ] Full Time	[ ] Part Time	[ ] Regular	[ ] Temporary

Name: First Middle Last	Social Security #
	Telephone #
Address:	

How were you referred to our company?	[ ] Ad	[ ] Agency	[ ] Relative	[ ] Friend	[ ] Walk-in	[ ] Other
Have you been employed by us before?	[ ] No	[ ] Yes	Dates:	Locations:		
Have you ever been convicted of a criminal act?	[ ] No	[ ] Yes	If yes, please explain: (Conviction will not automatically exclude you from employment)			
Are you legally allowed in the U.S.?	[ ] No	[ ] Yes	If hired, federal law requires documentation to work verifying your identity and legal authorization to work in the U.S.			

EDUCATION

	NAME	CITY / STATE	# of YRS	GRADUATED	DEGREE/MAJOR
High School:					
College/University:					
Trade School:					
Other:					
List any other education, training, special skills or certificates that you possess related to the job for which you are applying:					
List any machines or equipment that you are qualified and experienced at operating:					
List all computer software programs and systems with which you are experienced:					
Salary Desired:					

May we contact your present employer?	[ ] No	[ ] Yes	(if yes) Phone #:

(continued)

TABLE 9.2 *(Continued)*

WORK HISTORY
Start with your most recent employment, including self employment, military and volunteer experience.
This section must be completed even if submitting a resume.

Employer:			Telephone:	
Address:				
Employed from (Mo/Yr):	To (Mo/Yr):	Income Starting:	Income Ending:	Title:
Job Duties:				
Reason for Leaving:				

Employer:			Telephone:	
Address:				
Employed from (Mo/Yr):	To (Mo/Yr):	Income Starting:	Income Ending:	Title:
Job Duties:				
Reason for Leaving:				

Employer:			Telephone:	
Address:				
Employed from (Mo/Yr):	To (Mo/Yr):	Income Starting:	Income Ending:	Title:
Job Duties:				
Reason for Leaving:				

Employer:			Telephone:	
Address:				
Employed from (Mo/Yr):	To (Mo/Yr):	Income Starting:	Income Ending:	Title:
Job Duties:				
Reason for Leaving:				

IMPORTANT—READ BEFORE SIGNING
I certify that the information in this application is true and complete. Any false statements, concealments, or omissions are grounds for refusal to hire or immediate dismissal, if hired.
I authorize (YOUR COMPANY NAME) to investigate and verify the information contained in this application, which may include contacting my schools and former employers, and for (YOUR COMPANY NAME) to keep and preserve such records. I understand that, if hired, my employment is at will and may be terminated without cause and without notification by either the Company or me. THIS APPLICATION DOES NOT CONSTITUTE A CONTRACT FOR EMPLOYMENT, EXPRESS OR IMPLIED. If employed, I agree to adhere to the Company's rules and regulations.

Signature   **Date**

TABLE 9.3 Weighted Evaluation Scale. The following is a sample weighted evaluation scale. (Note: One column is the weight of importance you assign to each category and the other is how you rate the candidate.)

Candidate's Name:

Position:

Performance Category	Weighted Importance 1 (Low) – 5 (High)	×	Candidate Rating 1 (Low)–5 (High)	=	Total Score
Design Skills (hand)	3		5		15
Design Skills (CAD)	4		3		12
Selling Skills	5		1		5
Design Skills (hand)					
Design Skills (CAD)					
Selling Skills					
Time Management Skills					
Organizational Skills					
Communication Skills					
Previous Employment					
Reliability—Work Ethic					
Team Player					
Past Work History					
Professionalism					
Product Knowledge					
Follow-through					
Motivated					
Enthusiastic					
Cultural Fit					
TOTAL					

Note: Make this work for you by adding or deleting any categories and by changing any of the assigned weights. What may be the most important categories for one may not be for the other.

TABLE 9.4 Rate Schedule for Commission Plan

Employee:	Location:
Effective Date:	Date of Previous Schedule:

Design Fees	Gross Profit %	Commission Rate (% paid)
Appliances and Countertops		

Design Fees	Gross Profit %	Commission Rate (% paid)
Plumbing Products, Kitchen and Bathroom Cabinets, Door and Cabinet Hardware	42.00 and over	13
	40.00–41.99	12
	38.00–39.99	11
	36.00–37.99	10
	34.99–35.99	9
	32.00–33.99	8
	30.00–31.99	6
	25.00–29.99	4
	Less than 25.00	0
Appliances and Countertops	20.00 and over	12
	17.00–19.99	10
	14.00–16.99	8
	10.00–13.99	5
	Less than 10.00	0

Commission Payment Schedule	
Design Fee	
Project Deposit	
Project 2nd Payment	
Project 3rd Payment	
Project Final Payment	
Project Costing Completed	

I understand that this Commission Rate Schedule is subject to change without notice.

Employee's Signature:	Date:
Manager's Signature:	Date:

Copy Distribution:

Personnel File (original); Employee; Branch Manager; General Manager; President; Accounting

TABLE 9.5 Health Insurance Payroll Deduction Authorization

I. Instructions

Complete Sections II, III and IV.

Complete the applicable enrollment forms in Section II.

Return ALL forms to HUMAN RESOURCES within five days.

II. Election of Coverage

[ ] No	I waive health insurance. I understand that if I initially waive health coverage, I may be subject to enrollment limitations. For more information, contact the Human Resources Department. For more information, please call the Human Resources Department.
[ ] Yes	I elect health insurance coverage. Health insurance is effective the first of the month following 90 days of employment.
	INSERT HEALTH PLAN NAME HERE Complete Enrollment Application—including signature and date
	INSERT DENTAL PLAN NAME HERE Complete Enrollment Application—including signature and date

III. Covered Individuals

I elect coverage for:		
[ ] Employee Only	[ ] Employee + One	[ ] Employee + Family

IV. Authorization (sign and date)

I hereby request coverage for the group health insurance for which I am or may become eligible. I certify that the individuals I have enrolled are eligible dependents. I authorize my employer to make the necessary payroll deductions required for this insurance.
This payroll deduction authorization supersedes and cancels any health insurance deduction authorization I currently have on file.

Employee's Name:
Employee's Signature:
Date Signed:
Location:
COMPANY USE ONLY: Effective

TABLE 9.6 Employment Status Form

Employee #:	Employee Name:

CURRENT POSITION/ WAGE

Job Title:		Branch / Department:	
Pay Rate:	Per:		Since:

NEW POSITION/ WAGE / STATUS

Changes checked below are to be effective:

[ ] Status Change	From:	To:		
[ ] Exempt [ ] Non-Exempt	[ ] Commission	[ ] Non-Commission	[ ] Part Time [ ] Full Time	
[ ] Transfer	From:	To:		
[ ] Job #:				
[ ] Job Title:				
[ ] Wage Rate:	Per:			

APPROVALS (Route in the following order)

Manager:	Date:
General Manager:	Date:
Human Resources Manager:	Date:
President:	Date:

SUPPORTING INFORMATION

Duties to be added or deleted:
Comments on Performance:
Other:
NOTE: Once approved, two copies of this form will be returned to the requesting Manager for appropriate distribution.

TO BE COMPLETED BY HUMAN RESOURCES

Copies Sent:	HRIS (Human Resources Information System) Updated:

TABLE 9.7 Employee Performance Evaluation

Name:		Title:		
Location / Department:		Due Date:	Period Covered:	
APPRAISAL TYPE	[ ] Introductory	[ ] Promotion / Transfer	[ ] Annual	[ ] Other

EVALUATION CODE	
E = Excellent	Performance consistently above standards with minimal supervision
C = Competent	Performance fully meets Company's standards
U = Unsatisfactory	Performance falls below minimum standard
NA = Not Applicable	

SUPERVISOR RATING OF EMPLOYEE		
Rate the Following:	**Eval. Code**	**Comments**
1. Proficiency in Field/Specialty Degree of competence. Professional manner.		
2. Administrative Effectiveness Skill in planning, organization and implementing work assignments or projects.		
3. Leadership Skill in getting work done through formal or informal direction of others.		
4. Judgment/Decision Making Degree of analysis, objectivity and foresight used to make decisions.		
5. Relationships Ability to work effectively with subordinates, peers, and superiors.		
6. Initiative and Resourcefulness Amount of drive and creativity. Ability to start and accomplish work. Degree of supervision needed.		
7. Supervisor Skill Demonstrated ability to select, train, motivate, and develop subordinates. Degree of sustained contribution from work group.		
8. Communication Expression of verbal or written ideas. Method and manner of speaking. Ability to observe and listen.		
9. Professional Development Commitment to professional growth through development of skills and knowledge.		
10. Adaptability Efficiency under stress. Receptiveness to change/new ideas. Poise and/or courtesy in tough situations.		
11. Attitude and Cooperation Degree to which employee is supportive of Company's directives, decisions and policies. Accepts and profits from criticism.		
Overall Rating **When determining this rating, take into consideration the rating for major accomplishments**		

(continued)

TABLE 9.7 *(Continued)*

STRENGTHS:	AREAS FOR IMPROVEMENT:

EVALUATION SUMMARY:

Briefly summarize employee's performance:

FOR INTRODUCTORY PERIOD EMPLOYEES:	FOR REGULAR EMPLOYEES:
[ ] Satisfactory completion of introductory period	[ ] Satisfactory completion of employment year
[ ] Delay introductory period Reeval. Date:	[ ] Delay continued regular status Reeval. Date:
[ ] Less than satisfactory completion of evaluation Recommended Termination Effective:	[ ] Continued unsatisfactory performance Recommended Termination Effective:

SIGNATURES:

(The employee's signature means that the performance evaluation was reviewed with him or her. It does not necessarily indicate that the employee agrees with the evaluation.)

Employee:	Date Signed:
Direct Supervisor:	Date Signed:
General Manager:	Date Signed:
President:	Date Signed:

EMPLOYEE COMMENTS:

Write any comments you wish to make regarding your evaluation:

TABLE 9.8 Employee Self-evaluation

EVALUATION CODE	
E = Excellent	Performance consistently above standards with minimal supervision
C = Competent	Performance fully meets Company's standards
U = Unsatisfactory	Performance falls below minimum standard
NA = Not Applicable	

SUPERVISOR RATING OF EMPLOYEE		
Rate the Following:	**Eval. Code**	**Comments**
1. Proficiency in Field/Specialty Degree of competence. Professional manner.		
2. Administrative Effectiveness Skill in planning, organization, and implementing work assignments or projects.		
3. Leadership Skill in getting work done through formal or informal direction of others.		
4. Judgment/Decision Making Degree of analysis, objectivity, and foresight used to make decisions.		
5. Relationships Ability to work effectively with subordinates, peers, and superiors.		
6. Initiative and Resourcefulness Amount of drive and creativity. Ability to start and accomplish work. Degree of supervision needed.		
7. Supervisor Skill Demonstrated ability to select, train, motivate, and develop subordinates. Degree of sustained contribution from work group.		
8. Communication Expression of verbal or written ideas. Method and manner of speaking. Ability to observe and listen.		
9. Professional Development Commitment to professional growth through development of skills and knowledge.		
10. Adaptability Efficiency under stress. Receptiveness to change/ new ideas. Poise and/or courtesy in tough situations.		
11. Attitude and Cooperation Degree to which employee is supportive of Company's directives, decisions and policies. Accepts and profits from criticism.		
Overall Rating		
Comments:		

(continued)

TABLE 9.8 *(Continued)*

MAJOR ACCOMPLISHMENTS DURING EVALUATION PERIOD:			
Employee: Briefly identify goals/projects or other accomplishments.	Eval Code:	Evaluator: Briefly summarize employee's performance.	Eval Code:

GOALS AND OBJECTIVES FOR NEXT EMPLOYMENT YEAR
List your goals and objectives. Your Manager may modify these during the review of your performance.

SIGNATURE	
Employee:	Date Signed:

Return this completed form to your supervisor by the agreed upon date of _____

TABLE 9.9 Time Sheet. Recording Instructions: Round off all items to the nearest quarter hour. Use military time. Example: 1:00 to 1:07 record as 1300; 1:08 to 1:15 record as 1315

Day	Date	Time In	Meal Break	Time Out	Time Out	Time In	Explanation of Hours Not Worked	ACCOUNTING ONLY	
								Regular	Overtime
	01/16								
	02/17								
	03/18								
	04/19								
	05/20								
	06/21								
	07/22								
	08/23								
	09/24								
	10/25								
	11/26								
	12/27								
	01/28								
	02/29								
	03/30								
	04/31								

Codes		Military Time Conversion Chart			
		Hours		**Minutes**	
Sick	S				
Vacation	V				
Holiday	H	7:00 am	0700	15	.25
Dock	D	8:00 am	0800	30	.50
Sick/Vacation	S/V	9:00 am	0900	45	.75
Jury Duty	JD	10:00 am	1000		
Workers Comp	WC	11:00 am	1100		
State Disability	SDI	12:00 pm	1200		
		1:00 pm	1300		
		2:00 pm	1400		
		3:00 pm	1500		
		4:00 pm	1600		
		5:00 pm	1700		
		6:00 pm	1800		
		7:00 pm	1900		

Employee's Signature:	Date:
Supervisor's Signature	Date:

Routing Instructions: The immediate supervisor and employee must sign the time sheet prior to submitting. Completed time sheets are due to Accounting on the 1st and 16th day of each month.

TABLE 9.10 Leave Request

Employee:	Position:
Department:	Location:
Date:	[ ] Full Time [ ] Part Time

TYPE OF LEAVE REQUESTED		
[ ] Vacation	[ ] Maternity	[ ] Military
[ ] Sick	[ ] Other	

First Day Off Work:	Return Date:	Number of Days Off:
Reason for Request:		
Employee's Signature:		

ELIGIBILITY
Number of Vacation Hours Accrued:
Amount of Sick Leave Available:

APPROVALS	
Personnel or Payroll:	Date:
Supervisor:	Date:
Owner/Manager:	Date:

TABLE 9.11 Employee Conference Summary

To:	Date:
From:	
Subject:	

Issues Discussed:

Specific Examples:

Employee's Response:

Requirements Set and/or Actions Taken:

(continued)

TABLE 9.11 *(Continued)*

Timelines and Specific Goals Set:

Plan for Follow-up:

SIGNATURES	
Employee:	Date:
Supervisor:	Date:
Owner/Manager (as necessary):	Date:

TABLE 9.12 Termination Notice

Employee:	Position:
Address:	Department:
	Location:
	Phone:

Last Day of Work:
Reason for Termination:
I have received my final pay and vacation check in the amount of $
I have returned all items, equipment or documents with the exception of:
To be returned by:

I will receive any commissions due me at the time normally computed.

I have been informed of my right to continue any group health insurance I now have at my own expense. The employer has no other obligations to me, as I acknowledged at hire, that I accept that this employment is at the will of the employees and the employer and may be terminated at any time without cause.

Employee's Signature:	Date:

TO BE COMPLETED BY THE MANAGER

Employee's Name:		Position:		
Last Day of Work:	Type of Termination:	[ ] Voluntary	[ ] Discharge	[ ] Other
Reason:				

Company Property	Date Returned	Item	Date Returned
Car		Final Check	
Keys		Insurance Forms	
Credit Cards			
Uniform			
Company Manuals			
Employee Receivables			
Completed By:		Date:	

Return completed forms to Human Resources Department along with any employee-related materials.

TO BE COMPLETED BY HUMAN RESOURCES

Date Received:	LDW (Last Day Worked):	Effective Date of Term:

SUMMARY

This chapter was a continuation of the important subject of HR management. We discussed the five most important things you must do to build the very *best* team of employees. We covered the importance of having a formal training program that starts day 1 and never ends. The importance of creating an employee policy and procedures manual was explained. Conducting employee performance evaluations was explored. Disciplinary and termination procedures were discussed in depth. HR forms that you can use in your business are included at the end of the chapter

REVIEW QUESTIONS

1. Explain why a policies and procedures manual is a valuable tool in business. (See "Policy and Procedures Manual" page 177)
2. Describe various types of work arrangements. (See "Alternate Working Arrangements" pages 181–182)
3. Define "termination for just cause" and provide examples. (See "Termination for 'Just Cause'" pages 190–191)
4. Explain the purpose and value of an annual performance review. (See "Measuring Employee Performance" pages 184–185)

Marketing

Marketing is the third and final segment of the three main management areas within companies. (Finance and human resources are the other two areas.) Many business leaders believe that marketing is the lifeline of business success because nothing happens until a sale is made.

Learning Objective 1: Explain the importance of charging a design fee or retainer, and explain the difference between the two.

Learning Objective 2: Discuss the importance of developing a marketing plan and marketing budget.

Learning Objective 3: Define branding and company image.

Learning Objective 4: Describe effective means of advertising, promotions, and public relations.

Learning Objective 5: Discuss social media and how you can integrate it into your overall marketing plan.

As a small business today, you have lots of company and lots of competition. The Small Business Administration (SBA) estimates that there are over 5 million small businesses with fewer than 20 employees in the United States America . . . and that's an astounding 90 percent of all the businesses in the nation. Between 7,000 and 8,000 of these are kitchen and bath (K&B) businesses.

We know that no sales will be made without customers. That is what marketing is all about—finding customers, enticing them to look at, and then buy your products and services.

- Marketing is the process through which you create and keep customers.
- Marketing is the matchmaker between what your business sells and what your customers buy.
- Marketing covers all of the steps that are involved in tailoring your products, message, distribution, customer service, and all other business actions to meet the desires of your most important business asset—your customers.
- Marketing relies on two-way communication between seller and buyer.

Balanced

MARKETING AND SALES ARE NOT THE SAME

Too many people, including K&B owners, confuse the terms "marketing" and "sales." They believe that "marketing" is a high-powered or dressed-up way to say "sales." But selling is not a substitute for marketing, even though the sales function is one of the ways to communicate your marketing message.

A sale is the point at which the product is offered, the case is made, the purchasing decision occurs, and the business-to-customer exchange takes place. Selling is an important part of the marketing process, but it is not, and never can be, a replacement for it.

Pieces of the Marketing Puzzle

- Requires a written plan and budget including co-op dollars (defined later in this chapter).
- Must be measurable and achievable.
- Typically includes ads, promotions, public relations, and selling.

THE BIG PICTURE: THE MARKETING "WHEEL OF FORTUNE"

If you could get an aerial view of the marketing process, it would look like Figure 10.1. Every successful marketing program, whether for a billion-dollar company or a one-person operation, follows the same marketing cycle. Follow this "Wheel of Fortune" to go around the cycle, starting at the top right and circling clockwise.

Marketing begins with customer knowledge and cycles around to customer service before it begins all over again. It is the strategic plan for your business.

It involves . . .

- product
- development
- pricing
- packaging
- distribution
- communication . . .

. . . of the marketing message, including the steps involved with making the sale. Unless you manufacture your own cabinets, countertops, and the like, you will not be involved in every step in the cycle, but it takes all of these steps to complete the whole cycle.

FIGURE 10.1 Marketing is a continuous cycle.

As you loop around the marketing wheel, here are the steps you encounter:

- Get to know your target customer and your marketing environment.
- Tailor your product, pricing, packaging, and distribution strategies to meet the customer, market, and competitive realities of your business.
- Use your customer and product knowledge to create and project marketing messages that will grab attention, inspire interest, and move your customers into action.
- Go for the sale, but that's not all.
- Once the sale is made, move into the customer service phase, where your business works to ensure customer satisfaction so that you can convert the sale into an opportunity for repeat business and word-of-mouth advertising.
- After the sale, use follow-up communication to build referrals of new potential customers.

In marketing, there are no shortcuts. To build a successful business, you cannot just jump to the sale or even to the advertising stage—you have to go through the entire marketing process.

To Fee or Not to Fee

In the K&B industry, businesspeople often limit marketing to communication, product selection, and showroom development. However, the decision to include a design/retainer fee in your business strategy is also a part of marketing. An overview of the typical design fee/retainer systems used by professionals in the K&B industry follows.

Do you charge a fee? What do you charge? Do you apply the entire amount toward the sale? These are all great questions. In addition to these questions, professionals in the K&B industry often have heated debates regarding just what the "perfect" design-fee system is.

The business model dramatically influences the type of fee best charged. Additionally, the experience base and reputation of the firm and/or individual designer and what the local competition does have a significant impact on the ability of the organization and/or the person to charge a fee.

The first impression the firm and designer gives also influences how and when a fee is charged. Most profitable firms agree that some type of fee/retainer system is an important part of qualifying leads and effectively managing time. However, business leaders also are first to admit that, for many designers, it is hard to stand in front of a client and ask for a fee: There is a fear of losing the project because clients do not understand the fee schedule.

You may have heard designers talk about projects they lost (projects that might not have been profitable anyway) because of the client's reluctance to pay a retainer fee.

Experienced designers have found that having an organized fee schedule properly presented to a qualified prospect means the client has a vested interest in buying from them and therefore the client becomes a qualified lead.

Firms that always charge a fee seem to have a deep appreciation for the value of creativity. As one designer said, "Ideas are my stock in trade. I am a design professional, and it is my job to pull together a set of decisions that make sense functionally, economically, and aesthetically. This planning is invaluable, and ought to be paid for."

Before discussing the fees, here is a brief overview of typical fees charged under different business models.

Kitchen and Bath Dealership

K&B dealerships make the majority of their profits from selling cabinets and countertops—installed. Other products might be added to this mix. For these types of firms, a flat design fee or a percentage retainer fee determined by the estimated budget for the project is typical. The copyright ownership of the plans remains with the design firm. The plans are not released to the client if a contract is not signed. These fees may or may not be applied to the project when orders for products are placed. These fees are normally paid with an initial deposit and a final retainer fee when the project documents are presented. The designer and company share the fees after all associated direct costs are paid.

Design/Build Construction Firm

Charging for design and other preconstruction services is becoming common among major remodeling companies. Normally, a percentage fee (with a minimum fee established for smaller projects) is charged and billed in a three-tiered project.

1. A feasibility study that produces a master plan for the entire project, including drawings, written scope of work, and construction estimate (guaranteed to be within a specified percentage of the actual cost to construct) begins the process.
2. Design costs are then billed for the design process.
3. A separate fee is charged for working drawings and all communication with staff architects during the project.

The plans remain with the design firm. They may or may not be released to the client if a contract is not signed to complete the work.

Independent Designer

Independent K&B designers follow a business model closely aligned with interior designers. Typically independent designers are compensated for their planning services, and the plans become the property of the client. They may or may not receive a commission or finder's fee for products specified or from firms referred to. Professional ethics is at issue around these payments. The National Kitchen & Bath Association (NKBA), the American Institute of Architects, and the American Society of Interior Designers, among others, have ethical standards that require clients to be notified of any fees being paid to any design professionals collaborating on a project.

Independent designers may charge a flat fee for the conceptual planning part of the project and then an hourly fee to create the project documents and assist in sourcing and/or shopping. In other scenarios, an hourly fee is charged throughout the entire process.

As you can see, specific types of fee structures work well with specific business models. Following is a review of the pros and cons of various design fee systems.

Flat Design Fee

A flat fee is charged to complete the conceptual design and preliminary budget. Fees range from $200 to $2,500 in the K&B industry. In some cases, plans are released to the client; for others, they remain the property of the design firm. Typically a simple design fee form is signed, with monies collected before the planning process begins or in a two-payment tiered system.

Note: Confer with your legal counsel when considering selling plans. Much like an architect, you will need errors and omissions (E&O) insurance if you are selling a design plan that may be construed as a document a consumer can build from. Your legal counsel may recommend you include a specific disclaimer on your plans.

Pros
- Flat fees are easy for clients to understand. Consumers are typically more comfortable with this method than with hourly fees.
- Flat fees can be adjusted for different types of projects or for different designers with varying skills.
- Flat fee can be easily combined with a "measure fee," which covers your first visit to the home.
- Flat fees are easier to divide between the design professional and the business owner.

Cons
- Flat fees may not reflect the actual hours professionals need to devote to the planning process. A way to avoid this is to list the number of times you will meet with a client, the number of solutions you will present, and the number of changes made to plans for the fee, with an hourly fee included in the contractual documents for work above and beyond the services included in the flat fee.
- Designers who are compensated with a percentage of a flat fee may focus too much attention on fees and not sales.

Hourly Design Fee

The second system is an hourly charge for design time and project documentation time. An hourly fee is charged for the time the designer of record and backup staff spend preparing drawings, researching product, and writing specifications. Typically, hourly fees are used when no product is being sold.

A comment from author Ellen Cheever, CMKBD:

> For independent designers who expect their entire professional income to be generated from hourly fees, it is critical when building the business plan to understand the reasonable number of hours an individual can bill. There are approximately 235 productive days in one year after the elimination of Saturdays, Sundays, holidays, vacations, and average sick leave. Translating productive days into hours, based on seven hours per day, there are 1,645 potentially billable hours per employee. This should be further reduced by 5 percent for coffee breaks and such, leaving 1,563 hours. Experience suggests that the most efficient designers can expect to bill 75 percent of these productive hours, or approximately 1,200 hours. Therefore, an independent designer who has budgeted $5,000 per month for their overhead costs and expects to generate $75,000 in pretax income needs to bill these 1,200 hours at $120 per hour to generate $150,000 ($15,000 safety net included). Hourly charges range from a low of $35 to a high of $150 within the K&B and interior design industries.

Pros

- Hourly charges insure the designer is compensated for all time devoted to a project.
- A well-organized designer can easily keep track of all hours devoted to each project.

Cons

- Consumers often feel they are billed too many hours. The designer who bills by the hour only is not compensated for his or her years of experience that often results in an excellent—quick—solution. This is why many seasoned professionals charge a flat-rate conceptual fee first followed by an hourly fee for project documentation.
- Very clear project documentation is required to track the hours charged to each job with an explanation of services provided.

Conceptual Design Fee Combined with an Hourly Documentation Fee

This combination approach uses a flat fee or a percentage of the estimated budget as a conceptual design retainer, which is then followed by hourly fees for the designer of record and/or staff members to prepare the proper documentation.

Pros

- This system allows the designer to be compensated for the ideas he or she offers during the initial phase of project development. A multitier hourly charge for various members of the design team can then be applied to the client's account as work is performed.
- The design retainer contract can easily list a conceptual fee and the charges associated with other designers.

Cons

- Such a system requires very accurate budgeting skills up front to insure that clients understand the costs associated with conceptual design solutions being presented.

Retainer Fee

A retainer fee is a percentage of the preliminary budget estimate arrived at during the first visit to the client's home or upon plan review in the showroom. The fee ranges from 2 percent to 10 percent of the midrange budget point. Therefore, on a project estimated at $40,000 to $60,000, the midrange point is $50,000. A 5 percent retainer fee would be $2,500. When retainer fees are used, typically the plans do not become the property of the client: Copyright ownership remains with the firm. The retainer fee is applied to the contract when products are sold. The fees are collected in one payment at the beginning of the planning process or as a two-phase payment system.

Pros

- The fee varies based on the complexity of the project. This system works very well for seasoned designers with outstanding reputations in their community.

Cons

- Designers must be skilled in establishing accurate budget ranges at the job site and presenting potential solutions that intrigue clients.
- This system is difficult for newcomers to institute because of the significant payment at the beginning of the design process.

Ellen Cheever, CMKBD, recommends how to use the fee information:

> We have described the most typical fee structures used in the kitchen and bath industry. There are endless variations on these systems employed by successful members of our industry. Our goal has been to highlight the most successful systems for the new business owner and general managers/sales directors proposing a change in their companies' structure and for existing business owners considering reformatting their fee-based compensation program.

MAKE THE TIME

How many times have we heard kitchen and bath owners say that they just do not have time to market? The answer to that is easy. *Make the time*.

Think of it this way. If marketing is the process through which a business creates and keeps customers, then marketing is the difference between being "in business" and being "out of business." Looked at it this way, marketing is the single most important process in any business, including yours.

Before You Go Much Further

A January 2005 article in *Remodeling* magazine noted that barely 29 percent of remodelers surveyed prepared a marketing plan and budget each year and that 80 percent spent 3 percent or less of their annual revenues on marketing (Figures 10.2, 10.3). What was holding them back? Nearly 20 percent said they had more leads than they could handle, which is not the case in today's downturned housing market. Seventy-two percent of respondents back then said they could not afford marketing or did not have the time or know how to do it. Today's competitive market requires that business owners know how to market and budget for it if they want their business to survive and grow.

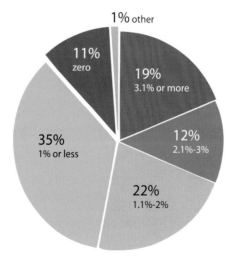

FIGURE 10.2 Annual Marketing Expenditures as a Percentage of Revenue

Source: Remodeling *(January 2005).*

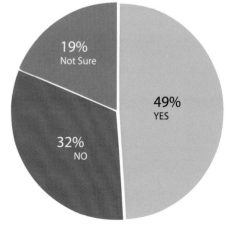

FIGURE 10.3 Do You Spend Enough Money on Marketing?

Source: Remodeling *(January 2005)*

TABLE 10.1 Measuring Market Strength

	Yes	No
You and those who help run your company have a complete understanding of the products and services that you offer.	❏	❏
You have knowledge of the competition.	❏	❏
You are aware of and responsive to the threats and opportunities that exist in your business world.	❏	❏
You have a clear understanding of who your potential customer is and what it will take to make that person, willing to buy from you.	❏	❏
You think not just in terms of making the sale but rather in terms of developing mutually beneficial long-term relationships with your customers.	❏	❏

Measuring Your Market Strength

To determine whether your marketing is strong, rate yourself to see whether you think your business does well in the areas listed in Table 10.1.

YOUR MARKETING PLAN AND BUDGET

A marketing plan lays out your analysis of the situation in your marketplace, along with your strategies and how you'll use the various elements of your marketing mix (such as advertising, promotions, public relations, website, social media, pricing, selling skills, etc.) to execute that strategy. It also includes sales projections and a budget for your marketing expenditures.

Very few dealers in the kitchen and bath industry develop a formal, written marketing plan each and every year. A few owners/managers may do a simple spreadsheet marketing budget. This may work in the short run, but to really succeed and to be ready for changes and challenges, you need to write a well-thought-out plan each and every year. Use this planning process as an opportunity to gather new information, reexamine your strategies, and refine your tactical marketing and sales efforts. If you're not sure whether spending the time to do this each year is worth your time and effort, write and follow a plan and you'll see how much better your company performs. Once you experience the success that follows, you will become an advocate of marketing planning.

Do not try to rate the success of your marketing based on sales figures alone. Sales may be strong in the short run, in spite of a weak marketing program, but it is unusual for them to stay strong unless you shore up the marketing effort.

Too many K&B owners/managers think that marketing plans are only for the big guys. The truth is that in just a few pages, you can write a marketing plan for your business that will turn your marketing efforts into a planned investment rather than a hopeful risk. The next 11 steps explain how.

Step 1. State your business purpose. Start with a one-sentence summary of your business purpose.

Example: To offer unique designs, quality products, and superior installation of kitchen and bath products for both new construction and remodel projects.

Step 2. Define your market situation. In a single page, describe the changes, problems, and opportunities that you will face over the upcoming marketing plan period. In analyzing your situation, consider these factors:

- **Your customers.** Are they undergoing changes that will affect their buying decisions?
- **Your competition.** Are there any new businesses competing for your customers buying decisions? Are existing competitors doing anything new or different that will make them more threatening to your business?

- **The market environment.** Do you anticipate economic changes that will affect your business? Will there be any physical changes to your building or showroom? Will your place of business still be in the best location for your customer base?

Step 3. Set goals and objectives. Your marketing plan details the program you will follow to reach your business goals and objectives. State your goals and objectives up front.
- Your *goal* defines *what* you want your marketing plan to achieve.
  Example: To increase sales by 5 percent and do higher-priced projects.
- Your *objectives* define *how* your will achieve your goal.
  Example: To increase sales by introducing a new line of higher end cabinetry and adding plumbing products to our offering.

Step 4. Define your market. You must define your target customer in order to:
- Select marketing tactics that will appeal to your prospects.
- Make effective media decisions to reach these prospects.
- Create advertising messages and promotions that appeal to the unique interest and emotions of your prospects.

Step 5. Advance your position, brand, and creative strategy. Your marketing plan should state your company's position and brand statements, along with the creative strategy you will follow, so that all marketing efforts implemented over the marketing plan period advance a single, unified image for your company. Here are some definitions to help you with this step:
- **Your brand.** The set of characteristics, attributes, and implied promises that people remember and trust to be true about your business.
- **Your position.** The available, meaningful niche that your business, and only your business, can fill in your target customers' minds.
- **Your creative strategy.** The formula you will follow to uphold your brand and position in all of your marketing communications.

Step 6. Set your marketing strategies. The next component in your marketing plan details the strategies you will follow, including:
- **Product strategies.** Will you be introducing any new products or services during the new marketing period?
- **Distribution strategies.** Will you be altering the means by which you get your product and service to your customer?
- **Pricing strategies.** Are you considering any special deals, payment options, rebates, or other pricing offers?
- **Promotion strategies.** This part of your marketing plan describes how you will support your marketing strategies through advertising, promotions, and PR.
  Once your strategies are set, you will spend time implementing an orchestrated and well-planned marketing program rather than reacting to far-flung ideas all year long.

Step 7. Outline your tactics. The next section of your marketing plan outlines the tactics you will employ to implement your strategies. For example, if one of your strategies is to introduce a new line of cabinets, the sequence of tactics may look like this:
- Review and select an ad agency and develop ad concepts.
- Develop a direct mailer concept and mailing list.
- Develop a product and service brochure.
- Develop a publicity plan.
- Add to your Web page.
- Place ads in "home" magazines.
- Print and send direct mailers.
- Generate local market publicity.
- Train staff.
- Unveil product at special event.

Step 8. Establishing your budget. Your plan must detail what your marketing program will cost. Avoid simply adding a few percentage points to last year's budget. A good guideline is to budget a certain percentage of total company sales. In the K&B industry, this ranges from 2 percent to as much as 10 percent with an average being about 5 percent of total sales. Then study your goals and objectives. Decide what advertising, promotions, and PR will help communicate your message the best. (See the "Sample Budget Form for Marketing" later in the chapter.)

Step 9. Blueprint your action plan. In this part of your plan, you bring together all of your strategies and tactics into a single action plan. One easy way is to prepare an action agenda in calendar form for each month of the year. Simply describe in four columns the action, the budget for that action, the deadline, and the person responsible for each step.

Step 10. Think long term. Include a targeted list of the market development opportunities you will research over the coming year for positive action and future marketing plan periods. Your expansion analysis might focus on the development of one or several of these areas:

- New or expanded business locations to serve more customers
- New geographic market areas outside your current marketplace
- New customers different from those represented by your current customer profile
- New products and/or services that would inspire additional sales
- New pricing strategies
- New customers service programs

  Choose only one to three opportunities to explore each year, and commit to producing an analysis before developing next year's marketing plan.

Step 11. Use your plan. This step is the easiest and most important. *Use your plan!* Share it with your staff. Use it to keep yourself on track as you manage your business to marketing success.

Timing Is Everything

The first half of the year is considered prime time in the K&B industry—it's when consumers often decide to do kitchen or bath remodels. Studies have shown that the decision timing for discretionary home improvements such as kitchen and bath remodels probably is impacted by anticipated bonuses and tax refunds. It's also possible that problems with existing kitchens and baths became all too clear during the holidays—creating a never-again sense of determination. Additionally, there is the simple psychological impact of a brand-new year—it is a goal-setting time of the year. People reflect on their lives, think about their jobs, and decide what's important for the family.

MARKETING BUDGETS

Kitchen and bath businesses may find it extremely valuable to focus their marketing efforts on the first half of the year.

The most important commitment you can make to your marketing program is to stick to it. What does commitment mean?

- Establish a marketing budget.
- Spend the funds on the planned marketing programs.
- View the allocation as an important business investment.
- Manage the programs well.

How Much Should You Spend?

Use a percentage of your forecasted sales for the marketing budget. For retail-oriented businesses, like most K&B dealers, the percentage should be in the 3 percent to 7 percent range, which would include co-op dollars from vendors.

There are a number of other ways to budget.

- **Arbitrary method.** This is best-guess budgeting. The budget is between an intuition and experience, often using the numbers from the last year or two as the benchmark.
- **Competitive parity.** This might be thought of as keeping up with the Joneses. Your budget is based on awareness of how much your competitors are spending and how your business compares in terms of size and strength.
- **Goal-oriented budgeting.** This is a spend-what-is-necessary approach. It involves a serious look at what you expect your business to accomplish over the coming year and what level of marketing is necessary to accomplish the task.

What Percentage Is Right for You?

As you contemplate how much your business should allocate for marketing, consider these points:

- **Nature of your business and your market.** A business-to-consumer or business-to-contractor business requires more spending than business-to-business firms (e.g., attorneys and accountants).
- **Size of your market area.** The bigger the area, the bigger the budget.
- **Your competition.** If you are the only game in town, that's one thing; if there are ten K&B dealers in town, that's another. If you're currently the underdog and want to take on the leaders, you must spend accordingly.
- **Your objective and task.** The most important consideration in setting your budget is to understand what you want to accomplish with your marketing. Look at your sales and profit goals. The more aggressive they are, the more you will have to budget.

Partner with Suppliers

Schedule a meeting with each of your major vendor partners prior to the start of a new year and review where you have been, where you are, and where you want to go. Hold this meeting with the local rep and his or her boss (a decision maker). Instead of waiting for things to happen, be proactive and make them happen. By developing a plan together and knowing where you want to go, you will have a much better chance of achieving your goals. (See Table 10.2 for a sample vendor marketing plan.)

TABLE 10.2 Annual Vendor Marketing Plan

COMPANY NAME:

I. Historical Data	
	A. Purchases (2 yrs ago):
	B. Purchases (1 yr ago):
	C. Purchases (this yr):
	D. Gross Profit on Sales (2 yrs ago):
	E. Gross Profit on Sales (1 yr ago):
	F. Gross Profit on Sales (this yr):

II. New Year Projections	
	A. Projected Purchases Next Year
	B. Projected Gross Profit Next Year

III. Display Products	
	A. Changes This Year
	B. Changes Need to Be Made Next Year

IV. Ideas on How to Grow Sales and Margins in the Next Year	
	A.
	B.

(continued)

TABLE 10.2 *(Continued)*

V. Advertising, Promotion, and Public Relations Plan for Next Year		
What	**When**	**How Much**

VI. Problems/Issues to Be Discussed	

VII. Ideas on How to Strengthen the Partnership	
	A.
	B.

Take Advantage of Every Co-op Dollar

You can dramatically stretch your advertising/promotional dollars by utilizing co-op funds. Surprisingly, statistics indicate that less than 50 percent of co-op funds are used over the course of a year. One reason this happens is that too few industry professionals know what programs are available to them from their supplier partners. Also, many business owners do not take the time to clearly understand the supplier partner guidelines/rules for co-op funding to apply.

Many distributors and manufacturers provide money for advertising/promotion if the activity or ad promotes their products by including the product name and/or logo. In addition to traditional advertising, some co-op funds also cover photography, logo development, literature creation, and other specialized promotional material.

When discussing co-op programs with your supplier partners, make sure you know the answers to the next questions.

- Who pays the initial cost?
- How is invoicing submitted?
- Is the message approved beforehand, or is a copy of the information submitted with the invoice?
- What specific requirements are in place within the co-op program?
- What activities are covered, and what activities are not covered?

Can You Afford Professional Help to Develop the Advertising Segment of Your Marketing Plan?

If you decide you just do not have the expertise to develop your advertising program, there are many excellent agencies out there. Some create advertisements, logos, images, and do the entire placement. Others do all of this plus public relations (more on this later). None is inexpensive, but this may be an option for you (see Figure 10.4, Table 10.3).

Hire an Advertising Professional

Being a successful kitchen/bath dealer or designer does not make someone an ad designer. Regardless of your location, there are usually a few good design companies in the area. Some affordable national agencies specialize in the kitchen and bath dealer business. Tell them about yourself and let them design your image or advertising campaign for you. They may create something you had never thought of before.

These people are the professionals in their field. Let them produce the best ad for you and your budget. Give them enough insight and direction to get them started, and then see what

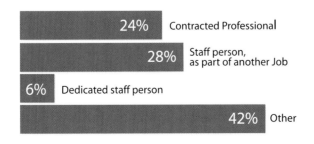

FIGURE 10.4 What's the plan? Creating and tracking: Who creates your marketing materials?

TABLE 10.3 Sample Budget Form for Marketing

Year:			
Sales from Prior Year:			
Percentage of Sales for Marketing: 5%*			
Total Annual Marketing Budget: $100,000			
Marketing Source	**Total Annual Dollars**	**Timing**	**Person Responsible[†]**
Magazine ads	$16,000	6 × Year	
Direct mail	12,000	Monthly	
In-Store Promotions	9,000	1 per quarter	
Update Web site	5,000	Ongoing	
Home shows	7,500	1 per year	
Radio ads	9,000	1st 2 quarters	
Television ads	12,000	1st 2 quarters	
In-home parties	4,000	1 per quarter	
Professional PR help	6,000	Ongoing	
Social media	2,500	Ongoing	
Kitchen tour	7,500	1 per year	
Charitable events	7,500	3 per year	
Miscellaneous	2,000	Ongoing	

*Includes approximately 1.5% in vendor co-op dollars
[†]Varies by company

they develop. Having someone else's unbiased view is a great way to get feedback. Do not forget that the final decision is always yours.

Once you have your plan in place, monitor the leads generated.

If your sales budget is $ 2,000,000 and you budget 5 percent for your marketing program that is $100,000. You might figure 10 to15 percent of this for outside professional help. The balance will be budgeted for other marketing initiatives planned by your firm and/or held in reserve for unexpected opportunities.

KNOWING WHO YOUR CUSTOMERS ARE

If you already know who your customers are, how they heard about you, and why they bought from you, you are unique. In a remodeling magazine survey, only about one-half of the respondents differentiated between qualified and unqualified prospects, and only about one-half tracked their lead-to-sale ratio. With today's lead tracking software, there is no excuse not to track each and every lead (see Figures 10.5, 10.6).

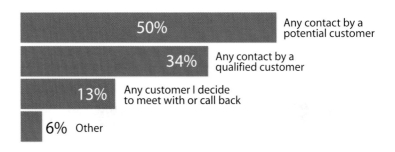

FIGURE 10.5 What's the Plan? Creating and Tracking: How Do You Define a Lead?
Source: Remodeling *(January 2005)*

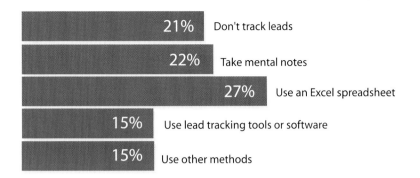

21% Don't track leads

22% Take mental notes

27% Use an Excel spreadsheet

15% Use lead tracking tools or software

15% Use other methods

FIGURE 10.6 What's the Plan? Creating and Tracking: How do You Track Your Leads?
Source: Remodeling *(January 2005)*

Most K&B owners know some of the answers to these questions, but unless they collect hard data and do serious market research, there is a lot they don't know. You, the business owner, may think you work for yourself, but you don't. You work for your customers.

Using NKBA's Business Management Form System

You should maintain an organized record to register leads visiting your organization. The NKBA has a lead system for its members that includes a registration card, record and register, and analysis form. You can use this tool to track everyone who comes to your firm and how they came to call on you.

Anatomy of a Customer

An important part of knowing your customer is differentiating who's who among your clientele. Such market segmentation is the process of dividing your customers into segments that share distinct similarities. Here are some terms and what they mean:

- **Geographics.** Segmenting customers by regions, counties/municipalities, states/provinces, zip codes, and the like.
- **Demographics.** Segmenting customers into groups based on things such as age, gender, ethnic background, education, marital status, income, household size, and so on.
- **Psychographics.** Segmenting customers by lifestyle characteristics, behavioral patterns, beliefs, values, and attitudes about themselves, their families, and society.
- **Geodemographics.** Also called cluster marketing or lifestyle marketing. Based on the old adage that birds of a feather flock together; people who live in the same area tend to have similar backgrounds and consumption patterns.

Collecting Information about Your Customers

Target marketing starts with customer knowledge. Learn everything you possibly can about the person who currently buys from you, then you can direct your marketing efforts toward others who match the same profile.

Do-It-Yourself Fact Finding

You can get a good start on conducting customer research without ever walking out the front door of your business.

- Review addresses from invoices and group them into areas of concentration.
- Survey customers. Ask clients to sign a register when they come through the front door. Get names, addresses, and so on, and ask "How did you hear about us?" Have salespeople ask the same thing. Keep track of the answers.
- Track responses to advertisements and direct mailers.
- Study Web reports to learn about prospects who visit you online.

Who Are Your Customers?

If you are the typical kitchen and bath business, you deal in mid- to high-end products. So who are your customers?

- Identify the right client profile.
  - Homeowners with combined incomes of $100,000 or more
  - Homeowners whose homes are 10 years or older
  - People over age 35, especially the "Baby Boomer" segment
  - People who like to cook/entertain/enjoy their homes
- Identify the right neighborhood.
  - Owners of mid- to high-priced homes
  - Owners building new mid- to high-priced homes
  - Owners remodeling either the kitchen or bath (home office, library, entertainment center, fireplace surrounds, etc., if you deal in those products)
  - Owners with vacation/second homes
- Identify key influences.
  - New construction home builders (mid to high end)
  - Remodel contractors who specialize in kitchen and baths
  - Interior design professionals who specialize in residential work

Certainly more criteria should make up your customer profile, but this list covers a large part of it. Knowing this information, as well as the facts you will learn from your surveys, will tell you where to advertise, how to promote, and what kind of public relations to incorporate into your marketing plan.

ARE YOU OFFERING THE RIGHT PRODUCT/ SERVICE PACKAGE?

Did you know that the best products are not sold, they are bought? If you are a good marketer, when it comes time to purchase, you are not selling anyone anything. Instead, you are helping customers to select the products and services to solve their problems, address their needs, or fulfill their desires. You are helping them buy.

As a result, you devote the bulk of your marketing efforts to the steps that take place long before money changes hands.

These efforts involve:

- Targeting customers,
- Designing the right product/service package, and
- Communicating your offerings in terms that address your customers' wants and needs.

Then, when customers are ready to make the purchase, all you need do is facilitate a pleasant exchange and make sure that your customers feel good about trading their money for the right product/service.

Making Customer Service a Core Value

In small businesses, customers can get lost in the workload shuffle. They can be overlooked, treated like intrusions, asked to wait too long, and confronted with rules that send them right out the door. That should not happen—and it will not happen if you understand and apply the following basics of customer service.

- **"Services" and "service" are not the same thing.** Services are what you provide to customers as part of your total product offering. Service is how well you do what you do—how well you deliver what you are providing to the customer.

- **Service leads to customer loyalty.** Products lead to sales, but service hooks clients for life. To improve your service, consider these four steps:
  1. **Create a service guarantee.** Assure customers that you will meet or exceed promises. Make the guarantee straightforward and liberal (no small points), relevant and substantial (worth the effort it takes to request it), available immediately (no management approvals required), and easy to collect.
  2. **Listen for hints of dissatisfaction.** Compensate customers—on the spot—by offering upgrades, discounts, or premiums when something goes wrong. Do not wait for a complaint.
  3. **Every month, spend time brainstorming on how to enhance your customer service.** Aim to create a service level that amazes customers and baffles your competitors.
  4. **Do a customer satisfaction survey on all sales of $5,000 or more.** Make it quick and simple. Offer an incentive for customers to take time to share their shopping experience with you. (See the "Showroom Customer Service Satisfaction Survey" later in this chapter for a sample form.)
- **Loyal customers are the best customers.** Loyal customers are the lowest-cost and highest-volume customers you will ever find. They reduce the cost side of your profit and loss statement. Loyal customers are new business ambassadors, spreading your message and serving as in-person advertising for your business. Referrals from happy clients should be your number one source of new prospects.
- **Indifference sends clients away.** Many clients do not "fire" a business because of poor-quality products, high pricing, or blatantly bad service; they leave because they felt they were treated with indifference—they were made to feel they were unimportant. Fight indifference with an obsession for customer care and service.
- **Use customer complaints to lead your business to service improvements and satisfied clients.** Follow these four tips:
  1. Talk to your customers.
  2. Encourage complaints.
  3. When you receive a complaint, first fix the customer, and then fix the problem.
  4. Encourage customer "pickiness."
- **There is no such thing as "bad" customers.** There are only good customers and non-customers.
- **Bad news travels faster than good news.** When you do a good job for clients, they may tell five people. However, when things go poorly, they are likely to tell 20 people. It is often not fair, but that is how it is.
- **It takes a great company to make a great customer.** If you want satisfied customers, make customer satisfaction a core value of your company. Insist that your employees always treat your customers with respect and courtesy. 10 Ways to Ensure Customer Satisfaction
  1. Get to know your customers, recognize them as individuals, and treat them like friends and valued partners.
  2. Create a team of great service people within your business.
  3. Anticipate your clients' needs.
  4. Communicate often with your customers.
  5. Thank customers for their business.
  6. Encourage customer requests and respond with tailor-made solutions.
  7. Bend your rules to keep loyal customers.
  8. Provide extra services to high-volume and longtime customers.
  9. Make dealing with your business a highlight of your customer's day.
  10. Teach your customers to expect your company's customer service—and keep your standards so high that no other business can rise to your level.

Answer These Questions about Your Business
- What does your product/service do for your customers? How does it make them feel?
- How is your offering different, more unique, and better than your competitor's offering?

- How is it better than it was even a year ago?
- What do customers do if they are displeased or if something goes wrong?
- Are there any other products or services that you might offer that would make you even more customer friendly?
- What do you sell? How much? How many? What times of the year do they sell best?

The better you can answer these questions, the better you will understand your business. And the better you understand your business, the more able you are to steer its future.

Analyze Your Product and Service Mix

Let's assume you do offer a complete complement of K&B products. But do you have any idea which category generates the biggest amount of sales and profitability? If not, Table 10.4 is an example of a product and service sales and profitability analysis, where GP stands for gross profit.

Do the same exercise with your top vendors. Determine which are the most profitable, and emphasize those in your selling efforts.

Let the Cash Register and Market Knowledge Steer Your Business
- Sell what people want. More and more customers (especially those 75 million Baby Boomers) are looking for one-stop shopping and turnkey jobs. Do you offer this? Should you?
- Promote the products your customers do not know you offer.
- Are your current sales 90 percent kitchens (like the majority of your peers)? Why not promote bathrooms, home offices, entertainment centers, and so on?
- Push your winners. Your product-revenue analysis exercise will tell you what they are.
- Bet on products and services with adequate growth potential. If you do not offer installation as part of your package, should you do so? The right reasons would be that your customers want it and it would bring in added revenues.

TABLE 10.4 Product and Service Sales and Profitability Analysis

Product/Service	Sales	% of Sales	GP %	GP $	% of GP $
Cabinets	$1,200,000	60%	40%	$480,000	64.6%
Countertops	150,000	7.5	22	33,000	4.4
Plumbing	65,000	3.25	35	22,750	3.1
Lighting	50,000	2.5	45	22,500	3.0
Design Fees	35,000	1.75	100	35,000	4.7
Installation	500,000	25	30	150,000	20.2
Totals	$2,000,000	100%	37.16%	$743,250	100%

KNOWING WHO YOUR COMPETITORS ARE

Every business has competition. Even if you are the only K&B business in town, you still have competition. Because kitchens are big-ticket sales, you are working with clients who may need a new kitchen, but they also need a new car and they want to take that trip of a lifetime. In this case, you are competing for the client's dollars. Competition is the heart of all sports, and it is also the core of the free enterprise system and business as we know it.

Competition is the contest between businesses for customers and sales. Competition is a good thing, and here is why:

- Competition promotes product upgrades and innovations.
- Competition leads to higher quality and lower prices.
- Competition enhances selection.
- Competition inspires business efficiencies.
- Competition dictates that you must render great service.

Defining Your Direct Competition

On an annual or regular basis, ask yourself these questions:

- Who does our business really compete with? When prospects start to consider redoing kitchens, what other businesses do they think of? Other kitchen dealers, the big box stores, local shops, a remodel contractor, or you?
- How does our business rate among all these other players?

Create a list of all of your competitors, especially the main ones, and for each, assess these three factors:

1. The competitor's strengths when compared to your business
2. The competitor's weaknesses when compared to your business
3. What your business could do differently to draw this competitor's customers over to you

"Mystery Shop" Your Competitors

Here is a great exercise that should be done on a regular basis (at least once a year). You, one of your sales associates, a friend, or an interior design professional should "shop" every one of your main competitors. Use Table 10.5 as a guideline, and report back to the whole team what the results of the survey were.

TABLE 10.5 Shopping Your Competition

Competitor Name:
Competitor Address:
Date of Survey:

Fill in the blank or rate each item 1 (low) to 5 (high):

Location and accessibility (easy to find, visibility, good location)	1	2	3	4	5
Parking (closest to building, enough spaces, etc.)	1	2	3	4	5
Overall appearance of building	1	2	3	4	5
Outside signage	1	2	3	4	5
Front window displays	1	2	3	4	5
Front of building and parking well lit	1	2	3	4	5
Cleanliness of sidewalk and walk-up area	1	2	3	4	5
Front door (signage, hours, etc.)	1	2	3	4	5
First impression as you step through the door (open feeling, well lit, colors, displays, etc.)	1	2	3	4	5
How quickly were you greeted?	1	2	3	4	5
Did the initial contact try to qualify you?	1	2	3	4	5
How well did they qualify you?	1	2	3	4	5
Was the feeling of the showroom consistent with the price point of products? (high end, medium, low)	1	2	3	4	5
Quality and cleanliness of the public restrooms	1	2	3	4	5
Did the showroom layout flow?	[ ]Yes			[ ]No	
Were the displays good looking and up to date?	[ ]Yes			[ ]No	
Were there any "holes" in the displays?	[ ]Yes			[ ]No	
Was the showroom clean?	[ ]Yes			[ ]No	
Were salespeople workstations well located?	[ ]Yes			[ ]No	
Were the desks and work areas neat?	[ ]Yes			[ ]No	
Did display products have model numbers?	[ ]Yes			[ ]No	
Did display products have prices?	[ ]Yes			[ ]No	
Was there a kids' area?	[ ]Yes			[ ]No	
What main products were displayed?					

Fill in the blank or rate each item 1 (low) to 5 (high):

Were there VCRs/DVDs and educational tapes	[ ]Yes	[ ]No
Did they offer product brochures?	[ ]Yes	[ ]No
How big was the showroom?	Sq. ft.	
How many sales consultants were there?		
Were the displays well lit?	[ ]Yes	[ ]No
Was their quote form customer-friendly?	[ ]Yes	[ ]No
Did they have a good mix and diversification of products?	[ ]Yes	[ ]No
Were the products on display current and up to date?	[ ]Yes	[ ]No
Did they offer coffee or refreshments?	[ ]Yes	[ ]No
If so, how were they served (paper cups, china mugs, promotional mugs, etc.)?		
Was there a closing area?	[ ]Yes	[ ]No
Were their quotes done by hand or computer?		
Based on the above answers:		
What is your overall rating of the showroom?	1　　2　　3　　4　　5	
What is your overall rating of the people?	1　　2　　3　　4　　5	

Other Comments:

BUSINESS IMAGE AND BRANDING

It takes years of hard work, creativity, and money to develop a strong, positive image/brand of a business. We'd like to share an example of how a K&B dealer totally reinvented his business and spent the past 10 years creating an all-new brand and image.

Case Study: Bella Domicile

Bella Domicile, headquartered in Madison, Wisconsin, opened its doors in 1963 and for 40 years operated under the name of Modern Kitchen Supply. Their image in the marketplace was "we sell moderately priced kitchens for new construction and remodel." Building contractors were a large part of their business.

In 2003 the owner of the business, Dan Luck, took a bold step and changed the business name and location. The new name, Bella Domicile, means "beautiful home." Dan wanted to get away from the image of kitchen only and moderately priced only to an image of a company that supplies products for virtually every room in the home. The new tag line says "Kitchen – Bath – Office – Living Room – Any Room—We'll make room for everything." In addition, the new image reflects a much wider range of pricing—from gorgeous higher-end projects to the more modest ones.

In addition to the name change, the company changed location from a large, older building where it fabricated laminate countertops to a brand-new 8,900-square-foot great-looking building. It now outsources the countertop business. It has a well-thought-out marketing plan that has redirected its target audience from mid- to lower-priced jobs and building contractors to a more upscale retail (homeowner) community.

To help ensure the success of this dramatic change, the company added new products and services. It offers installation on all projects, employs award-winning designers, and operates a very well-run business. The company has an annual business plan, marketing plan, and budget. It has a great Web site (www. belladomicile.com) featuring its core values, people, projects, and much more. It is very visible on several social media sites, does a number of innovative promotions and events throughout the year, and has won several honors and awards, which it is not shy about sharing with clients and prospective clients. Remember, we're talking about image and branding.

The company is active in local community charitable functions, and Mr. Luck and several of his staff members are active in a number of professional industry-related associations (NKBA, ASID, NARI, etc.).

So after 40 years of one image and one brand, this company has totally reinvented itself. The end result has been very rewarding for the owners, employees, vendors, and clients of this very innovative, progressive, and well-run business.

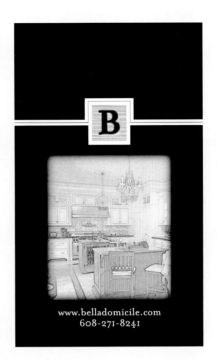

Source: Bella Domicile; provided with permission.

Source: Bella Domicile;
provided with permission.

Source: Bella Domicile; provided with permission.

(continued)

Source: Bella Domicile; provided with permission.

Analyze Display Effectiveness

How much and what type of sales volume should each of your displays generate? Any visual merchandising book or college marketing course tells you that the efficiency of any retail sales environment is judged by comparing square footage to sales per display and/or sales per square foot of display space. This formula works well for high-volume retail organizations in the housewares arena—and even in fashion. In the kitchen and bath dealership environment, it is a little different: Successful firms often have several different types of displays.

- Some displays create a statement about who you are in the marketplace. These displays may feature the most expensive products in your mix and therefore actually may reflect a low percentage of your total volume.
- A second tier of displays represents the majority of your sales in style, finish, and price range. Try to create a popular look in an entry-level (affordable) price version as well as a similar look with add-on or step-up features.
- The third type of displays consists of smaller vignettes. They typically demonstrate one center of activity in the kitchen, giving you more opportunity to show small areas of popular materials you sell or emerging materials you would like to give a try. A note of caution: Do not overdesign these vignettes. Packing every possible detail into a small vignette can result in a display requiring an investment equal to a larger one that has more typical cabinets stretched between the highly designed, architecturally detailed elements.

Displays are not a part of your inventory. Plan to change displays on a regular basis. Change high-style displays and vignettes every two to three years. Change the hardworking "foundation" displays every three to five years.

Many successful managers have a five-year plan for their showroom, which includes display change-out schedules. To keep your displays current, fresh, and ahead of your competition, you should have a completely new showroom look every five years. Such planning is important to manage the expenses for this marketing endeavor and its impact on cash flow.

Customers' First Impression of Your Showroom

Step back, if you can, and pretend that you are a customer. What would your first impression be of these areas?

- Company name
- Company signage
- Logo and colors
- Advertisements
- Business accessibility
- Customer parking
- Front window displays
- Front door signage
- Cleanliness of walk-up to the front door
- Immediate impression when entering your business
- Employee attire
- Manner of greeting showroom prospects
- Lighting and cleanliness of your showroom
- How are incoming calls answered?
- Voicemail message
- Web site impression Web site
- Neatness of workstations neat

Everything adds up to what image your business projects, and you have control over all of it.

Using the sample survey form in Table 10.6, have a few friends to rate their first impression of your business.

TABLE 10.6 Showroom Personnel Telephone/Customer Service Survey

	Always	Sometimes	Never	Don't Know
DOES HE OR SHE. . .				
Answer the telephone in three rings or fewer?	4	3	2	1
Answer the telephone with a cordial salutation, company name, and an offer of help? (For example, "Good afternoon, ABC Company, how may I help you?")	4	3	2	1
Avoid placing calls on hold for more than one minute?	4	3	2	1
Tell callers they will be "connected" rather than "transferred"?	4	3	2	1
Speak clearly on the telephone?	4	3	2	1
Thank customers for calling?	4	3	2	1
Ask customers to call again?	4	3	2	1
Allow callers to hang up the phone first?	4	3	2	1
Give customers full attention?	4	3	2	1
Exhibit a helping attitude toward drop-ins?	4	3	2	1
Offer visitors a chair or a place to sit?	4	3	2	1
Understand the importance of customer service?	4	3	2	1
Display a commitment to customer service?	4	3	2	1
Know that the job is a customer service position and not just clerical?	4	3	2	1

Scoring: Add all the numbers you circled and compare your total with these scores:

    51–56 Great! Very customer service-oriented

    41–50 Pretty good, with a little training

    31–40 Mediocre; needs attention and guidance

    19–30 Time for a serious talk

    14–18 Needs to be replaced

COMMENTS:

What Is It Like to Be a Customer of Your Business?

Pretend that you are a first-time customer and experiencing your business from a stranger's point of view. Or ask an impartial person to do the survey for you. Have them call and visit the business, send an email, look at your Web site, review advertisements—then have them give you all of their impressions. Ask them to use the "Mystery Shopping" form that you are encouraged to use with your competitors.

Are Your Marketing Communications Consistent?

Pull samples of advertisements, signs, brochures, letterheads—everything with your name and logo—line them up, and ask yourself these questions:

- Does your business name and logo look the same every time so you make a consistent impression?
- Do you consistently use the same type style?
- Do your marketing materials present a consistent image in terms of look, quality, and message?

If not, it may be time to make some changes. Does the image you are trying to project really reflect where your business is today? It is okay to change; in fact, rolling out a new name and/or image could be both fun and rewarding.

ESTABLISHING YOUR BRAND

A brand is the sum total of the experiences your customers and potential customers have with your company. A strong brand communicates what your company does, how it does it, what makes you different, better, and unique. Over time it establishes trust and credibility. Your brand lives in everyday interactions with your customers, the images you share, the messages you post on your Web site, the content of your marketing materials, and your posts on social media.

Perhaps you're thinking "We are a small, kitchen and bath dealer, we hardly need a brand." Wrong! You *do* need a brand. Many K&B dealers "ride" the brand name of the cabinets and other major products that they carry and don't spend time, energy, and money trying to develop their own brand identity. Unfortunately, they are missing a valuable opportunity.

Here are several tips that you can follow to help you develop a strong brand on a small budget:

- **Be unique.** What products or services do you offer that make you unique in your market place? Offering turnkey projects when your competition only sells cabinets makes you unique.
- **Grow your community.** As a small business, you have a number of opportunities to grow your online and offline communities. You can do this on Twitter, Facebook, your small business blog, Instagram, or other social networks. You won't be able to be everywhere at once; focus on one or two sites where you can best build your community and invest your time and resources there.
- **Build superior products and services.** Generate the most creative designs. Make yourself a one-stop shopping destination for the kitchen, bath, home office, and more. Offer installation, and strive to be the best at all of this in your marketplace. When you do this, people will start talking about you.
- **Have a good name and logo.** A strong brand is easily recognizable, and recognition starts with the name of your business. The name appears on your business cards, letterheads, Web site, social networks, promotional materials, and pretty much everywhere in print and online to identify your company. It's not only imperative to have a recognizable name; you must also have a logo that people will associate with the name. A good logo builds trust, and a strong logo helps pull your brand together.

- **Find your voice.** What you say is important, but don't overlook *how* you say it. Your company's voice is the language and personality you and your employees will use to deliver your branding message and reach your customers.
- **Be consistent.** Many small businesses mistakenly change their messaging depending on the audience. For example, a company may use a serious tone on its Web site but a light-hearted tone in its social media. Doing this can confuse your customers and potential customers. To build and maintain a strong brand, you must ensure that every aspect of your brand is as good as your products and services. You must be *consistent* in presenting your brand. Work hard for brand consistency because it leads to familiarity, and familiarity leads to trust.
- **Keep every promise.** Although this is common sense, many small businesses tarnish relationships with customers by failing to keep promises. Happy, satisfied customers who feel good about your business are your best source of referrals, and referrals should be your number one means of securing new customers.
- **Stand for something.** Stand for something that your customers can connect with emotionally. Support a local charity, have a customer-is-always-right philosophy, have the most professional-looking and acting installation crew, or do something else that makes you stand out from your competition.
- **Empower your customers.** You are not in control of your brand; your customers are! People can become your brand's ambassador, spreading your ideas and brands to their own networks. Ultimately, successful brands recognize that if they help their customers succeed, the customers will in turn help the brands succeed.
- **Deliver value.** Value doesn't mean the lowest price. It's everything else that you offer: quality products, great service, well-trained employees, a family-owned business, years of experience, awards and certifications, and so much more. When you deliver great value, your brand will succeed, and price will no longer be the most important thing on your customers' minds.

In summary, branding makes selling easier. People want to buy from companies they know and trust will be there well into the future. A brand puts forth that promise. With a well-managed brand, your company hardly needs to introduce itself. Within your target market, people will already know you, your business personality, and your promise based on what they have seen and heard through your marketing communicators.

FINDING AND FILLING A MEANINGFUL MARKET POSITION

Positioning involves figuring out what meaningful and available niche in the marketplace your business is designed to fill, filling it, and performing so well that your customers have no reason to allow anyone else into your market position.

The tricky thing about positioning is that it's not something you do to your business; it's something the market does for you. Customers position your company in their own minds. Your job is to lead them to their positioning conclusions through your branding and marketing communication efforts.

How Positioning Happens

When people learn about your business subconsciously, they slot you into a business hierarchy. For example, they may consider you:

- **A me-too business.** If the mind slot—or position—for your business is already taken, consumers do the equivalent of filing your message into the trash bin. If your offering simply duplicates what's already out there, you're dead on arrival, or close to it. The only hope for resuscitation is to find and promote a meaningful point of difference. It had better be a pretty convincing distinction, though, because you're going to have to convince people that (1) your difference is worth hearing about, and (2) your difference is worth changing for.

- **A similar but different business.** If your marketplace has three other K&B dealers but you're the only one that offers a turnkey package of design, products, and installation, you have a meaningful point of distinction. If you communicate that distinction well, you are apt to win a clear position in the minds of the consumer.
- **A business offering brand-new distinctions.** If you can be the first to fill a market's needs, you have the easiest positioning task of all. But you must jump into the market skillfully and forcefully enough to win your way into consumers' minds before anyone else can. Let's say you are the first K&B dealer in your marketplace to offer a complete selection of products and services, making you the only business to offer one-stop shopping, including design, particular products, and installation. This is important because it will make you first in consumers' minds.

WHY IT'S IMPORTANT TO HAVE A GREAT WEB SITE

Years ago, consumers would have gone straight to the Yellow Pages and then either given you a call or stopped by your business. Small businesses still spends hundreds of dollars a month on their phone, the Yellow Pages, local advertising, letterheads, business cards, and the like. Many spend a lot more to locate their business in the most customer-friendly place possible. All of these things are important to success.

Many people (especially Baby Boomers) still go to the Yellow Pages, check out flyers that come in the mail, or ask neighbors and friends about which business to call for a kitchen and bath remodel. But to finalize their decision, make their final choice, and put their plans into action they'll investigate on the Internet. Most people look and ask for the website of businesses that are suggested to them.

Today we live in an era of the Internet, the most powerful, most accessible dynamic communication system known to humankind. Most of us turn immediately to the Internet for answers to the simplest quests to find products and services or just someone to help us.

How often do you log onto your computer and go to someone's website to check out a company, its products, its services, its price, or simply to get a phone number or directions? We're betting that you do a lot of this. So do your clients.

For prospective clients, a website should answer who, what, why, how, how much, and how a business can help them. For your business, it is the best chance you have to fully and completely express who you are, how and why you are different and unique, and why you're able to provide the value people are looking for.

After all the searching, calling, querying, and referrals, the final piece in the buying process can be your website. It goes a long way toward making your business the consumer's first choice to handle their kitchen or bath remodel project.

The worst thing you can do is to continue to spend thousands of dollars in local advertising, promotions, and best location and not have a website. A really good website!

Investing in your website may be the best marketing investment you can make. Your website can, sell, persuade, and show prospective clients every facet of your business, skill, ability, and talent. You get to show everyone how capable, knowledgeable, experienced, and successful, your business is.

Having the very best website in your geographic marketplace is one of the best marketing tools you have and developing and maintaining it should be a priority.

A New Business Card Idea

A picture of your latest project is worth a thousand words, but a customized CD can provide much more to a prospective customer.

New Business Card Idea

Create a CD as a marketing tool. You can include music, video clips showing your crew at work, a voice-over describing the type of work your firm does, and/or still photographs. A link to your company's website is possible as well. Such a CD is a great tool to leave with the consumer, rather than a printed brochure. It is also much easier to update, and is relatively inexpensive.

Advertising

The opportunities to spend money on advertising are unlimited. Some are good and some are not. Your job—not an easy one—is to identify the advertising media that will help you accomplish your overall marketing strategy goal. What media will your clients be looking at and listening to? If your clients are at the higher end, the *Penny-Saver* flyer is not right for you, but an upscale home and garden magazine in your area might be. Here is a list of just some of the media available:

- Yellow Pages
- Newspaper
- Radio
- Television
- Regional magazines
- Trade magazines
- Email
- Website
- Direct mail
- Truck signage
- Door hangers
- Yard signs
- Billboards

You will probably decide to use a combination of several of these advertising venues. Devise some way of tracking the results of your different advertising activities so you can determine which ones paid off. Possibly offer a gift, special, or some other incentive for responding to an advertisement. At the very least, have your designers/salespeople ask, "How did you hear about us?" Follow this by tabulating all of the responses so that you can determine what works and what doesn't.

DEVELOP AN ADVERTISING CAMPAIGN

Do not plan your advertising campaign impulsively by simply reacting to media salespeople dropping in. Have a plan and schedule. (See for example the sample in Table 10.7).

Public Relations

Public relations (or simply "PR" as it is often referred to) is a terrific means to help get your message out. PR is the art of keeping your name before the public in a positive way other than through paid advertising. Good PR is the best and most economical way to let people know who you are and what you do. PR can be article about you, your company, your employees, projects you have done, awards you have won, new products and just about anything that a magazine, newspaper, radio, or television station thinks might make good reading, listening, or watching. Free publicity can expand awareness of both you and your business. The public (your clients) puts more credence in this type of "advertising" because

TABLE 10.7 Sample Marketing Timeline Action List

JAN	FEB	MARCH	APRIL	MAY	JUNE
Magazine	Magazine	Magazine			
Direct mail	Direct mail	Direct mail	Direct mail	Direct mail	Direct mail
	In-store promo	In-store promo			
Web site update	Web site update	Web site update			
	Home show				
Radio ads	Radio ads	Radio ads	Radio ads		
TV ads	TV ads	TV ads			
	In-home party	In-home party			
PR help	PR help	PR help	PR help	PR help	PR help
Social media	Social media	Social media	Social media	Social media	Social media
	Charitable event	Kitchen tour	Charitable event		

they know a third party developed it; it was not paid for. PR resources are usually free. The challenge is to get the attention of editors, writers, and reporters because your competition is trying to do the same thing.

Good PR rarely just happens. You have to make it happen. Either you or a paid professional PR person has to schmooze the listed sources, and you have to present them with something that they believe their readers, listeners, and watchers will be interested in. Good PR takes time, effort and creativity, but the results can be very beneficial.

Here are successful PR activities which should be in your plan every year:

- Enter design competitions.
- Schedule professional photographs of your better projects.
- Maintain a list of editorial contacts (regional and national).
- Submit your work to regional and national publications.
- Participate in high-profile charitable events.
- Network with your client base and allied professionals.
- Become the go-to kitchen and bath expert in your marketplace.

Promotions

There are many opportunities to spend money on promotions. Once again, your challenge is to decide where you will get the biggest bang for your buck. Here is a short list of some promotion ideas:

- Home and trade shows
- Showroom open house
- Sales
- Educational seminars hosted in your showroom
- "Lunch and Learn" type programs for ASID, AIA, and so on
- Host trade association meetings
- Cooking demonstrations
- Charity functions
- Parade of Homes/Street of Dreams participation
- Kitchen tour sponsorships
- Designer show house participation
- Celebrity cookbook signing in the showroom

GETTING YOUR WORK PUBLISHED

You have successfully marketed, sold, and produced another high-quality project—a project that you are proud to have your name on, one you want to share with others. You take some snapshots to pass around to friends and family. You gather people at your office for show and tell. And that's about it.

Occasionally, though, a project comes along that has a special quality that screams to be published. Perhaps your design focused on an architectural detail, such as a barrel ceiling. Or it is an historic landmark in your city. More likely it is just a beautiful project with extraordinary attention to detail. Or it may be the emphasis on universal design, the environment, or another specific issue. The project is right for publication. The question is: How do you do it?

Presenting your work in major consumer publications may seem too formidable to undertake on your first attempt, but there's nothing mysterious about working with local media for some profitable publicity.

Taking the Mystery out of Local Publicity

When it comes to getting kitchen and bathroom projects published, the qualities needed are:

- Clarity of the materials you send to editors.
- Persistence in contacting the right people.
- A spirit of helpfulness when you are working with editors.

Working with Editors

All three of these qualities will be important when working with editors.

The most important aspect regarding media relations is cultivating relationships with local editors. To do this successfully, make an effort to understand the editors' news needs and send them the right kind of information in the right format often. They'll appreciate your efforts and, in turn, will keep you in mind when they have a need for specific information. It may not happen overnight, but, like any good investment, it will pay dividends over time.

The next tips can assist you in cultivating editor relationships:

- **Understand that publicity differs fundamentally from advertising.** It is not something that you pay for outright. Editors are under no obligation to use your material. They may use part of it, change it, or add other material to it.
- **Submit material in an easy-to-understand format.** Print news releases double-spaced, and make them only as long as is absolutely necessary. Answer the questions who, what, when, where, why and how in the beginning of the release.
- **Be persistent in a friendly and helpful way with editors.** Offer material that presents interesting information to readers. If you have doubts about the appropriateness of your news, call or email the editor before submitting it.
- **Call editors a few days after you send the material.** Do this to verify that the information was received and considered. Ask what type of information the editor would like to see in the future.
- **Offer to serve as a source of information.** Make you case as a good source for future articles on kitchen/bathroom trends, design, and related topics.
- **Time your material appropriately.** Work with editors to find out when they need material on remodeling or an interview about K&B design trends.

Occasionally, an editor will make the first contact. It is likely that those kitchen and bath business owners who live in larger cities may have already been or will be approached by an editor of a local newspaper or magazine. Most city magazines and newspapers feature home and design sections three to four times a year. Editors are always looking for projects with an interesting story.

Always respond to requests for material from major magazines. Also, keep any inquiry letters you may receive in your magazine reference file. When you have material they may be interested in, you will have the name of the editor to contact.

If you aren't on anyone's contact list, write or call the home editor, offering to write an article or proposing an idea for a future story.

Become a Local Expert

If you have built up a reputation with local editors, and they turn to you for information regarding kitchen and bathroom design, approach them with the idea of an "Ask the Expert" column or write a rough draft of a short article that you can submit weekly or monthly. The editors may appreciate having the so-called expert appear in their papers. In return, you will receive great publicity for your firm.

You could invite readers to write in with their remodeling questions or problems; your answers would display your expertise and knowledge. Or you could create articles using general concepts, such as trends, remodeling expectations, working with a pro, universal design, environmental issues, and the like.

The syndicated column "Ask the Builder" featuring Tim Carter of Cincinnati started out in just this fashion. He became the local expert by asking and answering some of his own questions in the column, and readers soon responded. As the column became successful, eventually it was syndicated in 100 cities. He is now not only a local expert but a national one and has carved a niche for himself and his company.

Many home and garden shows offer educational seminars on a variety of subjects. Offer to do a session on styles, trends, and what's new and exciting in the world of kitchens and baths. This is another opportunity to become the local expert.

Going National

As stated earlier, getting your work published in a national publication may seem like an impossible task. This is not necessarily true. Large national magazines employ a network of editorial scouts, sometimes known as stringers. In each major metropolitan area, someone is regularly contacting designers, architects, and builders on behalf of the magazines, looking for projects and story ideas. These scouts will ask to see photos (it is a plus if you have "befores" as well as "afters") and plans of installations you have done. When they find a project they like, the scouts will want the address of the location. Next, they will take their own scouting shots to submit to the magazine's editors. When this happens, ask if you can help by driving the scout to the location. Doing this gives you the opportunity to tell the scout more about your company and an opportunity to "sell" your project. Point out details the scout might otherwise miss or explain why something was done the way it was.

The scout will shoot the photographs and submit them. If the editor decides to do a story about your design, the magazine will probably arrange for additional professional photography suitable for their publication.

The two leading trade magazines in our industry, *Kitchen & Bath Design News* and *Kitchen & Bath Business*, run articles on special projects in almost every issue. Try to get yourself published in one of these. Then frame and hang the article on your "Wall of Fame" in your showroom.

Submitting Projects

If your geographic location is not large enough to merit a scout in the area, you can write or submit projects to the magazines yourself. When submitting projects, there are several points to remember. Begin with what makes a project publishable from an editor's standpoint. NKBA compiled the next list with the help of national design editors.

1. Projects must be well designed (meaning they meet or come close to meeting NKBA's Kitchen and Bathroom Planning Guidelines).
2. Simple and charming projects are appealing. So are elegant and classic ones.
3. Huge projects cannot be photographed because the room cannot be fully captured in one or two photos.
4. Large, expensive rooms that are too extravagant or ostentatious are not favorable.
5. Very small rooms may not offer enough visual interest and may be difficult to photograph.
6. Warmth is important. Cold, stark rooms have little photographic appeal.
7. Very dark woods are difficult to light and photograph because details and highlights get lost.
8. High-gloss cabinets are hard to photograph, making certain projects less publishable.
9. Bathrooms can become mirror nightmares. Too many mirrors and reflections cause problems with lighting for photography and make it difficult to position camera equipment.
10. Rooms decorated with busy wallpapers or fabrics are less likely to be chosen.

It is important to note that these are not hard-and-fast rules; rather, they are guidelines that will help you determine which projects have the best chance of being selected for publication.

Once you do choose a project, submission is easy. Editors want to see:

- **Floor plans.** It is not necessary to redraw plans; make copies of the ones you shared with clients.
- **Perspective renderings.** Again, simply make copies of the ones you shared with clients.
- **Photographs.** Major national publications and many regional or city publications do not require professional photographs. Scouting snapshots are fine. If the project is accepted, the magazine will arrange for its photographers.
- **Professional photography.** Professional photographs of your projects will better portray your work in your portfolio, brochures, and ads; on your website and for other marketing activities. Most trade magazines and many smaller consumer magazines often use the professional photography supplied by designers.
- **"Before" photos.** In addition to shots of the finished project, "before" photos sometimes are helpful to submit.
- Never send originals photos or plans. Editors are conscientious about returning material they receive if you enclosed stamped, self-addressed envelope, but there is always the chance that your materials will not be sent back. In such a case, you would lose documentation of your work.
- **Design statements.** Take the time to write some notes about the project. Catch the editor's interest with a brief summary of the design concept, the problems you encountered, and how you solved them.

   For a consumer magazine, explain how the project meets the homeowner's needs.

   For a professional or trade magazine, you might describe any technical, architectural, or installation problems you solved.
- **Send material to only one or two magazines.** Try to establish a rapport with the editors. Be aware of which magazines seem to feature the kind of projects you do.

   Two of the best resources for NKBA members for getting their work published are the association's *NKBA Magazine* and its annual professional design competition. In addition, NKBA works closely with other publications, providing a vehicle for members to reach consumers on a national level. The NKBA Marketing team has formed strong partnerships with all of these publications and may help direct you in your efforts. As a professional courtesy, do not submit the same project to more than one magazine at a time. Send it to one publication, and wait for the editor's response. Give editors at least six weeks to get back to you; travel and press deadlines often keep them from responding quickly. If the first magazine you approach chooses not to publish your project, then send it to another. If you do send a project to more than one magazine at the same time, tell each editor that other magazines have received the same material.

- **Do not be discouraged if your material is returned "Thanks, but no thanks."** Many times an editor has just seen four white kitchens and you have sent in the fifth. To keep readers turning the pages, editors look for variety.

   Editors also consider other factors when choosing projects, some logistical and some technical. If their publication does its own photography, they may need more than one project in the same area to make the expense of flying in a photographer worthwhile. You might work with others designers in your area to give the editor and photographer several projects to consider. Whenever you finish an outstanding project, submit it right away. An editor may have photography scheduled in a neighboring state/province, making it easy to work you in.

   Sometimes a project is turned down because it is too difficult to photograph, even though the design has merit. As mentioned earlier, it takes special skill in lighting to photograph high-gloss cabinets or very dark woods and rooms that feature mirrors.

   Keep in mind that just because an editor says no the first time does not mean he or she won't consider another project from you. If the editor takes the time to explain the reasons for rejecting your first submission, take it as a good sign. Select another project and submit it. In the cover letter, mention any previous publicity the project has received—a local newspaper story or even your own local advertising.

When the Editor Calls

Much of the discussion thus far has focused on what to do if a project is not accepted for publication. If an editor receives material on a well-designed project that meets the needs of the magazine, chances are good that it will be selected for publication. The editor will contact you to inform you that the project has been selected. A professional photo session will be arranged, and additional information will be secured from the designer as well as the client. For this reason, it is essential to get permission for publication from clients before you go to the trouble of querying an editor about a project. If clients have had a good experience with you, chances are they will want you to get this recognition; most feel honored to have their homes featured in local or national magazines. But clients should be warned that professional photography could take a full day and possibly longer. Clients will be expected to sign a release form giving the publication permission to take and use photos in a number of ways, not necessarily limited to a single feature.

The magazine's editorial staff should inform you of when the project will be published. If no one is able to provide an exact date at the time the photography and interviews take place, you will be contacted later with a publication date.

Exposure in a consumer magazine—national, regional, or local—can do a great deal for your business. Acknowledge that fact and formally thank the editor and the magazine for the opportunity. Follow-up is not only good for increasing your chances of repeat business from customers; it also increases your chances of future exposure in the same magazine.

Remember, you have to promote your own company because no one else will.

Meet the Press: Tips for Preparing a Press Release

There is a general assumption that getting your company mentioned in the local paper is free publicity. Yes, it is publicity—but it is not free. In fact, if done poorly, it can be a most costly experience in futility.

The vehicle for most PR efforts is the tried-and-true press release. Press releases do work. The *Columbia Journalism Review* found that a single issue of the *Wall Street Journal* had 111 stories taken from press releases word for word and only 30 percent of these stories had additional facts collected by reporters. More to the point, an estimated 80 percent of all published newspaper and magazine stories began as a press release to promote a service or product and build image.

A press release is a written document with a clear headline, quotes and facts with attribution to support a news story, background on the featured company, release date, and basic contact information for follow-up.

Can the average remodeler write a good press release? Most have no experience and lack the necessary writing skills, making the result less than satisfactory.

Here are eight tips to help you prepare your next press release and increase your chance of seeing it in print:*

1. **Make sure it is newsworthy.** Avoid blatant, self-serving puffery which will cause you to lose credibility with an editor.
2. **Write well so it doesn't have to be rewritten.** Save the editor time.
3. **Use a style guide.** Most newspapers use the *Associated Press Stylebook*.
4. **Develop a great lead.** Make the editor want to read further.
5. **Use an inverted pyramid writing structure.** This means the most important information is up top; the least important, at the bottom. Editors are forced to select articles that fit the column inches available. With the inverted pyramid approach, editors can cut off as much as they need to make it fit without diluting the message.
6. **End with a boilerplate paragraph about your company:** Who you are, what you do, and contact information.
7. **Include photos.** If photos are available, include them either attached to an email, on a disc, or as prints.
8. **Proof carefully.** Then proof again.

If this is all more than you bargained for, there are good reasons to hire an agency:

- An agency has experience.
- It can prepare the press release in a manner recognized by an editor as professional.
- A submission from an agency is seen as a third-party submission.
- An agency may have already established a relationship with several editors and maintain a media list.
- The cost of a professionally prepared press release (not an in-depth article) is small compared to the level of effort for an internal job.
- Most important, an agency typically employs professional writers.

SOCIAL MEDIA MARKETING

The following comments are by Nora DePalma of O'Reilly-DePalma, a marketing and public relations consulting firm.

"What's up with Twitter? Why would I waste my time telling people that I just had a cup of coffee?" The Internet and social media have turned marketing upside down for everyone, from small local businesses to the biggest companies in the world. You're not alone if you haven't the faintest idea if social media is worth it for your business.

In many ways, it is small local businesses that benefit the most from social media marketing. Strategic social marketing is low-cost, high-touch, especially when you expand your thinking about it to support not only marketing, but also sales and customer service. (Hint: For best results, connect your social marketing to an inbound marketing and lead nurturing initiative. People buy from people they like, and social media supercharges the ability for people to find you and, well, like you.

Done correctly, social media marketing conveys the business owner's and employee's personality, expertise, and values. Abrams Research reported in its 2012–2013 *Luxury* guide that consumers who connect with a brand on social media spend 20 percent to 40 percent more money than those who don't. It also states that young, affluent consumers care more about a company's narrative than its price tags.

---

*Adapted courtesy of *Remodeling* magazine, by Stephen Wilson, Biz-comm Inc.

"Done correctly" are the operative words. The biggest mistake in undertaking social media marketing is not being social. Social media marketing is like a giant networking cocktail party. Personality counts, interest in others translates into interest in you, and nobody likes a crashing bore who likes to talk about only him- or herself."

Definitions

Let's start by defining the different types of "channels" and "platforms."

Channels: Flying Camel, an Advertising, Design, and PR Agency define three channels for communications with your customers: paid media, earned media, and owned media.

- **Paid media.** This is traditional advertising, such as buying a magazine ad or a radio ad or a home show booth. Or it can be paid search advertising or online banner advertising. Paid media is any media where you pay to reach an audience and you have complete control of the message. As such, it is the least credible messaging. But a well-targeted, highly visible, and creative advertising commitment is the fastest route to business "brand" awareness.
- **Earned media.** This is traditional PR, when a reporter, editor, or blogger does a story about your business or products or interviews you and quotes you in a report. Earned media is the most credible messaging but you have the least amount of control over timing and messaging. It is generally less costly than paid media but requires a high level of human resource commitment to build relationships and understand the needs of reporters and editors.
- **Owned media.** Owned media are the audience for your company who wants to hear from you. Social media falls into this group, as does your newsletter list of past and current customers, your Web site visitors, social media fans, followers, and blog readers. As with earned media, the out-of-pocket cost is much lower than paid media, but the human resource commitment is the highest of the three.

Platforms: Social media encompasses a wide variety of digital platforms that enable creative self-expression while bringing together people with like-minded interests. There are several categories of social media.

- **Blogging.** If you have resources to do only one thing on social media, make it a blog. Blogs can be connected to your Web site or can even *be* your Web site. They make it easy to post updates continually on your Web site, which makes your site more attractive to search engines. You can create blogs on numerous platforms, from the super-easy Blogger or Tumblr to the feature-rich Word Press, and they make it easy to share design inspirations, images and video. Build traffic by finding similar blogs and leaving comments (non-self-promotional, please)! Respond to comments on your blog.
- **Microblogging.** This is the social media category that includes Twitter, where your posts are limited to 140 characters. That's pretty micro. Twitter can be used to share your blog posts and posts by others but is also a great place to meet and network with like-minded individuals in a chat-style format. Designers and kitchen and bath industry pros gather at regular times for chats, on microblogs such as #KBTribeChat.
- **Photo sharing.** Photo-sharing social media encompasses numerous platforms, from places to upload albums to sharing sites, such as Pinterest and Instagram. Photo-sharing sites are magnets for visually oriented designers and also attract a strong female audience that can be helpful to K&B professionals. The downside is copyright risks in two ways. You're at risk of (1) having your own images used without your permission and (2) if you share images for which a photographer has not granted you universal rights. Protect yourself by knowing the usage rights for any professional photography, and do not use images taken by anyone else. Protect yourself from being victimized by a copyright violation by watermarking your images with your business name, so that it the sharing of your images far and wide benefits you.
- **Video sharing.** The biggest video sharing site is YouTube, which also happens to be one of the top search engines after Google itself (which owns YouTube). Men tend to watch

more videos related to home improvement than do women. But interesting content, defined as everything from kitten videos to entertaining ads to "Gangnam"-style dancing, can attract women and men of all ages. It's quite easy to share YouTube videos. If you upload one, you can increase views by embedding it on your blog or on other blogs. Vimeo has the same embedding capabilities, but with a few more options to improve the visual displays of videos.

- **Social communities.** Social communities include Facebook, LinkedIn Groups, Google+ Circles, and Hangouts, and include design-focused and home communities, such as Modenus and Houzz. Participation in social communities is a give-and-take relationship, so this route requires daily monitoring to respond to questions and outreach as well as reaching out to build your network.

10 Tips to Make Social Media Work for You

Doing social media correctly means it needs to be social. Learning how to use social media marketing effectively can take up its own book, but here are 10 tips to help you get started.

1. **Start by listening.** Choose a platform, and then watch and read what other do and say.
2. **Find your tribe.** Most of our industry trade magazines have done stories and profiles on social media leaders, so start by following them and watching their interactions to find more like-minded folks. Make connections through K&B-related groups on LinkedIn, and participate on Twitter chats at #kbtribechat every Wednesday at 2:00 p.m. ET or the interior designer chat #intdesignerchat every Tuesday at 6 p.m. ET.
3. **Be likable.** Provide fun, helpful, and emotionally uplifting experiences at every touch point.
4. **Follow the 50–30–20 rule** for content. This applies whether it's a 500-word blog post or a 140-character tweet.
   - 50 percent of content you share or create should be of interest to others, although it can be loosely related to your brand message.
     - A kitchen designer might relate stories about local food, recipes, and comment on food blogs.
     - A bathroom showroom might share stories about wellness or comment on fitness sites.
   - 30 percent of content can be related to your brand message, but in an entertaining way.
     - Images of past projects
     - Videos of how a kitchen remodel happens
     - Tips and tricks for successful remodels
   - 20 percent of content is your brand message.
     - Sales announcements, client endorsements, information about your team
5. **Be a person, not just a brand.** Convey a sense of who you are.
6. **Compliment and recognize others.** Even profile others, featuring stories, images, or interviews. Profiling someone is flattering and eminently sharable.
7. **Think like Hallmark.** Greeting card companies create the images and write the prose that makes it easy for people to keep in touch. Create content that people want to share with their friends. Think nostalgia, pets, and kids. Post fun quizzes and interesting questions.
8. **Professional profiles should be engaging and compelling.** Build a likable profile where people researching K&B remodeling will go in your market area.
9. **Focus on quality, not quantity.** Large social media followings can be beneficial, but so can small if you carefully cultivate a following, just as you carefully cultivate contacts offline.
10. **Use social medial to boost you PR.** Find local reporters and editors who do stories about kitchen and baths and follow them to see what interests them. Share and comment positively on their work.

What Does Social Media Cost?

Social media is "free" like PR is "free." While you may not pay for the end result, it takes an investment in time. For social media, plan on 30 minutes per day in conversations and commenting, plus a couple of extra hours a week to create or curate images, stories, and ideas.

Social media also requires a comfort level with written or visual communications. If that's not your thing, you may want to consider hiring some help. Outside expertise typically is based on an hourly rate or a monthly retainer, not unlike a PR or marketing consultant, with rates all over the board. As with hiring any expert, check references and request example of how they have helped small businesses like yours. By helping, we don't only mean the ability to grow a large number of followers. Ask specific questions of how their social expertise has helped clients to increase their business.

SALES AND SELLING

As mentioned earlier, some people believe marketing and sales are one and the same. They are not. Marketing is that whole broad picture. Selling is part of marketing, the most important part, because with no sales, there will be no marketing. A formal definition might be this: Sales is a component of the marketing process whereby your company, either directly or indirectly, contacts, convinces, and contracts with customers to purchase your products and services.

This very well may be the most important section in this entire book. Yours is a selling business. Yes, you design great projects, show great products, and offer outstanding services, but all of this will go for naught if you don't sell them. Your total existence depends on making the sale. Nothing happens until the sale is made! Without sales there would be no showroom, no computers, no vehicles, no desks, and no people. Everything depends on sales (solid profitable sales) being made. Having said that, ask yourself whether you do a good job in teaching and practicing selling skills. If you are honest, your answer probably is no.

Industry resources do a great job in teaching design and product knowledge skills, but often neglect the all-important selling skills. Whether your business consists of are a staff of 1 or 20, you must commit to becoming the very best selling business in your marketplace.

Selling is an art, a learned skill and anyone can learn to be a great salesperson. You may like the design end of the business best, but without learning and practicing great sales skills, you may not stay in business long enough to use all those terrific design skills. Learning selling skills is not rocket science. It's a skill that can be easily learned in fewer than six months. With continual practice, you can turn your team into a dynamic selling machine.

Someone once said that "a salesperson is the most important person in the business world." This certainly holds true in the K&B industry.

There are numerous books, tapes, CDs, seminars, and courses (including several NKBA courses-) on selling skills. As the selling skills of your sales team improve, productivity will increase, and the company will make more money. Plus, you will have happier, more satisfied clients (and more of them).

HOW TO GET STARTED

There are three very important things you must do to build the very best selling team possible. They are:

1. **Delegate someone to be in charge of your sales team.** If yours is a small business, like most kitchen and bath dealers, this responsibility will fall on you, the owner. This makes good sense because likely you are the strongest salesperson in your business.

2. **Develop a formal, written, comprehensive sales skill training program.** Include what, when, who, and how the program will be implemented. This training program should be ongoing and never-ending.

3. **Implement your training program with everyone who has any contact with your customers** . . . even if they are not part of the everyday face-to-face selling team. Do a sales training session at least twice a month. Include lots of interaction and role playing. Teach a skill and then have everyone practice until it is perfected.

The selling process is made up of a number of steps, and each step is designed to lead to the closing of the sale. Each and every step must be learned and practiced. There are no short-cuts! Every book you read on selling skills talks about the various steps in the selling process. Some authors say there are five steps; others will say there are as many as 10 or 12. In trying to customize the process to our industry, we've broken the selling steps down into seven easy segments. They are:

1. Prospecting for clients
2. Initial contact
3. Qualifying clients
4. Presenting products and services
5. Meeting objections and concerns
6. Closing the Sale
7. After-sale follow-through

It is important that sales staff gather information about the client's project in an organized way. The NKBA Business Management Form System, available to members, includes an excellent survey form for both kitchen and bath projects and should be the road map when gathering information from the client before the planning process begins.

Seven-Step Selling Cycle

Following is a brief description of what is involved with each of the seven steps in the selling cycle. Memorize these steps. It is important that you go through the selling process one step at a time, doing a good job with each step. Skipping a step or not doing a thorough job with each diminishes your chance of getting that all-important order.

Step 1. Prospecting for clients. This step involves finding potential buyers for the products and services you sell. Many—perhaps even the majority—of your prospects are referrals from happy clients. In addition, all your marketing efforts (advertising, promotions, your website and public relations) are geared to "drive" clients to your business. Without prospects, you will not need the next six steps!

Step 2. Initial contact. This can be a referral from a satisfied client. It can be someone who has seen one of your advertisements or is making the initial telephone call to your business. All of these, plus prospects' initial impressions of the drive-up, your store front, the first step through the door, and how they are greeted, are part of the initial contact. You only get one chance to make a good impression, so make sure everything you do and say will make clients want to stay for your entire presentation.

Step 3. Qualifying clients. Besides writing the order, this is the most important step in the selling cycle. Within the first few minutes of face-to-face conversation, the salesperson needs to determine if spending more time with a prospective client is worthwhile for both your business and for the prospect. This is when you have to ask a number of open-ended questions, encouraging clients to open up and tell you why they drove to your store in the first place. Questions such as:

- Who are you?
- Have you visited our store before?
- What is your project?
- What is your time frame?

- Do you have a designer?
- Do you have a builder?
- Have you been shopping other places?
- Where is the project?
- What is your budget?

Ask additional questions if you require more information to determine if it will be worth your time and prospects' time to continue. Proceed to Step 4 only if you believe doing so will be beneficial to both of you.

Step 4. Presenting products and services. This is when you start selling yourself, your company, and your products—and in that order. Each of these has a "value- added" component—that are valuable to prospects. These things include your being a CKD/CBD or CMKBD or your years of experience, length of time the company has been in business, and if the company offers one-stop shopping (i.e., all the products and services required to do a turnkey job), and others. This is where you also demonstrate products, talk features and benefits, and sell "value" over "price." When you add value, price becomes less important.

Step 5. Meeting objections and concerns. Every client will have some concerns, even objections. Your job is to determine what they are, to answer them, and to make them go away. Do this by asking the right questions and being a great listener. You should be listening at least two-thirds of the time during the selling process. If you aren't able to make the objections and concerns go away, your chances of being successful are very limited.

Step 6. Closing the sale. This step is why you spend all that money to drive clients into your dealership and why you go through steps 1 through 5. Writing the order/ closing the sale is what it is all about. If you do a good job in Steps 1 through 5, closing the sale should be almost a given. But do not forget that you have to ask for the order. There are a number of ways to do this, and with experience, you will know when the time is right.

Step 7. After-sale follow-through. Many businesses ignore and don't take advantage of this step. The little things like a handwritten thank-you note, a small thank-you gift, doing a customer satisfaction survey (see Tables 10.8 and 10.9 for sample survey forms), asking for referrals and rewarding those who give them to you, getting testimonials (and using them in your Web site or marketing materials and finally using that all-important past customer database to keep your name in front of them to try to promote additional business and referrals.

There is more to it, but learning sales skills is easier and quicker than earning a CKD certification. Make this an important part of your overall marketing plan.

Two important parts of selling skills are learning how to sell *value*: company value, product value, vendor value, and individual staff person value. The second part is learning how to sell *features and benefits*.

With the Internet becoming such an important part of the consumer's buying habits, it's more important than ever before to understand why selling value is important. When you add value to your selling proposition, you make price less important. So many K&B professionals allow price to be the most important piece of the selling effort that they forget to sell the many value features of your business.

We would encourage you to identify the five most important *value* features of your business: things that make you different, better, and unique in comparison to others in your marketplace. Here are a few examples:

- Number of years in business (if five or more)
- Family owned
- Offer turnkey projects including installation

TABLE 10.8 Showroom Customer Service Satisfaction Survey

Customer Name:
Address:
Phone:

We have recently completed a design project with you. We appreciate your business and thank you for the opportunity to serve you.

In order to help us do a better job in our showroom operation, we are asking our clients to complete this Customer Service Satisfaction survey. We have enclosed a self-addressed stamped envelope for your convenience.

Fill in the blank or rate each item 1 (low) to 5 (high):

My overall impression of your showroom	1	2	3	4	5
The selection of products on display	1	2	3	4	5
Being waited on in a timely manner	1	2	3	4	5
My salesperson was friendly and accommodating	1	2	3	4	5
My salesperson was knowledgeable and helpful	1	2	3	4	5
My quote was completed in a timely manner	1	2	3	4	5
My quote was complete and accurate	1	2	3	4	5
Your prices were competitive	1	2	3	4	5
My products were delivered on time	1	2	3	4	5
The delivery process was easy	1	2	3	4	5
Your invoicing was timely and accurate	1	2	3	4	5
My overall evaluation of my salesperson	1	2	3	4	5
My overall evaluation of your showroom	1	2	3	4	5
If you used our Web site, how would you rate it?	1	2	3	4	5

General Comments:

TABLE 10.9 Design Project Client Survey

1. What would you consider to be our greatest asset?

   Design ❏   Service ❏   Installation ❏   Product ❏   Other _____

   Comments: _____
   _____

2. What would you consider to be our greatest weakness? _____
   _____

3. Were your communications with us handled satisfactorily?   Yes ❏   No ❏

   Comments: _____
   _____

4. Do you feel the design service retainer was a benefit for you?   Yes ❏   No ❏

   Comments: _____
   _____

5. Was the designer available when needed?   Yes ❏   No ❏

   Comments: _____
   _____

6. Was your kitchen or bath ordered, delivered, and completed in a timely and satisfactory manner?
   Yes ❏   No ❏

   Comments: _____
   _____

7. What could we have done to make your project better? _____
   _____

8. Do you have any suggestions regarding the design process that could help us serve our clients better?
   Yes ❏   No ❏

   Comments: _____
   _____
   _____

(continued)

TABLE 10.9 *(Continued)*

9. Do you have any suggestions for our installers that could help serve our clients better?

   Comments: _____

   _____

10. Do you feel our service/warranty work is:

    Below Average ❏   Average ❏   Above Average ❏   Not Required ❏

11. Would you do business with us again?   Yes ❏   No ❏

    Why? _____

    _____

12. Is there anything you would recommend to others who are considering a project like yours?

    _____

    _____

13. How did you find [Firm's Name]?

    Advertising ❏   Yellow Pages ❏   Building Sign ❏   Other _____

    Referral—Name: _____

14. What was the deciding factor for you in selecting [Firm's Name]? _____

    _____

15. If you were the owner of [Firm's Name], what would you do to make us a better company?

    _____

    _____

16. May we place your name on our customer referral list?   Yes ❏   No ❏

17. Any other comments? _____

    _____

    _____

We certainly appreciate you taking time in helping us with this survey, so we may give the very best service.

Name (Optional): _____

Address: _____

Phone: _____

- Award winning (include what they are)
- Best-trained and educated staff
- Lifetime warranty on projects

Once you've identified your main value points, start including them in every area of marketing communications (Web site, brochures, ads, and social media).

Then meet with each member of your sales team and help them identify their very own individual value points. Here are a few examples:

- Interior design education/experience
- CKD, CBD, ASID certification
- Number of years of experience
- Awards and recognition received
- Schools and seminars attended
- Professional trade affiliations

Now that you've identified these important value points, you must learn to articulate them to your clients. It must be done in an effective way. Here's a great book that your team should read on this important subject: *Brag!: the Art of Tooting Your Own Horn Without Blowing It*" by Peggy Klaus (New York: Warner Books, 2004)

Another piece of the selling puzzle is learning to sell both the *features* and the *benefits* of your company, your services, your products, and your vendors. The most important part of this selling skill is understanding that f*eatures tell* and *benefits sell*. This means that features are something special, unique, and different about an item; benefits are what make the features important to the customer. Here are some examples of features and benefits:

Features	Benefits to customer
In business 25 years	Will be here for the long haul
Family-owned business	More personal than a large corporation
Installation of products sold	Continuity of project
CKD certification	Years of education and experience
PVD finish on faucets	Lifetime warranty
Kitchen cabinet door spice kit	Spices are easily accessible
Four-bin recycle center in cabinets	Convenient recycling of waste

As soon as you meet new prospects and learn about them and their project, you must start adding the value points to your conversation. When you move on to talking about your fine products and services, you have to articulate not only their features but you must explain to what the benefits of that feature means to prospects. Every time you highlight a value point and emphasize a benefit, you make price less of a concern for the prospect.

After the Sale Follow-Through

If you have done an excellent job with the completed project and you have happy clients, you can do several things to make them clients for life and utilize them for future client referrals. You should work as hard with your past clients as you do looking for new clients. Word of mouth can be your best (or worst) form of advertising and public relations.

Here are several suggestions for follow up after the project is completed.

- Call the client. Ask: "Did the project turn out as well as you had hoped?" "Are you completely happy with the end results?" "Is there anything else we can do?" "Thank you, again, for the opportunity of working with you."
- Send a thank-you note, personalized and handwritten.
- Make a personal visit to the job after clients have settled in.

- Take pictures of your special projects and get testimonial letters. Use these in a scrapbook, on your Web page, on a CD, and on your social networks.
- Ask clients if they would distribute referral cards to friends, family, and neighbors. Reward them with a small gift, such as a gift card for coffee, for each referral card brought to the showroom. Give clients a larger reward if the new prospect buys from you, perhaps dinner for two at a local restaurant.
- Make a follow-up telephone call three months, six months, and one year after the job has been completed. Ask: "Is there anything we can do?" (touch-up, adjust a hinge, straighten a door, etc.).
- Make clients feel like they received a warranty for life.
- Build a past client database and continue to communicate with them on a regular basis using e-newsletters, emails, special announcements, and the like. They bought a kitchen this year; maybe they will buy a bathroom or entertainment center from you next year.
- Ask clients if you can host an in-home party for their friends and neighbors to show off their beautiful new dream kitchen.

Keep those happy clients working for you.

YOUR SALES TEAM NEEDS A STRONG LEADER

It's often been said that "to be a great leader of salespeople, make them follow you, not the rules." We know that the majority of K&B dealers in the United States and Canada fall into the small business category (50 or fewer employees). We also know that in most of these businesses the number one salesperson is the owner. As the business grows and new salespeople are added to the company, it's important that they have a strong leader. We've already discussed the importance of developing a formal, written sales training program. In order to maximize the benefits of this program, someone must be in charge of it often this will be the owner of the business. We also know that "selling" may not be a favorite of that owner's daily activities. Most kitchen and bath designers would much prefer to design and not have to sell, but unless yours is a design-only business, every designer must learn to also be a great salesperson. Remember, nothing happens until the sale is made. No sales . . . no business . . . no employment!

A list of sales leadership traits follows. If you are the head of sales at your business, how many of these traits do you have?

- **Lead (manage) by example.** Don't preach things that you don't do yourself. Lead by doing, not telling.
- **Develop and maintain a positive attitude.** This is one of the biggest steps you can take toward your success and the success of your people.
- **Set and achieve goals together.** Don't set quotas, set goals. Review progress at least monthly.
- **Take sales inquiry calls.** Stay on top by knowing what customers want and sharpening your selling ability.
- **Make cold calls with your staff.** Accompany them on a regular basis.
- **Make follow-up phone calls.** Keep in touch with prospects to find out what it will take to turn them into customers.
- **Take some customer complaint calls.** Make calls to dissatisfied customers to learn what you need to do differently. **Make calls on lost sales.** Determine why you lost the sale.
- **Make customer thank-you calls after the sale.** A personal call from the boss or owner can be a great beginning to a relationship.
- **Visit job sites with your salespeople.** Ensure that all work is being done to your high standards.
- **Call satisfied customers.** Learn what they liked (and didn't like) about working with your company.
- **Ask for feedback:** from your sales team, vendor reps, and customers.
- **Back your sales team.** When a customer has a problem, defend the capability of your people and tell them you will respond to their complaint only after you've heard both sides.

- **Say positive things to your staff on a regular basis.** Encourage success with support.
- **Encourage, don't reprimand. Everyone makes mistakes, even you.** Encouragement and positive reinforcement will help prevent future mistakes. Be a coach, and offer support.
- **Don't play favorites.** This will damage team morale.
- **Be inspirational.** Send messages that will inspire your team.
- **Offer rewards and give awards for exceptional work.** Incentives work. Offer incentives that anyone can achieve.
- **Make your business a pleasant place.** Clients should enjoy visiting and staff should enjoy working for you.
- **Be known as someone who follows through and gets the job done.** This is important for both your staff and your clients . . . or else you will die on the job.
- **Keep your eyes open for opportunities to improve or sell more.** When you take advantage of opportunities and get results, it will inspire your whole team.
- **Train, train, train!** Continue to pursue training for yourself and train your staff on an ongoing basis.
- **Manage others *and yourself*.** Be a leader.

Staying in Touch with Clients on a Regular Basis

There are many ways to keep you and your company on the mind of your clients and prospects. Here are some suggestions.

- Holiday cards are a common tool in the industry.

    The most popular time for sending out holiday cards is during December. But how many cards do you receive to celebrate St. Patrick's Day, Groundhog Day, St. Valentine's Day, or Halloween? Here are some ideas for customized cards you can create.
    - Halloween: "Remodeling your kitchen or bath is a tricky business, but working with you is a real treat."
    - St. Valentine's Day: "We love our customers! Thank you for helping make us such a success!"
    - St. Patrick's Day: "Happy St. Patrick's Day to all our friends. The luck of the Irish was upon us when you chose us as your designer. Thanks!"

    Birthday cards are another special way of recognizing your customers.
- Newsletters are an excellent tool for keeping in touch with your clients. Attractive, lively newsletters can communicate valuable information in an interesting, easy-to-read format. They position your company as an expert. Costs can vary, depending on whether you produce it yourself or have it professionally prepared. Newsletter may be in digital or print format with print being far more costly.

    To create a high-impact, user-friendly newsletter:
    1. Keep articles short and easy to read.
    2. Two sides of an 8.5 × 11" sheet are all you really need. Do not make the newsletter longer than four pages.
    3. Include articles about your company, such as awards received, certificates earned, new staff, special charity projects in which you're involved, and the like.
    4. Design the print newsletter to be a self-mailer.
    5. Use the newsletter to inform past and potential clients about promotions, sales, new products, and services.
- Call clients of completed projects occasionally to see how things are and if there is anything you can do. The perception will be that you really care. Take pictures of the finished projects for your scrapbook.
- Throw neighborhood parties at a client's home after the project is completed. Ask your clients if they know of any potential prospects that can be invited.
- Ask for referrals. Those who refer are very special supporters of your company. Let these clients know that you value their support.
- Develop a thank-you gift program to give clients at the end of the job. A gift lets customers know that you value the business that they have given to your company. The gift does not have to be large or expensive, but it needs to show sincere thanks.

When purchasing a gift, it is recommended that you buy something that will be around the house for a considerable time. Wine, cheese, candy, and flowers are not recommended, since these are consumable items.

Some examples of appropriate gifts:
- Nicely organized binder containing project information, such as warranties, paint color reference numbers, important telephone numbers, and before and after photos of the project.
- Attractively framed, professional photo of the finished project. Not only will clients appreciate this, but neighbors will see it when it is displayed.
- Magazine subscription that will keep coming as a reminder of your great service.
- Pen-and-ink sketch of the home, matted and framed.
- Something fitting with a client's hobby or personal interests.
- Coordinating silk or dried flower arrangement.
- Attractive brass or ceramic planter with a healthy houseplant.
- Fruit or ornamental tree for the yard.
- Cutting board with your company name on it.

Promotional Ideas

Here are more tips to boost your exposure to new clients.

- Present slide shows using a continuous loop in a showroom display of your work. Add music to make it more engaging.
- Offer cooking classes to demonstrate your products.
- Have a large photo album in your showroom with before and after photographs of your projects (8×10" photos make the greatest impact).
- Display magazines in your showroom with "Designed and Installed by . . ." tabs indicating your published projects.
- Create a binder with testimonial letters from past customers.
- Use your own personalized graph paper for layout and design.
- Provide new customers with a "remodeling survival kit," consisting of a picnic basket or cooler with microwavable entrees, gift certificates, and coupons for meals out.

SUMMARY OF HOW TO BUILD A MARKETING PLAN

- **State your business purpose.** Use one (to the point, clear, concise) sentence on the purpose of your plan.
- **Define your market situation.** Describe the changes, problems, and opportunities that you will face over the coming marketing plan for:
  - Your customers
  - Your competitors
  - Your products and services
  - The marketing environment
- **Set goals and objectives.** What do you want your marketing plan to achieve?
  - Grow sales
  - Sales the same but margin up
  - Fewer (or more) products/services
  - Larger, expanded target audience
- **Select a marketing strategy that appeals to targeted consumers.** Outline your tactics. Detail any strategy changes. If adding installation to your package, you will need to list all the things you will need to do to make this happen (both the internal and external issues).
- **Advance your position and brand strategy.**
  - Position. Your business niche—only your business can fill.
  - Brand. The characteristics and attributes of your business.
- **Establish your budget.** Do not use last year's budget.

- **Establish by total dollars to be spent.** Start with zero-based costs and build the budget, one step at a time.
- **Your action plan.** Describe in four columns the action, the budget for the action, the deadline, and the responsible party for each step along the way.
- **Think long term.** Begin looking ahead. Make a list of the market development opportunities you will research over the coming year for possible action in future marketing plan periods. Here are some examples:
  - New or expanded business locations to serve more customers
  - New geographic market areas outside your current market area
  - New customers, different from your current customer profile
  - New products or product packages that will inspire additional purchases
  - New customer service programs

New-Market Checklist

If you've started thinking about moving your location or opening an additional store, here are eight things that you should consider

1. Learn everything there is to know about the new market.
2. Calculate your investment in terms of equipment, personnel, training, and systems management.
3. Research the profit margins to make sure they're attractive enough to you.
4. Approach the new market as if you're starting a brand-new company. Develop a stand-alone business and marketing plan, and make sure your core business is healthy enough to support the start-up until it becomes profitable.
5. Perform some work as a test project before proceeding full speed.
6. To decrease your risk, consider hiring subcontractors before committing to employees.
7. Avoid putting your company's reputation at risk. Market the new entity separately until you're sure of its success.
8. Use your plan. Share it with others. Use it to help others (advertisement agency) help you. Use it to keep yourself on track as you manage your business to marketing success.

IN CLOSING . . .

To begin doing a better job of marketing yourself and your firm, you should, at a minimum:

- Develop a detailed, written marketing plan and budget.
- Stay in touch with your past customers for new business and new business leads.
- Develop your brand.
- Follow up on leads immediately before they grow stale.
- Use low- or no-cost awards to recognize sales improvement and high performance. Have your salespeople compare and swap effective selling techniques.
- Use public relations to maximum advantage. Target public activities that will be visible to your potential customers.
- Assess the competition; know your competitors' products, sales techniques, and current pricing.
- Seek and fully utilize co-op advertising dollars.

- Keep your advertising message simple, memorable, and reflective of your unique selling value. Build an advertising program with a consistent message—and stick to it.
- Profile your customers. Use advertising vehicles targeted to their income, lifestyle, and reading and listening habits.
- Analyze the most profitable product and service sales and concentrate sales and marketing efforts on those products and services.
- Develop a formal, written sales skills training program. Designate someone to be in charge of it, and implement it with your entire sales team.
- Make sure your company vehicles, showroom, and storefront are neat and clean and completely identify and positively advertise your firm.
- Respond to all callbacks promptly. Use them as a potential source of new business.

SUMMARY

Marketing is one of the three legs of your management stool. It requires planning, budgeting, and creativity. Developing a strong brand and image identity for your business is an important. By "mystery shopping" your competitors, you will learn about their strengths and weaknesses. Selling skills are a key component of business success. Changing times dictate that you have an outstanding website and that you should start utilizing social media in your marketing communications.

REVIEW QUESTIONS

1. Explain how to determine who your target customers will be and how to direct your message to them. (See under "Knowing Who Your Customers Are" pages 222–223)
2. Explain the benefits of charging a design fee or retainer. (See under "Hourly Design Fee, Flat Design Fee, and Retainer Fee" pages 212–213)
3. Explain why building a strong company brand and image is important to your overall marketing strategy. (See under "Establishing Your Brand" pages 235–236)
4. Explain why a great utilizing social media can help your overall marketing efforts. (See under "Social Media Marketing" pages 244–245)

Professional and Profitable Project Management

Although kitchen and bathroom installation projects vary in size and complexity, all professionals involved in the project must follow a methodical, sequenced procedure to ensure a profitable project and satisfied clients. This chapter covers the topic from the perspectives of the business owner/manager and designer of record. The text also details acceptable expectations for installers, designers, and customers to have about the management of an installation. Specific information about business models, pricing strategies, scheduling procedures, and acceptable minimum standards for ordering molding (sometimes spelled moulding) as well as installing cabinets are covered.

Learning Objective 1: List information to be gathered for the job site survey.

Learning Objective 2: Explain the purpose of developing and following a lead system.

Learning Objective 3: Describe the various tasks that take place once construction begins.

INTRODUCTION

The design specification responsibility and project management accountability are areas that most professionals in the kitchen and bath industry undertake regularly and feel quite competent in. However, these are the two areas where money is lost day in and day out.

Properly detailed plans and efficient project processing mean profits for the business, the satisfaction of a job well done, and clients who are happy with the results.

Successful project management is everyone's responsibility. The owner of the design firm, the designer of record, the warehouse team, the specified manufacturers, the installation crew/subcontractors—even the client—are all active participants in transforming a dream into reality.

PROJECT MANAGEMENT FUNDAMENTALS: FROM INFORMATION GATHERING TO VISITING THE FINISHED ROOM

Although installation accountability varies according to different business models, the process a project goes through from beginning to end is chartable. It is critical to understand all the steps so that you can lead a team or be a valuable member of one. Understanding how to organize this process will help to deliver a project on time, on budget, with profit, to happy clients.

The Planning and Estimating Process

Take Job site Survey

The design professional must understand the project and the job site survey. A survey collects information about site constraints, existing construction details, appliances, cabinets, fixtures, fittings, and product and style preferences. The survey may take place at the designer's desk as photographs and dimensions supplied by the consumer are reviewed, or it may take place via digital photographs and electronic communications when the designer is a distance from the project. More often, the designer visits the job site or studies the new construction plans with the owner, asking questions about the overall project. Gathering specific information about the proposed project is the foundation for:

- Identifying the client's needs and wants.
- Determining the type of a design retainer to be charged.
- Creating preliminary design solutions and making preliminary appliance recommendations or receiving and incorporating appliance specifications from the client or the client's agent (builder, architect, interior designer).

Create Budget Estimate

Proven, successful professionals talk about the budget early and often. In fact, many seasoned professionals present a ballpark estimate or price range to the consumer as early as the first meeting in the showroom or over the telephone. This approach to the business of design is of great value to the consumer because the budget determines or influences the scope of the undertaking.

Present the Conceptual Design

For some projects, giving the client one or more potential solutions to the space may be beneficial. Show the client a portfolio (paper or electronic) with photos of completed projects. At these meetings, allow clients to present their ideas for solutions. Encourage them to show pictures they may have gathered from books, magazines, or online sources.

Finalize Design Adjustments

Experienced designers understand the connection between the concept plans and the final selection of appliances, the cabinet wood species, finish, artistic enhancements, and decorative hardware. These designers know the importance of helping clients make decisions on the many seemingly small details early in the planning phase.

Often clients cannot understand why a designer specifies a dishwasher this early in the process or whether the choice between a pull and knob makes sense. Seasoned professionals know that these individual elements of a kitchen plan must be selected sooner rather than later to ensure that the project progresses smoothly and finishes on time and on budget. Similarly, in bath planning, the inclusion of a steam system in a shower is an important early decision because it adds the cost of a generator and impacts the size of a shower (which must now accommodate a bench or a seat).

Receive Firm Estimates

Once the design is detailed enough for the craftspeople to review, it's time to schedule and conduct an in-office review of plans or an actual job site visit. Then firm installation estimates and/or contracts for the installation portion of the project can be presented to the design firm, the builder, or directly to the client.

Make Material Selections, Identify Allowances

After the client approves the final plan, reviews contract documents, and selects cabinets and appliances, a second round of product selections takes place. The client selects the decorative materials for the kitchen or bath at this time, or the designer identifies allowances, which are listed in the contract. Sometimes the countertop surfaces are part of this second round.

Review Design with Installation Specialist

All projects that involve any construction typically will require a job site check and inspection by the installation specialist or the product manager for the design firm. This is particularly critical if the design firm retains contract installation specialists because then an installation contract separate from the material contract is presented to the client.

There can be no gray areas. Ballpark figures are not acceptable at this stage. Experienced craftspeople will not commit to an installation fee until they have seen the physical job site.

Confirm Estimates

Once all products have been selected and craftspeople's fees have been submitted, a review of the estimates is recommended to ensure pricing is accurate and complete.

Prepare Presentation and Working Drawings

After all materials are identified and/or allowances are settled on, and all appropriate craftspeople have reviewed the project, prepare the actual working drawings, contracts, color boards, and other presentation tools.

Finalize Additional Design Adjustments

Present the project documents to the client. Make final changes to the plan and/or contracts.

Sign Disclaimers

Clients may need to sign a specification approval or disclaimer along with the contract. For example, if clients are ordering natural cherry cabinetry, they may sign a specification approval, acknowledging the inherent color range in natural cherry, which remains even after the finishing process.

Sign Contract

Review all documentation. At this stage the plans become final. The client signs the contract and pays a deposit.

Make Final Surfaces/Materials Selections

Once the cabinets are ordered, the client selects or verifies decorative materials, such as backsplash tile, light fixtures, and floor materials.

The Scheduling and Ordering Process

As soon as the client signs the contract, the scheduling and ordering process begins. It is important that the designer or the firm's representative stay in touch with the client between the contract signing and the actual start date.

Schedule the Installation

- Inspect the job site, if this was not done earlier.
- Write the cabinet order and transmit after careful comparison to the final job site dimension check, and the floor plan to the elevation.

- Schedule the trade contractors' work.
- Complete the permit process.
- Create the job site workbook.
- Conduct the pre-installation job site conference.

Order and Receive all Noncabinet Products

Many firms have an absolute rule that no project begins until the design firm receives all materials and they are ready to go to the job site. Sometimes designers have a hard time understanding this. Inexperienced designers may be unaware that, in bathroom remodeling, for example, the shower/tub fittings must be on the job site early because the rough-in valve is installed during the framing stage. This is far earlier than when the fittings are installed against the finished wall material.

Pre-installation Communication

- The client receives regular updates.
- Include any homeowners' association or other organizations that have control over the job site in the scheduling and ordering process.
- Notify neighbors or other individuals affected by the work that the project will begin soon.

The Installation Process

Construction Begins

Once construction begins, it is important to carefully manage the job site to ensure that the following steps are done properly.

- The person responsible for managing the project inspects the site.
- Material is delivered.
- Complete demolition (or deconstruction if existing materials will be salvaged for reuse) is completed.
- Trash is removed. This should be done throughout the duration of the job.
- Rough construction and mechanical work:
  1. Footings and foundations
  2. Framing, walls, and roof
  3. Heating, ventilation, and air-conditioning (HVAC)
  4. Plumbing/Electrical
  5. Finished wall surfaces/preparation

Inspections

Building department inspections take place at this stage.

Prepare Room Surfaces

At this stage the walls are closed in and any second inspections required take place. Wall surfaces are sealed and primed.

Install Floor

There are two options at this stage:

- Option 1: In some projects, the finished floor material is installed at this point because it extends throughout the space. When the floor is installed at this stage, it should be covered with heavy-duty protective materials.
- Option 2: In other installations, flooring is installed after all other products.

Deliver Cabinets

Typically, the cabinets are delivered to the job site either boxed or blanket wrapped. The project manager plans for the job site access required by a large delivery truck. How will the cabinetry be removed from the truck tailgate (and by whom)? What path from the truck tailgate to the storage area or work zone will be followed (particularly important in inclement weather)? These are all important things to consider at the delivery phase.

At this stage, the second major payment is usually due.

Tips from the Masters

Seasoned professionals suggest these tips:

- **Set an appointment with the client**, preferably when daylight illuminates the room and after artificial lighting is installed so that the light levels that will be in place when the room is finished can be simulated for the inspection. Sometimes a client will use a construction light to carefully inspect every square inch of the cabinet surface. Other clients review each cabinet as it comes off the truck. Neither of these inspection techniques is proper. Materials should be inspected under the same light levels expected within the space and at a standing distance of 36″.

- **If payment is due at this time, the designer should alert the client that an invoice will be presented.** This is a good time to review change orders and to take care of other paperwork. Structure the appointment by suggesting that you first review the project, then go to another part of the dwelling or outside (it might be inside a warm car) to review the documents. A temporary job site office is an excellent meeting area.

- **Begin the punch list process.** (A punch list is a task or "to do" list.) Start developing the list in one corner of the room and methodically review the entire project with the client to identify items that may be of concern. Review those items one by one and specify whether they are:
  1. Acceptable according to industry standards. Be prepared to provide documentation.
  2. Repair, replacement, rework to accomplish before presenting the final invoice.
  3. Warranty work not affecting the final payment.
  4. An expectation issue to resolve later with the client.

- **Clients' unrealistic expectations during the punch list process can be a sensitive subject.** If the client expects something that is not possible to deliver, the designer must determine what is causing the unrealistic expectation. Was the client "oversold"? Or is the stress and frustration of a new construction or remodeling project getting the best of the client? Seasoned professionals suggest preparing the entire punch list first so that you can determine the percentage of realistic issues versus nonrealistic issues. Do not attempt to settle each item as you work around the room. Rather, complete the list and then review the items, one by one. Frequently, the unrealistic expectations can then be isolated and dealt with separately.

Install Cabinets/Decorative Hardware

Cabinets and moldings are installed at this stage. This is an important time for the designer to meet with the client and review the project. It is important for everyone to realize that the building business and the renovation industry is not an exact science. Reassure clients that you have their best interests at heart. Carefully detail any work to be replaced, reworked, and/or redesigned early so that these changes can be designed, engineered, priced, ordered, and received in tandem with the continuing work at the job site.

- Template countertops
  - For some design firms, the countertop order is placed along with the cabinets, and the countertop may already be onsite. More typically, the countertops are templated (measured) after the cabinets are installed.

- Finish decorative surfaces
  - Because there is down time between the countertop templating and its fabrication and installation, this is usually the ideal time to finish all trim work and decorative surface finishing.
- Install countertops
  - Clients can begin to see what their new space looks like.
- Install backsplash
- Install floor
  - Option 2: If flooring was not previously installed as described in Option 1, the floor is finished now.
- Prepare punch list—Draft 2
- Install appliances, fixtures, and fittings
- Prepare punch list—Final
  - Create the final punch list with the owner and the owner's agent.
- Complete decorative surface finishing
  - Install final decorative surfaces. Touch up those materials finished earlier, as needed.
- Install lighting fixtures
- Complete inspection process
- Complete the final certificate of occupancy.

At this point, the room probably can be inhabited. This is the normal definition of "substantial completion." Many contracts are written so that the final payment is due at "substantial completion," allowing the design firm to collect the final payment from the client with the understanding, by both parties, that there may be outstanding punch list items that need to be completed, as well as some warranty work that may be unfinished.

Postinstallation Review

- Say "thank you" to all involved.
  - Send a post installation communication to the client. Present clients with their warranty and perhaps a gift. Thank neighbors for putting up with the trucks, trades people, and the disruptions of a construction site.
- Review project/present final invoice
  - If not accomplished earlier, hold a final review of the project and present the final invoice to the client or the client's agent.
- Complete punch list/warranty work.

Prepare and Review Project Cost Accounting

This can be the most important phase of the project to protect future profits. Regardless of how well or how poorly a project goes, everyone's focus must be on getting the work done, fixing mistakes, keeping the client happy (to protect your referral), and collecting the last payment.

By consistently conducting post installation reviews, the management team will be able to identify areas of weaknesses and strengths within the organization and project management process. A process improvement plan can then be put in place for members of the organization as well as for subcontractors or contract installers.

Creating a Lead System

In order to continuously generate new business and new projects, the individual designer or the design firm keeps track of leads. Individual designers follow up on these leads.

The lead system is the basis for evaluating marketing and sales information and determining the number of leads generated by marketing activities in order to determine marketing cost per lead and by source. It is used to determine the quality of a lead by comparing source/average sales or source/percentage of closes. The system also provides a management tool for the sales manager and a cash flow indicator for the business manager.

Lead system forms provide:

- A record of prospective clients' contact and project information.
- Information for the sales consultant.
- Information about the lead source.
- A record of project sales activity.
- Statistical information for salesperson performance review.

A client registration card is used at home shows, traveling displays, group consumer meetings, or in any other situation where adequate time cannot be spent with a prospect. This record can be used to set up appointments for a showroom visit.

A prospective client record is filled out by the individual conducting the showroom visit with the prospect. Upon completion of the showroom visit, the prospective client record is processed and assigned to a sales consultant.

A company lead register assigns each lead a number that is logged on the company lead register from the prospective client record. The company lead register is reviewed weekly by you or your sales manager to oversee the sales process. As stages of the sale are completed by the sales consultant assigned the lead, the progress is noted under the appropriate column.

A sales consultant lead analysis is completed and maintained by the designer or the sales manager. Review companywide performance with the entire sales team. The specific information provided by the lead analysis can be used to identify areas requiring sales training for team members.

SUMMARY

This chapter explains how multifaceted successful project management is. The business owner must organize his/her team, defining everyone's jobs. All involved in the process must carefully manage clients' expectations, protect their comfort level, and honor their privacy while managing a job site under construction. To be successful, a systematic, organized approach to scheduling the work and protecting products on and off the job site is a critical responsibility of the project manager and/or installation team leader. This is of paramount importance in remodeling and important in new construction as well.

REVIEW QUESTIONS

1. What are important tasks that take place pre-construction? (See "The Scheduling and Ordering Process" pages 261–262)

2. List five installation projects that commonly take place during construction. (See "The Installation Process: Construction Begins" page 262)

3. What actions are recommended after construction is completed? (See "Post Installation Review" page 264)

Responsibilities of the Business Owner/ Manager

Owners/managers must lead an organization that follows a well-thought-out project management system. Such a systematic approach will result in better projects. Not bigger, fancier, or more elaborate projects, but projects that are better because they are backed by detail. These details include drawings, careful job site dimensions, accurate estimating, a proactive customer management program, an organized method of communication on the job site, and a well-structured cost accounting system. The value to the business is a bottom-line benefit of minimized profit erosion.

Learning Objective 1: Define the installation delivery system.

Learning Objective 2: Describe how to estimate projects and develop specifications.

Learning Objective 3: Explain warranties and the role of the cabinet company field representative.

THE INSTALLATION DELIVERY SYSTEM

The first step in successfully managing kitchen and bathroom projects is organizing the company's installation delivery system.

Historically, the kitchen and bathroom industry consists of four segments:

1. Manufacturers
2. Product representatives and distributors
3. Retailers, dealers, and designers
4. Contractors, installation specialists, and specific tradespeople

Their interaction and respective functions constitute the delivery system that provides kitchen and bathroom products and services. The success or failure of a project depends on how closely the various segments work together. A well-organized installation delivery system facilitates a successful working relationship.

If your installation department is unstructured or poorly trained, this can be the weakest link in your delivery system and negatively impact your success in this industry. If the installation process is unnecessarily long, the workmanship poor, or the job site messy, the client will not be happy with any part of the project. When clients are unhappy with the condition of the job site or quality of the work, they often blame the products and/or the kitchen designer and the firm that sold them the products rather than realizing that their disappointment is related to the installation under way.

Types of Installations

There are four major types of projects in the kitchen and bath industry:

1. Replacement
2. Remodeling
3. Room addition/teardown/build-around
4. New construction

A kitchen or bath *replacement* usually involves minimal changes in an existing design. An existing layout remains intact, and new products are installed. A replacement might include refacing existing cabinets and installing new appliances, countertops, and decorative surfaces. Or it might include upgrades in the cabinet quality, layout, or quantity, with all mechanical elements remaining in existing locations.

For a bathroom redo, a replacement project might include new vanity cabinetry and all-new fixtures, faucets, and surfacing. The new materials merely replace the old ones in their existing locations.

A *remodeling project* usually includes a new design for the space. A remodel generally requires new plumbing, electrical, and mechanical systems. It may include structural changes, such as wall removal, additions, or the installation of new doors and windows. This type of project usually requires building permits. A remodeling project requires the greatest amount of design and technical skills, management knowledge, and communication expertise on the part of the designer and project management team.

In a *room addition/teardown/build-around project*, a design/build firm combines remodeling work with new construction in the form of a major structural addition to an existing house or the partial/complete teardown of an existing structure that results in a new home. This type of project is very different from new construction because it involves working in an established neighborhood, not in a new subdivision or open land being converted to a residential community.

There are three key criteria for such a project: (1) the ability to join the new structure to the existing structure, (2) knowledge of building codes and (3) the skill to work within mechanical constraints when adding new construction to an existing home.

Typically, *new construction* is led by the builder if the home is built on speculation, meaning there is no owner at the time of groundbreaking. In the case of a new custom home, the owner and/or the agent (architect, build/design professional, interior designer) control the specification process.

JOB SITE DYNAMICS: NEW HOUSE VERSUS OLD HOUSE

The job site dynamics for a new home under construction versus an existing project being renovated are very different. Following are some of the key things that differentiate these two sites:

New Construction	Remodeling
Sometimes working with a homeowner	Always working with a homeowner
New materials and site	Working with existing conditions
Dirt and dust don't matter	Cleanliness matters
Client does not yet have emotional attachment to the home	Client is emotionally attached to the home
May not be neighbors to be concerned about	Neighbors to be concerned about
No details to match	Many details to match
Predictable schedule	Unpredictable schedule
No pets or children living onsite	Pets and children onsite
May be many homes under contract in one location	Usually project locations miles apart

JOB SITE DYNAMICS: SINGLE-FAMILY DWELLING VERSUS MULTIFAMILY

The type of dwelling significantly impacts the cost of installing projects, the project scheduling and site accessibility.

Detached Single-Family Dwelling	Multifamily High-Rise Dwelling
Designer works directly with homeowner and contractor	Designer works with commercial contractors, building superintendents, or other's agent rather than directly with owner
Scheduling determined between owner/owner's agent and kitchen designer	Restricted schedule for access for the apartment/condo; noise is a big issue
No elevators/delivery issues	Elevator size, availability, and protection requirements are extensive
No parking restrictions; reasonable distance from the workers' truck/delivery truck location and the site.	Parking restrictions exist; debris collection areas may be nonexistent or very limited
Working hours at discretion of designer and client, with normal courtesies extended to neighbors regarding early or late hours or weekends	Working hours may be limited
Protection needed inside the home only; no common areas involved	Protection of common areas required; before beginning work, take digital images of the public area leading to the work area, paying close attention to existing damage to door casings, floors, walls, and stairwells to eliminate uncertainty about damage at job completion

INSTALLATION SERVICE BUSINESS MODELS

There are many successful business models that could be applied to the installation portion of the project. Each of these models affect job site responsibilities as well as acceptable methods of communication with field personnel and accountability for errors or omissions discovered at the job site once the installation process begins. Each is distinguished by who manages the job.

Model 1: Design Firm with a Project Manager

In this model, a project manager acts as liaison between the designer and the company-employed field personnel. The project manager frees up the designer's time to focus on new sales. This business model can also let each individual focus on what they do best—design or organization. On the negative side, adding a project manager to the staff increases the firm's overhead. It also adds one more layer of communication to the job, and inevitably, for every additional person involved with the job, the likelihood of communication breakdowns increases. The biggest omission often involves details about the project that the designer is aware of (because of the many conversations with the client) that are not relayed to the project manager. It is also possible that the clients may "disconnect" as they learn that they are no longer dealing with "their" designer.

Model 2: Design Firm without a Project Manager

In this business model, it is the designer who manages the installation and directs all of the company-employed field personnel. A designer who shepherds the project from concept to completion serves the client well because small details resulting from conversation will not be lost. The client also benefits from working with the designer on an ongoing basis because job site trauma can be avoided. However, this type of arrangement puts the responsibility for detail-oriented project management squarely on the designer's shoulders. Eliminating the added overhead of a project manager might save money, but this can be determined only when the firm carefully evaluates the actual percentage of profit generated at the conclusion of the installation compared to the estimated profit margin. In the long run, the firm may earn more money if a skilled project manager runs the job, relieving the designer of this time-consuming responsibility.

The Company-employed Installer

Both models may include a company-employed installer or installers. There are pros and cons to working with a company-employed installer:

- Pros
  - The firm has more control over the quality of work on the job.
  - The firm has total control over scheduling.
- Cons
  - There is higher overhead for the design firm, this expense remains even when no work is being done by the installation employees.
  - The project can get sloppy without proper oversight.

With either model, the designer or project manager's responsibilities vary based on the installer's job description. Two systems are typical in North America, the *lead installer system*, and the *single* or *team installer* system.

With a lead installer system, a lead installer is responsible for overseeing the installation from start to finish. He or she will:

- Coordinate all subcontractors.
- Order materials when there are shortages.
- Perform the quality control pre-completion punch list.
- Write change orders.
- Collect payments.
- Serve as a liaison between the owner/owner's agent and designer. The focus here is on discussions around the progress of the project. All design questions or concerns are relayed to the designer without comment by the installation team.

Often a client will enjoy a well-managed project that moves along at a reasonable pace because of the lead installer's oversight of the project. The lead installer must be an excellent communicator between the client and the designer should a problem arise. The individual selected must be a good craftsperson as well as a good manager.

With a single installer or team installer system, a single installer or a team of installers has limited decision-making accountability. All communication goes through the designer/project manager. The installation team is responsible for accurately following the plans and specifications as they relate to the cabinet installation part of the project.

An installation team that reports directly to the designer may require an extensive amount of the designer's time, thereby preventing the designer from moving on to the next sale. The profit potential of a well-managed job needs to be carefully balanced by the volume sales that may be lost while the designer pays close attention to an ongoing project.

Model 3: Design Firm with Subcontractors

In this model, the design firm subcontracts the installation portion of the project to contract installers. Contract installers may report to a project manager or to the designer so the advantages or disadvantages are the same as they relate to designer/project manager.

The dynamics of working with an independent contractor retained to provide installation services are different from installers who are on the firm's payroll:

Pros:
- The independent contractor provides a fixed cost per job.
- The independent contractor is motivated to complete the project quickly.
- The design firm is not responsible for employee costs during lean times.

Cons
- The independent contractor may set aside only a limited time for pre-installation conferences.
- The design firm must work according to the contractor's schedule.
- The design firm has less control over the quality of the project.
- The design firm may not know the experience level of the independent contractor's team.
- The independent contractor may not have a high degree of loyalty to the design firm.

Model 4: Design Firm Provides Referrals Only

In this model, the design firm does not provide any installation services directly, but does provide a referral list of recommended installation specialists who report directly to the client and are retained under a separate contract with the client. The designer remains accountable for the finished product and typically is expected to have an oversight responsibility.

This business model is typical on new construction projects, where the kitchen designer is simply one of many suppliers to the builder providing casework for specific rooms in the home. The builder's trim carpenters often are expected to install the cabinetry.

Model 5: Design Firm Offers neither Installation nor Referrals

In this model, the design firm's responsibility is completed with delivery of the components. It does not offer installation services and does not recommend installation specialists.

This business model works well for simpler projects and for firms serving a skilled do-it-yourself client base or a contractor who has a long history of working with the firm. This arrangement is not successful on complex projects or for firms whose plans and specifications are riddled with errors, omissions, or inaccuracies.

Tips from the Masters

Regardless of the designer's responsibility during installation, experts suggest that making sure the job site construction, HVAC, and mechanicals are "as per plan" is time well spent before the cabinet installation begins.

Today's technology, extending channels of communication via digital photographs, video conferencing between the job site and the design firm's office, or mobile communication devices can increase the potential for success.

KEY COMPETENCIES OF INSTALLATION SPECIALISTS

For all of the business models outlined, experienced professionals recommend finding an installer who possesses:

- **A complete understanding of the local municipality permitting process and building codes.** The installation specialist must be able to communicate with inspectors onsite, understand permit posting requirements, and be knowledgeable about construction building codes.

- **A basic knowledge of kitchen and bathroom design.** Although not actually required to do the complete design, installers need to master the principles of design in order to make decisions in the field and communicate effectively with the designer.
- **A thorough understanding of carpentry skills.** Installers need a base of knowledge and experience in carpentry covering everything related to the construction of the shell, including constructing stud walls and other framing, installing doors and windows, the construction of the openings for doors and windows, blocking required for cabinet and fixture installation, and general finish trim requirements.
- **Specific and detailed knowledge of cabinet and countertop construction and installation.** These skills include everything from field measurement and survey work to actual layout and cabinet and equipment installation.
- **Familiarity with finish materials.** Installers work in tandem with other trades and need to understand the installation techniques for each of these materials and their impact on the cabinet and fixture installation.
- **A thorough understanding of all of the appliances and equipment items.** Installers must understand standard installation and mounting techniques as well as electrical, plumbing, and ventilation requirements.
- **Techniques for ceiling construction.** Installers must understand ceiling framing systems and know how to install ceiling joists and how to frame soffits in preparation for drywall, plaster, or other finishes.
- **A basic knowledge of mechanical systems.** Installers must be familiar with these mechanical systems: electrical, plumbing, gas, HVAC, and cooking equipment ventilation.
- **Adherence to job site safety.** In order to protect both people and property, installers need a clear understanding of established safety rules and procedures.
- **Excellent people skills.** To deal effectively with clients, installers must be able to get along well with people. Establishing good relationships with clients and working well with those involved in the installation process will support effective job site communication.
- **An appreciation for the importance of pre-installation conferences.** A pre-installation conference helps everyone involved clearly understand the specifics of the job.
- **Practice good job site management.** An understanding of, and adherence to, effective staging and sequencing is extremely important to ensure that the job finishes in a timely and efficient manner.
- **A mechanical aptitude and an understanding of how to maintain tools and equipment.** Although a cabinet installer first, the installer should also have general mechanical ability. This includes a familiarity with all types of tools and equipment and keeping equipment in good working condition.
- **Familiarity with legal issues.** Installers must be aware of liabilities at the job site and have a clear understanding of responsibilities before the work begins.
- **An understanding of installation and construction terms.** The complex nature of this profession requires installers to be familiar with a wide array of terms used by installers and other related trades working on the job site.
- **The ability to read design plans.** The installer should be able to read, interpret, and follow design plans pertaining to each job site.

DEVELOPING SUCCESSFUL WORKING RELATIONSHIPS

Relationship with a Subcontractor/Trade Partner

The best working relationship between your firm and a trade partner relies on a business relationship trade agreement and an organized approach to estimating and completing each job. A firm estimate is provided at time of proposal preparation, and a job site inspection sheet is signed before a project is under way. The importance of respect cannot be overstated.

Successful kitchen and bath designers actively engage their trade contractors as business partners, with clear, regularly scheduled communication, shared educational opportunities, and an agreed-to set of performance guidelines and expectations.

To ensure that there are no surprises, an agreement between the firm and the trade partners addresses these areas:

- Licensing and insurance.
- Job safety and OSHA (Occupational Safety and Health Administration) requirements.
- Onsite attire. Suggested minimum standards are:
  - Professional carpenter pants or unripped jeans are acceptable, sweatpants are not.
  - Always wear a shirt. Sleeveless T-shirts or shirts with offensive phrases or logos are not allowed. It is highly recommended the design firm encourage some type of uniform for the installation team, whether it is a generic recommendation for types of shoes, pants, and shirts, or a uniform.
  - Footwear: Flat soles, as opposed to waffle-bottom or hiking shoes, are recommended to minimize tracking in dirt and mud. Different shoes for indoor and outdoor work are recommended. No sandals or beach shoes permitted.
- Job site behavior. Suggested minimum standards are:
  - No smoking anywhere on the job site!
  - No music playing without prior agreement with the client as to volume and music choice.
  - No profanity anywhere on the job site.
  - Snack/lunch breaks in agreed-on designated area only. During nice weather, seek permission from the client to sit outside.
  - No flirting—with anyone!
  - No non-work-related chatter.
  - No discussions about delicate topics: religion, politics, etc.
  - No extensive personal conversations or texting via PDA or mobile phone while on the job site.
  - No possession or use of illegal drugs or alcohol on the job site.
  - Only use the restroom assigned to the project.
  - Never place any tools and/or equipment on any finished surfaces.
  - Maintain a neat and clean job site at all times.
  - All vehicles will be clean and in good condition. Leaking motor oil or transmission fluid on the client's driveway is unacceptable.

The installer promises the business owner/manager:
- To carry the necessary liability insurance and follow proper tax laws as instructed by their accountants.
- To communicate effectively in the English language and to be able to review the contractual documents, plans and specifications, directions to the job site, and other notes relating to a job.
- To manage the upkeep of the job site workbook as instructed by the designer/project manager. To accept, inspect, and safely store any material delivered to the job site.
- To contact the designer/project manager immediately if any unexpected construction constraints are identified such as the client requesting additional work product oversights, mishaps, or other problems that will require reorder. Where appropriate, these items will be maintained in an agreed-to punch list format.
- To not perform any work requested by the client without a signed change order.
- To maintain a proper, professional appearance; respect the client's neighborhood, property, and home; refrain from loud talking, smoking, foul language, loud music, or any other activity that the client deems disruptive or unprofessional.
- To contact the designer/project manager away from the client to facilitate a private conversation when design modifications need to be discussed.
- To provide scheduling for job site inspections, pre-installation job site conferences, and completion of punch list items as per the design firm's agreement.
- To submit invoices to the design firm on a regular basis, listing all work performed.
- To provide warranty work on their portion of the project.
- To respect all other subcontractors and/or contract installers working on the job site.

- To lay out all work ahead of time and stock all required materials required on trucks or vehicles in order to minimize time-consuming trips to a supply house.
- To maintain a pleasant, professional attitude with the client, avoiding any comments on the design, quality of the project, and reputation of the firm/designer. To never answer questions posed by the owner or owner's agent regarding design details. To immediately refer the owner or owner's agent to the designer of record or to proactively arrange a meeting/phone call/internet meeting in order to facilitate dialog between the designer of record and the client.

The business owner/manager promises the installer:
- To maintain a clear accounts payable process and adhere to the agreed-on payment schedule.
- To provide prompt payment according to an agreed-on schedule.
- To establish a job site workbook format and to prepare the plans in a consistent way so that the installation team becomes accustomed to working with the same type of material.
- To share market strategies and the firm's business model and to make sure the individual is invited to see completed projects in order to instill a sense of confidence on the installer's part about the opportunity for a long-term working relationship with the firm.
- To provide clean, accurate plans, specifications, and details.
- To never schedule the installer's time without his/her prior agreement.
- To provide information about the client's personality before the installation specialists arrive at the job site.
- To maintain an established review process to evaluate mistakes when determining who is going to pay.

SYSTEMATIC APPROACH TO PROJECT MANAGEMENT

Time Management

The business owner/manager must be expert in time management. Many books have been written about how to manage time effectively. Experts agree that a system needs to be in place to guide all individuals involved in a new construction or renovation project from beginning to completion. A paper trail (hardcopy or electronic) must be in place to effectively manage projects from development through installation.

Such a system helps to organize the design, estimating, and project management process and helps to manage time much more efficiently by providing the forms, checklists, and other information needed to manage a project from contract to completion.

Communication Technology

Over the last several years, there have been dramatic changes in the way jobs are managed thanks to improvements in communication technology. Changes will continue to develop in mobile device technology, Internet video communication, and Internet-based project management tools.

Today, successful designers use technology to assist in managing the job site conditions, communicating with consumers, and managing installers. It makes good business sense to work with a technology specialist so that your business systems are continually upgraded. You must be aware of the latest business management tools.

A Business Management System

A business management system is based on a series of reports, forms, and checklists organized to track and report on the progress of the project under development, as well as to capture the project's financial results. Such a tracking system protects your profits and minimizes any slippage while the job is under way.

A Sample Business Management Forms System

Here is an example of a business management forms system created by the National Kitchen & Bath Association (NKBA).

1. Lead System
   Client Registration Card
   Prospective Client Record
   Company Lead Register
   Sales Consultant Lead Analysis
2. Pricing Tabulation Forms
   Price Quotation
   Price Quotation with Cost Column
   A Contract Installer Agreement
   Subcontractor Agreement
3. Survey Forms
   Kitchen Design Survey Form
   Bathroom Design Survey Form
4. Drawing Document
   Plan Title Block
5. Estimate Form
   Estimate Form for Kitchen Design & Installation
   Estimate Form for Bathroom Design & Installation
6. Specification Forms
   Standard Specifications for Kitchen Design & Installation
   Standard Specifications for Bathroom Design & Installation
7. Contracts
   Standard Form of Agreement for Design & Consultation Services
   Design Fee/Retainer Estimate Sheet
   Standard Form of Agreement for Design & Installation
8. Change Orders
   Change in Plans and Specifications
   Change in Plans and Specifications with Cost Column
9. Job Program Management Job Progress
   ChartTime Card
   On-site Project Communication Form
   Project Pre-installation Conference Detail List
   Project Production Start Checklist
   Pre-Close Punch List
   Final Inspection before Punch List with Client
10. Service Call System
    Pre-Completion Conference Detail List
    Customer Complaint Form
    Industry Feedback Response Form
11. Job Completion and Follow-up System
    Completion Report
    NKBA Limited Warranty
    NKBA Follow-up Letter
    NKBA Client Evaluation Form

Gathering Project Details

Interior designers, architects, and kitchen and bath designers all begin the planning process by learning about a client's wants and needs. Regardless of where the information is gathered, an organized data collection system saves a tremendous amount of time because it helps the designer avoid overdesigning or redesigning a project.

The design survey form provides:

- Design information relative to the personal needs and desires of the client.
- A complete listing of equipment and materials.
- Construction information regarding the physical restrictions of the project.
- Information to develop a budget for the project.
- Project contact information.

A special note for renovation projects: Information about site constraints, existing construction details, appliances to be reused, window and door dimensions as well as HVAC is critical when planning work in an existing structure.

Project Documents

Some successful kitchen and bath designers present the consumer with one or more concept drawings, accompanied by a budget analysis or budget range, before completing detailed plans. Other successful firms gather information from the client, establish a budget for the project, and immediately begin developing a full set of completed plans for presentation. Both systems work. But a system that includes a concept design presentation eliminates time-consuming drawing preparation and is advantageous if the designer is struggling to clearly understanding the client's initial requests.

Regardless of the system used, the plans need to clearly detail the solution for the client. For a detailed overview of a complete set of project documents, refer to the NKBA Professional Resource Library volume: *Kitchen & Bath Design Presentation*.

Estimating

The project estimating system provides the designer with an organized way to gather estimates.

The price quotation provides:

- A document to record individual price quotations and cost figures on projects, other than installed remodeling jobs.
- The client with a written price quotation and dated price protection.
- A system to prevent discrepancies between multiple quotations.

Installer/Subcontractor Agreement

The agreement forms provide an organized way to detail exactly which work the contractor/subcontractor will be completing at the job site, what the payment schedule will be, what documentation the firm has supplied to the contractor/subcontractor for the preparation of the estimate, and the general conditions established by the design business, which must be adhered to by contractors/subcontractors on the job site.

Material Selection and Specification

Design firms follow different business models for material selection. Some design firms offer a turnkey service, providing all components necessary to complete the project and charging fees to cover the time and expense of assisting consumers with all their selections. Other firms focus on cabinets, countertops, and appliances. Regardless of the type of business model, materials need to be selected or allowances provided.

List the exact equipment and materials for the project by manufacturer name, model number, or specific product description. Written specifications should acknowledge problems with matching old materials and new materials. Phrases such as "match as closely as possible within the installer's normal sources of supply" and "surfaces or materials to blend" are much better than simply saying "to match."

- Supply kitchen cabinetry, as per plans and elevations dated month/day/year (or some other agreed-upon system), with all specified finished ends, moldings, and decorative hardware.
- Cabinets to be XYZ brand, full overlay design with five-piece raised panel door style in cherry wood, stained Umbria Brown.
- Cabinet construction to be ¾" sides, tops, bottoms, and shelves; ½" back, 45-lb. commercially rated industrial board core with white melamine surfaces unless finished sides specified in cherry.
- All base and wall shelves to be similar material finished with 3 mm PVC edge tape on all four sides. All base and wall shelves to be adjustable on 5 mm faces.
- All hinging to be completely concealed, 120 degree opening, low profile six-way adjustable, demountable hinging.
- All drawers to be five-piece dovetail drawer boxes with under-mounted, full extension, self-closing drawer slides.
- Decorative hardware to be brushed nickel cup pull on drawers, and brushed nickel 1¼" pulls on all doors.

Performance

Outline the performance standards required for a particular operation or product. Specify exact fixtures and fittings. For example:

> Supply and install three-piece bathroom within 5" of main stack. Bath waste lines and water piping to meet existing codes, including necessary shutoff valves, cleanouts, and back vents.

Performance specifications are best suited for areas where there are codes to meet or where performance characteristics are clearly understood. In areas where performance characteristics are not specific, this type of specification leaves too much room for disagreement between client and installer.

Technical Specifications

Technical specifications should spell out each operation, detailing requirements for installation of the work:

> Build new interior partition to divide existing bathroom into two separate bathrooms. Supply top and bottom plates and studs 16" o.c., studs to be Douglas fir construction grade or equal. Install ½" drywall to manufacturer's specifications, tape all joints and spackle with two coats. Spackle all screw holes. Screws to be standard drywall screws. Install three-piece base, 1" × 4" #2 pine with ogee and oak shoe mold, shoe mold to be natural. Paint new wall with two coats of top quality paint, vinyl latex on new walls, semigloss on all wood trim.

Technical specifications should be used whenever possible and should include quantities dimensions and methods. Specifications for simple work need not be professionally drawn up in order to be sufficiently descriptive for communication between the installer and the client.

Contractual Agreements

Agreement for Design and Consultation Services

There are many ways kitchen and bath dealerships offer design services to clients. The design process for a kitchen or bath involves different sequential steps, which need to be factored into the design fee system employed by the firm. In some cases, different phases of the project are better planned with different fee structures. Therefore, the NKBA does not recommend a specific standard form of agreement for design and consultation services. However, the NKBA does offer a series of questions that the dealership answers to help to develop a personalized standard form of agreement for design and consultation services.

Agreement for Design and Installation and Change Order System

A legally binding agreement, or contract, that clearly defines the products, materials, and services that will be supplied by the kitchen specialist or the owner or owner's agent is a key step in the project documentation procedure. The contract typically has a provision covering how work will be handled if unknown job site construction issues arise.

Project information (without selling price information) from the contract is often included as part of the project documents used by tradespeople on the job site.

Change Order System

- Complete a change order whenever the client requests changes to the contract, specifications, and/or plans of the project.
- The changes should be explicit and priced in order to indicate any resulting credit or additional charges.
- All parties signing the original contract for the project are required to sign the change in plans and specifications form.

Estimating the Project and Developing the Specifications

In some businesses, the designer is responsible for gathering all costs and estimates from subcontractors' proposals, from countertop suppliers, and cabinet estimate costs and then applying the company's agreed to markup to the final contract documents. In other firms, a separate department prepares cost information and the contractual documents and the designer's responsibility is to present the proposal to the client and gain their acceptance.

It is critical that designers understand the basic elements of pricing. Here as a brief overview.

Standard markup: A standard markup is the multiplier amount (often expressed as a percentage) of the original cost you are adding to the cost to determine the sell price required to produce the gross profit your business is based on. For example, assume your desired markup is "Y":

Cost × Markup = Sell	$12,000 Cabinet order
Y = 0.0% $100 × 1.00 = $100	$12,000 × 1.00 = $12,000
Y = 33.0% $100 × 1.50 = $150	$12,000 × 1.50 = $18,000
Y = 37.5% $100 × 1.60 = $160	$12,000 × 1.60 = $19,200
Y = 39.0% $100 × 1.65 = $165	$12,000 × 1.65 = $19,800
Y = 42.0% $100 × 1.72 = $172	$12,000 × 1.72 = $20,640

Gross profit to price: You can determine what the sell price would be, given a particular profit, by using this formula:

$$\text{Cost of goods or services} \times 100 \text{ Selling Price} = 100\% - \text{Gross profit } \%$$

For instance, if a cabinet set costs $12,000 and your desired gross profit is 42%, you would calculate the selling price as follows:

Example 1: $12,000 Cabinets 42% Gross profit

$$\$12,000 \times 100 = \$1,200,000 = \$20,690$$

Selling price = 100 − 42 = 58

Example 2: $12,000 Cabinets 39% Gross profit

$$\$12,000 \times 100 = \$1,200,000 = \$19,672$$

Selling price = 100 − 39 = 61

Example 3: $12,000 Cabinets 36% Gross profit

$$\$12,000 \times 100 = \$1,200,000 = \$18,750$$

Selling price = 100 − 36 = 64

Example 4: $12,000 Cabinets 33% Gross profit

$$\$12,000 \times 100 = \$1,200,000 = \$17,910$$

$$\text{Selling price} = 100 - 33 = 67$$

Price to gross profit: If you are considering a particular price and want to know what the amount of your gross profit would be, you can figure that out too.

$$\text{Gross proft} = \frac{\text{Selling price cost}}{\text{Selling price}}$$

Using the cost and selling price from the previous examples, the gross profit would be calculated like this:

Example #1: $\$20,690 = \dfrac{\$12,000}{\$20,690} = 42\%$

Example #2: $\$19,672 = \dfrac{\$12,000}{\$19,672} = 39\%$

Example #3: $\$18,750 = \dfrac{\$12,000}{\$18,750} = 36\%$

Example #4: $\$17,910 = \dfrac{\$12,000}{\$17,910} = 33\%$

Tips from the Masters

Regardless of the firm's business model, the most important thing to understand is that it is not the designer's prerogative to change the firm's profit planning process.

Pricing Strategies and Methods

To help everyone involved in project management, a review of the fundamentals of pricing follows.

Three broad pricing strategies are used in the K&B industry:

1. **Lump-sum pricing.** The client is given one price for the project without listing items individually.

   Lump-sum pricing should be carefully detailed with all allowances noted so the clients know exactly what they are buying.

   Even when using a lump-sum contract, include a time-and-materials price to cover all unknown construction problems such as dry rot.

2. **Cost-plus pricing.** Each cost is identified and followed by an agreed-to markup factor. Normally, a not-to-exceed total is established.

   Cost-plus pricing is effective on jobs plagued with many change orders. Caution: The client may feel dissatisfied knowing the amount of the firm's markup.

   When using cost-plus pricing, add a contingency factor based on the historical performance of the estimator, salesperson, or company specialist. If an individual's past estimate numbers have not been accurate, adding a 2 percent to 5 percent slippage factor makes sense.

3. **Time and material pricing.** No final total cost is identified. Invoice the costs (plus an agreed-to markup factor) according to an agreed schedule.

4. Unit pricing. The unit price method, also known as the piece method, requires the company's management to assign a value to each installation operation or piece of material.

For example, each cabinet or foot of molding or miter cut carries a dollar point or value. A total is simple addition if a dollar value is used. Add points up and then multiply by an established value.

Unit pricing works well in the replacement market. It is harder to apply this method if there is a great deal of variation in cabinet configuration or architectural accoutrements and moldings used on the project.

5. Linear-foot pricing. Use the linear foot pricing method to quote a preliminary budget. Linear foot pricing is not as accurate as the other systems. Based on historical data, assign a linear foot price to base and wall cabinets with counters and/or tall cabinets.

6. Custom quotation method. Although it's the most time-consuming method, the custom quotation method (sometimes called "the stick method") is also the most accurate.

Use this pricing on a plan review or job site visit, a complete detailing of a material list, as well as a per-project labor estimate of the time required to complete the project. All costs for material, labor, permits, professional fees, cleanup and trash disposal are then added to identify a hard cost, and the profit margin is applied.

Most specialists in the industry agree that lump-sum pricing is the best way to build a profitable company with a satisfied client base. Use cost-plus pricing and time-and-materials pricing for projects where unknowns can lead to higher costs.

The Job Progress Management System

The job progress management forms provide:

- A review of the job and the status of each section
- An instrument for scheduling of the job as it progresses
- An outline of all information to review before installation begins
- An outline of all information and materials that the production department should receive before work on the project begins
- An organized way to communicate with individuals on the jobsite
- A systematic way to inspect the job site and specific check points to verify adherence to plan details and to gather information about corrective, add-on, or warranty work required to complete the project

The job progress chart is maintained by the expeditor or individual responsible for ordering labor, product, and/or material.

The onsite job communication form provides a simple way to manage written communications. Far better than notes written on the wall near the phone, or on sticky Post-it® notes left on a window, the form provides a clear format to direct a question or message to a colleague, the designer, another trade, or the client and provides for a written response.

The project pre-installation conference detail list is a useful management tool when the installation is the responsibility of the design firm.

The project production start checklist is used as a guide before the project starts. It is also useful if the designer transfers installation responsibility to someone else.

The pre-close-in punch list is a checklist that gives the lead installer, project manager, or designer responsible for the installation an opportunity to review the electrical, plumbing, HVAC, and framing work completed to date in preparation for a building department inspection. This review also allows the designer of record or their representative to check all mechanical, HVAC, and framing work completed to date compared to the project documents, ensuring that once equipment arrives and installation begins, all preparatory work will be properly positioned, complete, and to code.

The final inspection before punch list review with client is a check sheet that allows the lead installer, project manager, or designer responsible for project supervision to review the various equipment categories of the project, ensuring that the fit and finish of these materials are correct and ready to review with the owner and/or owner's agent. Such a checklist is an excellent way to make sure a project is closely reviewed by the responsible representatives of the design firm, with notations for corrective or replacement work made before the project is reviewed with the consumer.

Tips from the Masters

Your profits are protected when:

- You know your firm's estimating practices, and you make sure the entire organization follows them.
- You give special consideration to projects that are outside the firm's normal product offering or design expertise, are a distance away from the firm's marketing area, or involve a client who may be difficult to satisfy.
- You employ the concept of teamwork at critical points in the project.
- You make sure job site dimensions are double-checked, and you conduct a pre–job start conference.
- You produce complete and accurate product orders.
- You or your representative meet with the client on an ongoing basis.

Judgment Factors in Estimating: Special Conditions

It is clear that unit pricing has a number of advantages over other estimating methods. But even unit pricing cannot provide everything necessary to produce a complete and accurate estimate.

Many business owners/managers make sure unusual projects are reviewed by a member of the senior team. By analyzing the job for special conditions, features, requirements, company capabilities, and code requirements, better estimating of the real costs can occur.

Examine the job for any variations from the standard that could be covered by a unit-pricing system. Special access problems, such as unusual existing conditions, will greatly affect job costs and must be given special attention during the estimating process. An increase in time per craft or an increase in project markup factor should be considered.

In the kitchen and bath industry, some type of margin reduction will probably take place, particularly with full-service design/build undertakings on most projects. Given the reality that some margin loss is to be expected, this section focuses on the key elements of minimizing this erosion while doing the best job possible to manage the project, as well as job accounting.

Examples of Special Conditions
- **The project is far from your business location or is very complex.** For example, a large job that is located more than an hour from your showroom or place of business or involves a great deal of construction and low- to medium-price products that will require extensive job site assembly. Although mobile devices and video communication tools make it easier to supervise complex or far away projects, it is still a good business practice to increase the markup for such projects.
- **The site is hard to access.** For example, it is a bathroom on the third floor of a house with no windows large enough to accommodate materials. Extra costs will be incurred

to carry materials upstairs. If the stairway is narrow and standard 4 × 8″ sheets of drywall will not fit, there will be extra costs to cut the sheets and install a greater number of pieces. If the crew must maneuver a large whirlpool tub or shower unit up the stairway, it will require extra time, and that means extra costs. The company may need to repaint the stairwell at the end of the job to repair damage caused during the the job, which will add costs.

- **The installation is located in a house on a hill with no driveway to the house.** There will be an additional cost to transport materials up the hill.
- **Work inside a house will be done near areas with light-colored carpeting, antique furniture, and so on.** There will be an additional cost for the special care necessary to avoid soiling or damaging the valuable items.
- **Wall finishes require extensive repair or replacement work.** The cost of painting varies greatly, depending on the amount of preparation necessary. If many old coats must be scraped off, or if wallpaper must be removed from plaster walls (which may involve plasterwork), the cost will be much higher than for painting a clean, bare surface. The cost to comply with federal standards for managing lead paint removal must be estimated.
- **Job site access is limited or costly.** In some neighborhoods and in urban settings, parking is severely limited for trucks and other construction vehicles. When this problem is known to installers in advance, their estimate should reflect an extra cost for parking tickets, the cost of parking in a lot, and perhaps additional time to get to and from a job.
- **Restricted workdays.** If the workday is restricted by condo or co-op building regulations, you will have to extend the number of days projected for the project.
- **Animals or small children will be present during working hours.** There must be additional cost to compensate for their intrusions and for the additional care required.
- **Matching existing materials will be a challenge.** The necessary materials may not be readily available, and transportation costs may be high, or there may be special charges for things such as custom millwork.
- **The project is larger than the firm is accustomed to.** The possibility of being overwhelmed by a very large project is ever present in our profession. Experienced professionals counsel that you be prepared to handle "the big one."

Tips from the Masters

Sometimes a firm has an opportunity to work on a high-profile project. It may be for a famous client or a respected architect. These projects are usually much larger than your typical job and may include cabinetry for the entire house or an offer to work on a second residence at a distant location. Although these projects may be exciting and challenging from a design standpoint, they require special estimating and increased manpower to complete without jeopardizing the firm's overall profitability.

For these larger jobs, there will be more upfront design time, more collaboration with other professionals, and the need for additional subcontractors and supervisory people. You may be involved with more permits than you are accustomed to. The project may require a job site trailer and an on-site project manager. You may face longer lead times for specialty projects and longer and more costly cleanup. While working on the major, one-of-a-kind project, you may not have time to serve your other clients properly or work on new project presentations.

Estimating for Large Projects

Estimating Design Costs

Professionals advise caution when accepting such a special project or large commission. Integrating these projects into your normal workflow requires expert estimating.

Charging Design Fees

For unusually large projects, a three-tier design system, beginning with a fee to cover the conceptual plans, followed by a project documentation fee, and concluding with a selection service fee, is a good way to make sure you are properly compensated for this type of time-consuming project.

Estimating Labor and Materials

Experienced professionals accustomed to working on large, complex projects advise that money is often lost in labor miscalculations on such projects. Insist on firm proposals or estimates with specific times identified for project segments from subcontractors or best-guess estimates from your internal team.

Allow Enough Time to Manage These Projects

Large or complex projects require an extensive amount of attention by the designer of record. Job site visits, meetings with allied professionals, and the selection process might take up far more time than the professional normally sets aside for a simple kitchen or bath project. It is critical that the designer allow enough time for these extra responsibilities within the normal workday in order to service the owner and/or owner's agent without losing the needed momentum of new business.

Staging

Carefully plot the production or the project's staging, allowing you to work on the large project in tandem with (rather than in place of) your current installations under way, without limiting your ability to continue prospecting for new clients.

Know Who Is on the Design Team

It is critical to know the entire group of professionals who will be working on a large project and exactly what your responsibilities are within that team. Business managers also stress the importance of maintaining control over your portion of the project. Sometimes an influential client may intimidate a designer, or a well-known design professional may push the kitchen specialist into a product specification or design detail that does not reflect good planning. Both of these situations can lead to profit slippage.

Charge Enough

Some designers think a larger job can carry a smaller margin. Just the opposite is true. A large, time-consuming project that does not generate the company's projected profit margin possible from a series of smaller projects should be avoided. Savvy, skilled designers urge you to charge *more*—not less—for these large projects.

Measurement Standards

Determining material quantity needs and measuring standards used in the estimating process are described next.

- **Round all figures up to the nearest even number.** Most building materials are bought in 2″ dimensions, so the materials will be the same for a 14″ wide kitchen addition as for a 13″ 6″ addition, and there will be little or no difference in the labor.
- **Round up material quantities to the nearest even number.** Do this not only because of 2″ dimension increments but because rounding allows for necessary waste. And, when using simple, even numbers, mistakes in arithmetic are less likely.
- **Figure all walls with window and door openings as solid.** The slight savings on materials that would result if you accounted for all of these openings is more than offset by additional labor needed to cut around the openings.

Figures 12.1 through 12.5 show basic formulas that installers typically work with.

Length × Width = Square Footage

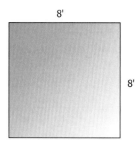

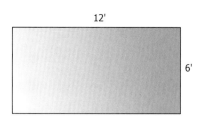

FIGURE 12.1 To calculate square footage, multiply length × width.

8' × 8' = 64 square feet

12' × 6' = 72 square feet

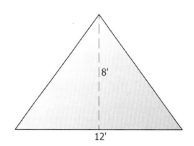

FIGURE 12.2 To calculate square footage of a triangular area, multiply width × height × ½.

8' × 12' × 1/2 = 48 square feet

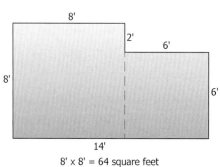

FIGURE 12.3 In a rectangle with an offset, calculate the square footage for the two rectangular areas and add them together.

8' × 8' = 64 square feet
6' × 6' = 36 square feet
64 sq. feet + 36 sq. feet = 100 sq. feet

Simply add up the footage on all sides, and the total is the lineal footage:

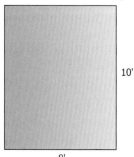

FIGURE 12.4 To calculate lineal footage, simply add up the footage on all sides. The total is the lineal footage.

8' + 10' + 8' + 10" = 36 lineal feet

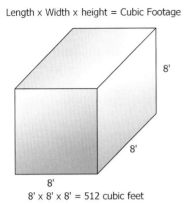

Length x Width x height = Cubic Footage

8' x 8' x 8' = 512 cubic feet

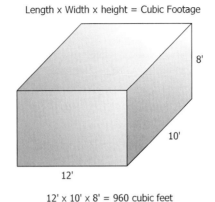

Length x Width x height = Cubic Footage

12' x 10' x 8' = 960 cubic feet

FIGURE 12.5 To calculate cubic footage, multiply length × width × height.

Protecting Your Profits

Unfortunately, common mistakes made in project estimating or project production result in profit slippage.

Three Major Causes of Profit Slippage

1. Material slippage
- Insufficient quantity of materials delivered to the site
- Material price increases
- Damaged materials delivered to the site

2. Labor/subcontractor/sales slippage
- Production errors and/or product ordering errors
- Poor job management by production manager or lead installer (carpenter)
- Bids not secured from subcontractors: working in an open-ended forum

3. Contract/client slippage
- Taking costly steps to please the client
- Numerous and undocumented change orders
- Unclear contract specifications

Maintain a Clear Purchase Tracking System

To protect your estimated profits, the firm must have an effective purchase order system.

If your firm is a large one, a single purchasing agent offers these advantages:

- Quantity buying
- Multiple orders
- Volume freight discounts

Whether the firm is large or small, the paper or electronic purchase order is an important part of job costing and needs to flow through from estimating sheet to accounting. This allows you to match up the purchase order amount with the actual invoice amount.

Warranties

The Magnusen-Moss Warranty Act is a U.S. federal law that governs warranties on consumer products. (For Canadian dealers, there is no equivalent to the Magnusen-Moss Warranty Act governing the content of manufacturers' warranties except for specific product categories, such as motor vehicles.) All dealers in the United States and Canada should take the time to read and understand suppliers' warranties to be aware of what you may be required to do.

Review with your legal counsel manufacturers' warranties and the warranty you plan to offer.

Definitions

Full Warranty

These are summaries of the federal minimum standards that permit a written warranty to be designated as a "full" warranty:

- The warrantor must remedy the problem without charge in a reasonable time to conform to the terms of the written warranty.
- A warrantor may not impose any limitations on the duration of any implied warranty on the product.
- A warrantor may not limit the damages for breach of the warranty unless the exclusion of limitation conspicuously appears on the warranty.
- After a reasonable number of attempts by the warrantor to remedy defects or malfunctions in the product, the consumer is allowed to choose either a refund or replacement without charge. If the warrantor replaces a component part of a product, the replacement includes installing the part without charge.

Limited Warranty

A warranty that does not meet the federal minimums. Such warranties must be conspicuously designated as "limited" warranties.

Implied Warranty

Defined in state law. This means a product will do what it's supposed to do. In all but seven states, a seller may negate the implied warranty by declaring in writing that a product is sold "as is" with no warranty.

ROLE OF A MANFACTURER'S REPRESENTATIVE

It is customary in the kitchen and bath industry to ask a manufacturer's representative to visit a job site. Sometimes this visit allows the dealer/designer to show the rep an innovative and beautiful project.

More often, the visit is a result of unresolved matters involving the product quality, specifications, and warranty replacement work. From time to time, a dealer will request a field inspection by a rep to resolve issues where a consumer feels a product needs replacement but the dealer knows it is within acceptable industry standards.

Unresolved matters involving quality issues and other concerns precipitate the need of a field inspection by the rep. The dealer and designers are responsible for in-depth product knowledge and for presenting the product accurately. The dealer or client's agent is also responsible for ensuring the products were installed according to the manufacturer's recommendations and industry standards.

The manufacturer's rep should resolve only those quality issues that are directly attributable to product.

Field Inspection

The goal of a field inspection is to end up with a completed job and a happy customer. To reach this goal, you should have a clear agreement about the roles the dealer principal/designer and manufacturer's rep will each play during such a visit. First, fully inform your rep of the situation.

Provide as many details as possible before visiting the job site. Tell the rep everything—from how the customers were to work with to how much money they still owe you. Make sure you tell the representative exactly what's wrong with the installed product.

As respected cabinet company representative, John Morgan of Morgan Pinnacle, LLC states:

> If one of my customers tells me that the drawers are binding when opened and closed, as a rep, I know to check out the drawer issue with the factory prior to the visit. If the drawers are binding, chances are that when I call into the plant they will already have seen a similar occurrence and have a ready solution. If it is a new issue, it gives the manufacturer time to research it and advise me as to what path we need to follow to try to find a solution. It is important to show up prepared.

Second, remember that you and the representative are on the same team.

Four recommended guidelines for job site visits are discussed next.

1. **The manufacturer's rep should never visit the job site without the dealer representative.** The dealer or agent needs to be aware of everything discussed.

   This guideline applies not just to job site visits but also to telephone calls, emails, and other types of communication. The dealer should be included in all forms of communication about the issue.

2. **The manufacturer's rep is just that—a manufacturer's representative.** His or her focus is on the product and whether or not it conforms to the manufacturer's standards and was installed according to manufacturer guidelines.

   Another example by John Morgan:

   > If a customer is concerned about warped doors, I show up with a level. I look for shims to see if they were installed properly. If the complaint is cabinets are out-of-square, I walk into the door with a square in hand. I am prepared to find and report quality issues that are genuinely attributable to the manufacturer.

   > The client that has not been managed well by the dealer and has unrealistic quality expectations around a product should be immediately referred back to the dealer. The rep's sole focus is to report issues that concern his/her product, complaints based on other products or poor installation are not the manufacturer representative's responsibility.

3. **The manufacturer's rep is not carrying a checkbook.** It is not uncommon for the consumer to assume that there is a deal (discount, rebate, free product) to be had when the rep arrives onsite. As leverage, the consumer may start by pointing out every conceivable imperfection or may ask for a resolution one issue at a time.

   A good rep first observes and records all issues raised by the client. The rep never addresses them one by one. The best resolution to any issue is one presented after a review of the entire project. This allows all parties to agree on the scope of the issue under review. If possible, a product replacement or repair, not money, should be the solution. It is more beneficial to the manufacturer to have a satisfied customer than to have the customer live with a cabinet he or she is still not happy with after receiving a monetary credit.

4. **The manufacturer's rep, the dealer, and possibly the installer should confer before any major product replacement solution is offered to a client.** A conference should be held before the visit, and discussions should be held away from the job site if there is an issue of shared responsibility for the quality issue raised by the client.

Communications

Technology has improved communications between all concerned parties involving repair or warranty work involving a manufacturer's representative. In the past, sharing a job site concern with a manufacturer representative required scheduling a job site visit during which photographs were taken. Before the digital photography, the film had to be developed and a report had to be written. All of this information was then sent via the mail service to the plant for review and recommendations. Today's technology eliminates time and distance issues, allowing for an expedited resolution.

Words of Caution
- **Electronic communications—email or online meetings with a specialist at a manufacturing facility miles away—never take the place of face-to-face meetings.** Having a manufacturer's representative travel with you to a site often reassures the designer of record and client that issues under discussion are being attended to with great regard for a quick, effective solution.
- **Technological innovation is ever evolving.** One particular mobile device or application may be considered "the best" today, but a new product launch might replace it tomorrow. Using technology effectively means looking for new, improved systems or methods of communicating. From a dealer's point of view, this is another reason to have a positive business relationship with all manufacturer representatives. These individuals travel throughout their regions, or even nationally, and are exposed to successful business systems and technological applications used by other specialists. Therefore, these individuals can share valuable insights and information.

Tips from the Masters

According to John Morgan of Morgan Pinnacle, LLC: "Being a trusted advisor to my kitchen and bath dealers is by far the most important part of my job. I see the trends as they start, I know what is selling and what is not and, most importantly, I witness what makes the successful dealers successful. Your rep can be an incredibly valuable resource to you in bettering your business."

How Technology Is Being Used Today
- **During project inspections.** As a project is inspected, imperfections in the finish or areas of concern often are marked with painters' tape. The representative may take digital photos on his/her tablet during the walk-through. Applications exist that allow users to circle, highlight, or otherwise note issues directly on the photograph. These images can be sent immediately to the manufacturer's facility for review by the appropriate personnel. This method eliminates much of the time spent investigating and reporting on the issue under review.
- **To access experts.** A specific question or concern that requires an expert's attention "back at the plant" can be facilitated through a real-time interface. The representative can stand in the area under discussion and stream live video to team members at the manufacturing plant. It may be a hinge that is not functioning correctly. The engineer at the plant can ask the rep to zoom in for a closer shot. It's almost as if the manufacturer's specialist is with the group on the job site.
- **Videos can also be used in other applications.** Perhaps space in a showroom is going to receive a new display. Video can be sent to the manufacturer allowing the marketing team to see the entire showroom and the space that is being allotted for the new display.

A note about security: People not accustomed to working with online communication systems are concerned that when something is posted, everyone is able to see it. This is not the case. Communications between the manufacturer's rep and the manufacturer's personnel can be securely delivered with access to the information provided only to approved parties.

IMPORTANCE OF JOB COSTING

Once the project installation is complete and final payment has been made, scrutinizing job costs and comparing them to the original estimate can lead to business changes that result in increased profits on future undertakings.

Not many years ago, job costing was a daunting task. Matching up invoices, purchase orders, and sale slips was done by hand and involved piles of paper. Today even though a number of software programs can make our lives easier, but many kitchen and bathroom dealers still do not bother to job cost. It's like walking a tightrope without a net!

Tips from the Masters

- Maintaining daily time records is critical for understanding the amount of time spent on a project from a planning and estimating stage. For hourly employees, it is equally important that their time be posted to the job.
- Job comparative costs should be posted as invoices are received. If the actual invoice differs from the estimate by an agreed-to percentage factor, the responsible staff member should explain the difference.
- Job costs should be scrutinized on a monthly basis to look for areas where profits are slipping away.

SUMMARY

The business manager must select among competing business models in regard to the type of projects the firm services as well as the type of relationship he or she has with various contractors, subcontractors, and installation professionals. The business manager establishes not only the company's profit margins but the strategic pricing used to prepare estimates. He or she is also responsible for considering job site conditions that may impact the standard markups applied. The business manager is responsible for fostering a positive relationship between his firm and manufacturers' representatives.

REVIEW QUESTIONS

1. List five business attributes that an installer should promise to deliver to a business owner if he or she is employed by the firm as a member of the team or as a subcontractor. (See "The Installer Promises the Business Owner/Manager" pages 273–274)

2. State the differences among the three pricing methods discussed. (See "Pricing Strategies and Methods" pages 279–280)

3. What are the four main types of projects in the kitchen and bath industry? (See "Types of Installations" page 268)

4. Differentiate between a material specification and a performance specification on a project. (See "Material Selection and Specification" and "Performance" pages 276–277)

Responsibilities of Designer of Record

A designer's success is not only defined by the beauty and creativity of his or her design solutions. Professional accomplishment in K&B design also includes familiarity with the details of construction and production installation, thorough and accurate estimating skills, project management expertise, and the people skills to work with the many personalities involved in transforming a beautiful plan into a beautiful room.

> *Learning Objective 1: Explain the designer's role during the project documentation process*
>
> *Learning Objective 2: Recognize the importance of establishing a good relationship with the installer.*
>
> *Learning Objective 3: List the types of problems designers may encounter with cabinet installation.*

"WIN-WIN" STRATEGY

Designers who "win" understand both the design and the installation process. This understanding allows them to produce award-winning projects, on time, and on budget. These designers have a strong working relationship with trade partners and installers and have satisfied clients, who may refer them to others.

Successful designers:

- Have in-depth product and industry knowledge.
- Participate in the industry; stay informed about design trends and new product innovations.
- Create projects based on the accepted guidelines published by the NKBA.
- Are effective communicators from the design and sales process through the installation process.
- Are organized.
- Understand that their conceptual plans are little more than a drawing until they've assembled the team necessary to order, receive, and install the individual elements of the plan.

DESIGNER'S ROLE DURING PROJECT DOCUMENTATION PROCESS

The designer has a variety of responsibilities during the project proposal and project management process, depending on the business model chosen.

Model 1. Designer is responsible for all aspects of the planning process.
In this business model, the designer is solely responsible for client contact in the showroom, during the planning process (in the showroom or on the job site), estimating the cost of the project, ordering the material and monitoring material delivery. If the firm installs product, the designer is also the project liaison orchestrating site preparation, material delivery, and installation.

Model 2. Designer works with an in-house or outsourced drafting department and transfers project management responsibility to a production manager.
In this business model, the designer's primary responsibility is client contact and creating concept design solutions. The designer meets with the client in the showroom or in the home and creates the concept solution. These concept sketches are then transferred to an in-house or outsourced design department that interfaces with the designer of record to create the working drawings and complete estimating. Once the project is sold, the design department may also be responsible for ordering material. The project is then handed off to a production manager, who assumes responsibility for job site management and serves as liaison between the designer, the client, and the installation team.

Model 3. Designer works with a design associate during the planning process.
In this business model, there is a team of two individuals: the designer of record and a design associate. The design associate may interface with other people in the design firm or may serve as the drawing source. Typically, the design associate is responsible for assisting the client in making surface selections, securing estimates and proposals from subcontractors or contract installers, and preparing job site workbook materials. In some organizations, the design associate has more project management responsibility, allowing the senior designer to focus on design and selling, as opposed to project management or the technical details associated with the ordering process. Alternatively, installation may be supervised by the designer and design associate, as detailed in model 1, or the project may be transferred to a production manager, as outlined in model 2.

Relationship between the Designer and the Installer

Experienced professionals suggest the next foundation points for developing a good relationship with the installer.

- **Your goal is to make the installer's job as easy as possible.** Installers primary goal is to make the design look good.
- **Leave egos at the door.** Include the installer in design reviews and any "What should we do?" discussions. Installers should never make negative comments to the client about the designer or the designer's work.
- **Establish a communication system.** The communication system that exists between you and the installer includes the client when appropriate and takes place away from the client when appropriate.
- **Easy access.** Designer and installer are readily available to one another via text, telephone, pager, or email.
- **Designer includes the installer in praise given for a job well done.** Sharing photographs of completed projects and inviting the installation team to celebrations at the job site are some ways of sharing the finished project with these hardworking professionals.

SUCCESSFUL DESIGNERS ARE DETAIL ORIENTED

The profits resulting from your design will only be as good as the initial job site survey and measurements taken. Minimize measuring mistakes. Successful firms often have another staff member accompany the designer to the job site after the contract is signed to double-check measurements, and take a "committee" approach to reviewing the cabinet order acknowledgements or other purchase orders.

The second most important element in profitable projects is a clear set of project documents. According to the NKBA, a complete set of project documents consists of seven items:

1. A "before" floor plan, with electrical notations. Digital photography in the project package helps.
2. An "after" floor plan that includes all cabinet nomenclature in a clear and easy-to-read format. On the floor plan, include cut-out and overall dimensions for appliances, the countertops' actual depth, and appliance doors/drawers.
3. Dimensioned elevations that match the floor plan perfectly. Too often, changes are made in the floor plan that are never translated to the elevation.
4. An electrical plan, with construction details for a simple project. A separate construction plan may be required for more complex projects.
5. Copies of all the appliance or equipment spec sheets (taken from the Internet, not from outdated catalogs).
6. A completed contractual document spelling out all of the products supplied and work completed.
7. A system to document changes made during the project.

Figures 13.1 to 13.5 comprise a set of sample kitchen plan documents meeting these standards.

UNDERSTANDING CONSTRUCTION CONSTRAINTS

In addition to detailed design plans, the designer of record must understand construction constraints. To minimize the stress surrounding a project installation, make sure your team has a shared knowledge base of industry-accepted product standards and that these standards are shared with the client throughout project design, ordering, and installation phases.

Creating realistic product expectations begins when the design professional first meets the client. During every step of the planning process, the client must be informed about material and equipment limitations as well as the proper sequence of the selection process. Clients need to understand that wood characteristics are very different from wood defects—and that wood characteristics are magnified under a natural finish.

It is equally important for clients to appreciate how the realities of the construction process and hand-crafted precision, as well as the natural movement of wood, affect the details of the design.

Common oversights often made when presenting the details of the project to the owner or the owner's agent can result in a dissatisfied client. If the client requests a design detail, a product specification, or a process change that is not aligned with industry recommended procedures: insist on a notation in the contract documents. Some firms use waivers.

Definition

Waiver

A form clients sign when a decision they make does not coincide with the designer's best judgment.

- If the appliances are not selected before the cabinet order is placed, the client must sign a waiver stating that placing an order for cabinetry prior to the confirmation of appliance selections can lead to delays if changes are made.
- Similarly, firms use a waiver if the client supplies the appliances.
- Waivers are also often used when clients select a natural finish on wood cabinet doors.

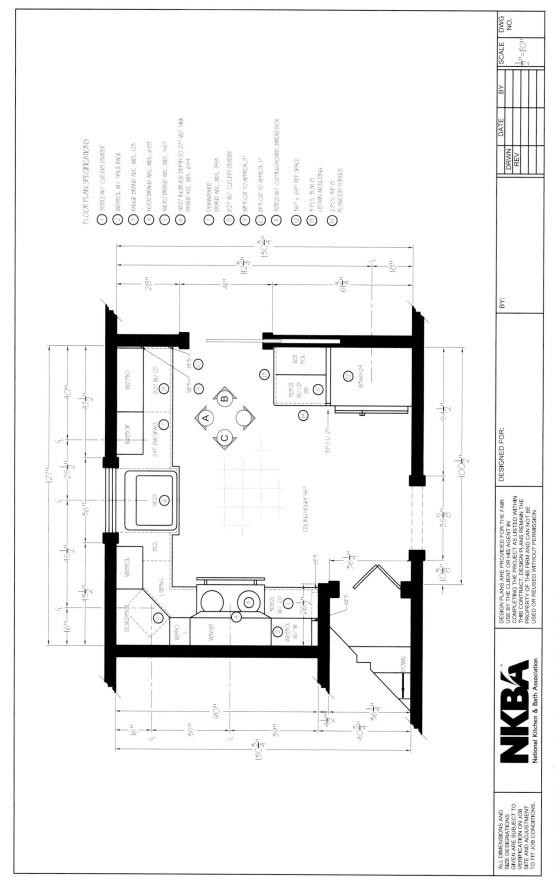

FIGURE 13.1 Kitchen floor plan. (Concept by Mary Galloway)

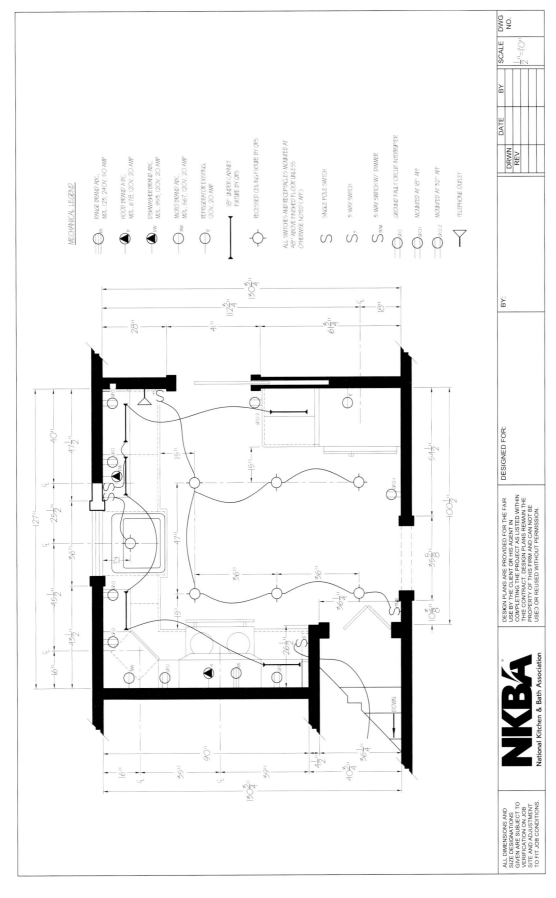

FIGURE 13.2 Kitchen mechanical plan. (Concept by Mary Galloway)

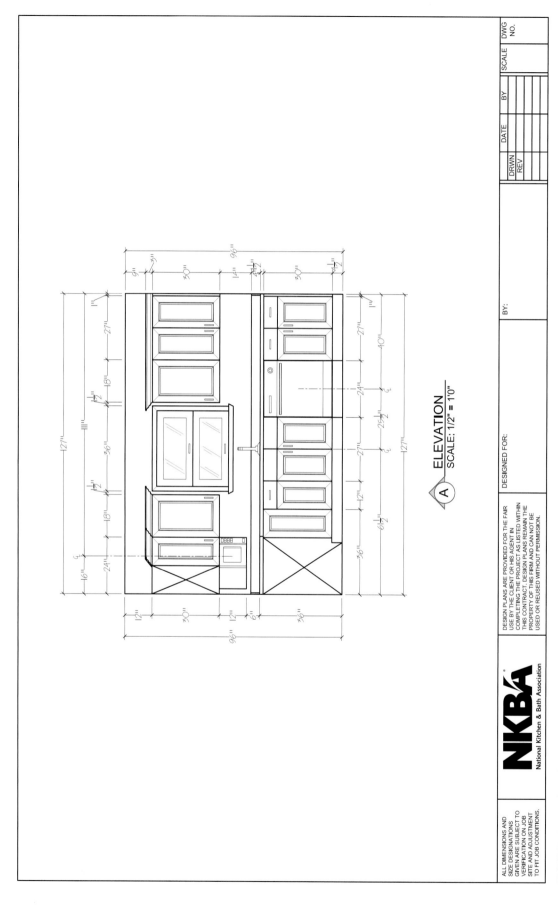

FIGURE 13.3 Kitchen elevation. (Concept by Mary Galloway)

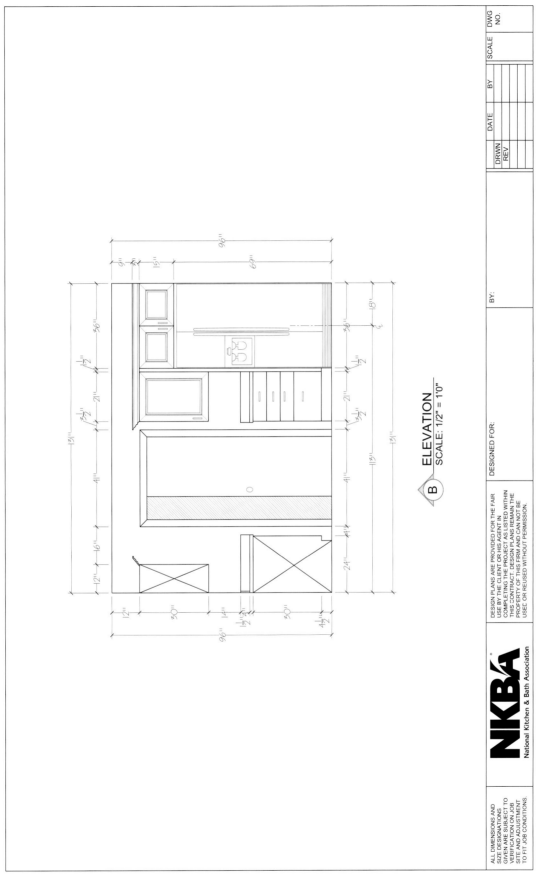

FIGURE 13.4 Kitchen elevation. (Concept by Mary Galloway)

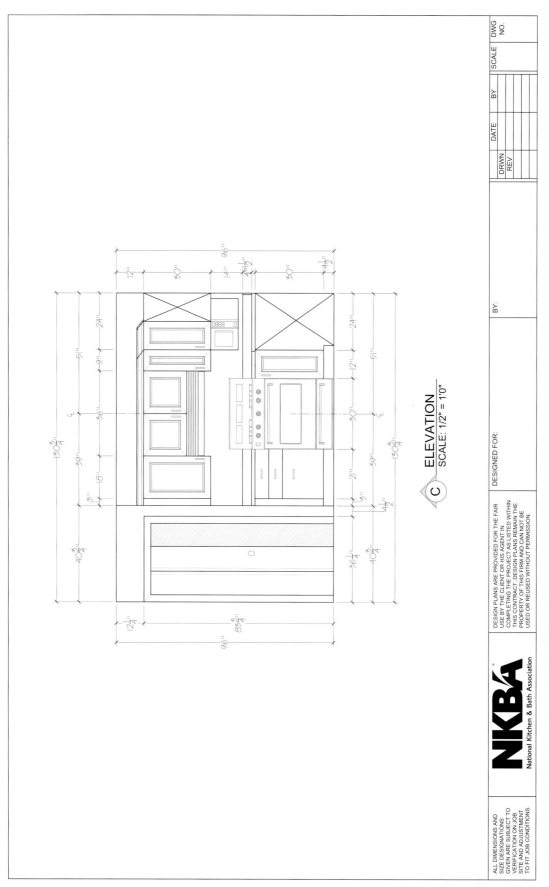

FIGURE 13.5 Kitchen elevation. (Concept by Mary Galloway)

Tips from the Masters

Use this checklist to verify that all the details have been covered.

Client/Design Information

- ❏ All job data included: proper names, address, email, telephone, job location, directions.
- ❏ Assigned a job number.
- ❏ Have complete design drawings, including floor plan and elevations:
    - ❏ All dimensions are in inches and fractions of an inch or in metric sizing.
    - ❏ All overall dimensions total equal individual wall segment dimensions.
    - ❏ Wall heights are indicated.
    - ❏ If no soffit, installed wall cabinet heights are indicated.
    - ❏ Allowances are made for out-of-square corners.
    - ❏ Special dimensions for peninsula and island placement are noted.

Job Site Special Conditions/Conflicts

- ❏ Out-of-square and out-of-plumb corners and walls are noted.
- ❏ Flooring conditions that may affect cabinet installation noted.
- ❏ Conflicts between electrical receptacles/switches and cabinets and/or backsplash decorative material noted.
- ❏ Conflicts with phone jacks noted.
- ❏ HVAC supplies and returns noted.
- ❏ Plumbing fixture centerlines located.
- ❏ Door and window casings located with widths noted.
- ❏ Waste supply lines located.
- ❏ Power/gas line for range and wall ovens located.

Cabinetry and Layout

- ❏ NKBA Guidelines followed to greatest extent feasible.
- ❏ Base cabinet and wall cabinet individual dimensions correspond to overall total dimension.
- ❏ Fillers provided where necessary for door and drawer clearances.
- ❏ Fillers provided at 90-degree inside corners.
- ❏ Proper door hinging provided.
- ❏ Any special conditions or cabinet modifications provided.
- ❏ Finished ends at wall cabinets noted.
- ❏ Finished ends at base cabinets noted.
- ❏ Clearances between full overlay doors/drawers and moldings adequate.
- ❏ Clearances between full overlay doors/drawers and baseboards adequate.

(continued)

❑ Pulls for any special base cabinets noted.

❑ Pulls for any special wall cabinets noted.

❑ Allowance provided for waste in molding installation.

❑ Adequate clearances provided for aligning tall cabinets.

Island/Peninsula Cabinets

❑ Cabinet dimensions are adequate.

❑ Framed half-wall, if used, is properly sized, with moldings and panels noted.

❑ Outside corner detailed.

❑ Scribe locations noted and method provided for.

❑ Toe kick detailed.

❑ Paneling for exposed sides noted.

❑ Cabinet orientation indicated, if nonstandard.

❑ Locations of built-in switches indicated.

❑ Any other special conditions noted.

Countertops

❑ Lengths verified with base cabinets.

❑ Overhang dimension noted at open ends and adjacent to specific appliances.

❑ Raised sections indicated with method of support detailed.

❑ Lowered sections indicated with method of support detailed.

❑ Special conditions have been fully detailed in design drawings.

❑ Backsplash locations indicated, and fit and finish noted regarding end caps and splash/deck joint.

❑ Radius and/or angled corners are dimensioned.

❑ Edge treatments described.

❑ Cutouts located by centerline and dimensioned.

Appliances

❑ Appliance specification cut sheets available.

❑ Clearances between appliances and cabinet doors/drawers specified.

❑ Downdraft ducting provided for.

❑ Ventilation duct path for hood noted.

❑ Dishwasher clearances adequate.

❑ Range clearances adequate.

❑ Cooktop dimensions verified with countertop.

❑ Wall oven dimensions coordinated with cabinet.

❑ Disposal located, with respect to the side of sink, and switch location noted.

❑ Microwave specified and located.

❑ Refrigerator specified and located.

Glass Shelving/Counter Section/Cabinet Doors or Other Special Decorative Material

❑ Type, location and sizes indicated.

❑ Quantities scheduled.

❑ Tempered _____ Non-tempered _____

Hardware

❑ Quantity indicated allows for two extra (for contingencies or to give to owner).

❑ Clearances required at 90-degree inside corners verified with cabinet fillers.

About the Fit (Relationship between Adjacent Materials and Equipment)

In both new construction and renovation work, consumers need to understand that the building envelope may not be level (see Figure 13.6), plumb (see Figures 13.7 and 13.8), or square (see Figure 13.9). Therefore, cabinet reveals and scribing fillers must be part of the cabinet plan.

Definitions

Level surface

A surface without bends, curves, or irregularities. Normally refers to a horizontal surface.

Plumb surface

Perfectly straight. Normally refers to a vertical surface.

Square corner

Two surfaces connecting at 90 degrees (a right angle) with no bends, curves or irregularities in either surface as it radiates out from the corner.

Out of Level Floor

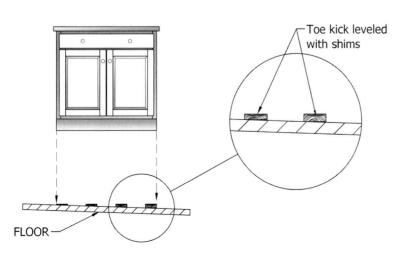

FLOOR

Toe kick leveled with shims

FIGURE 13.6 Example of an out-of-level floor.

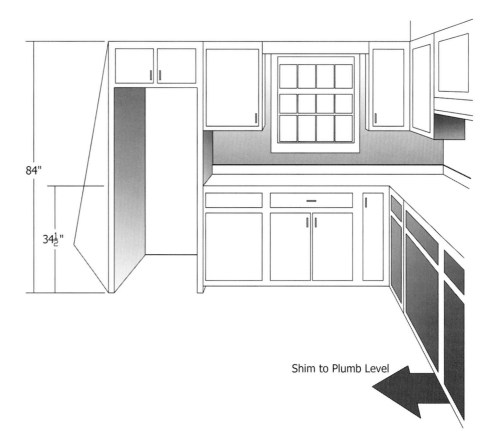

FIGURE 13.7 Shim to level cabinets.

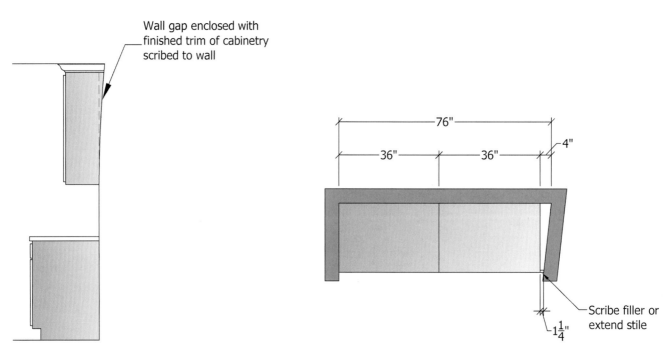

FIGURE 13.8 Example of an out-of-plumb wall.

FIGURE 13.9 Example of an out-of-square corner.

Impact of an Imperfect Room on the Cabinet Layout

Fitting Cabinets between Walls

Cabinets must be installed plumb and level even in rooms that are not plumb, level, and square. Doing this becomes troublesome if cabinets are installed between two walls. Accentuating the problem is the fact that computer-generated design programs always assume the room is level and plumb and will attempt to fit exact-size cabinetry in an opening.

For example, experienced designers never place two 36"- (914-mm) wide cabinets in a 72"- (1,829-mm) wide area. When the cabinets are leveled in an enclosure with walls out of plumb, the two 36" (914-mm) cabinets will not fit because the 72" (1,829 mm) space only exists along the back wall, not along the face of the cabinets 24" to 25" (610 mm to 635 mm) in front of that wall surface.

Extended stiles on framed cabinetry or separate fillers (sometimes called "scribes") are always used when cabinets are fit between walls to provide room for job site adjustment. (See Figure 13.10.)

Scribing also takes place if cabinets extend to the ceiling. (See Figure 13.11.)

Fit between Cabinets

There is less fit flexibility in a full overlay cabinet because the door covers the entire case. In a framed cabinet, there is an extended frame that gives the installer more room to adjust cabinet sizing.

Regardless of the case configuration, cabinets at right angles to one another, cabinets at right angles to an appliance on the return run, angled or diagonal cabinets in corners, or cabinets that are less in depth than adjacent units with crown molding attached all require scribing space. Clients must appreciate why these scribes are used and what the visual reality is of a crown molding scribed to the ceiling. (See Figures 13.12 to 13.17)

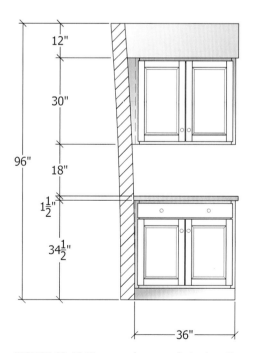

FIGURE 13.10 Diagram of an out-of-plumb wall with cabinets using a scribing method or extended stile.

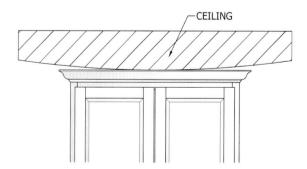

FIGURE 13.11 Diagram of an out-of-level ceiling.

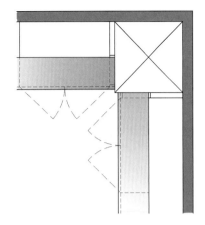
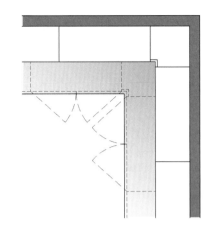

FIGURE 13.12 Diagram of base and wall cabinets butting one another in a 90-degree corner.

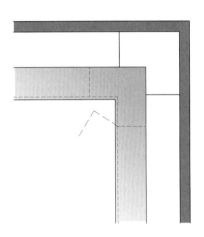
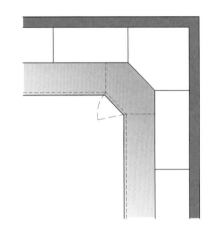
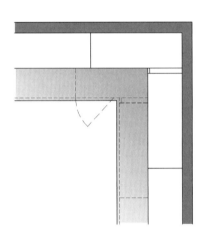

FIGURE 13.13 Diagram of base and wall special-purpose corner cabinet arrangements.

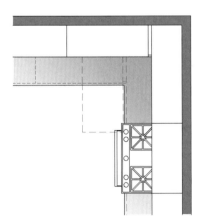

FIGURE 13.14 Diagram of full overlay cabinets at right angles to a cooking appliance with handles.

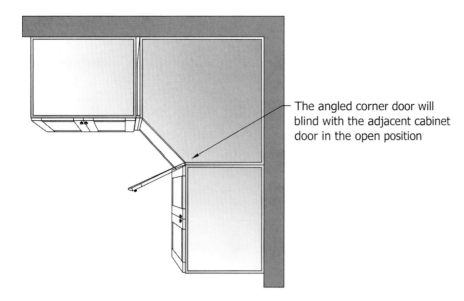

The angled corner door will blind with the adjacent cabinet door in the open position

FIGURE 13.15 Diagram of a typical diagonal wall cabinet installation without required fillers.

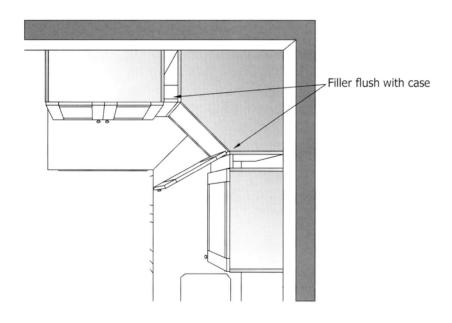

Filler flush with case

FIGURE 13.16 Diagram of a typical diagonal base cabinet installation with required fillers.

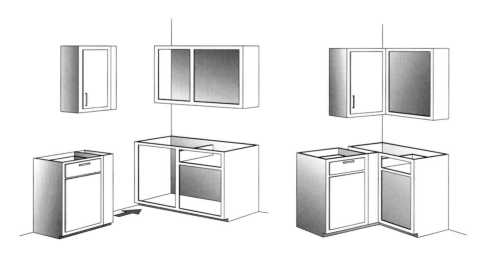

FIGURE 13.17 Diagram of a typical blind corner base installation.

Accommodating Adjacent Material Overhang Requirements

The countertop overhang extends beyond the side and the front of the base cabinet. Crown molding extends beyond the side and the front of a cabinet. The relationship of countertop and molding overhangs to the product they are installed on, as well as the walls they are set against, must be clearly detailed in the elevations. (See Figure 13.18) Don't forget to allow space around door and window casings for the cabinet end, countertop/backsplash overhang, and molding treatment. (See Figure 13.19) Clients must understand why slivers of wall space are often included in the kitchen design. (See Figure 13.20)

About Cabinet Door Movement

Door Stability: Swelling and Shrinking

It is the norm in the industry that wood used to manufacture cabinets has a moisture content approximating that which will be present in the finished installation. This is important in a cabinet with a factory finish. It is critical when unfinished cabinetry is shipped to a job site.

Until the wood is finished, there is a greater chance for it to absorb moisture from the surrounding atmosphere at the job site. Because of this concern, it is often specified that unfinished cabinetry cannot be delivered to a job site and stored in a non-air-conditioned space. For example, shipping cabinets built in Salt Lake City, Utah, to Key West, Florida, and then storing them in a non-air-conditioned garage on the job site can spell disaster as the wood swells in the new environment. Managing the delivery and installation process means keeping a careful eye on the moisture content at the job site.

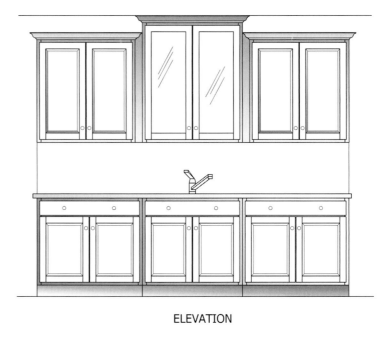

ELEVATION

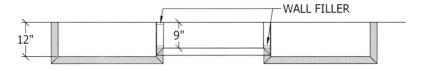

FLOOR PLAN

FIGURE 13.18 Elevation of typical installation of base and wall cabinets with overhanging crown molding and full backsplash.

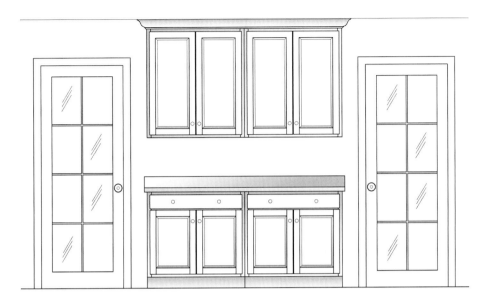

FIGURE 13.19 Elevation of similar typical installation with 4″ backsplash detail.

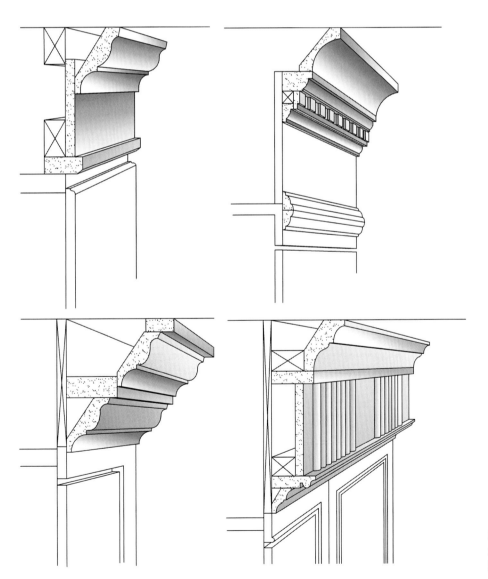

FIGURE 13.20 Diagram of wall space required for stacked molding installation.

Regardless of how carefully this process is monitored, it should be expected that doors will expand or shrink during heating and cooling seasons in the home. This is typically most evident the first year the wood is installed. Less movement can be expected after the first year.

One of the biggest misconceptions a consumer has is that the cabinet doors will be absolutely straight and that the margins between doors will be precisely the same dimension. Consumers often assume a door is defective and must be replaced because of a misunderstanding about acceptable wood movement.

The K&B industry is not scientific. Consumers must understand that the overall size of the door and the wood species selected affect how much that door will grow and shrink as it acclimates to the ambient moisture content in the air in the home.

One design firm includes this information in their project specifications:

> Once installed, expect to see some shrinking during the first winter months, and some swelling during the first summer as the kitchen adjusts to its new setting. Swelling is to be expected in our inset cabinetry, which allows 3/32" allowance between the case and our hand-sanded doors. If cabinetry is exposed to excessive moisture, the wood will swell more. For example, a 24"-wide door with a 20" panel could swell as much a ⅛"—all this movement is taken up on the pull side because the hinge holds the door stable. Should some swelling occur, do not sand and refinish the door, because of the expected reversal of the swell during the warmer season.

Framing will expand outward in all directions. This is the reason why paired doors or inset doors hit each other or get tight inside the front frame. It is also why full overlay doors are typically hung on the cabinet with a ⅛" gap between doors and cabinets.

Space between drawer fronts and drawers also must be considered in both frame and frameless cabinetry. The wider or higher the door front, the more chance of wood movement problems. Because of these expansion issues, drawer fronts are rarely made from a solid wood slab.

When five-piece doors are used, the door is designed for the panel to expand. Normally the panel is glued or pinned in the middle of the top and bottom rails, allowing the panel to move (grow) in width for seasonal expansion. In addition, or alternatively, the door engineering may include spacers (positioned in the rabbit groove of the door frame). These spacers are flexible, allowing the "floating" panel to expand without opening the frame joints or to shrink without causing a "rattle" sound because of a loose-fitting center panel.

Mitered doors usually have wider framing than stile-and-rail doors. Typically they are designed to have a small opening in the inside corner. This opening will close first during expansion before putting pressure on the mitered joint.

Panel staves are affected by increased moisture. A combination of staves growing at different rates and a slight increase in the radial direction are highly visible in painted doors. Framing joints also will be more visible with increased moisture.

Tips from the Masters
What Every Designer Should Know

- Some species expand more than others. Know the specs for the species the client has selected.
- The wider the framing, the more chance for expansion problems.
- Solid wood raised panels will expand more than plywood panels. Because of the monolithic nature of medium-density fiberboard (MDF) panels, they will not show stave (solid wood strips laid up to form the center panel in a wood five-piece door) movement lines in paint.
- Do not recommend mitered doors and inset doors for high-moisture areas.
- Show client examples of movement lines in painted wood panels.
- Show examples of what is acceptable and what would be replaced.

About the "Finish"

Caution about Samples

For many custom projects, a sample door is prepared for the client to approve or sign off on. Once the actual finishing process begins, the manufacturer will refer to this sample door to ensure consistency between the presented sample and the completed project. However, because of woodworking variables, differences can be expected between a finished product and an individual sample door. Consider these important factors:

- **Wood color and figure vary.** The actual project will be built from a different lumber unit from the door sample submitted; therefore, some tonal differences can occur.
- **Small samples and even a door sample will look different from a completed room.** Expect glazed finishes to vary from slightly lighter to slightly darker from the presented sample.
- **Timing is important.** If the sample reviewed is older than 30 days, the natural aging of wood and mellowing of finishes due to ultraviolet light will affect the color rendition. Typically, both wood and finishes darken with age. This is of particular importance in any white glazed finishes, which tend to mellow with age, and cherry or mahogany finishes, which dramatically darken with age.
- **Hand application is a human process.** Most important, hand-applied, artistic layered finishes will vary by the nature of their hand application. Cabinet manufacturer technicians are trained in application techniques; however, any hand-applied finish will bear the mark of the specialist, and his or her team, creating the project. Therefore, some application and appearance variations are to be expected in layered finishes.
- **Make sure you and your team are clear when discussing the names of finishes, door styles, and physical distressing techniques that the manufacturer offers.** The manufacturer might have a finish name that includes a specific distressing package. Yet another manufacturer might have a finish that you enhance by selecting one of a variety of distressing packages. Clients might not understand this and ask you for a specific style that they feel defines both finish and distressing. Look at the sample and walk through all the elements to make sure clients understand.
- **When showing the client thermal foil door samples and/or laminate door samples, discuss any concerns the manufacturer has listed in its warranty regarding possible damage to the finish should it come in contact with excessive heat.** (Some self-cleaning ovens may allow enough hot air to escape to be categorized as excessive heat.)

Natural Beauty of Wood

People have appreciated the natural beauty and versatility of wood for centuries. While certain characteristics are unique to select species, each tree—and its wood—varies in color, density, hardness, strength, grain pattern, and texture. Truly a product of its environment, a tree's growth and appearance are influenced by many factors. Just like people, no two trees are exactly alike.

This range of wood characteristics will show up in both solid and veneer materials. Make sure the client expects some color or grain characteristic variations between the actual cabinetry delivered and a sample. For those clients interested in a more repetitive wood graining, a laminate surface, rather than a real-wood product, may be more appropriate.

Pricing and Availability of Wood

Availability in the region of origin determines the starting point for pricing wood. Grading, a description of the appearance and performance characteristics of the wood, also affects the price. Quite simply, the more restrictions placed on natural characteristics, the matching required, or the higher the level of color or grain consistency specified, the higher the price. Additionally, shifts in demand throughout the world do occur, creating shortages that affect pricing.

Importance of Specifications

Veneer and solid wood grading restricts the naturally recurring characteristics of each wood species. Grading also limits color variation. Industry standards include six face grades and, within each grade, a range of appearances. The grades used are AA, A, B, C, D and E. Grade AA face appearance does not totally eliminate wood characteristics. The grading means the best quality contains the least natural characteristics. The higher the grade the more natural characteristics, with E grade permitting the greatest number of natural characteristics and repairs. A grade of matching or blending veneers is typically used on door backs.

Even with such attention to detail, wood is still a product of nature. Although certain characteristics are unique to each species, a piece of veneer produced from an individual log will have its own characteristics. This is the true beauty of wood.

Color Variations

Expect color variation within a species. Many factors influence wood color during the life of the tree, including the soil types and minerals found in the soil, along with water levels, available sunlight, and temperature.

Genetic composition also plays its part in creating variety within a species. Hardwood trees originate from seeds, root sprouts, and stump sprouts. Trees originating from seeds contain genetic variables from two parent trees, while sprouts from roots and stumps are genetically identical to the parent tree. Because of these variables, trees of the same species from one area might be quite different from trees of the same species from other areas.

Natural Wood Characteristics

Wood is a product of nature therefore it includes variations in color, grain patterns, and other characteristics including markings created by insects.

- **Bird peck.** Woodpeckers produce small holes, which are the starting point for brown to blackish mineral streaks. Bird peck is common in hickory and maple.
- **Gum spots.** Peach bark beetles and cambium miners are the main cause of gum spots. The feeding insects injure the living portion of the bark, leading to the formation of gum spots in the wood as the tree continues to grow. Also known as "pitch pockets," gum spots are common in cherry.
- **Mineral streak.** A mineral streak or stain is a darkened or discolored wood area caused by minerals the tree extracts from the soil. Mineral streaks, also known as spalting, are a natural by-product of the rotting process caused by a vast array of stain, mold, and decayed fungi found naturally on the forest floor. Mineral streaks appear as a blackish blue, well-defined line or area running parallel with the grain. Mineral streaks are commonly found in maple and birch and sometimes in oak and cherry.
- **Pin knot.** Knots vary in size, shape, structure, and color.
- **Ray flecking.** Ray flecking is visible in hardwood species that are quarter-sawn and have rays. The rays are strips of cells that extend radially within a tree and primarily store food and transport it horizontally. Red oak and white oak are noted for this characteristic.
- **Sapwood.** The sapwood of a tree conducts water up the tree stem and may contain some living cells. Sapwood can be lighter in color than hardwood. Sapwood usually comes from the outside of the tree as compared with the heartwood.
- **Worm track.** A worm track is a small, narrow, yellowish to brown streak caused by cambium miners feeding beneath the bark from the branches to the roots. Tiny burrows are filled in by new cell growth and become embedded in the wood as the tree continues to grow. Worm tracks, also called "pith flecks," are common in maple.

Inspecting the Finish on Wood Surfaces

Testing labs approved by the Kitchen Cabinet Manufacturers' Association (KCMA) adhere to this guideline for inspecting a finished wood surface:

> Lighting shall be from an overhead white fluorescent light with bulb(s) positioned parallel to the floor and having an intensity of 75 to 100′-candles (807 to 1076 lux) on the surface. View at an eye-to-specimen distance of approximately 30–36" (762 to 914 mm) and at an angle of approximately 45 degrees. Direct sunlight or other angle light sources, which will accentuate or minimize the effect, shall be avoided.

SUMMARY

Regardless of the business model being used, designers must be detail-oriented and organized. They must establish a good working relationship with the installer. Designers should also have a good understanding of how to deal with the many problems that can be encountered on the job site.

REVIEW QUESTIONS

1. Compare the three ways designers work (on their own or with others) during the project preparation process. (See "Designer's Role during Project Documentation Process" page 292)
2. Describe the ideal relationship between the designer of record and installation professional on the job site. (See "Relationship between the Designer and the Installer" page 292)
3. Explain how a five-piece wood door expands differently from a mitered wood door. (See "About Cabinet Door Movement" page 306)
4. State the guidelines approved by the Kitchen Cabinet Manufacturers Association for inspecting a finished wood surface on the job site. (See "Inspecting the Finish on Wood Surfaces" page 310)

Managing Client Expectations and the Job Site

You or one of your designers just signed a contract for a $50,000 kitchen remodel, and the project will start in 8 to 12 weeks. Your team knows what to expect during the waiting period and once the work begins. But the client may only remodel or build once or twice in a lifetime. Your entire company has the responsibility of not only doing a quality job but of keeping the client happy during the entire renovation.

The best plan is to organize the installation process and to maintain a high level of communication with the client, in person, by phone, and via email. There is no substitute for doing a first-class job in this all-important area.

Learning Objective 1: Describe the various roles performed by members of the project team.

Learning Objective 2: Outline the topics to be addressed during the preconstruction conference.

Learning Objective 3: Explain how to prepare and manage a punch list.

UNDERSTANDING "REMODELING FEVER"

It is helpful to remember how traumatic a renovation undertaking can be. It may be very emotional for the customer. The expression "remodeling fever" describes the natural stages of customer emotions during a typical remodeling project. Figure 14.1 shows this pattern.

The six stages are:

1. **Sales contract is signed, and the customer feels that a dream is about to be realized.** This is the highest degree of happiness, optimism, and satisfaction.
2. **Production begins.** Demolition, storage of materials in the customer's space, and designating a bathroom for the project bring the realization to customers that they will be under siege for a period of time.
3. **Watching rough carpentry shape the space quickly raises the customer's expectations.** The client may feel the job is going so well that it will be finished before the completion date.
4. **The slow pace of other work begins to take their toll on the customer.** Electrical and mechanical rough-ins, inspections and drywall, numerous workers of various levels of

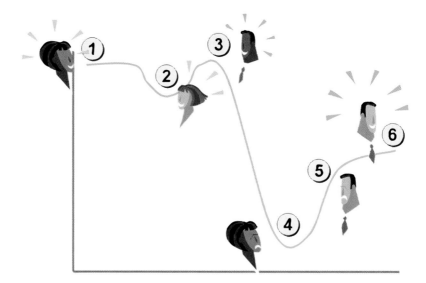

FIGURE 14.1 Remodeling Fever Graph

thoughtfulness roaming the house, unexplained delays, and work needing to be redone all cause anxiety. At the drywall stage, clients often hit bottom. There seems to be almost no visible progress, drywallers may arrive at odd hours to do what appears to be invisible work, and then the ultimate blow of drywall sanding, which creates a great deal of dust, can lead the most even-tempered of homeowners to feel that they have made a terrible mistake in undertaking a remodeling project.

5. **The trim-out stage, which appears so simple to the layperson's eye, moves ever so slowly.** A day's work makes almost no visible difference to customers. At this stage, customers feel that the job will never be finished. However, they do begin to have a good overall view of what the space will look like.

6. **Cabinets and countertops are installed.** Completion marks an improved outlook and a relief that the space will be the customers' to use and live in. In many jobs, goodwill is lost by the slowness with which the punch list is handled. Workers may mess up what was completed by the last worker. Painters touch up and leave drips on the newly finished wood floor, while the floor finishers scratch the newly painted base trim when they return to remove the drips.

Finally, the customers' lives return to sanity. They move back into the kitchen or bathroom and begin to enjoy the new space. Their appreciation of the installer begins to return and grow as time goes on. However, there was a long downslide during production, and it will be long time, if ever, before clients' satisfaction returns to the original level.

Recognizing this natural pattern of a remodeling project will motivate the dealer/designer to create a system to help clients live through it.

MANAGING THE CLIENT AND THE PROJECT

Step 1: Organize Team So Each Member Understands Their Responsibility

Building the team starts by giving everyone a specific job. Each team member has a specific role to play in successfully producing a project. Mix-ups occur when the individuals do not understand their roles. The following is a list of job titles along with their various responsibilities.

Owner/Owner's agent   The client assumes all decision-making responsibilities or delegates them to an individual identified as their agent. The owner's agent may be the architect, designer, builder, or business manager, or even a relative. To ensure a clear understanding of everyone's responsibility, provide a statement outlining the breadth and responsibility of your work if you will not be dealing directly with the homeowner.

Designer of record   The professional whom the client originally retains. The designer of record may be an interior designer, who invites a kitchen specialist to collaborate on the project. Alternatively, the kitchen firm's designer, whom the client was referred to or who met the client in the showroom, may be the designer of record. This individual is normally the member of the project team who is accountable to the client.

Co-designer   Can be an assistant to the designer of record, an individual who is contributing to the overall project, or one who is collaborating with the designer of record. The title "co-designer" can apply to an individual who focuses on one aspect of the project while the designer of record takes a holistic approach to the project, considering it in its totality.

Design associate/assistant   A team member hired by the kitchen/bath designer to assist in the planning process or in the project management. Clearly communicate the scope of responsibility of this associate to the team.

Site superintendent   An individual who supervises an entire site, usually consisting of more than one home, such as a new home development (or building in multistory structures). "Supers" are on the site to supervise and coordinate. On some projects, they spend a large amount of time scheduling so that the subs work to maximum efficiency. In high-rise living environments, the super oversees the work and ensures completion within the building covenants.

Project manager   An individual based off site who travels from job site to job site. Project managers can have responsibility for more than one job in different locales and give on-site direction—often specific instruction on the work for that day. A project manager orders material and schedules subs, among other duties. The owner of a remodeling company or designer of record often fills this role until the jobs become too numerous to manage.

Lead installer (carpenter)   A tradesperson who assumes management responsibility while continuing their role on the job.

Journeyman installer (carpenter)   The general definition of "journeyman" is a worker who has learned a trade and works for another person, usually by the day. In the context of union labor, a "journeyman" is an individual who has reached his or her status through apprenticeship and/or testing as part of a trade association or labor union. For a firm that does not retain union labor, the term "journeyman installer" or "journeyman carpenter" often applies to the most senior member of the installation team who has demonstrated capability through years of service.

Apprentice installer (carpenter)   An installer who is learning a trade by practical experience under skilled workers. An apprentice installer or apprentice carpenter is learning a trade from installers participating in an organized union, trade guild, or trade association. For a firm that does employ union labor, the term "apprentice" is used to designate an individual who is learning the trade.

Helper   A term used in the construction industry to designate an individual who is just entering the field and who assists in all activities. The helper allows the apprentice or journeyman to complete tasks in the most efficient way. For example, the helper might be in charge of unpacking materials, moving product in and out of the room, daily sweeping chores, and maintaining the truck in a neat and orderly fashion.

Most kitchen and bathroom installations require more than just a carpentry specialist. General contractors, subcontractors, plumbers, tile setters, and others are part of the installation team. There may be other professionals involved such as interior designer, architect, and home media consultant.

Who actually does what on the job site can be surprising. Just because a plumber is there to install the sink does not mean he cuts the hole in the countertop to put the sink in. The electrician might arrive to connect the oven but may expect an installer to be on site to place the oven in the cabinet opening.

The key question is: Who is accountable to the client, and who is paying whom? There are several possible arrangements. Kitchen designers have varied success working with builders. Clearly, the simpler the project and the more detail on the designer's plan, the better the new construction project will go when the kitchen firm does not manage the installation. For complex custom projects, a successful conclusion to the project (getting paid on time, having the contractor refer another project to you, and having the client happy with your work) will occur only when the kitchen designer checks the project at the framing stage to ensure the construction, HVAC, and mechanicals are "as per plan" and also insists that their installation team complete the cabinet set and additional molding installation.

Step 2: Forecast the Installation Timeline for the Client

Installation can be worst part of the project for clients. It disrupts their life and is inconvenient and messy. It can also be stressful because clients fear that, once the project starts, the contractor (you) and subs won't be available to work or answer questions.

Many of today's television shows create unrealistic installation timeline expectations for consumers. By providing work schedules, introducing clients to your reliable subcontractors, and helping them to prepare for the construction phase, you will protect yourself from such misconceptions.

It's important to make sure your team alerts homeowners when no one will be on the job. Your clients may expect something to happen every day and will get nervous when nobody shows up and nothing is happening. If there is a schedule change or delay, be sure it is "SOP" (standard operating procedure) to let the client know right away and modify the project timeline accordingly.

You or a project manager should track all of your firm's projects under way. These timelines should be updated at regular daily or weekly meetings.

Develop a detailed schedule for the complete project and share it with your client. Show time frames for demolition (or deconstruction), framing, building inspections, rough work, cabinet and appliance installations, finish work, and completion. Indicate when subcontractors will be there and who they are. Allow extra time for scheduling delays, hidden conditions, custom work, add-ons, or more elaborate plans. There are many excellent electronic systems available online to assist you or your project manager to map out each stage.

Delivering the Cabinets to the Job Site

As you prepare the project timeline, consider humidity control and site conditions before scheduling the cabinet delivery.

What affects moisture in the house?

- Is the house located in a high-risk area, such as near water?
- Is the house under construction? If yes, are the windows installed or open much of the time?
- Are tradespeople still putting up drywall or painting in the house? Grouting the tiled floor? Cementing garage or basement floors? These construction activities increase the moisture content in the air.
- Is the home climate controlled? Is there air conditioning? Dehumidification?
- Where are the components of the new kitchen being stored during construction? In the basement? Garage? Was there new cement poured on this site?
- Is there an indoor pool or a hot tub close by?

What you can do to minimize the risk of wood expansion?

- Educate the homeowners explaining that a relative humidity level of at least 50 percent must be maintained all year round. This might require air conditioning in the summer and a humidifier in the winter.
- Deliver all cabinetry (especially molding) to the job site at least three days before installation. Then the wood parts can acclimate to the environment, which will minimize molding joints opening up after installation.
- If joints do open up during construction, insist on climate control measures prior to adjustments/replacements.
- Be prepared to remove doors/drawers and put them in a climate-controlled area until the site is controlled.

When should a kitchen be installed?

- Windows and doors have been installed.
- Drywall is completed.
- Flooring is installed (and protected).
- Painting is completed.
- Cement work is mostly cured. (This varies, based on humidity levels, from geographic area to geographic area and at different times of the year. Check with your general contractor.)
- Home is climate controlled.

If wood is negatively affected by moisture, or lack thereof, door warpage will occur. Door warpage requires costly and time-consuming product replacement.

Definitions

Positive Bow

A convex curve in the door (when the wood member bulges away from the frame) (see Figure 14.2).

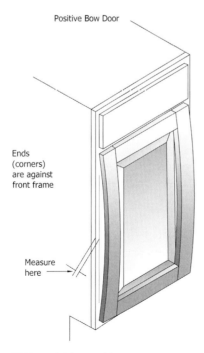

Positive Bow Door

Ends (corners) are against front frame

Measure here

FIGURE 14.2 A positive Bow.

(Courtesy of Conestoga Wood Specialties Corporation)

Negative Bow

When the cabinet door warps inwardly; a concave curve (see Figure 14.3).

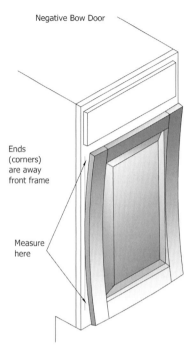

FIGURE 14.3 A negative bow.
(Courtesy of Conestoga Wood Specialties Corporation)

Twisted Door

When opposite corners twist away from the frame (see Figure 14.4).

FIGURE 14.4 A twisted door.
(Courtesy of Conestoga Wood Specialties Corporation)

Schedule

Many designers and production managers are fearful of committing themselves to specific dates for the project schedule—and for good reason. To the consumer one of the most frustrating elements of a project is the time it takes to complete the work. There are weather concerns, economic concerns, custom materials that need to be ordered, and other factors.

Mark Richardson, president of Case Design Remodeling Inc., suggests using the word "forecast" rather than "schedule" to help everyone understand the variable nature of the installation process (see the sample in Table 14.1).

Simply changing the language will not solve timing problems, but by providing a project forecast, you paint a more accurate picture for the client. In addition to the daily activity forecast or schedule, the client must understand:

- There will not be someone on the job site every day from 8:00 A.M. to 5:00 P.M. The nature of construction means free days (where no work takes place) are part of the process.
- Extended lead time between stone countertop templating and installation is the norm across North America.
- The payment schedule is part of the project forecast. Some punch list items, necessitating a separate job site work visit after "substantial completion," is to be expected.

Tips from the Masters

- If you have a question about a code, call or visit the inspector's office to get clarification. Or consult a contractor who has had experience with the code item—typically inspectors will not give advice due to liability concerns.
- Build time for inspection and reinspection into your schedule.
- Make sure it is clear who is responsible to wait at the job site for the inspector: you, one of the installers, or the owner or owner's agent. (If at all possible, a senior member of your team should be on site to welcome the inspector to ensure a clear understanding of any issues raised.)
- Check your work carefully. Your reputation will benefit from having your work ready and up to code. Inspectors get to know the better firms in their area. If they have no reason to believe you are going to try to slip something past them, they will work more closely with you.
- Get the inspector's name. Everyone likes to be addressed by name, and inspectors are no different.
- Be sociable—small pleasantries may help you establish an ongoing rapport with this professional.
- If the inspector flags (turns down) any part of the project, make sure you understand exactly what the violation is and what you must do to correct it. In some situations, the inspector may be wrong or the code may be vague. Be proactive and contact the appropriate department for clarification.
- Ask questions about future potential problems: Are there any areas of work coming up that you are not sure of? Take the time to ask about them while the inspector is on the job. You will be able to find out exactly what the inspector will be looking for when he or she returns to the job.

TABLE 14.1 An example of a project schedule chart.

PROJECT SCHEDULE

Project: _____
Calender Period: _____
Page _____ of _____

	Jan Wk 1					Feb Wk 2					Wk 3					Wk 4					Wk 5					Mar Wk 6					Wk 7				
Description Of Work	M 23	T 24	W 25	T 26	F 27	M 30	T 31	W 1	T 2	F 3	M 6	T 7	W 8	T 9	F 10	M 13	T 14	W 15	T 16	F 17	M 20	T 21	W 22	T 23	F 24	M 27	T 28	W 1	T 2	F 3	M 6	T 7	W 8	T 9	F 10
1 Deliver Cabinet/2nd Payment Due	×																																		
2 Remove Cabinet/Tops		×	×																																
3 Lay Out Kitchen On Floor				×																															
4 Rough Wiring					×	×																													
5 Rough Plumbing						×	×	×																											
6 Building Dept. Inspection									×	×																									
7 Patch Walls											×	×																							
8 Free Day/Clean Jobsite													×																						
9 Install Cabinets														×	×	×	×																		
10 Inspect With Client																	×																		
11 Template Granite																	×																		
12 Paint																		×	×	×	×														
13 Lay Vinyl Flooring																						×													
14 Install Moulding/Set Appliances																							×	×											
15 Free Days/Contingent Time																									×	×	×								
16 Install Granite																												×							
17 Trim-out Electrical																													×						
18 Hook-up Plumbing																														×					
19 Inspect With Client/3rd Payment Due																														×					
20 Touch-up Paint																															×				
21 Complete Punchlist																																×			
22 Clean Jobsite																																		×	

☒ = Projected

Step 3: Explain to Clients What to Expect during Remodeling

Provide clients with information on your website or a printed brochure on what to expect during the remodeling process. It is important for homeowners to understand that remodeling is not an exact science and that constant communication is vital. The introduction meeting is a good start, but there are a number of other issues to address with homeowners before the project begins.

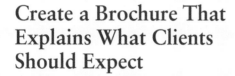

Step 4: Have Organized Collection and Staging Areas

You need an off-site staging area. Whether you have a warehouse or not, you need some organized way to gather products for a job before it begins and to receive those odds and ends that come in during the job. Without some type of staging area, time is wasted and that translates into money lost. Do not start a job until you have everything on hand.

Once on site, clearly define the actual work zone so the client, designer, and all installation professionals on site know which areas are off-limits and which spaces are accessible to crew members. It is also important to identify where delivered materials can be stored and where trash can be collected.

It is the responsibility of the project manager to prepare the client for the inevitable mess and up to the installation team to minimize it. An on-site planning meeting sets the stage for a successful project and helps determine how clients live and what precautions you should take in and around their home.

Our Craftsmen Are Coming . . .

The brochure should thank the clients for their order and for the opportunity to serve them. It should explain what clients can expect and what they can do to help make their project a pleasant experience. A brochure should contain the following information to help your client understand the process.

What to Expect

Designing a new project is great fun. Most people manage to focus on the future outcome while they endure the actual remodeling. But no one said it was easy!

The Job Is Starting!

You are excited and enthusiastic, but are you ready to deal with the disruptions to your home and your routine? If your project is extensive, you might consider moving out temporarily. If you are going to stay in the home, here are some strategies to help you through the experience.

- After the materials are ordered, your designer will schedule a pre-construction meeting at the job site with you and our project manager. Details such as where to place the lock box, store materials for the project and exchange messages will be discussed.
- Good communication prevents most problems, so make sure you agree on a system for staying in touch. The lead installer and project coordinator are usually the best contact people. Share your concerns as they arise. A minor adjustment early on might avoid a major expense later.

Do Not Panic!

If you discover a problem, get all of the facts, and then call your designer or project coordinator. Questions that do not need an immediate response can be left in the project binder. Problems are an inherent part of the remodeling process and we will work with you to alleviate your concerns and solve them as soon as possible.

Expect the project to feel like it is taking too long. There will be times—usually three to four weeks into a project—when it seems like not much is happening. During the first few weeks, there is a flurry of excitement following the demolition of your existing project and the creation of a new space. However, as we approach the fine details of the project, it is the quality of the work—not the speed—that will distinguish a [company's name] project.

Scheduling

About one month before delivery, our production manager will call to say which *week* you can expect delivery. Our production manager will call again to confirm the *day* of delivery.

Cabinets and other materials will be delivered to your home by van or semi-truck. You must provide a storage area until installation begins. Be sure to inform your insurance company (homeowner's policy) of this storage.

On the first day of installation, we will bring all the tools and materials that we will need for the work. Our production manager will contact you if there is any delay.

A typical project can take approximately eight to ten weeks from the time we arrive to start the work to substantial completion. This period can vary depending on the scope and complexity of the project. Small detail items may take longer. Please be aware, there will be days when no one is working at your job site. We will review the overall project schedule with you so that you are familiar with our plans. Our team arrives at approximately 7:30 A.M. and departs at 4:00 P.M.

Before Our Craftsmen Arrive . . .

- **Preparation Work.** Did you plan to do some of the preparation work yourself, such as removing old cabinets or flooring? Please check your contract. If any of this work is your responsibility, please have it completed before our installers arrive. This will avoid delays and/or extra labor charges.
- **Clearing the Decks.** If we are removing the existing kitchen, please remove everything you want to keep. Clear off the countertops and empty the cabinets. Even if you are only having new countertops installed, you should empty your cabinets because the work creates a lot of dust. Empty closets, too, if we have work to do in them.
- **Protect Your Valuables.** Paintings, hanging plants, knickknacks, anything

on your walls and adjacent walls should be moved to another room. Valuable antiques are irreplaceable and often fragile. We prefer not to move them. Please give them the care they deserve by making arrangements to have them moved in advance.

- **Debris.** Since all new cabinets have a protective wrapping, there will be an accumulation of cardboard, paper, and other debris. Old appliances and countertops may also be thrown away. More than likely, there will be a Dumpster placed on your property. Our production manager will determine with you the best location for this.
- **Safety.** We'll appreciate your cooperation in keeping everyone, including pets, out of the room being remodeled. Some of the adhesives are

toxic when wet, some cannot be removed from clothing, and power equipment and sharp tools are always dangerous when children are around. In addition, some products break easily when they are partially cut and fit. You will receive a better installation when all of the installers' attention can be concentrated on the work.

- **Contact Availability.** While it is not necessary for an adult to be present while work is in progress, we ask that you please place a permanent note beside your telephone where you can be reached. If an emergency occurs, we'll need to know how to reach you quickly. Lock boxes will be provided, if needed, so that our installers are able to enter your home if no one is present.

Before Our Craftsmen Arrive . . . —continued—

- **Dust Covers.** Sanding, sawing, and other preparation work creates dust. You may wish to cover furniture and other objects in rooms adjacent to the work area to protect them. Old sheets and inexpensive drop cloths are ideal for this.
- **New Construction.** New construction may leave plaster or drywall joint cement droppings on the floor. If your drywall or plaster contractor didn't clean up when he finished, please arrange to have it done before we begin.
- **The Installers.** Our installers are experienced and have received specialized training. Our product manager has reviewed your order for accuracy, has discussed it with the installers, and will have covered the details on your particular design. The installers are professionals and take pride in their knowledge and craftsmanship.
- **Leftovers.** On some products, we send a greater quantity to the job site for our convenience than what we've estimated for the job. The installers will return this excess to the warehouse. Normally, our installers remove all waste and debris for disposal. Please tell them if you want the waste pieces.

Things to Expect

- Most kitchen remodeling jobs require that water be cut off in part of the house during installation. Remember, dishes can be washed in the bathroom or laundry sink, though the use of paper plates tends to be the most hassle-free. Hot plates are convenient to use when your cooktop or range is out of working order. A little advance planning makes the inconvenience more tolerable.
- Our cabinets are high-quality construction, but doors, drawers, etc., are not given final adjustment at the factory. When our installer starts installing cabinets, you may notice some doors and drawers do not line up correctly. This is normal. The installer knows how to make adjustments in these situations. When installation is complete, he will ask you to inspect the job, and he will be happy to adjust any doors and drawers to your satisfaction. If a door or drawer is damaged in shipment and cannot be repaired on the job, we will gladly reorder the same item from the factory. This is your uniquely designed project and we want you to be pleased with it.
- Some scratches and splintering may occur if doors are shortened. Baseboards are vulnerable to damage when materials are fit to them. Our installers exercise the utmost caution, but some damage is inevitable. These chips, splinters, and scratches are not covered by your contract or warranty. Since they are usually of a very minor nature, most homeowners either touch them up or leave the marks until the next time the room is painted. We can recommend painters when you decide to repaint.
- **Change Orders.** During the remodeling process, you may decide to add a few additional items for our installation crew to complete. It is the perfect time with our people already on site and your lives already disrupted. Please be sure to have our lead installer prepare a change order for this work and note that it will add additional time to the project.

Water Leaks . . .

On most jobs, plumbing is disconnected, moved, and reconnected. Please check for water leaks several times following hook-up. Sometimes a leak is so slow that it may not be apparent until the following day. Your alertness will prevent water damage due to a sustained leak. If you do discover a leak, place a pan or bucket to catch the drip while you wait for the plumber. Please be sure that it is a leak, not just condensation, before calling.

After the Installation

- **Protect Your Investment.** Use the cleaning materials and methods recommended by the cabinet, counter, floor, appliance, and fixture manufacturers.
- **Appliance Literature.** All "use and care" booklets and warranties packed with your new appliances will be left inside the appliances. Read them carefully and file for future reference. If you need service on any appliance, you may call our office for the name and phone number of the factory authorized Service Company.
- **Moving Appliances and Furniture.** BE CAREFUL! Do not damage your new floor when moving objects over it. It is of utmost importance that heavy furniture or appliances not be dragged across floors. Heavy objects tend to settle into the floor somewhat. When you pull or push them, they are actually pushing against the slight dip of the top surface, which may cause damage.

While we have not touched on every item or obstacle that you will encounter during your project, we have tried to give you an overview of what to expect. Be patient and have faith in our crew to complete your project. The finished project will be worth the wait and serve you with years of enjoyment and beauty.

Again, thank you for your order; we look forward to working with you on your project in the future.

Tips from the Masters

Here are some questions to ask the client regarding staging the job:

- What hours can we work?
- What days can we work?
- What areas of the home do we need special permission to enter?
- Where is your security alarm system and how does it operate?
- Can we use a lockbox system during your project?
- If the home has wireless connectivity, may we access your wireless network? If not, is there a high-speed Internet line available to us in the work zone?
- Regarding children: What is their daily schedule? Who is responsible for them if they return home when parents are working?
- Are there any pet considerations?
- Are there any neighbor concerns?
- Where can we drop/store deliveries, notably the cabinets and/or crated, oversize bathroom fixtures?
- What do you want to salvage from demolition, and where do you want it stored?
- Where can we place the trash?
- Where can we place the portable toilet? Or which of your bathrooms can we use?
- Do you have snow removal service? How will plowing patterns affect the trash or storage areas?
- Where can we park our vehicles?
- Where can we post company signs?
- Where are your utilities (gas, electric, septic, communications) located?
- What furniture or shrubbery needs to be moved?
- What hours can we call you, and what numbers should we use (home, work, cell)?
- Can we install a phone/fax line for the duration of the project?
- How often do you want us to meet with/contact you?
- Do you understand our request that no family members or other unauthorized individuals spend time in the work zone and that all communication is best maintained between the designer or our appointed responsible project manager and the owner or your representative?
- What can we do to make the project more enjoyable for you?

Step 5: Conduct a Pre-construction Conference

The pre-construction conference with clients is an absolute necessity, especially for kitchen and bathroom remodeling projects. Hold it on site, immediately following the initial job site walk-through, and include the client, installers, subcontractors, and the designer/project manager.

At the conference, review the contract one more time to ensure that the client understands just what is and is not included. Because most clients have discussed a variety of options on a project, and compromises are often necessary to bring in a job on budget, it is easy for them to forget just what the specifications will be.

It is absolutely essential that the client make every selection for the project prior to or during the pre-construction conference. Many business owners/managers also insist all materials for the job be in stock or on site before work begins.

This meeting passes the chain of command from the designer to the project manager and the installer. If planning a lead installer model, make this clear to clients. They must understand that they will work with the lead installer rather than the designer. If a client continues to call the designer during the course of the project, the lead installer will not be able to take full control of the project or gain the respect of the client. Alternatively, the pre-construction conference gives the installation specialist an opportunity to thoroughly review the project with the designer/project manager and client.

In addition to instructing and explaining, the team needs to listen. Most clients have one or two pet peeves that concern them. One person might have concern about hammer marks on the trim but be completely oblivious to whether the wall insulation is installed properly. Another person might be concerned about air leakage or energy conservation. This does not mean that clients should set the standard of quality for installers, but it is advantageous to know what areas should receive extra care and attention if a client is to be satisfied.

The pre-construction conference establishes the line of communication among the firm, the installer, and the client. Good communication skills are important to the success of the project.

Where there is more than one client, designate one person to be the key decision maker and liaison to the firm's responsible project manager. This person should be responsible for handling payments and for initiating change orders.

Tips from the Masters
Sample Topics for Pre-construction Conference

- If there is a garage on the premises, set aside at least one bay for storage and staging of cabinetry, appliances, fixtures, and finishing materials.
- If there will be interior work, decide where the client's furniture, rugs, curtains, and other possessions will be stored. Discuss dust protection of adjoining rooms and disruption of the rest of the house. Advise that if a household member is allergic to dust; other living arrangements should be considered. Alternatively, the allergic person might move to a room on a floor unaffected by construction.
- When a kitchen is gutted and remodeled, there will be no working sink or appliances or even counter space. Find out where to temporarily locate the refrigerator. Possibly arrange to lend a hot plate and/or microwave oven to the client. Does the client wish to keep the removed cabinets, or will they be hauled away? (If the cabinets are the old, built-in-place type, which do not remove in one piece, make this clear to the client.) Give the client a clear picture of what will and will not be removed from the existing kitchen and what the completed space will look like. Impress upon the client the importance of emptying cabinets and removing valuable items prior to the start of the project.
- If a wall will be removed between the existing house and a new bump-out or addition, the timing of wall removal is of utmost importance to the client. Most installers try to enclose the bump-out or addition before tearing out, but this is not always possible. Keep the client informed about when the tear-out will occur. Opening up an existing house is just a construction project for an installer, but it is a heating, air conditioning, privacy, housekeeping, and security issue for the client.

(continued)

- Point out that any required matching (floor tiles, special molding, windows, doors, etc.) will match "as closely as possible from stock materials at existing local sources of supply." Even this phrase is subject to misunderstanding. Inform clients of potential differences, and encourage them to visit the supplier or view samples of what is available.

- Discuss everything, even the placement of electrical outlets. If the installer is working with designer's—(or architect's)—plans, all outlets should be shown and specified but should still be reviewed. Exact placement of outlets is important where appliances need to be connected or where the outlets are integrated into a tile backsplash with a pattern.

- Decide where to position a suspended light fixture. Will the junction box be centered on a bay window, the space, or to the anticipated location of a table? Electricians and installers often make this decision without consulting the client, leading to unexpected costs of moving it later, including a separate trip by the electrician, drywaller, and painter. "Who will pay for this?" can be a difficult discussion.

- Many clients have strong feelings about certain details, and they tend to assume that everyone working on the project shares their feelings. A client may plan to stain all trim and be astonished to find that the trim is finger-jointed. There is no way that the installation team, designer of record, or project manager can cover every possible area. However, close attention to past experiences, client comments, and the client's current living style are helpful in providing clues to areas of possible misunderstanding.

- For a bath remodel, make the client aware that there will be days during which it will be unusable. Assure the client of adequate notice and minimal downtime. The client should also understand that at the end of this period, the bathroom will be usable but not finished.

- When installing a bathroom on the second floor directly over a bathroom on the first floor, the plumber will have to tie-in below the sink on the first floor. Doing this requires opening up and patching the wall and painting the room or the affected wall. If only the wall is painted, it may or may not match the existing paint in the room. If this is not clarified, costs to repaint the entire room will be the subject of another unpleasant discussion about who will pay for it.

- Suggest changing all the accessible piping in a home with galvanized pipes to copper, CPVC (chrlorinated polyvinyl chloride), or PEX (cross-linked polyethylene) during construction. Point out that galvanized pipes rust from the inside out and ultimately clog. As the rust increases, the aperture gets smaller. When installing a new bath using the same horizontal galvanized pipes, there will be a noticeable drop in water pressure if more than one fixture is turned on. If you do not explain this, the client may understandably accuse the installation team of ruining the water pressure in the house and expect it to be corrected.

Each of the prior points are only a few of many possible misunderstandings illustrating the compelling need for a pre-construction conference. Forewarned is forearmed, and so a conference is a key part of a successful installation delivery system.

Step 6: Organize the Job Site
Project Binder

To ensure clear communication and to minimize down time, prepare a project binder, which remains at the job site at all times.

Documents to include:

- A map and written directions to job site; gate access information, if necessary
- Contract scope, omitting financial details
- Construction calendar
- Homeowner target dates for open selections
- Salvage report listing what to keep and where to put it
- Subcontractor list, with contact information and job scope details
- Cut sheets of materials, specifications, install sheets, product warranties
- Salesperson and homeowner's contact information, with email addresses and 24-hour emergency contact information
- Plans and elevations
- Permit and inspection reports
- Miscellaneous, such as receipts for homeowners
- Change order request forms
- Place for checks from homeowner

Step 7: Have a Plan to Manage
Change Orders

Any seasoned pro probably has horror stories in which they did not document changes and clients were surprised—perhaps even outraged—when the final bill was presented with the additional charges. In most cases, some type of negotiation followed, and the designer was never fully compensated for the changes requested by the owner. This is all because the changes were not documented step by step in a change order.

The purpose of a change order is to amend the original project specifications and documentation. Initiate a change order whenever a client requests goods or services outside those specified in the original proposal or whenever additional work must be performed because of the discovery of unknown, hidden construction contingencies. The installer, project manager, or designer can execute the change order, using an established format. Execute the change order and have it approved by the client in writing or via email before the work is completed. Part of the change order process is to make sure a copy is filed with the design firm's accounting department so that these changes are duly recorded and integrated into the payment schedule.

In new construction, the most profitable part of the sale for the builder or general contractor may be the "upgrades" or "changes" the homeowner requests. In the kitchen and bath design business, this is not the case. However, it is not uncommon for a change order item to carry a larger markup percentage than the full project markup because of the additional time it will take to execute the change as well as the additional risk/responsibility assumed by the designer or design firm as they "think through the entire project" to identify what parts of the project this change order impacts.

Whatever the markup factor is, most professionals agree that a deposit on the estimated work or the agreed-to price listed on the change order should be collected at the time of change order signing so the outstanding final payment never exceeds the final payment percentage established by the firm's business managers.

Change orders are so important that some firms will refuse to pay the designer's commission or additional charges listed on a subcontractor's or contract installer's bill if the proper change order process has not been followed.

Step 8: Expect a Punch List: Manage the List and the Client

Even though designers carefully explain all these types of technicalities and variables of a project, many seasoned professionals agree that problem jobs can still grow out of good jobs. Common reasons are:

- Imprecise communication from project manager to subcontractor/contract installer.
- Indecisive/incomplete preparation of punch lists with owner or owner's agent collaboration.
- Problems resulting from a disorganized job site, overscheduling with too many trades on the job at one time, and lack of respect for the client's existing property or the new materials being installed.
- A lack of urgency on everyone's part in completing punch list items. The items on this list are often simple initially but grow out of proportion as the client begins losing confidence in you and your team because the project just does not seem to get finished.

Clearly, the path to any profitable project is 100 percent accuracy in the design details, product specifying, measuring, and product ordering before the installation begins. In reality, once the installation starts, it may be quite evident that a 100 percent performance was not accomplished during the preparation for the project. Your commitment to excellence in communication and your expectation of professionalism from every person on the job site will make the difference. Creating an organized approach to managing the punch list is the best tool you can utilize to ensure the project is done on time, on budget, resulting in a happy client.

It is the designer's or project manager's responsibility to oversee the preparation of a list of items to be completed to the client's satisfaction. Here are some pointers from seasoned professionals.

- Focus on precise communication with clients. Maintain your business relationship with them through the end of the project. (You can become good friends later.) Make sure clients understand that some items on a punch list at the end of the project are to be expected. A punch list does not indicate poor workmanship. Make sure the clients understand that they have responsibilities in the preparation of the punch list, as do you and your craftspeople.
- Start the punch list early. Inspect the job site at several points, such as before the wall studding is closed in, just before the cabinets arrive, as soon as the cabinets are installed, and after the counters are in place. Keep a copy of the punch list in the job book.
- Talk to the client. Nothing will turn a good client sour faster than if days go by with no communication about the reordered parts or when the inspection will take place.
- Order replacements for missing items as soon as they are detected. Make sure you know where to ship these items if the location is different from where materials for a new job are accepted by your organization.

At the conclusion of the project, evaluate the punch list so that you can improve your presentation skills to clients and your project management abilities to help you avoid some of the following situations.

1. The consumer does not have a realistic expectation about product performance, wood species, door warpage, hand-applied glaze, the appearance of crown molding against an out-of-plumb ceiling, and so on. It is your job to make sure the client knows what they are going to receive before the product arrives. If the client's expectations are unrealistic, address their observation/complaint/question as soon as it is raised. Use industry standards to prove your case.
2. Products arrive damaged from the manufacturer or shipping company. It is the job of the job site installer, project manager, or other individual assigned to the site (or the warehouse manager's responsibility) to thoroughly inspect all products and note any defects immediately so that they can be repaired or replaced. Projects under the control of the designer being installed outside of your normal business area can be problematic. Experienced designers will visit a distant job site themselves or have a representative do so to receive and accept cabinetry delivery. Never leave this task to anyone on the job site who does not report directly to your firm.

Tips from the Masters

- Prepare a punch list once and then work against it. The client signs off on each item to ensure understanding and agreement.

- Start the punch list in one corner of the room and then move in a full circle around the space so that nothing is overlooked. Always look for one item that you know needs to be replaced or repaired and point it out to the clients so they are comfortable with you as the inspector on the project.

- If clients raise an objection that is not realistic such as a pebble-size imperfection in a stucco wall surface, or a worm tracking mark in a maple veneer, address the product quality level immediately. If necessary, use industry documentation to demonstrate that the product, as delivered, is within industry standards.

- Travel with portable construction lights in your car, because often designers meet with clients in the evening at the job site when there is no electricity or lighting in the room under construction. Keep in touch with your clients. Keep them informed as to progress. If any of the costs associated with items on the punch list are better categorized as change orders, provide a copy of the change order to clients. If there is any disagreement, handle it now so there are no surprises when the final bill is presented.

- When working on large, luxury projects, always include a punch list contingency fund dollar amount in your estimate, so if the client doesn't like one particular door on the job, you don't have to argue about the wood specification. You can replace the door, make the client happy, and protect your profits.

- Have a special area in your warehouse for any items received for a project that is in progress. All too often, small boxes arriving with hardware or another roll of wallpaper or a small under-cabinet light can get lost in a warehouse filled with large cabinet orders awaiting delivery. Have a special racking system by the front door of the warehouse that is divided into bins. Clip a label on the bin identifying the job name and number. Inspect any replacement material before storing in the bins. Send an email from the warehouse to the designer each time a replacement item arrives so both the warehouse staff and the designer in charge of the project can keep track of what has arrived. This makes it easier for the designer, who is responsible for all ordering, to double-check with a manufacturer/supplier if something misses its scheduled delivery time.

- If there are several items on the list, separate the punch list into each area of the house and for each source or manufacturer. You don't want the cabinet manufacturer to have to wade through your list of touch-up points for the plumber or the painter.

- Follow a routine. Update all punch lists at the end of the week on every project. Start checking with manufacturers, installers, or subcontractors on Thursday to make sure you have the correct update material for the punch list. Doing this makes it easier to schedule service work for the following week.

- Have a clear policy around punch lists and the installers on your team: no punch list/no specific information = no pay to the installer and no future jobs. Until clients sign off that the job is complete to their satisfaction, no final payments should be made to installers.

3. Items were ordered incorrectly, overlooked, or are incorrect because a change was made. Key areas of concern here are:
   - Incorrectly ordered molding.
   - Decorative hardware never ordered when the cabinets were ordered.
   - Appliance selections changed after the cabinet order was placed, resulting in appliance panels arriving at the job site that do not fit the final selection.
   - Decorative brackets or other architectural accoutrements that are shown on the plan, but never ordered by the designer.
4. Job site damage. Everyone visiting or working on the job site needs to be aware of how delicate materials are and how costly it is to repair/replace damaged product if a careless installer places a tool belt on a new counter or a ladder falls against a stainless steel appliance. Steps needed to minimize a punch list include:
   - Sweeping a job site clean every night.
   - The design firm managing a staging area in the garage or adjacent living space.
   - Installation team members (whether a direct employee, subcontractor or contractor) respecting each other's work.
   - A design firm providing proper dust barriers, drop cloths, and other protective coverings.

Step 9: Train Everyone on Your Team in "People Management"

Regardless of how hard you try, sometimes a frustrated client will get angry with you. Successful business owners, designers, project managers, and installers have a strategy in place to follow when clients are upset about the progress of a project, disappointed in an element of a project, or are just difficult people.

The most important first step in people management is to identify whether the distress is related to the relationship or to the project process.

Relationship-Related Distress
- Have all promises been kept relating to the project?
- Was something said to clients that could be perceived as rude or discourteous, or as indicating someone is not listening to their concerns?
- Do clients feel they might have made a mistake in choosing your design firm?
- Were you or anyone else on the job site argumentative or defensive with clients?
- Could a family disagreement or an unrelated household incident have sparked the client's unhappiness?

Project Process–related Distress
- Were all client design, product, and installation expectations met?
- Are the clients frustrated about the renovation or building process in general? Are they upset with other subcontractors on the project and is that rubbing off on you?
- Have clients been given false or misleading information? (It does not matter whether they were misled purposely or not.)
- Are the clients discouraged with the lack of progress on the project?
- Is the job site messy? Are clients' possessions and home protected as well as they could be?

Any one of these experiences can lead clients to be dissatisfied with an element of a project. In reality, the problem is not the product or project; it is the relationship or process they have with you.

SUMMARY

The designer of record must be equally as responsible as the business owner to the success of the project. Careful detailing of client requests, proper project documentation, and a keen understanding of the basics of woodworking as it relates to the industry are foundational knowledge for all designers. Being a team player is also a substantial contributor to success.

REVIEW QUESTIONS

1. State the difference in the responsibilities for:
   A. Designer of Record
   B. Co-designer
   C. Design Associate/Assistant (See "Managing the Client and the Project" pages 314–316)
2. List the six job site criteria used to determine if a project location is suitable for the delivery of wood cabinetry for storage. (See "Delivering the Cabinets to the Job Site" page 316)
3. Name five "Tips from the Masters" that help foster a positive business relationship between the designer of record/project manager and building officials responsible for issuing permits or job site inspections. (See "Tips from the Masters" page 319)
4. Restate why a pre-construction conference is critical in successful project management. (See "Conduct a Pre-construction Conference" page 324)

Industry Standards for Molding Order Procedures and Cabinet Installation

Designing a beautiful kitchen is only the beginning of creating a room the cook and family members can enjoy. Design professionals must also be familiar with accepted cabinet installation methods, as well as proper ordering procedures for decorative molding.

This chapter includes a system used by practicing professionals for ordering decorative molding, as well as a pictorial review of the methods used to install kitchen cabinetry. Professional designers can use the molding ordering information to correctly estimate the lengths of decorative materials needed. This information will prevent added expense incurred when the proper number of molding lengths are not on the job site at the start of the project. The detailed cabinet installation information also provides design professionals with the information required to supervise cabinetry installations.

Both of these topics are critical to protect the profits planned for a project.

Learning Objective 1: Describe the cabinet installation process.

Learning Objective 2: Explain methods used to align cabinets.

Learning Objective 3: State why it is important to determine the floor high point.

Learning Objective 4: Describe why a molding order is not completed by simply measuring the lineal footage of wall space.

ORDERING MOLDING

One of the most common mistakes made when ordering cabinets and decorative moldings is miscalculating the quantity of molding lengths needed to complete the project. When cabinet parts are missed on the order, ordered incorrectly, or not ordered in sufficient quantity, a great deal of time and money is wasted during the reorder process (see Figures 15.1 and 15.2).

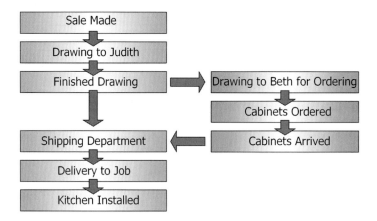

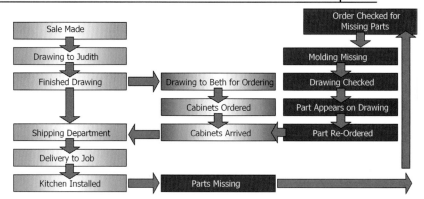

FIGURE 15.1 When something is missed, this is what can happen.
(Courtesy of David Newton, CMKBD)

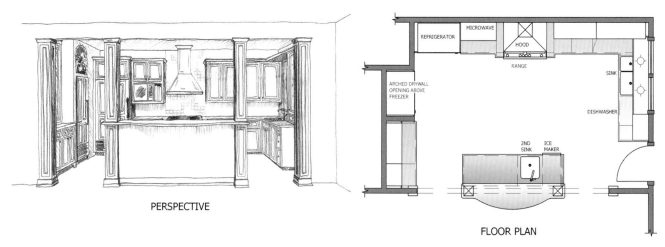

PERSPECTIVE

FLOOR PLAN

FIGURE 15.2 Ordering molding.
(Courtesy of Ellen Cheever, CMKBD, ASID and Jeffrey Holloway, CKD, CBD)

Joseph Matta of Masterwork Home shares his years of experience about the best way to lay out a molding plan for a kitchen or bath and calculate the proper lengths of moldings (see Step 1, Step 2, and Step 3). He breaks the plan down into six steps.

Step 1. Identify the projection of molding and lengths of molding available.

Determine usable length of molding based on manufacturer's specifications.

Select one corner to begin the molding length calculation.

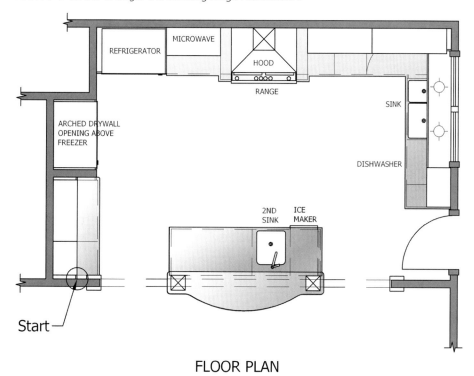

FLOOR PLAN

STEP 1 Select one corner to begin the molding length calculation; identify the projection of molding and lengths of molding available.

Step. 2. Add the lengths needed, rounding up to the next full foot.

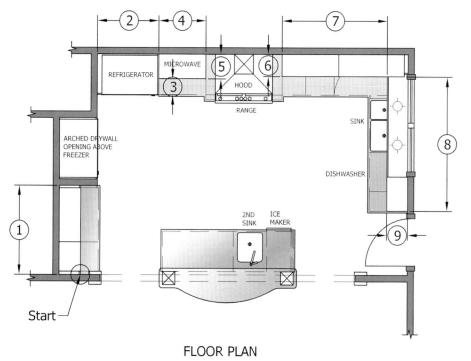

FLOOR PLAN

1. 54 1/2"	or	60"
2. 39 1/4"	or	48"
3. 9 3/4"	or	12"
4. 30"	or	36"
5. 15"	or	24"
6. 13 1/2"	or	24"
7. 67"	or	72"
8. 82 1/4"	or	84"
9. 13 1/2"	or	24"

STEP 2 Add the lengths needed

Step 3. Start with the longest length required; add the various lengths to determine the total number of pieces required from the proceeding step.

Step 4. Consider the wood selection.
Are there any molding splice joints? If so, add one length.

Does the wood specie graining require some wood sorting? If so, add at least one additional length.

Does the wood's finish vary to the point some selection will be necessary at mitered corner joints? If so, add a length.

Step 5. Allow for job site mistakes. Add an extra length.

Step 6. Explain to the client that you will allow for ordering extra molding to compensate for loss due to cuts, miters, damaged ends, or questionable grain/color continuity. Decide whether you're going to leave this molding on the job or return it to your stock.

HOW TO INSTALL KITCHEN CABINETS

The cabinet installation begins at the job site weeks or even months before the cabinets arrive and the dimensions are double-checked. The installation continues when someone inspects the job site again before installing the drywall. At this point, verify that the mechanicals, HVAC, and framing are as per plan. This step is critical on new construction projects to make sure workers follow the plan exactly. Measurement verification is necessary at this stage of new construction because it is common for windows to be 3" off or a wall to be perhaps as much as 4½" out of place. To avoid problems when the cabinets arrive, measure the entire site again and verify that the cabinets will fit as planned before closing in the room.

The installation draws closer with the delivery of the cabinets to the design firm's warehouse and/or the job site and a careful "transfer of title" takes place. Ideally, numbers on the outside of the packages coincide with numbers on the elevation and/or floor plan. The truck driver and the installation manager responsible for the project check the cabinets off as they arrive, inspecting each for damage and verifying the received items against an order acknowledgment and/or packing list.

The installation continues as the cabinets (boxed, shrink-wrapped, or blanket-wrapped) enter storage in a climate-controlled, safe area on the job site, protected from any damage that may occur as work progresses onsite.

The installation process continues when the installer arrives onsite and begins putting the cabinets in place.

Step 1. Review the floor plan at the job site, marking each cabinet off on the wall and/or the floor to verify once again that the mechanicals, HVAC, and framing are as per plan. This is a good time to stand back and evaluate your plan details one more time. Do you need to shift a filler for better balance, or modify a rollout shelf to accommodate the sink waste line rough-in? If there is a large, complicated island in the space, creating a template of the island in, (a) and (b) addition to verifying the mechanical rough-ins stubbed out of the floor is recommended. Installation experts consider this cabinet check and layout review a critical part of a successful installation. Last, establish the cabinet delivery route through the house, checking doorway widths and any tight corner turning radius.

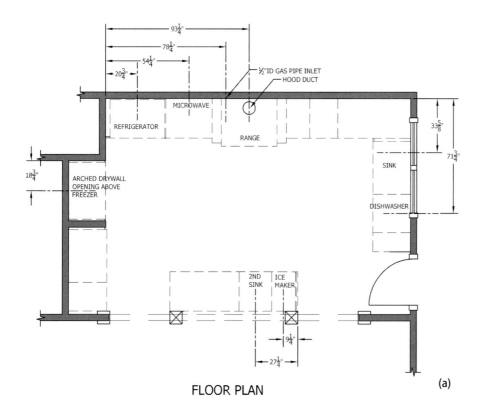

FLOOR PLAN   (a)

Perspective of Cabinetry Tracing

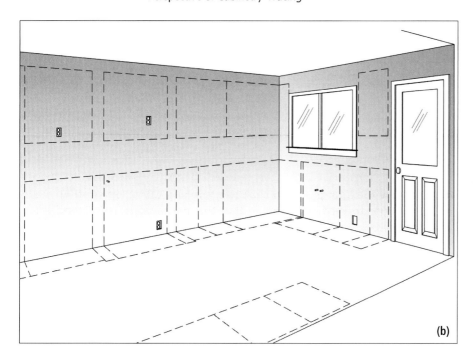

(b)

STEP 1, (a) and **(b)** Review the floor plan and cabinetry layout

STEP 2 Check the plans to make sure the correct cabinets have been delivered, and secure the room.

Step 2: Secure the work area

Step 3 (a, b, and c): Identify any out-of-plumb or out-of-level surfaces the cabinets will be installed against or upon. Check the floor level by measuring out 18" (457 mm) from the wall for vanity cabinets and 21" (533 mm) for normal kitchen cabinets. Use a straight edge and/or a long level to determine the high point in the floor. Many projects will have the high point of the room in a corner, as this is typically the place least likely to have settled. If this is the case, there may be so much drop at the front edge of the cabinets that the installer must scribe the back bottom edge of the base cabinets or shim up the front edge to meet the highest spot in the room. Be aware that some cabinets with toe kicks that are edge banded with flake board may hold up better if they are not cut for scribing.

On some projects, where the finished floor is installed before the cabinets, it must be completely protected before this work begins. If there is no finished flooring installed, double-check the overall thickness of the substrate as well as the finished floor. You may need a built-up substrate if all of the cabinets must be shimmed up so that the finished floor can continue into a recess for an under-counter appliance. This step is critical so that the appliance is not locked in and impossible to remove for service or replacement.

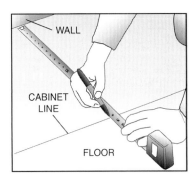

STEP 3(a) Check the floor level by measuring 18" from the wall for vanity cabinets and 21" for kitchen cabinets.

STEP 3(b) Determine the high point of the floor.

STEP 3(c) Plan on shimming the cabinets up or scribing the cabinets down to accommodate the floor high point.

Step 4: Transfer the high floor level mark to the wall and snap a plumb line at 34½" (876 mm) off the finished floor. Or set the laser to 34½" (876 mm) off the floor to determine the high and low spots. This tells the installer at what height the cabinets actually will be installed to ensure they are level at the normal countertop finished height of 36" (914 mm).

STEP 4 Transfer the high level mark to the wall and snap a plumb line at 34½" off the finished floor or set the laser to 34½" off the floor to determine the high and low spots.

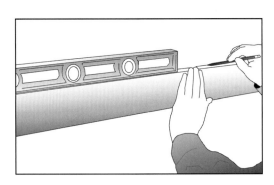

Step 5: Mark base or mid-high cabinet heights other than a standard 34½″ (876 mm): for example, a raised dishwasher installed at a 54″ (1,372 mm) height or a mid-height oven cabinet installed at 60″ (1,524 mm).

Step 6: Repeat the same "find the high point" exercise at the ceiling—finding the lowest spot on the ceiling wherever installing tall cabinets. This is of critical importance if cabinets will be installed to the ceiling. In the worst-case scenario, an out-of-plumb subfloor with a dramatic high point combined in a room with an out-of-level ceiling and a low point spells disaster if 96″- (2,438 mm) high units are trying to squeeze into a room with 96″- (2,438 mm) high ceilings. Reduce the toe kick on the tall units to accommodate such an out-of-square room.

Step 7: Based on the backsplash dimensions, mark another cabinet level for the wall cabinets; this may vary from 60″ (1,524 mm) above the finished 36″- (914 mm) high standard countertop to 24″ (610 mm) above that dimension.

Step 8. Use a straightedge to determine the high and low spots along the back wall surface. This dimensioning will direct where you will need shims behind cabinets to provide a flush face and a level surface.

Step 9. If cabinets fit between walls or turn a corner, check the corners with a framing square. Doing this enables you to adjust cabinets and countertops with a scribe that compensates for a tight wall, or finish with a filler to accommodate an out-of-square corner. Typically, the misalignment will be confined to the corner area, and the wall will not continue to run out of square its entire length. Be aware that the drywall compound used to finish the corner joint can cause a false read on a corner. Sometimes more accurate dimensions can be found near the floor, where the drywall compound is not present. It may also be necessary to set up a 3,4,5 triangle to test a larger area for squareness and get away from the corner for a better fit.

STEP 9 Determine the squareness of corners that cabinets will be placed against.

Here is how you use the mathematical equation to determine the squareness of a corner, and, if it is out of square,(i.e., if the corner is less than 90 degrees or more than 90 degrees):

1. Starting in the corner, measure out of the corner along one wall to a dimension of 36″ (914 mm). Mark the wall with pencil.
2. Return to the corner and measure out of the corner 48″ (1,219 mm) along the second wall. Place a mark at this point.
3. Measure the distance between these two marks. If the corner is square, the dimension between the two pencil marks will be 60″ (1,524 mm). If the dimension is less than 60″ (1,524 mm), the corner angle is less than 90 degrees and fillers will need to be cut down in width. If the dimension is more than 60″ (1,524 mm) inches, the corner angle is more than 90 degrees and fillers may need to be added or cabinet widths increased.

Step 10. Locate the wall studs. The floor supports base cabinets if they have attached toe kicks, or if they sit on a prefabricated subbase. Fasten the wall cabinets directly to the studs, or use a hanging strip that is first attached to the walls, with the wall cabinet then cantilevering off this strip. See Step 18 for an option to consider when installing against a finished wall.

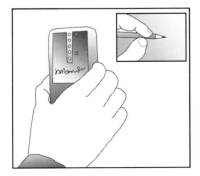 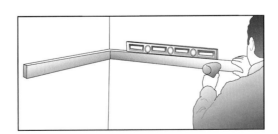

STEP 10 Using an electronic stud finder makes the process easier and more accurate. You can attach a hanging strip before securing the cabinets.

Tips from the Masters

Industry experts vary in their recommendations regarding what to install first: the base cabinets or the wall cabinets. Talk to your installation experts to ascertain their preference. The key to a satisfied client is protecting each cabinet after installation. This outline continues with the assumption that you will install the base cabinets first.

Step 11. Provide support for countertops for special cabinet considerations. Corner lazy Susan base cabinets normally have a clipped back corner, allowing them to be moved through normal interior door widths. Therefore, the back wall will need to be "cleated" so that the countertop is supported. This may also be required behind an opening for a cooktop/range top, behind the wall for a dishwasher or other appliance. It becomes of critical importance if oversize or unusually heavy countertop materials are being used. Special partial walls or other supports may be required for countertop overhangs, open shelf systems, or extended valance panels.

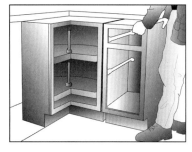

Step 12. Move the cabinets into the room and position. Start in a corner. Remove skids from under toe kicks. Remove doors and drawers and protect. Most installation specialists believe the one exception to this rule is for inset cabinet doors: The doors remain on the cabinet so that the installer can verify the door alignment during the installation process. If doors remain on the cabinet, take extra time to protect them from damage. Cover them, particularly if they are cherry wood and there is direct sunlight close by.

STEP 12 Move the cabinets into the room and position, starting in a corner. Remove doors and drawers and protect.

Framed and frameless cabinetries are similar, yet each has unique features. The process of installing framed cabinetry is a little more forgiving than for frameless cabinets. Install both plumb and level. Frameless units are more likely to rack if not shimmed and properly braced to avoid the twisting action caused by the tightening of screws where voids occur. Install the doors on the cabinets just before the final tightening of screws in the hanging strips. Doing this will immediately reveal any racking, so you can correct the situation before it becomes severe.

Step 13. For typical cabinets with a subbase (toe kick), align and shim a corner cabinet as necessary to ensure it is plumb. For decorative cabinets with furniture feet or columns/cabinet stiles extending to the floor, the original design should provide some means to modify the height. For example, decorative feet may incorporate a square scribing portion on the underside of the foot. It is cut to fit an unleveled floor or is removed completely if a level floor surface exists. Decorative molding can cover space resulting from an uneven floor between the floor and a shimmed column. If no such design adjustment exists, hold a job site conference to decide how to lower the cabinet without compromising the height required for adjacent appliances.

Use a clamping device to hold adjacent cabinets together while installing the proper screws.

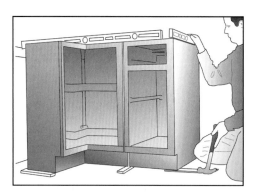
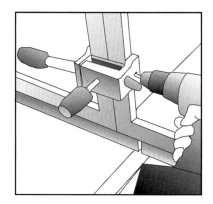

STEP 13 Align and shim a corner cabinet to ensure it is plumb. Use a clamping device to hold adjacent cabinets together.

A master installer uses proper screws and the proper tools to install cabinets, with the necessary force (just enough, but not too much) to avoid splitting the face frame. The master installer then pulls adjoining cabinets together with screws. To do this:

1. Drill starter hole approximately 6" (152 mm) from the top and bottom of face frame.
2. Insert and tighten screw.
3. After hanging, joining, aligning, and shimming all base and wall cabinets, tighten screws in the hanging strips.

Step 14. When shims are required at the back wall, place them directly over a stud. Then drill a pilot hole and screw the shim to the wall. Never use nails to fasten cabinets together or to secure cabinets to walls.

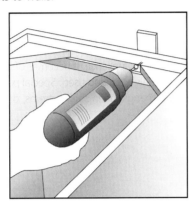

STEP 14 Drill a pilot hole and screw the shim to the wall. Never use nails to fasten cabinets together or to secure cabinets to walls.

Step 15. Cabinets that finish against a wall, against another cabinet that is deeper than the unit, or that meet one another in corners will require extended stiles or scribes (fillers). A scribing or filler strip allows the installer to attach an extra strip of cabinet finish material to the case and then fit it against an out-of-plumb wall. The filler is normally set flush with the case, with a decorative panel placed on the front of the filler. This decorative panel will include a detailed edge echoing the finish on the door in custom cabinet work. In stock cabinet work, the filler normally blends with the door finish but is a piece of plain wood or cabinet material set flush with the case. Alternatively, the filler can be an L-shape or U-shape element that has no detail but that can be set flush with the door.

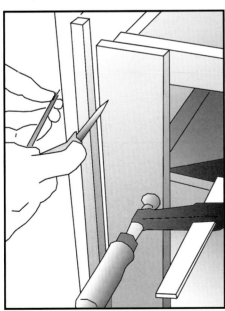
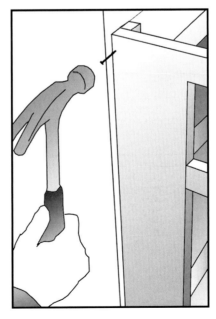

STEP 15 A scribing, filler strip, or extended stile allows the installer to finish the cabinet elevation against a wall. A marking compass and clamp are used to scribe the filler. A marking compass and clamp are used to scribe a filler.

Tips from the Masters

Trim the filler with a bevel cut, tapered away from the wall by several degrees, and add a $\frac{1}{32}$" to the width of the filler. Doing this allows the sharp edge of the filler to embed into the drywall and take away any slight imperfections in the cut or wall.

STEP 16 Use plywood or the cardboard containers to protect the base cabinets.

To scribe a filler, start by setting a marking compass to the width of the gap. Then place a strip of $\frac{1}{2}$"- (13 mm) wide masking tape along the filler board in the area where it needs to be trimmed. Clamp the board to the end face frame of the cabinet, and trace the wall contour with the compass. Remove the board, and cut along the scribed line with a jigsaw. The scribe will now mirror the wall dimension.

Step 16. Now cover the base cabinets for safety. This is a must. One of the main causes of scratches and indentations on base units is the installer's belt buckle or tape measure. *Be aware!* Install temporary plywood countertops or recycle the cardboard the cabinets came in to protect the cabinetry and provide a place for the installers to set their tools as they install the wall cabinets.

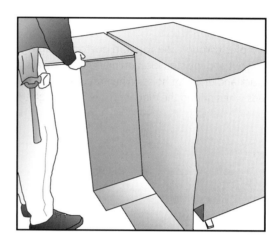

Step 17. Now the installation moves to the tall and wall cabinets. If the design includes tall cabinets and the tops are to be at the same height as wall cabinets, install the "talls" just after the base units. They will then determine the precise height of the wall units.

A team of two installers is most efficient, but individual installers can work by bracing the wall or by using special tools designed to temporarily hold a wall cabinet in place while the installer secures the unit to the wall. Sometimes a hanging strip supports the wall cabinets. If the cabinets are to be installed against a finished wall, such a plan will compromise the wall finish. A better alternative is to cut strips 1" × 2" (25 mm × 51 mm) strips 19½" (495 mm) (for an 18" splash height), tapping them into the wall at the countertop height. The cabinets can then rest on these strips, or legs, until they are adjusted and screwed into place.

Normal base cabinets finish at 34½" (876 mm) tall and are then topped by a 1½"- (38 mm) thick countertop, making the finished base cabinet 36" (914 mm) off the finished floor. Backsplash height dimensions range from 15 to18" (381 to 457 mm) high in U.S. cabinet manufacturing standards. International cabinet standards often call for a 16" to 24" (406–610 mm) backsplash area. Therefore, there is no industry standard. The elevation plans must clearly note what the backsplash dimension is from the top of the finished countertop to the bottom edge of the wall cabinet. It is important to have good elevations with accurate measurements and details so the installer knows what the designer is thinking.

STEP 17 Install a hanging strip to support wall cabinets during the installation.

Although splash heights vary, determine the distance from any cooking surface to the underside of the ventilation hood by local codes and the appliance manufacturer's specifications. Do not specify this height or agree to any job site change recommendations without first verifying distances dictated by the building authorities or the manufacturer.

Step 18. Much like base cabinet installation, wall cabinet installation starts in a corner. Wall cabinet corners may have a diagonal front, which requires fillers on either side to ensure the diagonal door can swing clear of adjacent units. Alternatively, a square corner cabinet occupying 24" (610 mm) of wall space in each direction (called a pie cut cabinet) may be used. Or a blind corner cabinet may be installed on one wall, extending into the corner, with a second wall cabinet (separated by a scribe to ensure handle clearance) fitting against this cabinet at a 90-degree return. When installing a blind corner cabinet, some manufacturers leave the blind portion open so it appears to omit a door. Closing this blind area off with light-grade plywood or a panel will keep the owner's items from falling into the void left after installing the adjoining cabinet. The last typical option is to install two wall cabinets at right angles to one another (separated by fillers and/or scribes) or finished against a boxed-in corner arrangement.

STEP 18 Much like a base cabinet installation, wall cabinet installation also starts in a corner.

Step 19. Before lifting any upper cabinets into place, the installation specialist normally predrills screw holes through the top and bottom hanging rails of the cabinet. Following the cabinet layout and the stud location marks on the walls, transfer the measurements to the cabinet back and drill pilot holes. When used properly, this system ensures that the installer will hit studs when driving the mounting screws through the finished back of the cabinet, passing through the hanging rail and the drywall to the stud behind.

STEP 19 Proper planning will ensure that cabinet backs are drilled correctly to hit the wall studs.

Step 20. The sequence for installing wall cabinets resembles the sequence used for base cabinets. Some installers assemble groups of upper cabinets as a single unit; other specialists prefer to hang each unit individually. A bar clamp is used to hold adjacent cabinets together and fasten loosely. The face frames remain aligned, flat, level, and plumb. Such alignment is critical; any twist in the cabinet box or case will affect the fit of the doors.

Step 21. When the last upper cabinet is secure, install all soffit or molding treatments. Then reinstall the shelves, interior accessories, and doors on the cabinets. Next, drill for the decorative hardware if the manufacturing facility did not. Although it is easier to lay out hardware on the back of the door, drilling from the back may cause a "blowout" as the drill bit exits the face side of the cabinet. Clamp or hold a block on the face side of the door/drawer to reduce the likelihood of this happening, or drill from the front of the panel.

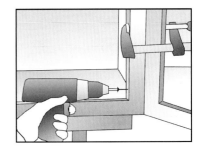

STEP 20 Use a bar clamp to hold adjacent cabinets together so the face frames remain aligned, flat, level, and plumb.

The elevation plans must clearly call out the exact location of the hardware. For example, a pullout wastepaper basket cabinet probably will have the pull located in the center of the door, while other doors will have the pull opposite the hinge side. In many kitchens, drawers and doors feature different hardware. For some cabinet styles, the width of the stiles and rails determines hardware placement. Any mistakes are costly and necessitate replacing full drawers and/or doors.

Tips from the Masters

Never leave the job site with doors out of alignment. If the doors are put back on the cabinets, adjust them before you leave. Otherwise, clients undoubtedly will call you complaining the cabinets and doors are crooked.

Step 22. Once the cabinet set is completed, methodically move around the room to adjust all door hinges and all drawer hardware to align the doors and drawers. At this time, putty any holes and/or finish touch-ups. Vacuum all cabinets, inside and out, and wipe with a damp tack cloth before the client inspects them.

STEP 22 (a) and **(b)** After the cabinet set is complete, adjust all the door hinges and drawer hardware. Make sure all the doors are aligned properly.

Step 23. Sweep the entire job site clean and dispose of all trash daily. Keep protective coverings on the cabinetry. Remember, clients waited weeks, if not months, for the cabinets to arrive and made substantial payments on the project to date. Their first impression about the fit and finish of the cabinets can make a dramatic difference in how they perceive the overall quality of the job.

SUMMARY

Industrial standards for the procurement of moldings and the installation of cabinetry must be understood and followed by all team members. This chapter outlined the procedures for such work.

REVIEW QUESTIONS

1. What is another name for an extended stile? (See "Step 15" page 341)
2. List three reasons to allow for ordering extra molding. (See "Step 6" page 336)
3. Describe the conditions that require scribing, filler strips, or extended stiles. (See "Step 15" page 341)

Index

Abrams Research, 244
Account Edge Pro, 73, 74
accountants, 71, 73, 76, 85–86,
    91, 92,
accounting, 11, 67–68, 70, 73, 85
accounts payable, 9, 71–72
accounts receivable, 9, 71–72, 97, 102,
    105, 114
accrual method, 70, 71, 86, 98, 110
action plan spreadsheet, 31–32
advertising, 209, 211, 215–217, 221,
    225, 237–238, 240, 243, 245,
    248, 258
advisory board, 65–66
agreements, 44, 48, 50, 59, 74–75,119,
    122–123, 135, 150, 190, 272–273,
    275–278
apprentice, 313
assets, 9, 59, 72, 95, 97, 105, 121
at–will employment, 189
audits, 76, 135, 149

backsplash, 261, 264, 299, 306–37, 326,
    342, 346
balance sheet, 9, 40, 72, 80, 85–87,
    95–97, 110
bankruptcy, 123
base wage, 152
Bella Domicile, 230–232
benefits, 48, 125–127, 136, 142–143,
    152–153, 155, 157, 170–171, 182,
    189–190
blogging, 245
bookkeeper, 71, 76, 85, 91,
bookkeeping, 3, 68–70,
bottom line, 73, 106, 110, 132
    See also net profit
branding, 230, 235
Brown, Jr, H. Jackson, 123
budget, 77, 80, 98, 108, 217–218, 260
budget spreadsheet, 80

building permits, 262, 268, 271, 321
business insurance planning worksheet,
    128
business interruption insurance, 124
business management system,
    274–275
business model, 15
business plan, 35–36, 45
business strategy, 25, 26
buying groups, 63–64

cabinets, 260–263, 277, 280, 287, 299,
    300–311
C corporation, 38, 47
Canada Deposit Insurance Corporation
    (CDIC), 65
Canada Revenue Agency, 46, 47, 55, 60,
    65, 149
capital, 10, 119, 133
car expense, 134
Casey, Leonard V., 20–21
cash disbursements, 70, 72
cash flow, 57, 76, 86, 99–102
cash flow analysis, 40, 85, 98
cash flow statement, 80, 86, 101
cash method, 70
CDIC, 65
certificate of occupancy, 264
chamber of commerce, 34, 64, 65, 74,
    77, 124
change order, 278, 327–328
chart of accounts, 80, 85–87, 91,
check–and–balance, 71
classified advertisements, 160–161
COBRA, 190
codes, 121, 140, 268, 271, 277, 321, 346
collateral, 57, 59,
color variations (wood), 319–311, 339
commission, 152, 154, 156
company lead register, 265
compensation, 151–152,

competency models, 145
competitive analysis, 38
compressed workweek, 181
construction, 121, 260–262, 265, 268,
        271–274, 276–277, 282, 293, 301,
        316, 319, 322–331, 340
co-op, 221
co-op monies, 39
copyright, 123
corporations, 45, 47–48, 50, 73, 81, 92
cost of goods sold (cogs), 73
cost plus pricing, 279–280
credit rating, 57
creditors, 72
crown molding, 303, 306, 330
current ratio, 105
custom quotation method, 280
customer base, 10
customer service, 3, 224–225, 230–232

debt, 115
deductions, 131, 132, 133–134
demographic profile, 51–52,
DePalma, Nora, 244
depreciation, 55
design/build firm, 16
design associate, 313
design survey, 276
designer of record, 313
designer's studio, 15
disability insurance, 125
disciplinary procedures, 188
disclaimers, 123 –125, 261,
distribution channel, 25
dividends, 48
domain name, 18
door alignment, 343, 347
Door stability, 306
double taxation, 48–49
double–entry system, 71
draw, 154–155
Dunn & Bradstreet, 9

EBIDA, 98
economies of scale, 126
elevations, 261, 277, 293, 299–306
employee skills inventory, 145–146
employment contracts, 158
entrepreneurial innovation assessment, 5–8
Equal Employment Opportunity (EEO), 162
errors and omissions, 121, 125
estimating, 260, 272, 276, 278, 281–283,
        285, 292
excise taxes, 132
executive summary, 35, 37
exempt employees, 150–152

exit strategy, 17
expense journal See also cash
        disbursements 70
expenses, 81, 92

Facebook, 235, 246
factory direct, 18
Fair Labor Standards Act (FLSA), 151
FDIC, 65
federal income tax, 136
federal reserve bank, 65
federal taxes, 132
Fields, Debi Rose, 2
filler strip, 299, 301, 303, 305, 340, 342,
        345–346
financial ratio analysis, 103
financial statement, 103
fire insurance, 125
fiscal year, 71, 77, 86
five–year business statement, 30, 33
fixed assets, 95
fixed expenses, 92
fixtures, 260, 268, 272, 277, 324, 326–327
flex time, 181, 144
Flying Camel, 245
401(k), 50

general ledger, 71–72
general partner, 47
general partnership, 44–45, 47–48,
Google, 245–246
gross margin, 105, 106, 108, 119
    See also gross profit
gross profit, 9, 73, 81, 106, 110, 278
gross profit margin, 92, 107, 109, 116
gross profit margin adjustment, 107
gross profit margin ratio, 104
gross receipts, 133
gum spots, 314

hangouts, 246
health insurance, 125–126
Health Maintenance Organization (HMO),
        126
health savings account (has), 126
Hollingsworth, John, 24
HOUZZ, 246
human resources, 9, 39, 68, 122, 140–144,
        151, 173
HVAC, 262, 271, 272, 276, 280, 299, 316,
        340

incentives, 152, 153
income statement, 40, 73, 80, 85–86,
        90–93, 98
    See also operating statement

income tax, 132
independent contractor, 149–150,
Independent Insurance Agents of America, 124
individual investor, 59
inspections, 261–263, 272–273, 280–281, 286, 288, 316, 321, 327–328
installation checklist, 299–301
installation delivery system, 267
insurance, 121, 122, 124, 126
interest-bearing account, 110
Internal Revenue Service (IRS), 55, 60, 71, 132, 149
interviewing, 164–167
intuit quick books premiere, 73, 74
inventory, 9–10, 71, 74, 97, 101, 113–114
investors, 73
Individual Retirement Account (IRA), 50
Internal Revenue Service (IRS), 133–136

job applications, 162
job costing, 10, 73
job description, 146–148,
job progress management system, 280
job sharing, 182
job site survey, 260
Johanson, Berenson LLP, 150
journeyman, 17, 313

Kitchen & Bath Business, 241
Kitchen & Bath Design News, 64, 241
Kitchen Cabinet Manufacturers' Association (KCMA), 315

lead installer, 313
lead system, 265
leadership traits, 1, 3–4
level surface, 301
liabilities, 72, 95, 97, 105, 121
liability insurance, 126
licenses, 43, 50
life insurance, 127
limited liability, 47–48, 49, 133
limited partnership, 44–45, 47
linear-foot pricing, 280
LinkedIn, 246
liquid assets, 95
location, 10
long term liabilities, 97
long–term planning, 11, 20
Luck, Dan, 230–232
lump–sum pricing, 279

Magnusen–Moss Warranty Act, 285
manufacturer representative, 286–289
margin analysis, 80

margins, 109
marketing, 3, 11, 38, 209–222, 235–247
markup, 79, 106–108, 111
Matta, Joseph, 336
mechanics liens, 120
media, 245
mentors, 12, 17, 39, 65, 124, 174–175
mineral streaks, 314
mission statement, 24
Modenus, 246
molding, 263, 277, 280, 299–300, 303, 306, 307, 316–317, 326, 330, 333–348
Morgan, John K., 287–288
Mrs. Fields Cookies, 2
multiplier, 108
mystery shop, 11, 227

National Federation of Independent Business (NFIB), 131
National Kitchen & Bath Association (NKBA), 3, 34, 65, 74, 103
needs assessment, 175
negative bow, 322
negligence penalty, 134
net income, 73, 86, 92, 132
net profit, 92, 106, 110
    See also bottom line
networking, 3, 63–65, 245
NKBA certification, 177
nonexempt, 150–152

one-year action plan, 29–30
operating expenses, 81–83, 92, 106
operating income statement, 71
operating profit, 106, 108,
operating statement, 73
    See also income statement
operational costs, 48
orientation, 173–174
OSHA, 273
outsourcing, 142
overhang, 300, 306
overhead, 79
owner equity, 97
owner's agent, 314–315
owner's disability insurance, 127

P&L statement, 76–77, 86, 88–90, 115
partnerships, 38, 44, 47, 50, 133
payroll, 9, 133
performance evaluations, 184–187
permits, 43, 50
personal liability, 48

Pfeif, Melvin, 56–57
photo sharing, 245
piece method, 280
pin knot, 315
plumb surface, 301–303
policy and procedures manual, 174, 177–180,
positive bow, 317
preconstruction conference, 325–326
Preferred Provider Organization (PPO), 126
press release, 243–244
pro forma, 40
professional development, 176–177
profit and loss statement (P&L), 9, 73, 88–90, 93–95, 106–107
profit margin, 85–86, 101
profit slippage, 285
profit–sharing plan, 50
project documentation, 292
project manager, 315
public relations (PR), 238–240
punch list, 263–264, 273, 281–282, 319, 328

quick ratio, 105

ray flecking, 315
recruiting, 159–160,
regulations, 144
regulatory issues, 142
remodeling fever, 313–314
résumés, 162–163
retainer, 209, 211, 213, 247, 258
Richardson, Mark, 319
Rohl, Ken, 114

S corporation, 38, 47, 49, 71, 133, 136
Sage 50 Complete, 73, 74
salary, 153–154, 157
sales, 3, 81, 109, 132, 210, 247–248
sales revenue, 91
sales tax, 51, 132
sales volume, 109
SCORE, 56
scribing fillers, 301, 303
self-funded, 19
self-insure, 114
SEP, 50
shareholder, 48
short term liabilities, 97
short–term planning, 11
    See also One–Year Action Plan
short-term planning, 20
shrinkage (door), 306

single-entry system, 71
site conditions, 267–269, 281–282, 299, 316–317, 324, 328, 330
site superintendent, 313
Small Business Administration (SBA), 46, 56–58, 65, 132, 209
small business resource guide, 136
small business tax calendar, 134
small claims court, 120
social communities, 246
social media marketing, 244–247
sole proprietorship, 38, 44, 46, 50, 133
specifications, 259, 261, 268, 270–271, 273, 275–278, 283, 285–286, 301, 312, 325, 327, 329, 336, 346
square, 301–303
staging area, 324
stakeholder, 27, 28
standard markup, 278
start-up issues, 54
stick method, 280
stockholders, 59
strategic business plan, 21
subcontractor, 29, 108
substantial completion, 264
substantiation, 134
swelling (door), 312

target audience, 17
target consumer, 26
tax bracket, 133
tax credit, 132, 134
tax deductions, 44
tax identification number, 51
taxes, 60
telecommuting, 144, 182
templating, 263–264
termination, 189–191, 207
time and materials pricing, 279
toe kick, 300, 341–343
trademark, 18, 50
trial balance, 72
turnkey project, 20
twisted door, 319
Twitter, 244
types of installations, 268

U.S. Tax Reform Act of 1986, 48
unit pricing, 280–281
United States Postal Service (USPS), 113
unlimited liability, 44–45
use tax, 132

vendors, 3, 61–64, 72, 109, 219
venture capital firms, 55, 58
vertically integrated business model, 27

video sharing, 245–246
virtual small business tax workshop, 132

waiver, 293
warpage (door), 317
warranty, 285–286
weighted evaluation scale, 169, 195
Wellborn Cabinet, Inc., 1

wood characteristics, 314–315
workers' compensation insurance,
  114, 127
work zone, 262, 324
worm tracks, 315, 329
write-offs, 132, 134

YouTube, 245

If you enjoyed this book, you may also like these:

Kitchen Planning 2e,
by Kathleen Parrott, Julia Beamish, JoAnn Emmel
and Mary Jo Peterson
ISBN: 9781118367629

Bath Planning 2e,
by Kathleen Parrott, Julia Beamish, JoAnn Emmel
and Mary Jo Peterson
ISBN: 9781118362488

WILEY